essent

JNI

JAVA™ NATIVE INTERFACE

R O B   G O R D O N

Prentice Hall PTR
Upper Saddle River, NJ 07458
http://www.phptr.com

ISBN 0-13-679895-0

90000

9 780136 798958

Library of Congress Cataloging-in-Publication Data

Gordon, Rob
    Essential JNI: Java Native Interface / Rob Gordon
      p. cm.
    Includes index.
    ISBN 0-13-679895-0 (paper)
    1. Java (Computer program language) 2. Application software.
    Title.
    QA76.73.J38G665   1998
    005.13'3--dc21   97-44105
                                                        CIP

Editorial/Production Supervision: *James D. Gwyn*
Acquisitions Editor: *Gregory Doench*
Series Editor: *Alan McClellan*
Manufacturing Manager: *Alexis R. Heydt*
Marketing Manager: *Kaylie Smith*
Editorial Assistant: *Mary Treacy*

© 1998 by Prentice Hall PTR
Prentice-Hall, Inc.
A Simon & Schuster Company
Upper Saddle River, New Jersey 07458

Prentice Hall books are widely used by corporations and government agencies for training, marketing, and resale. The publisher offers discounts on this book when ordered in bulk quantities. For more information, contact: Corporate Sales Department. Phone: 800-382-3419; FAX: 201-236-7141; E-mail: corpsales@prenhall.com; or write: Prentice Hall PTR, Corp. Sales Dept., One Lake Street, Upper Saddle River, NJ 07458.

Printed in the United States of America
10 9 8 7 6 5 4

ISBN 0-13-679895-0

Prentice-Hall International (UK) Limited, *London*
Prentice-Hall of Australia Pty. Limited, *Sydney*
Prentice-Hall Canada Inc., *Toronto*
Prentice-Hall Hispanoamericana, S.A., *Mexico*
Prentice-Hall of India Private Limited, *New Delhi*
Prentice-Hall of Japan, Inc., *Tokyo*
Simon & Schuster Asia Pte. Ltd., *Singapore*
Editora Prentice-Hall do Brasil, Ltda., *Rio de Janeiro*

essential
JNI
JAVA™ NATIVE INTERFACE

Titles in the PH/PTR essential series:

Essential JNI: Java Native Interface

Essential JMF: Java Media Framework
  Designing Media Players

Essential JTAPI: Java Telephony API
  Designing Telephony Projects with Java

Series Editor Alan McClellan is coauthor of the best-selling *Java by Example*, *Graphic Java: Mastering the AWT*, and *Automating Solaris Installations: A JumpStart Guide* (SunSoft/Prentice Hall). He is an award-winning software technical writer with over ten years of experience in the computer industry.

For Kathy, Matthew, Kilian and Kieran
who define my place in the world.

Contents

Chapter 4   NATIVE TYPES, SIGNATURES AND OTHER DETAILS 49

Chapter 5   OBJECTS AND CLASSES 65

Chapter 6

ARRAYS AND STRINGS 95

Chapter 7

EXCEPTIONS 121

Chapter 8

MONITORS   135

Chapter 9

JAVA AND C++   151

Chapter 10

CONVERSION OF C STRUCTURES 185

Chapter 13   AN NT SERVICE APPLICATION   291

Chapter 14   DEBUGGING NATIVE METHODS   317

Chapter 15

Appendix A

Appendix B

Appendix C   **STRUCTCONVERTER REFERENCE** 463

Appendix D   **JAVAH REFERENCE** 471

PREFACE

Before we plow an unfamiliar patch
It is well to be informed about the winds,
About the variations in the sky,
The native traits and habits of the place,
What each locale permits, and what denies

Virgil
The Georgics

What This Book is About

The subject of this book is the Java Native Interface (JNI) Application Programming Interface (API). The JNI was introduced in release 1.1 of the Java Development Kit (JDK) as distributed by JavaSoft. This book covers the entire API for the JNI including the enhancements introduced in release 1.2 of the JDK. Where there are minor differences between various 1.1 point releases, these are discussed.

Who Should Read This Book?

This book is written for the software engineer who needs to make Java and C or C++ talk to one another. Experience with C/C++ and Java is assumed. This book also assumes some familiarity with both UNIX and Win32 platforms.

If you are a Java programmer who needs to step outside the Java Virtual Machine to take advantage of some platform-specific functionality, this book will show you how. If you are a C programmer responsible for putting a Java front-end on a legacy application, this book will show you how. If you are a

C++ programmer wanting to take advantage of an existing C++ class library, this book will show you how.

Further, this book covers these topics for both UNIX and Win32 platforms. Okay, now turn around and walk to the sales counter.

Structure of This Book

This book can be thought of as having three distinct parts. The first part, roughly the first eight chapters, covers the JNI API in great detail. The second part, the remaining chapters, covers some general issues involved with native method programming. The third part, a series of appendices, contains reference material, both for the JNI and for tools introduced in this book. There is also an appendix that compares the JNI with the old-style native method programming model introduced in JDK 1.0. The last appendix offers a brief discussion of native methods, applets and security issues.

The early chapters contain plenty of simple examples intended to highlight the essential features of the API. No attempt is made to place JNI function calls into large, complex examples that obscure their salient features.

The first part of the book takes a walk-before-you-run approach. After an overview of the JNI in Chapter 1, Chapter 2 presents a JNI version of the classic "Hello World" example. Chapter 3 then follows with examples of some of the more common JNI operations before plunging into the syntactical details of the JNI in Chapter 4.

With all that work behind you, Chapter 5 through Chapter 8 provides detailed coverage of the remaining JNI functions.

The second half of the book deals with a series of general topics on using the JNI to integrate Java code with non-Java code. Chapter 9 presents an approach for mirroring existing C++ classes in Java. Chapter 10 introduces a tool for the automatic conversion of C structures into Java classes and an accompanying set of adapter functions for copying data between an instance of a C structure and a Java object.

Chapter 11 starts with a collection of Java classes that provide a high-level interface to serial and parallel ports. Throughout this chapter the native code for targetting these classes for both POSIX and Win32 platforms is presented and discussed. The Java package used in this chapter is the *portio* package which is freely-available from Central Data (www.cd.com) as well as being included with the examples at the Prentice-Hall ftp site.

Chapter 12 and Chapter 13 deal with the Invocation API. Chapter 12 is a broad discussion of the mechanics involved with starting a Java Virtual Machine from a C/C++ application. Chapter 13 provides a very specific example of this facility, namely, starting the Java Virtual Machine (JVM) as an NT service. This chapter is for NT developers who wish to use Sun's JVM as an engine for their Java applications.

Chapter 14 presents some approaches to debugging a Java application that includes native code. Finally, Chapter 15 is dedicated to changes and enhancements to the JNI in the JDK 1.2.

Whose Java?

This book covers the Java Native Interface API. To use the Java Native Interface API, you will need to run your Java code on a Java Virtual Machine that supports the JNI. The list of JVM vendors supporting the JNI is growing, but a sure bet is the JVM distributed by Sun. The Sun JVM, the Java Core classes and the JNI are available as part of the Java Development Kit (JDK). The JNI is supported starting in release 1.1 of the JDK.

To download the JDK, surf to the JavaSoft download site

```
http://java.sun.com/products/jdk/1.1/index.html
```

and follow the instructions. The JDK 1.2 release is available from:

```
http://java.sun.com/products/jdk/1.2/index.html
```

Downloading Example Source

The source code to the examples in this book is available at the Prentice Hall ftp site, ftp.prenhall.com. This site is available via anonymous ftp. The following sequence of steps illustrates how to download the *Essential JNI* examples. You type the bold.

```
% ftp ftp.prenhall.com
Connected to iq-ss3.prenhall.com.
220 iq-ss3 FTP server(UNIX(r) System V Release 4.0) ready.
User (iq-ss3.prenhall.com:(none)): anonymous
331 Guest login ok, send ident as password.
Password: <type your user name, e.g. username@someisp.net>
230 Guest login ok, access restrictions apply.
ftp> bin
ftp> cd /pub/ptr/professional_computer_science.w-022/
gordon/essential_jni
250 CWD command successful.
ftp> get ejni_ex.tar <or ejni_ex.zip>
200 PORT command successful.
150 ASCII data connection for ejni_examples.tar
    (38.11.232.6,1099) (19818 bytes).
226 ASCII Transfer complete.
20184 bytes received in 5.93 seconds (3.40 Kbytes/sec)[1]
ftp> bye
Goodbye.
```

(1)

---

1. Do not take these file sizes and transfer times at face value. A test run generated these values.

The `ftp` directory named in line [1] contains two examples files described in the following table.

File Name	Format	Size
`ejni_ex.zip`	zip	452KB
`ejni_ex.tar`	tar	1.55MB

These two files include makefiles for both Win32 and Solaris.

After downloading the examples, unzip or untar the file in a directory of your choice. Users of a UNIX zip utility should be careful to use the `-a` flag with unzip so that CR/NT sequences are properly converted.

Extracting the files will create a directory named `ejni`. Within the `ejni` directory will be another directory, `examples`.

The directory `ejni/examples` is known as the *examples directory* throughout this book.

Building the Examples

Before the examples can be built and run, some environment must be set up.

Setting Up the Environment

Two files are included with the example files that describe the appropriate environment settings. The file `csh.env` is provided for UNIX csh users. It is easily modified for other shells. The file `win32.bat` is provided for Win32 users. Both files must be modified to specify the location of your JDK and the location of your examples directory. Specifically, two environment variables are provided, `JDK_HOME` and `EJNI_HOME`, which point to these locations.

Additionally, these files define an appropriate setting for the `CLASSPATH` environment variable, adding the directories required to run the examples.

Finally, there are some platform-specific environment variables that need to be set.

Solaris Environment

The environment variable `LD_LIBRARY_PATH` is set within the `csh.env` file. The directory in which the example native libraries are installed is added to your existing value.

The Solaris build assumes you are using Sun's compilers. Be certain to modify the CC settings in `EJNI_HOME/Makefile.master` to point to the proper installation directory, or comment it out and use your environment settings.

The examples in Chapter 9 require Rogue Wave's Tools.h++ class library. If you have this software, you will need to set the relevant macros in

EJNI_HOME/Makefile.master to the appropriate values. If you are a UNIX user and don't have the Tools.h++ software, remove the target chap9 from the SUBDIRS macro in EJNI_HOME/Makefile. Your enjoyment of this example will be necessarily limited to viewing the source.

Win32 Environment

Win32 users can use the batch file win32.bat located in EJNI_HOME to set up their environment for building the examples. The file win32.bat batch assumes you are building using Microsoft's compiler, specifically Visual C++ and cl.exe. The appropriate environment for running cl from the command line is set using the vcvars32.bat batch file shipped with Visual C++. This file is located in your Visual C++ bin directory, typically \Program Files\DevStudio\VC\bin. vcvars32.bat should be run before running win32.bat.

If you get the message "Out of environment space," you will need to use the command command from the DOS prompt as shown below.

▶ • User Input   **Increasing DOS Environment Space**

`C:\> command /e:8192`

This setting will only be in effect for the current DOS shell. To set this value permanently, add the following line to your CONFIG.SYS file.

`shell=command.com /e:8192 /p`

How To Build

Once the environment is set up you are ready to build. On Solaris, the following make commands, executed from the EJNI_HOME directory, build the Java class files and native libraries.

▶ • User Input   **Building on Solaris**

`% make all; make install`

On Win32 systems, the nmake command is used to build the example Java class files and native DLLs. This command must be executed from the EJNI_HOME directory.

▶ • User Input   **Building on Win32**

`% nmake TARGET=all /f nmake.mak all`

When the build is complete, all the class files live in `$EJNI_HOME/classes` and all the native libraries live in `$EJNI_HOME/`*platform*`/lib` where *platform* is either `sparc` or `win32`. Tilt the slashes appropriately for Win32 platforms.

A Word About the Examples

All of native coding examples are written in either C or C++. As you will learn, the syntax for calling a JNI function differs across the two languages.

In the first part of the book, through Chapter 8, all of the examples are written in C++. Therefore, whenever a reference is made to the *first* argument to a JNI function, it is understood not to count the `JNIEnv` pointer argument that is present in a C call of a JNI function.

The examples directory contains a directory for each chapter. Within the chapter directory is a directory for each example. Example 1 in Chapter 5 resides in `ejni/examples/chap5/example1`.

A `README` file in each `exampleN` directory describes how to run the example since the book does not actually show all the examples running.

Some Conventions

All code listings, output, all variable, method and function names that appear in the text, command names, directory names, and all URLs appear in `courier`.

User input appears in **`bold courier`**.

Special terms, upon their introduction, and parameters to be substituted for appear in *italics*.

Pseudo-code and labels within figures appear in helvetica.

Help From Fellow Travellers

There are at least two list-servers available for JNI programmers. The first deals directly with native method programming. On the jnative-l list you will find discussions of JNI as well as old-style JDK native method programming, Microsoft's Runtime Native Interface (RNI), Netscape's Java Runtime Environment (JRE) and, to a lesser extent, problems with incorporating native code with various browsers.

To subscribe to this list, send an e-mail message to majordomo@lists.tele-port.com with the text

```
subscribe jnative-l
```

in the body of the message.

It is not unusual for questions related to native method programming to appear on the Advanced Java list. To subscribe to this list, send mail to majordomo@xcf.berkeley.edu with an empty subject and the following body:

```
subscribe advanced-java your_email_address
end
```

Do not use this latter list injudiciously. It is heavily patrolled by self-appointed experts who spend as much time telling people their question is not sufficiently "advanced" as they do providing answers to those question that they deem worthy of their consideration.

To stay in step with updates and enhancements to the JDK and the JNI, you may want to register with the *Java Developer's Connection (JDC)*. To do so, follow the link off the JavaSoft home page (`java.sun.com`). As a member of the JDC, you are eligible for Early Access APIs. This is also the place to submit and track bugs. The JDC is a free service from JavaSoft but you do have to register.

A Word About Borrowed Words

Reading the quotes at the beginning of each chapter is a requirement for successful completion of this book. Too many late nights were spent finding them and too many phone calls were made acquiring permission to use them for you to ignore them.

Why include them at all? A guy who takes writing seriously has to do something to catch the eye of the reviewers at *The New York Times Review of Books*. Besides, it was fun trying to decorate the often bland minutia of a programming API with the distinguished dress of great ideas. I don't know if it worked, but I highly recommend all the quoted authors. Well, I can take or leave Nietszche. As for Hobbes, I think he had it backwards. We are heading toward where he thinks we began.

ACKNOWLEDGMENTS

When I grow up I want to work on computers and I am going to write a book but I won't have any kids so I can finish it.

Matthew Gordon
6 years old

That these words are being written is proof that a father of three very high-energy, as the politically correct, early childhood educators are wont to say, boys, as the not so politically correct, exhausted parent is willing to acknowledge, can finish a book.

What the presence of these words on paper can not even begin to hint at is the extent to which finishing a book depends on the patience, perseverance, forbearance and tolerance of, no, not the author, but the people closest to him: his wife and his three sons.

Kathy deserves a big thanks because, well, if she had a nickel for every time somebody asked her how she puts up with me, she would be a rich woman. What more need I say?

Then there are little ones: Matthew, Kilian and Kieran. If they were not in my life, I may not have undertaken this. It is a long story so you will have to take me at my word. When they get older, I will explain it to them, although as intuitive as they are, I suspect they have an idea even now.

Beyond those close to me who helped by their forbearance, there are many more who helped by their active participation. Steve Talley was with me as every chapter came off the printer providing critique both fair and fast. Peter Rivera, who must now hold some sort of record for pre-publication review of

Java books, also lent his sharp eye to reviewing an early draft of many chapters. Dave Geary provided spiritual support to the very last day.

Four additional technical reviewers, Buzzy Brown of the IBM Retail Store Solutions Group, John Gray of the University of Hartford, Francoise Duclos of Kodak, and Jeff Barr all provided valuable input after thorough readings of the manuscript.

There are numerous people at Prentice Hall, many nameless, who helped get this book from my computer to your bookstore. Greg Doench provided a steady hand from beginning to end. Jim Gwyn took care of many details I did not pretend to understand. Gail Cocker-Bogusz and Lisa Iarkowski helped minimize document processing-related headaches and contributed much to the layout of this book. Julie Bettis was a painfully thorough copy editor and went beyond the call of duty in the home stretch.

The boys at QuickStream Software (www.quickstream.com), Shawn Bertini and Eric Westerkamp, besides having a pretty slick 100% Pure Java web-based document management product, offered their native method programming experience gained from their forays into not-so-pure Java. Chapter 10 and Chapter 12 owe a lot to Shawn's skills. However, in spite of his brain-power, Chapter 12 would not have happened without the kind and timely help of Richard Brame.

Jeff Roloff and Emilio Millán at Central Data (www.cd.com) were generous enough to review Chapter 11 and allow me to distribute their *portio* package with the example code available with this book. Dr. Val Veirs of Colorado College gets credit for helping me understand that such a chapter would be useful.

Aaron Naumann of the Software Productivity Consortium (www.software.org) planted the seed which grew into Chapter 14. Aaron was also kind enough to review a draft of this chapter. Appendix E was subject to last minute reviews by Bill "Billy" Birnbaum of Sun Microsystems and Raman Tenncti and Sailesh Krishnamurthy of Netscape Communications. Besides having the most lyrical names of all the people who helped, these three agreed to a very short turnaround time for providing their input.

A handful of people expert at adjusting fonts, aligning text, numbering paragraphs and importing raster files into FrameMaker deserve a tip of the hat. Without Paul Kasper, Scott Hudson, Kris Trierweiler and Lou Ordorica (rhymes with Topeka) I would have been more frustrated at times than I already was.

Leah Kral, Richard Willems, and Craig Lindley helped in small but very measurable ways, all of which fall under the heading of helping me out in a fix. John Kelin's contribution, the compilation of Appendix A, falls under this heading also, but was far from small.

There were three people who were there when I (and my family) needed them: Patrick Hamilton, Susan Gordon and Rebecca Felts. Their contribution to this book is indirect, yet considerable. And then, there is my peripatetic brother, John. He dropped from the sky two days before my deadline and entertained my boys while I put the finishing touches on this beast.

I am also deeply grateful to a few people who, although not directly contributing to this book, have been important in the evolution of my thinking of myself as a writer. Barbara Huber, S.C., Michael Gardner, Richard Skorman and Kathryn Eastburn have supported my writing in other, non-technical venues over the past five years. There is also my father-in-law, Dr. R. B. (Bob) Sullivan, who, perhaps more than anyone else, convinced me I could arrange words on a page.

Finally, I owe a big thanks to Alan McClellan who, besides being the editor of the Essential Java series, is a friend and mentor. It is an immeasurable boost when a writer as talented as Alan is supportive of one's own writing. I am grateful for his invitation to be a part of this series.

Chapter 1   *WHY JNI?*

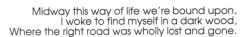

> Midway this way of life we're bound upon,
> I woke to find myself in a dark wood,
> Where the right road was wholly lost and gone.
>
> Dante
> *Canto I, The Divine Comedy*

Introduction

Procter & Gamble spent a bundle touting its Ivory Soap as 99 and 44/100 per cent pure. That was good enough to sell millions of bars of soap. Sun Micro systems is spending a bundle promoting 100% Pure Java and "Write Once, Run Anywhere" applications. The 100% Pure Java and "Write Once, Run Anywhere" efforts are noble goals, certainly, but not always possible. The mere presence of the `native` keyword in the *Java Language Specification*[1], and the emergence of the Java Native Interface (JNI) as part of the Java Development Kit (JDK) 1.1 are acknowledgments by Sun and within the industry that there exists an honest need to get work done outside of the Java Virtual Machine.

This, of course, comes as no surprise if you are building Java applications. 100% Pure Java is desirable and necessary in applet development when you want visitors to your Web page to be able to run your applet regardless of where and on what type of platform they reside. However, Java has increased in popularity partially because of its strength as an application development

---

1. *The Java Language Specification*, James Gosling, Bill Joy, Guy Steele, Addison-Wesley, 1996.

1

language. The breadth of its functionality, the clarity of its design, and its integration with the Internet have all contributed to its allure as a language for developing large-scale applications.

Virtual Machine, Real Machine

In a world of many hardware vendors, the idea of "Write Once, Run Anywhere" only makes sense in the context of a *virtual machine*. A virtual machine runs atop various operating systems and processors and provides a uniform execution environment. For our purposes here, the type of virtual machine in which we are interested is a virtual machine that executes Java bytecode, or a Java Virtual Machine (JVM). The JVM executes Java bytecode and performs system-specific operations on behalf of a Java application.

The problem with large-scale applications is that they often run up to and past the edges of the JVM. They need to run on real machines and they may have performance requirements more stringent than the limits of a user's patience waiting for a Web page to load. As attractive as the idea of complete platform-independence is, it will become a reality only if and when the computer industry is reduced to a single platform, either through a new spirit of cooperation among vendors, or the existence of only a single vendor. Until then, the big hitters, for all the talk of open standards, will never be doing things exactly the same way.

Even if the JVM matures to the point where it becomes unnecessary to consider the details of the real machine, there is still the issue of existing, or legacy, code. Nobody, especially management, likes to throw away well-worn code. If you want to integrate existing code with Java code, you will have to leave the confines of the JVM. Existing device drivers, databases, embedded applications and application libraries abound. The continued use of such code often will be an economically wise decision, overwhelming any purely aesthetic plea for 100% Pure Java.

The designers of the Java language knew all of this. That is why they provided a way out of the virtual machine and into the nether world of native code. Like Proctor & Gamble, the language designers were humble enough to realize their JVM was only 99 and 44/100 per cent of the solution. At least for now. How matters shape up in the future, with Just-In-Time (JIT) compilers addressing performance concerns and a shrinking base of legacy code as more applications are transitioned to Java, is still an open question. However, I would not bet a single dollar that the need for some native escape hatch will go away in my lifetime.

Convinced of the need for some mechanism for getting at native code, there still remains the question posed by the title of this chapter: Why JNI? After all, JDK 1.0 provided a native method interface. There is also the Netscape Java Runtime Interface (JRI) and Microsoft's Raw Native Interface (RNI). What does the JNI provide that these other interfaces do not provide?

JNI and Binary Compatibility

The short answer to this question of what advantage the JNI provides over RNI and JRI is binary compatibility across multiple versions of the JVM. For a short answer, this is a mouthful, so elaboration is in order.

A Java application that uses native methods depends on the execution of code running directly on the host hardware. Java code is compiled to Java bytecode and is executed by the JVM. The JVM acts as an intermediary between the bytecode and the host hardware. Native code, on the other hand, can be thought of as running outside the JVM. It is platform-specific object code.

This native code typically exists in a dynamically loadable library that was built using the host machine's native compiler and linker. The contents of this library are necessarily platform-dependent since the object code generated by the native compiler is necessarily processor-specific. Beyond that, there may be all sorts of code in that library that references platform-specific devices or an application-specific database interface. In any case, the dynamically loadable library contains binary objects.

If the binary objects in a library built for platform X adhere to the JNI Application Programming Interface, then that native library can be used, without rebuilding, with any JVM that supports the JNI on platform X. If vendor A and vendor B both provide a JVM with JNI support on machine X, then any library using only JNI calls to interface with the JVM will work with either or A or B's JVM.

Contrast this with the native method interface implementation in JDK 1.0 and Microsoft's RNI. Both of these approaches pass a Java object to the native side as a C structure. This is certainly a straightforward treatment of an object and familiar to anyone who has done C++ programming. The problem with this simple approach is that it exposes to the native method programmer a memory layout that is not specified by the *Java Language Specification* and, therefore, not guaranteed across different implementations of the JVM.

Memory Loss

Exposing object memory to the native code further requires the native programmer to be mindful of memory management issues. If, as in RNI and the JDK 1.0-style native method programming available in the JDK, you deal with Java objects as pointers (i.e. an address), there exists the possibility that the Java memory management system may move the object to which you have a pointer, invalidating it. The results of this would be unpredictable, to say the least.

What happens if the memory which the native pointer points to gets garbage collected? Unless the native programmer is careful to ensure this memory would not be garbage collected, or moved due to garbage collection, strange things could happen. Programs whose memory disappears out from under them have been known to crash.

The JNI solves this problem by giving the native code access to Java objects through an object reference. This reference remains valid during native code execution in spite of any memory management work done by the JVM.

The JNI Solution

This exposure of a particular object layout was rightly considered unwise by the developers of Java and others within the industry. But this was only part of the motivation for the development of the JNI. The number of competing "solutions" was seen as an obstacle to a consistent Java environment. Three major competing approaches were available: Sun's JDK 1.0-style approach, Microsoft's RNI and Netscape's JRI. The "right road was wholly lost and gone."

The attempt to resolve these competing models started with a summit of the three big players. To make a long story short, the three big players, Sun, Microsoft and Netscape, got together and agreed upon very little. What understanding was achieved at their meetings resulted in the Java Native Interface. If you are familiar with the JRI, you will see much of its influence on the JNI. For its part, Microsoft still ships the RNI and has given every indication that it has no intention of supporting the JNI.

The JNI solves the problem of exposing JVM implementation details from the native code in four ways:

- By providing opaque references to Java objects, thereby hiding object implementation from native code.

- By placing a function table between the JVM and native code and requiring all access of JVM data to occur through these functions.

- By defining a set of native types to provide uniform mapping of Java types into platform-specific types.

- By providing flexibility to the JVM vendor as to how object memory is handled in cases where the user expects contiguous memory. JNI calls that return character string or scalar array data may lock that memory so that it is not moved by the memory management system during its use by native code.

These are some of the problems in RNI and JDK 1.0-style native method programming that the JNI corrects. However, beyond fixing these shortcomings, what are some of the general features available in the JNI of which you can take advantage?

Features of the JNI

So far, we have answered the question "Why JNI?" from the perspective of "Why JNI as opposed to the JDK 1.0 solution?" or "Why JNI as opposed to RNI?" It is time to consider the JNI on its own merits; in other words, "What does the JNI offer that makes it attractive?"

Let's look at some of the major pieces of the JNI functionality. Subsequent chapters cover all these areas in great detail. This discussion is simply to whet your appetite.

Invoke Java Methods

The JNI lets you call Java methods from any class in accordance with class visibility rules, that is, any class in the classpath or loaded by a class loader.

Create Objects

The JNI lets you create Java objects for any class in accordance with class visibility rules.

Access Class Variables

The JNI lets you access Java class variables for any class in accordance with class visibility rules.

Access Instance Variables

The JNI lets you access Java instance variables for any instance to which you have a reference.

Throw and Catch Exceptions

The JNI lets you throw exceptions to be handled by Java code. Also, native code can catch exceptions thrown by either Java methods or JNI function calls.

Native Critical Sections

The JNI provides monitors which can perform as mutexes in native code.

Load Classes

The JNI lets you write a class loader that uses native code to create a Java class from bytecode.

Create a JVM

The JNI defines a mechanism for creating an instance of the JVM from within an arbitrary native application.

A bit more needs to be said about this last item. The JNI defines a handful of functions under the larger heading of the Invocation Application Programming Interface. This gives a native application access to the full power of the JVM. The best example of this is a browser capable of launching a Java applet. This power was only obscurely present in the JDK 1.0-style of native method programming. The JNI defines this functionality in a clear and usable way.

Summary

The need for integrating native code with Java applications is no secret. 100% Pure Java is a noble goal, and appropriate for some applications. However, as the popularity of Java increases and its power is brought to bear on a wide range of problems, and as more existing applications are made web-friendly, more development projects are going to look to native methods to accommodate their requirements.

In the ancient days of JDK 1.0, before the Summit of Three, there were competing and inadequate solutions to the native method programming problem. Today, there are still competing solutions. At least one of them, however, the Java Native Interface has improved and asserted itself, by virtue of its association with Sun, as a "standard." Netscape has added support for the JNI in its Communicator 4.03 product. Its competitor, Microsoft's RNI, makes no claim to serve anything but the Windows platform.

This chapter has provided a brief introduction to both the rationale of the JNI and some of its features. It is time to write your first native method.

Chapter 2

HELLO JNI WORLD

An adequate sense of tradition manifests itself in a grasp of
those future possibilities which the past has made available to
the present.

Alasdair MacIntyre
After Virtue

Introduction

In order to situate this book within the short, yet illustrious, tradition of programming books, it seems appropriate to begin with an example from the relatively ancient days of programming languages.

So, with a nod of respect to Messrs. Kernighan and Ritchie, this book
begins with the ever useful "Hello World" example. Never mind the obvious.
Never mind that you may never need to do such a trivial task. There is much to
be learned from this example and that is why it has lasted nearly twenty-five
years.

Unlike pure Java code, using the JNI involves much more than simply creating a Java source file and using `javac` to build a class file. An application
combining Java code with some platform-specific code requires additional
steps to build a native library and interface it with the Java code. Further, some
of those steps differ in details depending on the platform for which the application is to be targeted.

7

The Big Picture

An overview of the steps employed to integrate native code with a Java application will be helpful before we look at the individual steps.

A `native` method in Java is identified using the `native` keyword to modify the method declaration. When the `native` keyword is used to identify a Java method, no body is defined for that method within the Java class in which the method is declared. Instead, the body of the `native` method is contained in a separate C/C++ source file.

For each `native` method declared, a C/C++ function needs to be written. A tool, `javah`, provided with the JDK, takes as input a Java class file and generates an ASCII C function prototype for each `native` method declaration. Each prototype defines the calling protocol the JVM uses to execute a `native` method. The prototype also constrains how the native function is written by defining its input (formal arguments) and output (return value).

With this overview in mind, let's look at the individual steps involved in writing `native` method code.

The Steps

In this section the steps necessary for integrating `native` method code with a Java class will be described. As we get into the details of actually generating the appropriate files, a simple "Hello World" program will serve as an example.

Identify Native Functionality

You are interested in the JNI for one of two reasons. Either you have existing code which you do not want to rewrite and you want to use within a Java application, or you are writing a Java application, some parts of which are best written in C/C++.

Although the JNI does not limit you to C or C++, you will see that `javah` assumes a C/C++ calling interface between Java and native code. If you choose to implement native code in another language, you will at least have to guarantee that arguments passed from the JVM to a `native` method honor your platform's C function call protocol. Alternatively, you could implement the C function prototypes as wrappers to calls into another language environment. In either case, it is your responsibility to get the call stack correct when calling into another language.

This books limits all discussion of `native` method programming to C and C++.

Describing the Interface to the Native Code

If you want to interface Java code with legacy applications, you presumably understand the interface to your existing code. You can describe, probably using ANSI C function prototypes, an API to your existing code. The challenge when integrating legacy code with Java is mapping the formal arguments of the Java native methods onto the formal arguments of your existing API. In this case, you generally have two choices:

- Model legacy data in Java and define the appropriate methods for manipulating this data. The native method implementation then serves as a wrapper that, possibly, massages the arguments to the native method and sends them to the appropriate legacy call(s).

- Map the existing interface directly onto your Java native method declarations.

Of these two approaches, the latter is the easiest to implement, but the former offers an opportunity to enhance the design of older applications that may not have been designed using object-oriented techniques and could benefit from Java's encouragement of these techniques.

Each of these approaches is treated in detail in later chapters. Chapter 9 discusses the former as it applies to the use of legacy C++ object libraries. Chapter 10 discusses the second as it applies to the conversion of C structures for use with Java objects.

If you are writing native code from scratch, that is, Java development is driving the design, you have much more freedom in your native code implementation. The native method declaration will define the API to which your native code has to be programmed. The function prototypes generated by javah ensure this.

Writing the Java Code

Declaring a native method within a Java class is as simple as the use of the native attribute keyword. A class can signify that any of its methods will be implemented with native code by simply preceding the method name with the native keyword and not supplying the body of the method. From a syntactical perspective, the abstract keyword and the native keyword are identical. Both defer the implementation of the method. In the case of an abstract method, of course, a subclass defines a method. In the case of a native method, the method is defined within a C/C++ source file.

Because a code snippet is worth a thousand words of English prose, here is an example that illustrates the point of the above paragraph. Note the use of the native keyword in line [1].

Listing 2.1 *A* native *Method Declaration*

```
// File: AClassWithNativeMethods.java
// A really simple example of a class containing
// a native method.
public class AClassWithNativeMethods {
    public native void theNativeMethod();
    public void aJavaMethod() {
        theNativeMethod();
    }
}
```

(1)

Beyond the native keyword, there is nothing special about this Java source code when defining and invoking a native method.

Using javac to Generate Class Files

Once your classes are defined in Java source files, you need to run javac to generate the class files. For example, to generate Java bytecode for a java class Clazz, the following command is used.

 **User Input**   **Running** javac

```
% javac Clazz.java
```

The next step in writing native methods requires the class files as input, so you can't proceed without first creating them.

Using javah to Generate Include Files

Once the Java class files that include native method declarations are generated, ANSI C function prototypes for that method need to be generated. These prototypes are generated using the javah tool that comes with the JDK. You will want to run javah on all the class files that contain native method declarations.

javah takes as input the names of Java class files that contain native method declarations. The files named must reside in a directory named in the CLASSPATH environment variable or by the -classpath command line option of javah.

User Input   **Using** javah **to Generate Function Prototypes**

```
% javah -jni AClassWithNativeMethods
```

The -jni option in the above example tells javah to generate a JNI style function prototype. This may be stating the obvious, so a little history is in order. The native method support in JDK 1.0 is quite different from the support introduced in JDK 1.1. In fact, the term JNI specifically refers to an API defined by JDK 1.1 and extended in JDK 1.2. javah, however, still provides the ability to generate function prototypes that adhere to the native method programming model defined by JDK 1.0. To generate old-style function prototypes, use the -stubs option to javah and consult Appendix B for more details.

As output, javah produces a C header file that defines an ANSI C function prototype for each native method declared in the input class file.

By default, the output file name is determined by the fully-qualified class name of the input class. For a class named Clazz, defined in the package myPkg.tools, the name of the generated header file is myPkg_tools_Clazz.h. If Clazz is not a member of a package, the header file generated would be Clazz.h. The -o option may be used with javah to explicitly name the header file.

The generated header file is then available for inclusion (i.e. #include) by the C/C++ source file containing the implementation of the native methods. The output file from our example javah invocation above will be placed in a file called AClassWithNativeMethods.h.

Just to put a little meat on this bony description, the contents of this file are shown below.

Listing 2.2 javah-***Generated File*** AClassWithNativeMethods.h

```
/* DO NOT EDIT THIS FILE - it is machine generated */
#include <jni.h>
#ifndef _Included_AClassWithNativeMethods
#define _Included_AClassWithNativeMethods
#ifdef __cplusplus
extern "C" {
#endif
/* Class: AClassWithNativeMethods
 * Method:    theNativeMethod
 * Signature: ()V
 */
JNIEXPORT void JNICALL
   Java_AClassWithNativeMethods_theNativeMethod(
      JNIEnv *, jobject);
#ifdef __cplusplus
}
#endif
#endif
```

Each function prototype will contain at least two arguments, always preceding any additional formal arguments to the `native` method. The first of these, the Java execution environment, is an opaque reference to the JVM execution context in which the `native` method is running. This value is of type `JNIEnv`. The second argument, sometimes an object reference, sometimes a class reference, can be thought of as a *this* reference. It refers to the object instance or class of which the method is a member. You can see that it does so using a special type `jobject` in the case of an object instance reference. In the case of a class reference, the formal argument will be of type `jclass`. All other arguments to the `native` method defined in the declaration appear after the *this* reference. There will be more on the arguments to `native` methods later.

A few other things are worth noting.

First, the generated file includes the file `jni.h`. This file contains all the relevant JNI definitions.

Second, the file is generated such that it suppresses C++ name mangling. The `#ifdef __cplusplus` takes care of this. Of course, the function bodies themselves can be written in C++. All the `#ifdef` does is inform the compiler that these functions will be called using the C language naming convention.

Third, the comments contain a line introduced by `Signature:`. What follows is a description, called a *signature*, of the function, its arguments and return value, in terms understandable by the JNI.

Fourth, even though the Java declaration of `theNativeMethod` has no arguments, the generated function prototype has two. As mentioned above, these two arguments will appear in every native function prototype generated by `javah`.

Fifth, two `#define` macros, `JNIEXPORT` and `JNICALL,` appear in the function prototype. The definitions of these are platform-dependent. At this point, you should trust that JNI does the right thing. The curious can look in `$JDK_HOME/include/`*platform*`/jni_md.h` where *platform* is, for example, `solaris` or `win32`.

Finally, in tones most ominous, you are warned not to edit a file generated by `javah`. Being a product of Catholic schools, I take seriously such warnings. You will have to buy another book if you want to learn what happens if you disregard this advice.[1]

If `javah` is rerun with the same arguments, the previously generated header file would be overwritten without warning.

---

1. Okay, I confess, I have edited a `javah`-generated file by hand. But only after having read and thoroughly understood this entire book.

Writing Native Code

Up to this point, all the steps have been platform independent. Now comes the time when you need to write a C/C++ function. That you are even reading this book means you have some job to do that most likely can not be done in Java. Chances are you have requirements specific to a particular platform, whether it be manipulating a serial port on a UNIX machine, starting a Java application using NT's Service Manager or using legacy code from an existing application. In any case, it is time to do some platform-specific work.

The output of the previous step, a header file with ANSI C function prototypes, of course, purposely constrains the writing of the function implementation. By providing a tool such as `javah`, Sun is not only making the job of writing `native` methods easier, but it is enforcing an interface between the world of Java code, the JVM and the world of C/C++ code. Writing to this interface is the task of the native code author. This interface imposes three constraints:

- Every function implementing a `native` method takes a `JNIEnv` pointer as its first argument and an object reference as its second argument.
- The types of the input arguments are defined by the JNI.
- The type of the return value is defined by the JNI.

In our example, the header file which enforces this interface and contains the function prototypes is `AClassWithNativeMethods.h`. This file must be included in the file which implements the `native` methods declared by the Java class `AClassWithNativeMethods`.

The implementation of our `native` method is shown below. Notice the inclusion of the java-generated file `AClassWithNativeMethods.h`. Also, notice that all our `native` method does is print, as promised, `Hello JNI World`.

Listing 2.3 *Hello JNI World*

```
/* File: theNativeMethod.c
 * Implementes theNativeMethod of class
 * aClassWithNativeMethods
 */
#include <stdio.h>
#include "AClassWithNativeMethods.h"
JNIEXPORT void JNICALL
Java_AClassWithNativeMethods_theNativeMethod(
    JNIEnv* env, jobject thisObj) {
      printf("Hello JNI World\n");
}
```

Notice that the two macros `JNIEXPORT` and `JNICALL` find their way into the file that defines the `native` method implementation.

Building a Library

This final step in merging Java and C/C++ code is where all the beautiful machine virtuality provided by Java and all the portability provided by C/C++ can be bid farewell. In the world of compilers, linkers, and library archival tools, the purity of thought one maintains while building those elegant, pattern-like Java classes becomes sullied. One is quickly reminded of the purpose of all those computer science courses.

Okay, it is not that bad, but this is where platform specificity really gets specific. Suffice it to say at this point that you need to:

- Compile your C/C++ code, pointing to all the right places for inclusion of `jni.h`.

- Build a library containing the object files of your native function implementations.

In the Solaris world, for example, this would be a Shared Object Library. In the Windows and NT world, this would be a Dynamic Link Library. In the latter case, at least, there are integrated development environments which do a fair job of hiding some of the subtleties of this task.

These two types of libraries are identified on their respective platforms with special suffixes.

Table 2.1 *Native Library Descriptions*

Platform	Library Description	Suffix
Solaris	Shared Object Library	`.so`
Win32	Dynamic Link Library	`.dll`

For our "Hello World" example, we will build a Shared Object Library for Solaris. First, let's assume that the environment variable JDK_HOME points to the directory in which the JDK is installed. This will allow cc to find the required include files. In the example below, note the mention of two directories using the -I flag. The first is sufficient to include jni.h. The second is required to get at jni_md.h, a JDK include file that defines some machine-dependent values. This file is included by virtue of including jni.h.

▶ **• User Input**   **Building a Native Library on Solaris**

```
% cc -I$JDK_HOME/include -I$JDK_HOME/include/solaris \
        -G -o libNative.so \
        theNativeMethod.c
```

This cc command, with the -G option, will generate a Shared Object Library. The lib prefix and so suffix are added to satisfy both a Solaris convention and a Java requirement. In the case of multiple C sources, they would all be included on the command line.

The Win32 analog to using the -I flag on Solaris platforms is the /I option. Most integrated development environments (IDE) also provide a mechanism for supplying preprocessor directories. For the example, the Microsoft Visual Studio allows for setting preprocessor directories from the Preprocessor Category under the Project->Settings->C/C++ tab.

In a similar fashion, most IDEs will explicitly support the construction of a DLL through a specially configured project. The Win32 analog to the -G option above is the /dll option to the Microsoft link-editor (LINK.EXE).

Loading and Invoking the native Method

As mentioned earlier, invoking a native method looks exactly like invoking a regular Java method. There is, however, an extra step required to load the native method library into the JVM.

To load native code, the class method System.loadLibrary must be invoked. A typical way of doing this is by placing a static initializer block within the class that declares the native methods. This is a sure way to guarantee the library is loaded and the native method name resolved when the native method is invoked. According to the *Java Language Specification* (12.4.1), code within a static initialization block gets executed when the class is *initialized*. A class is initialized at its first *active* use. An active use includes the invocation of a method declared by the class. This would include a native method invocation and, therefore, you can be guaranteed that the library containing the code that implements the native methods will be loaded if the loading is done within the class declaring the native methods.

If you elect to put the `System.loadLibrary` in the body of another class, you must be certain that class is initialized before your application tries to invoke a `native` method. Failure to load the native library before invoking a `native` method will result in an `java.lang.UnsatisfiedLink-Error` being thrown by the JVM at the time of attempted `native` method invocation. If this occurs, the `getMessage` method of the thrown object will return the name of the `native` method that could not be found.

In our example, we provide the `static` block within the class `Main` that contains the `public static` method `main`, the first method invoked at application start-up.

Listing 2.4 *Loading Native Library and Invoking* `native` *Method*

```
public class Main {
static {
    System.loadLibrary("Chap2example1");
}
    public static void main(String[] args) {
        AClassWithNativeMethods
            c = new AClassWithNativeMethods();
        c.theNativeMethod();
    }
}
```

(2)

On UNIX systems, the Java run-time adds `lib` to the front of and appends `.so` to the argument to `System.loadLibrary`. In line [2] you can see that these strings do not appear in the argument to `System.loadLibrary`. Likewise, on Win32 systems, the suffix `.dll` is appended to the value named in the `System.loadLibrary` method call. This allows the name to be specified in a platform-independent way. The following table makes clear the translation for UNIX and Win32 platforms.

Table 2.2 *Native Library Naming*

Platform	`System.loadLibrary` Argument (e.g.)	Library Name
UNIX	Example	libExample.so
Win32	Example	Example.dll

In order for `System.loadLibrary` to find your native library, the directory in which the Shared Object Library file resides must appear in the `LD_LIBRARY_PATH` environment variable. On UNIX systems, the `LD_LIBRARY_PATH` environment variable is a colon-separated list of directory names. This value can be verified using the `echo` command.

• User Input   Verifying `LD_LIBRARY_PATH` **on Solaris**

`% echo $LD_LIBRARY_PATH`

On Win32 systems the `PATH` environment variable is used to locate dynamic link libraries. The `PATH` value is a list of directory names separated by semicolons. On Win32 systems, the `PATH` value can be verified using the DOS shell echo command, with a slightly different syntax.

• User Input   Verifying `PATH` **value on Win32**

`C:\> echo %PATH%`

On both platforms, the list is searched in order for a file which matches the modified argument to `System.loadLibrary`.

Returning to Listing 2.4 we will look at how the `static` block containing the `System.loadLibrary` [2] can be modified a bit to provide more robustness when loading a native library. By wrapping the call to `System.loadLibrary` with a `try` block and a supporting `catch` clause, the program can test whether or not a library was successfully loaded and take some appropriate action. In the following example, the `try-catch` block is used to test the availability of a specific version of a native library.

Listing 2.5 *try-catch* **When Loading Native Library**

```
public class MainWithTry {
static {
    try {
(3)        System.loadLibrary("Chap2example1beta");
(4)    } catch (Error e) {
        System.out.println("Using current version");
(5)        System.loadLibrary("Chap2example1");
    }
}
    public static void main(String[] args) {
        AClassWithNativeMethods
            c = new AClassWithNativeMethods();
        c.theNativeMethod();
    }
}
```

If the first `System.loadLibrary` fails in [3] a `LinkageError` is thrown. After being caught in [4], a second attempt to load the native library is made [5]. Note the need for catching a `java.lang.Error` object. Failure to find a library or an error during loading a library results in a `Linkage-Error` being thrown which extends `java.lang.Error` and not `java.lang.Exception`.

Alternative Loading Strategy

The above example, and all of the examples in this book, show the native library being loaded in a `static` initialization block within the class in which the `native` methods are defined. This is not a requirement. The only requirement is that the `native` methods be available (i.e., loaded by the JVM) before you attempt to use any of them.

That leaves open the possibility of loading a native library within the main-line execution stream of a program. Listing 2.6 illustrates placing a call to `System.loadLibrary` in the `main` method.

Listing 2.6 *Loading at Runtime*

```
public class MainRTLoad {
    public static void main(String[] args) {
        System.loadLibrary("Chap2example1");
        AClassWithNativeMethods
            c = new AClassWithNativeMethods();
        c.theNativeMethod();
    }
}
```

(6)

(7)

This approach works as long as the load [6] of the class containing the `native` methods, in this case, `AClassWithNativeMethods`, takes place before the reference to the method [7].

Loading Problems

Probably the most frustrating obstacle to early success with the JNI are problems involved in loading `native` methods properly into your Java application. In an attempt to avoid these frustrating experiences, a discussion of some of the most common problems and possible solutions will be undertaken.

Incorrect lookup path   If your native library can not be found by the JVM, you will get one of two possible errors.

- If you attempt to load a library in a `static` block and this fails, a `java.lang.UnsatisfiedLinkError` will be thrown at the first attempt to invoke a method presumably in that library. The `getMessage` method of the thrown object will return the name of the method your code was trying to invoke.

- If you are loading in the main-line of your application, a `java.lang.UnsatisfiedLinkError` will be thrown as soon as you attempt to load the library. As in the above case, the `getMessage` method of the thrown object will return a message to the effect that the library could not be found.

If either of these conditions occur, the first culprit is, on UNIX systems, your `LD_LIBRARY_PATH` environment variable and, on Win32 systems, your `PATH` environment variable. Check to make sure the value contains the directory in which your library lives.

Improper library name   This problem causes the same errors as above. As far as the JVM knows, it can't find the library you asked for. Check the argument to `System.loadLibrary` to make sure it is what you expect. Also make sure any `.so` or `.dll` suffixes do not appear.

One very specific example of this problem is seen when running a Java application under `java_g`. `java_g` is the version of the JVM for use with debuggers. When `java_g` is executing, `System.loadLibrary` appends `_g` to the name of the native library passed as an argument. If you are on a Win32 platform and run `java_g` and the following load is issued:

```
System.loadLibrary("myNativeLib");
```

the VM will look for a file named `myNativeLib_g.dll` in the directories named in the `PATH` environment variable. On UNIX platforms, the JVM will try to load `libmyNativeLib_g.so` from the directories named in the `LD_LIBRARY_PATH` environment variable.

Improper signature match   If the number and types of the formal parameters in your `native` method declaration do not match the number and types of the parameters in the function prototype, your `native` method name will not get correctly resolved and a `java.lang.UnsatisfiedLinkError` will be thrown. This condition can occur if you have changed the `native` method declaration without using `javah` to regenerate the function prototypes. Or, if you have been naughty, this problem can arise if you manually edited the function prototypes. One particular manifestation of this problem is testing classes outside a `package` and then placing them in a `package` without using `javah` to regenerate the `native` method function prototypes.

When any of these above problems is confronted, there are some tools helpful in getting at the specific cause. On UNIX platforms, both the dump and nm tools report symbol information about a library. A analogous tool, dumpbin, is available on Win32 systems. These tools are most helpful in allowing you to match your expectations for native method names against what the library has recorded.

Building and Running Your Java Application

Hopefully, with all the potential problems behind us, we can now print Hello JNI World from native code invoked by a Java application.

 **User Input** **Compiling and Running a Java Application**

```
% javac Main.java
% java Main
```

Program Output **Running on Solaris**

```
Hello JNI World
```

Feels good, doesn't it?

The Steps in Pictures

Now the preceding 1000 or so words will be turned into a picture.

In the diagram below, the files you produce are shaded. All others are automatically created. Tools you run appear in ovals. All other symbols represent data files.

The compile and link-edit steps have been labelled generically and shown separately. Although this is technically correct, these steps are often combined into one by the development tools supported within different environments.

Figure 2-1 *Steps for Integrating Native Code*

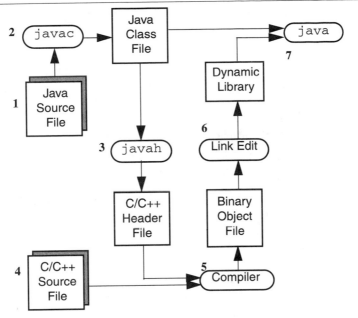

The condensed version of the steps described in the preceding section and the above figure is provided below.

1. Write Java source file.

2. Run Java source file through `javac` to produce class file.

3. Run Java class file through `javah` to produce function prototypes.

4. Write C/C++ source to functions prototypes generated by `javah`.

5. Compile C/C++ source file to produce object files.

6. Run link editor on object file to produce a dynamically loadable library.

7. Run `java` on class file produced in (1) ensuring that this class file invokes Java method `System.loadLibrary` naming library created in step (6).

The following table shows a bit of the specifics for UNIX and Win32 platforms.

Table 2.3 *Platform-Specific Build Tools[a]*

Description	Solaris	Win32
Compile	cc	cl
Link-Edit	ld	link

a. Visual Age C++ from IBM uses `icc/ilink` for these steps. Borland products use `bcc/blink`.

Many compilers allow options intended for the link-edit to be named on the compiler command line. When building libraries that are intended to be loaded dynamically, these flags can be quite helpful. These flags differ across platforms. Required flags for Solaris and Win32 platforms are shown below.

Table 2.4 *Flags for Dynamic Library*

Description	Solaris	Win32
Compile	-G	/LD
Link-Edit	-G	/dll

Of course, on Win32 platforms with a feast of IDEs from which to choose, much of this detail is hidden from view. For instance, in the Microsoft Visual Studio, all you need to do is build your `native` method code in a project explicitly configured for DLL support.

Summary

Take a deep breath. If you have been paying attention, you have successfully completed writing your first Java application using `native` methods. You are at the end of Chapter 2 and you can now do something useful.

Granted, we did not touch the input from the JVM—the arguments to the native function—nor did we return any value. We have deftly sidestepped many of the details of JNI. Instead, we have focussed on the process of incorporating `native` methods into a Java application. We have gone through all the steps necessary to create a Java application which uses C/C++ code.

Additionally, the keyword `native` has been introduced and rendered innocuous. We have met `javah`, that handy little utility that turns `native` method declarations into ANSI C function prototypes. We even gave you a glimpse of how we are going to help you with a variety of platforms.

In the next chapter we will get a little more dirty with the details and see how arguments passed from Java are manipulated in a C/C++ routine.

Chapter 3

SETTING JAVA VARIABLES, INVOKING JAVA METHODS

Moreover I hate everything which merely instructs me without
increasing or directly quickening my activity.

Johann Wolfgang Von Goethe

Introduction

Okay. You're on a roll. You knocked off that `Hello JNI World` example
in no time. You're feeling confident. Thinking, maybe, you can hit those
schedule milestones. Maybe even pull them in a little.

Good. Herr Goethe would be happy. If he weren't dead.

At this point, most programming books would delve into some detail about
data types or other esoteria. We, however, are going to quicken our activity,
pick up the pace, put aside the niceties of computer-generated salutations, and
learn something deserving of your high salary.

In this chapter we will answer the question: "How do I do something meaningful using JNI?" In Chapter 4, we will take a break and discuss some necessary details of the JNI.

For now, we will look at performing the following operations using the JNI:

- Setting the value of a Java instance variable
- Setting the value of a Java class variable
- Getting the value of a Java instance variable
- Getting the value of a Java class variable
- Calling a Java instance method
- Calling a Java class method

A series of examples will cover each of the above operations. These examples are intended as a quick reference. After you have assimilated the details to be learned in future chapters, you can refer to these examples as memory aids.

Before we jump into the examples, a general word about using the JNI functions is in order.

What Is All This Talk About C and C++?

The JNI is designed for use with either C or C++. This means that all the JNI functions can be invoked as either entries in a function table or as methods of a C++ object.

Every `native` method function prototype generated by `javah` declares a JNIEnv pointer as the first argument. Native code written in C treats the JNIEnv pointer as a pointer to a table of functions. For example, to call the function GetFieldID in this table, the proper C syntax is:

Listing 3.1 *Calling a JNI Function From C*

```
JNIEXPORT void JNICALL
Java_myPkg_func(JNIEnv *env, ...) {
    (*env)->GetFieldID(env,...);
    //...
}
```

Note that all JNI functions called by C require the JNIEnv pointer as their first argument. C++ avoids the redundant appearance of the JNIEnv pointer by providing in-line methods that hide the JNIEnv argument to the JNI call. This gives the C++ JNI code the feel of invoking a method on a JNIEnv object with the JNIEnv pointer acting like the hidden *this* argument.

Listing 3.2 *Calling a JNI Function From C++*

```
JNIEXPORT void JNICALL Java_myPkg_func(
                              JNIEnv *env, ...) {
    env->GetFieldID(...);
    //...
}
```

This syntax for calling JNI functions in C++ should come as no surprise since a C++ object maintains pointers to its methods in a similar fashion.

Throughout this book, we use env as the name of the JNIEnv argument passed to the native function.

Some of the Basics

What follows are examples of common operations performed by native code using the JNI. These examples illustrate operations on both static and non-static variables and methods.

Recall that an instance variable, or non-static field, is a variable created and initialized as part of each newly created object. A class variable, or static field, is created when its class is loaded by the JVM. A single variable applies across all instances of a class. A similar distinction holds for static and non-static methods. Static methods are associated with a class, non-static methods are associated with an object. The examples will show how the JNI treats non-static and static references a bit differently.

The examples also highlight just how an access modifier applied to a variable or method does not constrain access from native code. In the Java language, an object's private instance variable is hidden from all but that object's instance methods. Using the JNI you can violate the normal Java access constraints. Namely, if a native method has a reference to an object, it can access both private variables and private methods. The examples below illustrate how native methods can get at both instance and class data of any scoping flavor.

Setting Java Object Data Fields

We are now going to look at how to set both instance and class variables using native methods. The following examples distill these operations to their essence to illustrate exactly what steps need to be taken.

Two examples are offered. In the first, an object accesses the instance and class data of another object using the latter's public methods.

In the second example, an object of one class uses its own native methods to access private and protected data of an object of another class. An OO no-no, but possible.

In both cases, the class SomeVars contains the data we will access. SomeVars appears below.

Listing 3.3 SomeVars: *Target Java Class for JNI Field Access*

```
public class SomeVars {
private              int aPrivate = 0;
protected            int aProtected = 0;
public               int aPublic = 0;
private static       int aStaticPrivate = 0;
protected static     int aStaticProtected = 0;
public static        int aStaticPublic = 0;
public void printAPrivate() {
   System.err.println("A Private = "+ aPrivate);
}
public void printAProtected() {
   System.err.println("A Protected = "+ aProtected);
}
public void printAStaticPrivate() {
   System.err.println(
      "A StaticPrivate = " + aStaticPrivate);
}
public void printAStaticProtected() {
   System.err.println(
      "A StaticProtected = " + aStaticProtected);
}
public native void setAPrivate(int val);
public native void setAStaticPrivate(int val);
}
```

The SomeVars class defines:

- Three instance (non-static) variables, one each of private, protected and public
- Three class (static) variables, one each of private, protected and public
- Four public methods that allow for printing of non-public data
- Two native methods for setting its own private data fields

Two different mechanisms for accessing SomeVars' data fields will be illustrated. First, we will access SomeVars' data fields through its own methods, setAPrivate and setAStaticPrivate. Then, we will access these data fields through native methods of another class.

Native Access to an Object's Own Data Fields

Below is the C++ code for the two `native` methods, `setAPrivate` and `setAStaticPrivate`, both of which set the value of a data field in the `SomeVars` class. In the first, an instance variable is set. In the second, a class variable is set.

Listing 3.4 *Native Code for Setting Java Variables*

```
#include "SomeVars.h"
/* Setting a static variable */
JNIEXPORT void JNICALL Java_SomeVars_setAPrivate(
    JNIEnv *env, jobject thisObj, jint val)
{
    jclass clazz = env->GetObjectClass(thisObj);
    jfieldID fid = env->GetFieldID(clazz,
                                      "aPrivate", "I");
    env->SetIntField(thisObj, fid, val);
}

/* Setting a non-static variable */
JNIEXPORT void JNICALL
Java_SomeVars_setAStaticPrivate(
            JNIEnv *env,
            jobject thisObj,
            jint val) {
    jclass clazz = env->GetObjectClass(thisObj);
    jfieldID fid = env->GetStaticFieldID(clazz,
                            "aStaticPrivate", "I");
    env->SetStaticIntField(clazz, fid, val);
}
```

(1) `jfieldID fid = env->GetFieldID(clazz, "aPrivate", "I");`

(2) `env->SetIntField(thisObj, fid, val);`

(3) `jfieldID fid = env->GetStaticFieldID(clazz, "aStaticPrivate", "I");`

(4) `env->SetStaticIntField(clazz, fid, val);`

The first thing to note is how similar the two functions look. Each performs three operations:

1. Get `jclass` value of the Java class that declares the data field

2. Get the `jfieldID` for the named data field of this class

3. Set a value for that field

The difference is clear from the naming of the JNI functions. Compare lines [1] and [3]. In line [3] the name of the function for retrieving a `jfieldID` value makes explicit the fact that the field is `static`. Likewise, when setting a `static` field, the function `SetStaticIntField` is used (line [4]) rather than `SetIntField` as in [2].

JNI Rule To Remember 1:

There are different sets of functions for accessing static and non-static data fields.

Further comparison of lines [2] and [4] exposes two more subtle differences. First, note that in line [2] SetIntField, the function for setting non-static int fields, takes a jobject as its first[1] argument. On the other hand, SetStaticIntField takes a jclass as its first argument. This brings us to:

JNI Rule To Remember 2:

JNI functions which reference static data fields require a jclass reference as their first argument. JNI functions which reference non-static data fields require a jobject as their first argument.

This distinction makes sense if you think about the difference between a non-static or instance variable and a static or class variable. The value of the former is associated with its object, whereas the value of the latter is associated with its class. Hence, setting an instance variable is a function of a jobject argument and setting a class variable is a function of a jclass argument.

The second difference appearing between line [2] and [4] is the type-parameterized name of the setting function. Again, a naming convention makes explicit what type of field is being set. In this case SetIntField and SetStaticIntField are used. This introduces:

JNI Rule To Remember 3:

JNI functions for setting and getting data fields are named for the type of data being accessed.

In the next chapter we will go into more detail about how Java and JNI keep type information straight.

---

1. When counting arguments to JNI functions, I ignore the JNIEnv pointer since it does not appear in the C++ forms of the calls.

Making It Happen

The example we are considering performs a very common Java operation: a service class provides `public` methods so that client classes can manipulate its `private` data through a common interface, without direct access to that data.

That the two methods in this example are `native` does not change the relationship between the service class and its client. To make this point explicit, consider the following class, `SetSomeVars1`, which creates a `SomeVars` objects and invokes each of its `public` methods.

Listing 3.5 `SetSomeVars1`: *Driver Java Class for JNI Field Access*

```
import SomeVars;
public class SetSomeVars1 {
static {
    System.loadLibrary("Chap3example1");
}

public static void main(String[] args) {
    SomeVars v = new SomeVars();
    v.setAPrivate(300);
    v.printAPrivate();
    v.setAStaticPrivate(301);
    v.printAStaticPrivate();
}
}
```

From a Java programming standpoint, there is really nothing special going on here except, and this is important, the class `SetSomeVars1` uses `System.loadLibrary` to load the library in which the `native` methods are implemented.

And, for the sake of completeness, the output from running the `main` method from class `SetSomeVars1` is shown below.

• Program Output > **Invocation of** `SetSomeVars1`

```
A Private = 300
A StaticPrivate = 301
```

Native Access to Another Object's Data Fields

In this section we will see how `native` methods have access to all data fields, regardless of Java access modifiers.

An intermediary class, SetSomeVars2, is used to declare the native methods rather than declaring them within the class containing our static main method. This way, the native methods need not be static as required by the Java language rule that prevents a non-static reference from within a static method.

Listing 3.6 SetSomeVars2: *Target Java Class for JNI Field Access*

```
import SomeVars;
public class SetSomeVars2 {
public native void setAPrivate(SomeVars v, int val);
public native void setAProtected(
                SomeVars v, int val);
public native void setAPublic(
                SomeVars v, int val);
public native void setAStaticPrivate(
                SomeVars v, int val);
public native void setAStaticProtected(
                SomeVars v, int val);
public native void setAStaticPublic(
                SomeVars v, int val);
}
```

Observe that SetSomeVars2 declares six native methods. All of these methods take a SomeVars reference as their first formal parameter. We will see from the native code that this parameter references the object whose data fields will be manipulated. Of the six native methods, three set a non-static field and three set a static field. Let's look at one implementation from each of these sets of three. Specifically, we will look at setAPrivate and setAStaticPrivate.

Listing 3.7 *Native Code Accessing Private Data Fields*

```
/* Accessing An Object's Private Data */
JNIEXPORT void JNICALL
Java_SetSomeVars2_setAPrivate(
                JNIEnv *env,
                jobject thisObj,
                jobject someVarsObj,
                jint val) {
    jclass clazz = env->GetObjectClass(someVarsObj);
    jfieldID fid = env->GetFieldID(clazz,
                                "aPrivate", "I");
    env->SetIntField(someVarsObj, fid, val);
}
```

(5)

Listing 3.7 (cont.) *Native Code Accessing Private Data Fields*

```
/* Accessing An Object's Private Static Data */

JNIEXPORT void JNICALL
Java_SetSomeVars2_setAStaticPrivate(
                JNIEnv *env,
                jobject thisObj,
                jobject someVarsObj,
                jint val)
{
    jclass clazz = env->GetObjectClass(someVarsObj);

    jfieldID fid = env->GetStaticFieldID(clazz,
                            "aStaticPrivate", "I");
    env->SetStaticIntField(clazz, fid, val);
}
```

(6)

In many respects, this code is not unlike the code from the previous example. Three similar steps are involved in setting a data field in one object from another.

1. Get a `jclass` of the `someVarsObj` parameter.
2. Get a `jfieldID` for a named data field.
3. Set a value for that field.

The major difference is the source of the argument for the call to `GetObjectClass`. The third argument to the native function, `someVarsObj`, is a reference to a `SomeVars` object. So, in lines [5] and [6] above, the function `GetObjectClass` will return a `jclass` value for the `SomeVars` class. Subsequent calls to get the field ID and set the field value will use this `jclass` value.

Making It Happen

Running this program will leave no doubt as to the ability of one object to access the `private` data of another using `native` methods. A small driver application, class `Main`, shown below, creates a `SomeVars` object and a `SetSomeVars2` object.

Listing 3.8 SetVars2Driver: *Driver Java Class for JNI Access Private Data*

```
import SomeVars;
import SetSomeVars2;
public class SetVars2Driver {
static {
    System.loadLibrary("Chap3example2");
}
public static void main(String[] args) {
    SetSomeVars2 s = new SetSomeVars2();
    SomeVars v = new SomeVars();
    s.setAPrivate(v, 100);
    s.setAProtected(v, 101);
    s.setAPublic(v, 102);
    s.setAStaticPrivate(v, 201);
    s.setAStaticProtected(v, 202);
    s.setAStaticPublic(v, 203);
    v.printAPrivate();
    v.printAProtected();
    System.err.println("A Public = " + v.aPublic);
    v.printAStaticPrivate();
    v.printAStaticProtected();
    System.err.println("A StaticPublic = " +
                v.aStaticPublic);
}
}
```

Methods invoked on the SetSomeVars2 object are used to set values in the SomeVars object. Using SomeVars own methods for printing confirms that the private data fields in the SomeVars object have changed.

• Program Output Invocation of SetVars2Driver

```
A Private = 100
A Protected = 101
A Public = 102
A StaticPrivate = 201
A StaticProtected = 202
A StaticPublic = 203
```

With this proof in hand, it is worth stating another JNI Rule To Remember.

Native code can circumvent the constraints imposed by the Java language's data field access modifiers.

This rule should, if nothing else, serve as a reminder that native code can break all the rules when it comes to data encapsulation and good OO design.

Getting a Java Object's Data Fields

It will come as no surprise that getting data fields from a Java object within native code looks similar to setting the fields.

Let's add two `public native` methods to `SomeVars` to create a new class `SomeVarsWithGetters`. These new `native` methods will illustrate how to retrieve data fields from a Java object using native code. The declarations for the new `native` methods appear below.

Listing 3.9 *Getter Methods In class* `SomeVarsWithGetters`

```
public native int getAPrivate();
public native int getAStaticPrivate();
```

These is nothing surprising here, nor is there in the native implementation of these two methods. As noted in the discussion of the above example, how a native setter/getter is implemented is not a function of the access modifiers qualifying the declaration of a data field. Native setter/getter code differs only according to whether the data field to be accessed is a `static` or non-static variable.

Listing 3.10 *JNI Code for Getting Variables*

```
JNIEXPORT jint JNICALL
Java_SomeVarsWithGetters_getAPrivate(
                            JNIEnv *env,
                            jobject thisObj
{
    jclass clazz;
    jfieldID fid;

    clazz = env->GetObjectClass(thisObj);
    fid = env->GetFieldID(clazz, "aPrivate", "I");
(7)     jint val = env->GetIntField(thisObj, fid);
    return val;
}
```

Listing 3.10 (cont.) *JNI Code for Getting Variables*

```
JNIEXPORT jint JNICALL
Java_SomeVarsWithGetters_getAStaticPrivate(
                        JNIEnv *env,
                        jobject thisObj)
{
    jclass clazz;
    jfieldID fid;

    clazz = env->GetObjectClass(thisObj);
    fid = env->GetStaticFieldID(clazz,
                            "aPrivate", "I");
    jint val = env->GetStaticIntField(clazz, fid);
    return val;
}
```

(8)

Comparing this code with the native setter code above, it is clear the only difference in the JNI calls lies in the code that actually accesses the data within the Java object. In this example, we use `GetIntField` in line [7] and `GetStaticIntField` in line [8] rather than `SetIntField` and `SetStaticIntField`.

Invoking a Java Method

We have seen how to set and get `static` and non-static data fields in a Java class and object using native code. Now we will look at examples of invoking a Java method from native code.

Before we proceed, it is worth recalling some of the rules we learned about accessing data fields. We will develop similar rules for accessing Java methods.

First, we saw that different JNI functions exist for accessing `static` and non-static data fields. Second, we saw that the first argument to JNI calls depends on whether the operation applies to instance data or class data. Third, we saw that JNI functions are named according to the type of data they access.

A variation of each of these rules applies as well to JNI functions for invoking Java methods. We will make explicit these rules as the examples develop.

As with the previous example where data fields were accessed, we will look at both an object's access to its own methods and another object's access to those same methods. We will see again that there is no protection against native code invoking a `private` method on an object.

The class defined below is the Java source code for the class whose methods which will be invoked from native code.

Listing 3.11 *Java Source for* SomeMethods

```
public class SomeMethods {
private void aPrivateMethod() {
    System.err.println("SomeMethods.aPrivateMethod");
}
public void aPublicMethod() {
    System.err.println("SomeMethods.aPublicMethod");
}
private static void aStaticPrivateMethod() {
    System.err.println(
        "SomeMethods.aStaticPrivateMethod");
}
public static void aStaticPublicMethod() {
    System.err.println(
        "SomeMethods.aStaticPublicMethod");
}
public native void invokeAPrivate();
public native void invokeAStaticPrivate();
}
```

This class consists of six methods, two of which are `native`. First, we will examine how those `native` methods can invoke the other non-native methods. In the second example, we will explore how another object can invoke `SomeMethods'` `private` methods. In this section, we will focus on the `private` methods. As with setting and getting data fields, `private`, `protected` and `public` modifiers are meaningless within native code. Again, the interesting difference is between `static` and non-static methods.

Native Access to an Object's Own Methods

The native code that implements `invokeAPrivate` and `invokeAStaticPrivate` follows.

Listing 3.12 *JNI Code to Invoke Java Methods*

```
/* Invoke a non-static method */
JNIEXPORT void JNICALL
Java_SomeMethods_invokeAPrivate(
        JNIEnv * env, jobject thisObj) {
(9)     jclass clazz = env->GetObjectClass(thisObj);
(10)    jmethodID mid = env->GetMethodID(
                clazz, "aPrivateMethod", "()V");
(11)    env->CallVoidMethod(thisObj, mid);
}
```

Listing 3.12 (cont.) *JNI Code to Invoke Java Methods*

```
/* Invoke a static method */
JNIEXPORT void JNICALL
Java_SomeMethods_invokeAStaticPrivate(
      JNIEnv *env, jobject thisObj)
{
    jclass clazz = env->GetObjectClass(thisObj);
    jmethodID mid = env->GetStaticMethodID(clazz,
              "aStaticPrivateMethod", "()V");
    env->CallStaticVoidMethod(clazz, mid);
}
```

(12)

(13)

If you think this looks familiar, good. The JNI Rules To Remember must have had an impact.

It takes three operations to invoke a method:

1. Get `jclass` value of the Java class declaring the method.

2. Get the `jmethodID` for the named method from this class.

3. Invoke the method based on its object (non-static) or class (`static`).

The code in line [9] is identical to what we saw when accessing Java data fields. In both cases, a `jclass` is returned from `GetObjectClass`. Line [10] is not sufficiently different to confuse anybody. Instead of asking for a `jfieldID`, we ask for a `jmethodID`. Finally, in line [11], we use a JNI function whose name gives the correct impression that we are calling a method.

In lines [10] and [12] above, note the different calls for getting the `jmethodID` of a method. The call varies depending on whether the method is `static` (`GetStaticMethodID`) or non-static (`GetMethodID`).

In lines [11] and [13] above, a method is called using a JNI function whose name explicitly denotes whether or not the called method is `static`.

One detail we will gloss over for now is the appearance of `Void` in the name of the functions used to call a method. At this point, suffice it to say that, like the JNI functions for accessing data fields within a Java object, the naming convention for JNI method invocation functions includes mention of the return type of the method being called.

Native Access to Private Methods of Another Object

With what we have learned so far, this final example can be dispatched with rather quickly. The SomeMethodsInvoker class simply declares two native methods that take a SomeMethods object as an argument.

Listing 3.13 *Declaration of Natives That Take an Object as Argument*

```
public class SomeMethodsInvoker {
    public native void invokeAPrivate(SomeMethods s);
    public native void invokeAStaticPrivate(
                        SomeMethods s);
}
```

The methods declared in Listing 3.13 use the SomeMethods object reference to invoke its methods. The C/C++ code for these native methods is similar to the code in Listing 3.12 except that the GetObjectClass function uses the SomeMethods object reference argument to find a jclass value. This means that instead of calling one of its own methods, the native method invokeAPrivate is calling a method of a SomeMethods object.

Listing 3.14 *Calling* private *Methods of Object Passed as Argument*

```
#include "SomeMethodsInvoker.h"

JNIEXPORT void JNICALL
Java_SomeMethodsInvoker_invokeAPrivate(
                        JNIEnv *env,
                        jobject thisObj,
                        jobject someMethodsObj)
{
    jclass clazz;
    jmethodID mid;

    clazz = env->GetObjectClass(someMethodsObj);
    mid = env->GetMethodID(clazz,
                        "aPrivateMethod", "()V");
    env->CallVoidMethod(someMethodsObj, mid);
}
```

(14)
(15)

Listing 3.14 (cont.) *Calling* `private` *Methods of Object Passed as Argument*

```
/* Calling a private static method on object
 * passed as argument
 */
JNIEXPORT void JNICALL
Java_SomeMethodsInvoker_invokeAStaticPrivate(
                        JNIEnv *env,
                        jobject thisObj,
                        jobject someMethodsObj)
{
    jclass clazz;
    jmethodID mid;

    clazz = env->GetObjectClass(someMethodsObj);
    mid = env->GetStaticMethodID(clazz,
                "aStaticPrivateMethod", "()V");
    env->CallStaticVoidMethod(clazz, mid);
}
```

(16)

(17)

In lines [14] and [16] a class reference to the SomeMethods class is retrieved and then used in line [15] and [17] to get the method ID. No surprises here. By this time it may be just a tad boring but, before we move on, let's write a few more JNI Rules To Remember.

JNI Rule To Remember 5:

There are different sets of functions for invoking `static` and non-static methods.

JNI Rule To Remember 6:

JNI functions which invoke `static` methods require a `jclass` as their first argument. JNI functions which invoke non-static data methods require a `jobject` as their first argument.

JNI Rule To Remember 7:

JNI functions for invoking methods are named for the type of data being returned.

And finally, let's just drop a couple words from JNI Rule To Remember 4 and offer a revised formulation.

JNI Rule To Remember 8:

Native code can circumvent the constraints imposed by the Java language's access modifiers.

Making It Happen

Invoking Java methods from native code will now be illustrated using the above `native` methods.

A class `MainInvoker` drives the example by creating both a `SomeMethods` object in [18] and a `SomeMethodsInvoker` object in [21].

Listing 3.15 *Java Source for* `MainInvoker`

```
import SomeMethods;
import SomeMethodsInvoker;
public class MainInvoker {
static {
    System.loadLibrary("Chap3example2");
}
public static void main(String[] args) {
```
```
(18)        SomeMethods m = new SomeMethods();
(19)        m.invokeAPrivate();
(20)        m.invokeAStaticPrivate();
(21)        SomeMethodsInvoker s = new SomeMethodsInvoker();
(22)        s.invokeAPrivate(m);
(23)        s.invokeAStaticPrivate(m);
```
```
    }
}
```

The `SomeMethods` object invokes its own methods in lines [19] and [20]. In lines [22] and [23] the `SomeMethodsInvoker` object calls its own `native` methods, passing the `SomeMethods` object as an argument. From within those `native` methods, the `private` methods of a `SomeMethods` instance are invoked. The output follows.

• Program Output **Invocation of** `MainInvoker`

```
SomeMethods.aPrivateMethod
SomeMethods.aStaticPrivateMethod
SomeMethods.aPrivateMethod
SomeMethods.aStaticPrivateMethod
```

A Disclaimer of Sorts

It is a legitimate question to ask why a `native` method of one object would want to access the `private` data and methods of another object. The point is not that it is a good idea to do so, but that it can be done. Knowing it can be done, an application designer can take advantage of this capability or avoid it, depending on the requirements.

Returning a Value From Java Methods

In the preceding examples, every time we invoked a Java method from native code, we either used the JNI function `CallVoidMethod` or `CallStaticVoidMethod`. This pair of functions calls into Java to execute a method that returns void.

The JNI provides an entire suite of functions available for invoking Java methods based on the return type of the method. The parametric function prototypes for these functions look like:

```
<jniType> Call<type>Method(
                jobject, jmethodID, args...);
<jniType> CallStatic<type>Method(
                jclass, jmethodID, args...);
```

The functions are distinguished, first, by their return type and, second, by whether they invoke a `static` method or an instance method. Both, however, return the value returned by the Java method that they invoke.

In the next chapter, we will look at the JNI native types in more detail. For now, the following table describes how to replace the variable parts of the above function descriptions.

Table 3.1 *JNI Call Function Types*

Return *<jniType>*	Function Name *<type>*
jbyte	Byte
jshort	Short
jint	Int
jlong	Long
jfloat	Float
jdouble	Double
jchar	Char
jboolean	Boolean
jobject	Object
void	Void

As an example, to invoke a Java instance method that returns an integer, use:

```
jint retVal;
retVal = env->CallIntMethod(...);
```

When calling a function that returns a type that extends java.lang.Object, use:

```
jobject obj;
obj = env->CallObjectMethod(...);
```

This second construction generally requires some type of cast, especially if the object returned is an array. We will take a peek at how that works now, but we defer full coverage of JNI arrays until Chapter 6.

To invoke a Java method that returns an array object, use CallObject-Method and cast the return value:

```
jintArray intArr;
intArr = (jintArray) env->CallObjectMethod(...);
```

Of course, the same usage conventions apply to invoking static methods.

Non-Virtual Method Invocation

There is another set of JNI functions capable of invoking Java methods. These functions allow invocation of a method from anywhere up the chain in an object's inheritance hierarchy.

The `Call<type>Method` and `CallStatic<type>Method` set of functions invoke a method based on an object reference. This is the most common way of invoking a function, either within native code or within Java.

The non-virtual invocation functions effectively allow you to jump up the inheritance hierarchy when invoking a method and invoke a superclass's method. This is the motivation for the naming convention for the family of functions: you can circumvent the virtual method in a subclass in favor of one in the superclass.

Consider the following classes. The `Super` [24] and `Sub` [25] classes in Listing 3.16 provide a mini-hierarchy of Java classes.

Listing 3.16 *Java Source for* `Super` *and* `Sub`

```
(24)    class Super {
            protected String name;
            public String helloMsg() {
                return(name + " says Hello from Super");
            }
            public Super(String nm) {
                name = nm;
            }
        }
(25)    class Sub extends Super {
            public String helloMsg() {
                return(name + " says Hello from Sub");
            }
            public Sub(String nm) {
                super(nm);
            }
        }
```

The class `NVMain` in Listing 3.17 drives this example by creating a `Sub` object [26] and passing it to a `native` method [28].

Listing 3.17 *Java for* NVMain

```
public class NVMain {
    static {
        System.loadLibrary("Chap3example3");
    }
    public static native void nativeToString(
                                  Super obj);
    public static void main(String[] args) {
(26)        Sub sub = new Sub("Kilian");
(27)        System.out.println(sub.helloMsg());
(28)        nativeToString(sub);
    }
}
```

Before we look at any native code, consider the output that results from line [27]:

• Program Output   Invocation of helloMsg **from Java**

```
Kilian says Hello from Sub
```

As expected, this invocation of helloMsg reports it is coming from the Sub class. This call is the Java analog to the JNI Call<*type*>Method. We will contrast this to the non-virtual calls in native code.

Use of JNI Non-Virtual Functions

In the nativeToString method, we will see an invocation of the Super.helloMsg passing a Sub object as an argument. To highlight the differences between the different calling conventions, let's look at the implementation of the native method nativeToString which invokes helloMsg in three different ways.

Listing 3.18 *Implementation of* nativeToString

```
        JNIEXPORT void JNICALL Java_Main_nativeToString
          (JNIEnv *env, jclass thisClz, jobject aSub) {
          jboolean isCopy;
          const char* cstr;
          jstring jstr;
          jclass sclazz;
(29)      jclass clazz = env->GetObjectClass(aSub);

          // Call helloMsg() of object using class
          // reference derived from GetObjectClass(self)
(30)      jmethodID mid = env->GetMethodID(clazz,
                           "helloMsg",
                           "()Ljava/lang/String;");

(31)      jstr = (jstring) env->CallObjectMethod(
                           aSub, mid, NULL);

          cstr = env->GetStringUTFChars(jstr, &isCopy);
(32)      printf("Call*Method.helloMsg:%s\n", cstr);

(33)      sclazz = env->GetSuperclass(clazz);
          // Call helloMsg() of object using class
          // reference derived from GetSuperClass(self)
(34)      mid = env->GetMethodID(sclazz,
                           "helloMsg",
                           "()Ljava/lang/String;");

(35)      jstr = (jstring) env->CallObjectMethod(
                           aSub, mid, NULL);

          cstr = env->GetStringUTFChars(jstr, &isCopy);
(36)      printf("Call*Method.helloMsg:%s\n", cstr);

          // Call what amounts to super.helloMsg()
(37)      jstr = (jstring) env->CallNonvirtualObjectMethod(
                           aSub, sclazz, mid, NULL);

          cstr = env->GetStringUTFChars(jstr, &isCopy);
(38)      printf("CallNV*Method.helloMsg:%s\n", cstr);
        }
```

There are three sequences of JNI calls in the above code that get a method ID from some class, then invoke that method. Before we look at the code, let's look at the output from invoking the main method of NVMain from Listing 3.17 on page 45. This will give a context in which to discuss the behavior of the JNI functions.

• Program Output   **Invocation of** NVMain

```
Kilian says Hello from Sub
Call*Method.helloMsg:Kilian says Hello from Sub
Call*Method.helloMsg:Kilian says Hello from Sub
CallNV*Method.helloMsg:Kilian says Hello from Super
```

We saw the first line above. This was printed by [27] in the Java code. It is the standard invocation of an object method.

The second line of output is printed by line [32] after a call to CallObjectMethod in line [31]. This call to CallObjectMethod uses a class reference retrieved from the Sub object in line [29] and a method ID retrieved using the same class reference in line [30]. This results in calling the helloMsg of Sub object. The output confirms this.

The third line of output is printed by line [36]. In spite of using a class reference to the Super class returned by GetSuperClass [33] to retrieve the method ID in line [34], the helloMsg method of the Sub object is executed [35]. The Call<*type*>Method form of the JNI method invocation forces the method of a particular object to be invoked.

All that changes with the use of CallNonvirtualObjectMethod in line [37]. The same class reference as was retrieved in line [33] and the same method ID as was retrieved in [34] are used in the call to CallNonvirtualObjectMethod. Yet, a different helloMsg method was invoked. The fourth output line above as printed by line [38] confirms this. The helloMsg method from the Super class was invoked, not the implementation of helloMsg in the Sub class object.

Yet More Ways to Call a Java Method

We have seen three styles of invoking a Java method from native code. We have seen the Call<*type*>Method functions for invoking non-static methods. We have seen the CallStatic<*type*>Method functions for invoking static methods. We have also just seen the CallNonvirtual<*type*>Method family of JNI invocation functions.

You can take all you know about these functions and multiply it by three. Each of the JNI invocation functions implied by the parametric naming convention has two relatives. For example, to invoke a Java method that returns an object, there are the following three forms of Call<*type*>Method.

```
CallObjectMethod
CallObjectMethodA
CallObjectMethodV
```

More generally, for each return type, there are three invocation functions:

```
Call<type>Method
Call<type>MethodA
Call<type>MethodV
```

We have seen examples of the first style. The arguments are simply listed in the function call.

The second type of function call, e.g. `CallObjectMethodA`, takes a `jvalue` array of values for its third argument. For example, the arguments to `CallObjectMethodA` look like:

```
CallObjectMethodA(jobject, jmethodID, jvalue*)
```

We will see more about the `jvalue` array in Chapter 4. Additionally, the arguments to `CallObjectMethodV` look like:

```
CallObjectMethodV(jobject, jmethodID, va_list)
```

The third argument to this call is a variable argument list as defined by the ANSI C header file `<stdargs.h>`.

Summary

Are you still with me?

Good. Because you now know just enough to make you dangerous as a JNI coder. We have learned the difference between invoking JNI functions in C and C++. You have learned how to set and get data fields within Java objects using JNI. You have learned to invoke Java methods using JNI. You have learned a few handy rules to help us assimilate JNI details. Finally, you have learned that a great 19th century German poet, philosopher and mystic is dead. But, fortunately, you have not heard the last from him.

You are still, however, missing a few details. Some things were purposely ignored in this chapter so that the focus could be on some of the major functionality of JNI. In the next chapter, you will learn about those funny type names like `jint`, `jclass` and `jmethodID`. You will also learn the meaning of that cryptic quoted string that keeps appearing as an argument to JNI function calls.

In the next chapter you make a commitment to the details of JNI.

Chapter 4

NATIVE TYPES, SIGNATURES AND OTHER DETAILS

Concerning all acts of initiative and creation, there is one elementary truth, the ignorance of which kills countless ideas and splendid plans: the moment one definitely commits oneself, then providence moves too... A whole system of events issues from the decision, raising in one's favor any number of unforeseen incidents, meetings and material assistance which no man could have dreamed...

Johann Wolfgang von Goethe[1]

Introduction

If you are still with me you have, presumably, made a commitment. All hesitancy has dissipated and any urge to draw back has been squelched.

That's good. For all that you need, but could not have foreseen, to make complete sense of the Java Native Interface will now become available.

In this chapter the little holes left from last chapter will be filled. You will learn about the Java Native Types, those funny data types whose names begin with a j. You will also learn the details of those strange looking sequences of characters, the method *signature*, that appeared in some of the JNI function calls. Java Native Types provide a canonical mapping of C types to Java types. Signatures provide a mechanism for identifying Java methods and data fields using a character string.

This chapter also includes a brief discussion on passing arguments to native methods and some more details on that ubiquitous JNIEnv argument.

---

1. Although attributed to Goethe, there is some uncertainty as to whether he deserves credit for this quote. Meredith Lee, Executive Secretary of the *Goethe Society of North America,* writes that this quotation "is circulating broadly at the moment, but we have not been able to verify that Goethe said or wrote it. If I come up with something, we'll let you know."

Java Types

To accommodate different platforms, the JVM imposes a well-defined size on various types of data. In programming languages such as C, an `int` may be sixteen bits on one machine and thirty-two on another. As a virtual machine, the Java environment defines the size of the data types that it supports.

Java has two kinds of types: *primitive* and *reference*. Primitive types are either numeric or boolean. The numeric types are `byte`, `short`, `int`, `long`, `char`, `float` and `double`. Table 4.1 describes the format for these types.

Table 4.1 *Size of Java Primitive Types*

Type Name	Description
byte	8-bit two's-complement
short	16-bit two's-complement
int	32-bit two's-complement
long	64-bit two's-complement
float	32-bit IEEE 754 floating point
double	64-bit IEEE 754 floating point
char	16-bit Unicode

Additionally, the *Java Language Specification* defines the primitive type `boolean` which may have only one of two possible values: `true` or `false`.

In addition to the primitive types, Java defines reference types. Reference types either refer to a `class`, an `interface`, or an array. It is tempting to call these reference types pointers, and the *Java Language Specification* does, but when you are reading a book about native coding that contains lots of C/C++ examples, it is best to stay away from the term "pointer" when what you are really talking about is an object reference. In C/C++, pointers are addresses. In Java, addresses do not exist.

When writing native code, you must be aware of the Java type definitions so that when manipulating data from the Java world you use the corresponding native type. A common error is to think of a C ASCII character array as mapping directly into a Java `char` array. There may, of course, be a relationship between the two, but there is some massaging required to pass from one world to the other. Before we look at the details of that, let's take a look at Java Native Types.

Java Native Types

As mentioned, Java defines a virtual machine. The size of the types which this virtual machine supports are given above. However, what happens when you leave this virtual machine and do work on the real machine upon which your virtual machine is running? How do you map Java types to the native types on the real machine?

Fortunately, the JNI does this for you. For each type defined by the Java language, the JNI defines a corresponding native type. The types defined by the JNI are called Java *native types*. Within native code, the Java native types should be used when manipulating data shared with the Java application. We will see that all the JNI function calls take as arguments and return as values native types. This way, the correct mapping between Java types and native types is ensured.

Primitive Native Types

In the following table each JNI native type is listed with its corresponding Java type to its right.

Table 4.2 *Primitive Native Types*

Native Type	Java Type
jbyte	byte
jshort	short
jint	int
jlong	long
jfloat	float
jdouble	double
jchar	char
jboolean	boolean
void	void

With this mapping, the JNI ensures that the C type is the same size as its corresponding Java type.

All the native types in the above table are defined in one of two header files.

```
$JDK_HOME/include/jni.h
$JDK_HOME/include/platform/jni_md.h.
```

The header file `jni_md.h` declares those JNI types that may be defined by different platform-specific types. This file is generally used to define the

8-bit JNI type, `jbyte`, and the 64-bit JNI type, `jlong`. Each vendor of a JVM will ship its `jni_md.h` file in the JDK include/*platform* directory where *platform* specifies the name of the platform for which the JVM is targeted.

On Win32 platforms `$JDK_HOME\include\win32\jni_md.h` contains the following type definitions:

```
typedef long        jint;
typedef __int64     jlong;
typedef signed char jbyte;
```

On Solaris, the file `$JDK_HOME/include/solaris/jni_md.h` contains the following type definitions:

```
typedef long        jint;
typedef long long   jlong;
typedef signed char jbyte;
```

Comparing these two sets of `typedef`s, you can see that for 64-bit data, different platform-specific types are mapped onto the `jlong` native type.

As a convenience, `jni.h` defines two macros for use with `jboolean` variables:

```
#define JNI_TRUE      1
#define JNI_FALSE     0
```

Reference Native Types

In addition to the above type mapping, the JNI defines the following native reference types and their corresponding Java reference types.

Table 4.3 *Reference Native Types*

Native Type	Java Referent
jobject	Object
jclass	Class
jstring	String
jarray	array
jthrowable	Throwable

JDK 1.2 introduces a subclass of `jobject`, `jweak`, for designating weak references.

The `jarray` type acts as a superclass to native arrays with elements of various types. There exists a native array type for each Java primitive type as well as the `jobject` type.

Table 4.4 lists the native types for arrays and matches them with their corresponding Java type. The native array types can all be treated as subclasses of `jarray` when native code is written in C++.

Table 4.4 *Primitive Array Types*

Native Array Type	Java Referent
jobjectArray	Object[]
jbyteArray	byte[]
jshortArray	short[]
jintArray	int[]
jlongArray	long[]
jfloatArray	float[]
jdoubleArray	double[]
jcharArray	char[]
jbooleanArray	boolean[]

Note that for C++ compilations of native code, `jobject` is the superclass for all the other JNI native types. For C compilations, all the native types are typedef'd from `jobject`. These relationships are defined in `<jni.h>`.

Programming Considerations

Combined, the preceding three tables define what it means for a piece of data to be of the same type when used by both Java code and native code.

The programming implications of this are as follows:

1. The type of each actual argument passed to a `native` method as defined by function prototypes generated by `javah` will be one of the native types described above.

2. The type of each argument passed to all JNI functions will also be one of these native types.

3. All return values from native code should be of one of the native types.

4. Any native operations not involved in returning a value to the JVM or making a JNI function call may use regular ANSI C types (e.g., `int`).

5. When casting machine-dependent types to JNI native types, as when passing values to JNI functions or returning values to the JVM, be careful not to alter the intended value of data, for example, casting an `int` to a `jshort`.

Items (1)-(3) above describe an interface between Java code and native code. You should think of all calls to JNI functions and return values from native methods as communication with another machine, the JVM, that only speaks the language of native types. Item (4) basically says that when staying in Rome, it is okay to do as the Romans, and item (5) is really nothing more than a common sense programming rule.

The jvalue Type

The JNI introduces a special union type. The jvalue type is used as the element type for an array of values passed to some JNI functions. The jvalue type simply defines a union structure capable of taking any JNI native type as a value.

The definition of the jvalue type appears below.

Listing 4. 1 *Definition of* jvalue union

```
typedef union jvalue {
    jboolean z;
    jbyte    b;
    jchar    c;
    jshort   s;
    jint     i;
    jlong    j;
    jfloat   f;
    jdouble  d;
    jobject  l;
} jvalue;
```

In Chapter 5, we will look at using the jvalue structure when creating a new Java object within native code.

Field and Method Identifier Types

The JNI introduces two special native types which have no corresponding Java type but are necessary when using the JNI API.

jfieldID and jmethodID are used to identify data fields and methods, respectively, within Java class and instance objects. Each data field and method within a Java class has a unique identifier associated with it. The identifier is established when the class is initialized and retains its value unchanged until the class is unloaded. If a class is loaded, unloaded, and then loaded again, there is no guarantee that a given field or method identifier will have the same value across class loads.

Table 4.5 completely describes the usage of field and method identifiers. It lists the JNI functions that return field and method identifiers along with those JNI functions that require identifiers as input arguments.

Table 4.5 *Uses of Field and Method Identifiers*

Native Type	Returned by	Argument to
jfieldID	GetFieldID	Get<*type*>Field Set<*type*>Field
	GetStaticFieldID	GetStatic<*type*>Field SetStatic<*type*>Field
jmethodID	GetMethodID	Call<*type*>Method Call<*type*>MethodA Call<*type*>MethodV CallNonvirtual<*type*>Method CallNonvirtual<*type*>MethodA CallNonvirtual<*type*>MethodV
	GetStaticMethodID	CallStatic<*type*>Method CallStatic<*type*>MethodA CallStatic<*type*>MethodV

Table 4.5 introduces a notation you will see throughout this book. The <*type*> placeholder refers to either a Java primitive type with its first letter capitalized, or Object for a Java reference type.

When you need, for example, to set an int instance variable, you first get its field identifier in a jfieldID variable using GetFieldID or GetStaticFieldID and you then pass it to the JNI function, SetInt-Field.

Both jfieldID and jmethodID are pointers to opaque structures.

JDK 1.2 introduces four more functions that use field and method identifiers. These functions convert between identifiers and instances of objects defined by the java.lang.reflect package.

The following table shows the usage of the field and method identifiers in these newly introduced functions.

Table 4.6 *JDK 1.2 Uses of Field and Method Identifiers*

Native Type	Returned by	Argument to
jfieldID	FromReflectedField	ToReflectedField
jmethodID	FromReflectedMethod	ToReflectedMethod

Chapter 15 covers these functions in detail.

Method Signatures

Recall from the previous chapter the character strings used in calls to Get-MethodID and GetStaticMethodID. In a typical call to Get-MethodID, the jclass argument and the name of the desired method were followed by a character string known as a *signature*. The following example illustrates this.

```
jmethodID = env->GetMethodID(
                clazz, "valueOf", "()I");
```

Since a Java class may have multiple methods of the same name, a unique signature is used to identify a specific one. The *Java Language Specification* defines a signature as the name of a method and the number and types of its formal parameters.

A JNI method signature is a character string description of the formal parameters to a method and its return value. A method signature encodes information about the number and type of arguments to the method and the type of its return value. In the code segment above, the string ()I is read "a method with no arguments, returning an integer." Within a signature, the encoding of the arguments appears in the parentheses.

This is best understood through the use of examples. Consider the following abstract class below. The class aClass and its methods have been declared as abstract so that a syntactically correct example can be shown while omitting the method bodies. That a method is declared as abstract has no bearing on its type signature.

Listing 4. 2 *Java Source for* myProject.aClass

```
package myProject;

public abstract class aClass {

private int        anInt = 10;
private int[]      anIntArray;
private aClass[]   aClassArray;
private boolean    aFlag;

public abstract    void setString(String aString);
public abstract    String getString();
public abstract    void setInt(int anInt);
public abstract    int getInt();
```

Listing 4.2 (cont.) *Java Source for* myProject.aClass

```
private abstractvoid setMyClass(aClass a);
private abstractaClass getMyClass();

private abstractaClass[] getArrayOfClass();
public abstractvoid setStringArray(String[] name);
public abstractvoid setIntArray(int[] ints);

public abstractvoid
        setEmAll(String name, int[] ints, aClass a);

public abstract void getFields();
}
```

The JDK provides a tool to take the guesswork out of signature use in JNI functions. After the following class is compiled with javac, the javap command can be used to display signature information. When the -s option is used with the javap command, the method signatures are reported, depending on the presence of one of the -public, -protected, -package, or -private options. These options determine which method signatures are displayed.

Since aClass has private methods, the use of the -private flag will be used to display all of the method signatures.

▸ **User Input**　　**Use of** javap

% **javap -s -private myProject.aClass**

The output of this command is straightforward. Following each method, a comment contains the signature for that method. Both private and public methods are reported since the -private flag was used with the javap command.

```
Compiled from myproject.aClass
public abstract synchronized
    class myProject.aClass extends java.lang.Object
      /* ACC_SUPER bit set */
    {
    private int anInt;/*   I    */
    private int anIntArray[];/*    [I    */
    private myProject.aClass aClassArray[];
    /*    [LmyProject/aClass;    */
    private boolean aFlag;
    /*   Z    */
    public abstract void setString(java.lang.String);
    /*    (Ljava/lang/String;)V    */
    public abstract java.lang.String getString();
    /*    ()Ljava/lang/String;    */
    public abstract void setInt(int);
    /*    (I)V    */
    public abstract int getInt();
    /*    ()I    */
    private abstract void setMyClass(myProject.aClass);
    /*    (LmyProject/aClass;)V    */
    private abstract myProject.aClass getMyClass();
    /*    ()LmyProject/aClass;    */
    private abstract myProject.aClass
       getArrayOfClass()[];
    /*    ()[LmyProject/aClass;    */
    public abstract void
       setStringArray(java.lang.String[]);
    /*    ([Ljava/lang/String;)V    */
    public abstract void setIntArray(int[]);
    /*    ([I)V    */
    public abstract void
         setEmAll(java.lang.String, int[],
            myProject.aClass);
    /*    (Ljava/lang/String;[ILmyProject/aClass;)V    */
    public abstract void getFields();
    /*    ()V    */
    public myProject.aClass();
    /*    ()V    */
    }
```

(1)

The strings appearing in this output can be used as the third argument to `GetMethodID` or `GetStaticMethodID`.

To make complete sense of the above output, the following table is helpful. Each character or sequence of characters that may appear in a signature appears on the left, with its description on the right.

Table 4.7 *Signature Encoding*

Signature	Description
B	`byte`
C	`char`
D	`double`
F	`float`
I	`int`
J	`long`
S	`short`
V	`void`
Z	`boolean`
L<*fully-qualified-class*>;	fully-qualified class
[<*sigtype*>	Array of <*sigtype*>
(<*sigtype-list*>) <*return-sigtype*>	Method signature

Looking at line [1], we see the signature for the `setEmAll` method. Its formal parameters are described between the parentheses. Its first argument is a `java.lang.String`, followed by an integer (`int`) array followed by a `myProject.aClass` object. In both cases where a class is named, its description is terminated with a semi-colon. The final `V` denotes a `void` return.

In general, <*sigtype*> in the above table can be replaced by any of the values in the left column. Similarly, <*sigtype-list*> is a list of <*sigtype*> values that represent the arguments to a method. <*return-sigtype*> denotes a <*sigtype*> value returned by the method being described.

With the help of `javap`, determining the signature of a method is straightforward, nonetheless, it is not uncommon for this native coder to spend too much time debugging a `native` method only to find out the problem is a missing semi-colon, so, for emphasis:

JNI Rule To Remember 9:

Don't forget that semi-colon after a fully-qualified path name.

Signature and Constructors

Type signatures for constructors follow the same rules as those for instance or class methods. There are two things to keep in mind, though. First, the name for a constructor is always <init>. Second, even though both syntactically and semantically constructors do not return a value, their type signature should always include a V, signifying void, after the parenthesized formal parameter description.

Assuming a class, Foo, with a constructor as shown below:

```
public class Foo {
Foo(String[] list, int count) {
// do something constructor-like...
}
```

The JNI call to get its method identifier would look like:

```
jmethodID mid;
//...
mid = env->GetMethodID(clazz, "<init>",
                    "([Ljava/lang/String;I)V");
```

Notice the V following the parenthesized parameter description in the last line of the above code segment.

Type Signatures and Data Fields

The JNI uses a technique similar to method signatures to describe the type of a Java data field. GetFieldID and GetStaticFieldID both require an argument which describes the type signature of the data field for which they are to return a jfieldID value.

In this case, however, rather than a parentheses-enclosed sequence of multiple types, only a single type is described.

The class aClass appears below along with the type signatures for its data fields.

```
public abstract class aClass {
private int anInt;            // "I"
private int[] anIntArray;     // "[I"

// "[LmyPackage/myClasses/aClass;"
private aClass[] aClassArray;
private boolean aFlag         // "Z"
// ...
}
```

For example, when referring to the `anIntArray` field, the C++ call to `GetFieldID` would appear as below:

```
jfieldID fid = env->GetFieldID(clazz,
                    "anIntArray", "[I");
```

Another mistake that has kept this native coder scratching his head for an embarrassingly long time is using the improper type encoding when retrieving a data field of type `long`. In the hope you can be spared the same embarrassment:

JNI Rule To Remember 10:

The type signature encoding for a Java `long` is 'J' not 'L'. Repeat after me: "The type signature encoding for a Java `long` is 'J' not 'L'."

Be forewarned.

The `JNIEnv` *Pointer*

Every `native` method receives a `JNIEnv` pointer as its first argument. The `JNIEnv` pointer points to another pointer which in turn points to a table of function pointers. Each entry in this table points to a JNI function. The following diagram shows the relationships among these pointers.

Figure 4-1 *The* JNIEnv *and the JNI Function Table*

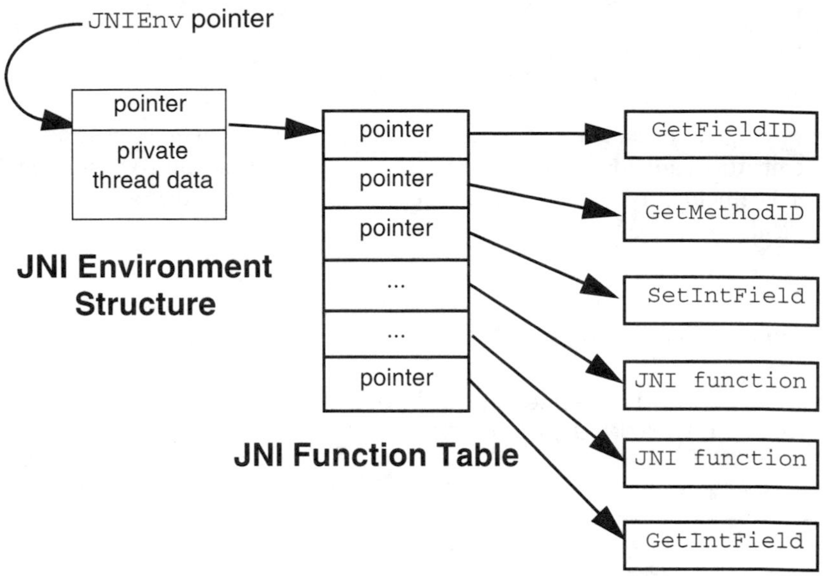

The JNIEnv pointer, besides pointing to a table pointer, may also point to some additional thread private data. This private data is defined by the JVM implementation. The JNI specification says that a JVM implementation may store thread-specific data in the area pointed to by a JNIEnv pointer. This means that the JNIEnv pointer can not be passed from one thread to another.

JNI Rule To Remember 11:

The JNIEnv pointer is only valid within the current thread.

Since a native method may be called from different threads in a Java application, each different invocation of that native method will have a different JNIEnv pointer passed to it. Passing this information to another thread will result in unpredictable behavior.

On the other hand, for a given method, from a given thread, the JVM guarantees that the same JNIEnv pointer is passed on each call to that method.

A Word About Passing Arguments

The rules for passing arguments to a `native` method are the same as those for passing arguments to a Java method. This could, possibly, go without saying if there weren't some confusion about how Java parameters are passed. However, this confusion, coupled with the slightly ambiguous conventions for C argument passing, motivates a discussion on this topic.

The ambiguous notion of 'pass by reference' has a different meaning in Java than some C programmers may assign to it. In C, one has address pointers and it is not uncommon, albeit slightly inaccurate, to refer to a pointer as a 'reference'. When a C/C++ pointer is passed to a function, it is not unusual to say a 'reference' is passed. Of course, it is more correct to say an 'address' is passed. This use of 'reference' muddies a bit the idea of a Java reference.

All arguments in Java are passed by value—even references. The following is excerpted from Section 4.5.3 of the *Java Language Specification*:

> *For every parameter declared in a method declaration, a new parameter variable is created each time that method is invoked. The new variable is initialized with the corresponding argument value from the method invocation. The method parameter effectively ceases to exist when the execution of the body of the method is complete.*

It is correct to say that a reference to a Java object is passed as an argument to a method. However, before the method is called, a copy of all of its arguments are placed on the call stack. For an argument that is an object, there exists at least two references to that object at method call time: the original and the argument value. Any changes made within the method to the object referenced by the argument value will show up in the object referenced by the original reference; they refer to the same object.

On the other hand, any variable of a Java primitive type may never act as a 'return parameter' for a function. Because all Java arguments are passed by value, this (perhaps) common practice for a C programmer is not available from a Java method, native or otherwise.

This subject gets even a bit more confusing when dealing with arrays and strings in native code. In order to affect changes made to strings and arrays in native code, a little extra work is required of the native programmer. As you will see, the JNI provides functions for getting at a contiguous memory representation of `java.lang.String` objects and Java arrays. It is the decision of the JVM whether this representation is a copy of the data in the Java object or a pointer into the object's memory. If it is a copy, then it is up to the programmer to make sure that any changes made to the copy are written into the Java object. The JNI also provides functions for this operation. Chapter 6 discusses the treatment of strings and arrays in detail.

Summary

The details of the JNI are now in place. With an understanding of the JNI native types and type signature, you have learned to treat data in native code consistent with its use by Java. You have learned about all the types acceptable as input to JNI functions. You have learned how to identify Java methods and data fields within native code using signatures. You now understand the point of the JNIEnv pointer. Finally, you have experienced the wisdom of Goethe. When you made a commitment, what you needed came your way.

In the previous chapter, you got a glimpse of the some of the basic JNI functions. In this chapter, you gained some knowledge of the details required to make those functions work. In the next chapter, we will take a close look at the JNI functions for manipulating objects and classes.

Chapter 5   OBJECTS AND CLASSES

In the fields before the flood
You'll be spilling blood
Like a native son

John Hiatt
Native Son

Introduction

By now you have spilled enough blood to qualify as a gender-neutral native child. This and subsequent chapters should start you on your way to native adulthood.

In this chapter, we will take a look at all of the JNI functions for dealing with objects and classes. Since the Java inheritance tree starts with objects, that is where we will start. After looking at how to manipulate objects in native code, we will move to Java classes.

Before we jump into the JNI functions dealing with objects, however, the subtleties of JNI local and global references will be discussed. Native code may maintain references to Java objects just as Java classes may. There is, however, a slight twist on the behavior of references held by native code.

JNI References

As a prelude to our discussion of JNI object manipulation, a few words need to be said regarding how the JVM treats object references in the nether world of native code.

Ignoring the primitive types for a moment, all one has for data in Java are object references. An object reference points to an object, but is not a pointer to an object. To say the latter would be to use a phrase that really has no meaning in Java. A reference is an opaque handle to an object.

All this is true in native code, too. But that is not the end of the story.

Code Natively, Reference Locally

As we saw in Chapter 3, when a `native` method declares a Java object as a formal parameter, an object reference is passed to the native code. To keeps its house in order, the JVM needs to track these object reference crossings into native code. The JVM needs to track these references for two reasons. First, it can not allow the object referenced within native code to be mistakenly released due to garbage collection. Second, the JVM must be free to move objects referenced by native code without undermining the operation of the native code.

The JVM tracks the use of object references within native code through a per transition registry. Upon each invocation of a `native` method, the JVM creates a table with an entry for each object referenced within the native code. The table is initially populated with any references passed as arguments to the `native` method and a slot for a possible `jobject` return value. References maintained in this table are known as *local* references.

In JDK 1.1, the distinguishing characteristic of local references is that they live only throughout the duration of the native call. When the native call is complete and control returns to the JVM, the registry is deleted and the local references are no longer valid. This is true even if the object reference is maintained in a static C variable.

In JDK 1.2, the user is given finer control over the life-span of local references. Specifically, the JNI provides functions for manipulating a stack of local references. Native code can *push* and *pop* local reference frames as necessary for allocation and release of blocks of local references.

To think of the different JNI versions using the same model, you can think of native function entry and exit as analogous to the pushing and popping of a local reference frame. Whereas local reference frames can be nested and are under user control in JDK 1.2, the JVM is entirely responsible for allocating and releasing local reference memory in JDK 1.1.

In both versions of the JNI it is important not to use a local reference when it is no longer valid. In JDK 1.1, a local reference becomes invalid after it is manually deleted or a native method returns. In JDK 1.2, a local reference becomes invalid after its stack frame is popped.

Listing 5.1 illustrates how this problem can arise. Here a static variable `savedReference[1]` is used in an attempt to store a local reference across native method calls.

Let's look at what NOT to do.

Listing 5.1 *A Bad Example of Using an Object Reference in Native Code*

(1)
```
static jobject savedReference;

JNIEXPORT void JNICALL Java_SomeClass_someMethod(
    JNIEnv *env, jobject obj, jlong val)
{
    savedReference = obj;
    //...
}

JNIEXPORT void JNICALL
Java_SomeClass_someOtherMethod(
        JNIEnv *env, jobject obj, jlong val)
{
    // Try to use savedReference...NOT!
    jclass clazz;
```
(2)
```
    clazz = env->GetObjectClass(savedReference);
    //...
}
```

Even if there were any guarantees in life, they would not involve what value is returned in line [2] above.

Here is the problem. Once `Java_SomeClass_someMethod` does its thing and returns, all bets are off regarding the value of `savedReference`. The only reference the JVM knows about is the one created for passing as the second argument to `Java_SomeClass_someMethod`. When `Java_SomeClass_someMethod` returns, the argument reference is no longer valid. It is a local reference, and local references are invalidated when control returns to the JVM.

You can think of the value of `savedReference` as an index into the local reference table created by the JVM. When control returns to the JVM after the call to `someMethod`, the table is destroyed, rendering the value of `savedReference` useless.

Upon return to native code during a subsequent invocation of `someOtherMethod`, a new table is created. The value of the entry in the local reference table to which `savedReference` previously referred is a mystery.

The code in Listing 5.1 would cause problems in either JDK 1.1 or 1.2. The same problem of an invalid local reference could manifest itself in another way peculiar to JDK 1.2. Consider the following code segment from the implementation of a `native` method. Note the calls to the JDK 1.2 JNI functions `PushLocalFrame` and `PopLocalFrame`.

Listing 5.2 *Use of* PushLocalFrame *and* PopLocalFrame

```
jclass clzz1, clzz2;
jobject obj1, obj2, localRef;
```

(3)
```
        env->PushLocalFrame(16);
        // ...
```
(4)
```
        obj1 = env->NewObject(...);
```
(5)
```
        obj2 = env->NewObject(...);
        // ...
        // A VALID reference to obj1
```
(6)
```
        clzz1 = env->GetObjectClass(obj1);
```
(7)
```
        localRef = env->PopLocalFrame(env, obj2);

        // An INVALID reference to obj1
```
(8)
```
        clzz1 = env->GetObjectClass(obj1);

        // A VALID reference to obj2
        clzz2 = env->GetObjectClass(localRef);
```

In this code segment, a local reference frame is created by the call to PushLocalFrame in [3]. While that frame is active, two local references are created, obj1 and obj2 in lines [4] and [5]. The use of obj1 in the first call to GetObjectClass in [6] is fine. The local reference obj1 is being used within the frame in which it was created. The next use of obj1 in line [8] is invalid because its defining frame was popped at [7].

The status of obj2 outside of its defining frame is no different. However, PopLocalFrame provides a mechanism for effectively passing a local reference from one frame to the next. After the call to PopLocalFrame in [7] above, localRef refers to the same object as was created and assigned to obj2 in line [5].

If a reference to an object created within native code needs to remain valid across native method calls or across local reference frames, local references will not do. To meet this need, the JNI provides *global* references.

Coding Globally

Before any more is said, the above code snippet will be modified to do the right thing.

Listing 5.3 *Use of* NewGlobalRef

```
static jobject savedReference;

JNIEXPORT void JNICALL Java_SomeClass_someMethod(
                JNIEnv *env, jobject obj, jlong val)
{
(9)     savedReference = env->NewGlobalRef(obj);
        //...
}


JNIEXPORT void JNICALL
Java_SomeClass_someOtherMethod(
        JNIEnv *env, jobject obj, jlong val)
{
    jclass clazz;
    // Try to use savedReference...safely this time!
(10)    clazz = env->GetObjectClass(savedReference);
        //...
}
```

A simple call to NewGlobalRef [9] solves the problem and removes the mystery. Unlike a local reference, a global reference lives until it is explicitly released.

After Java_SomeClass_someMethod returns, the savedReference will continue to point to the object to which the obj argument referred when originally set. The reference value will also remain valid for later use at line [10].

A global reference created by native code has the additional effect of preventing an object from being garbage collected even though native code may not be executing. Creating a global reference is a way for the native code to stake a claim on a Java object.

In doing what it is intended to do, a global reference will prevent an object you are finished with on the Java side of your application from having its finalize method called. This is relevant if, say, you are modeling native objects in Java and maintaining a table in native code that connects Java objects with native objects. You cannot override the object's finalize method to do cleanup on the native side and ever expect the finalize method to get called. The global reference will prevent the finalize method from ever being called.

This discussion leads to a new Rule To Remember.

JNI Rule To Remember 12:

A global reference maintained by native code will prevent the object referenced from being garbage collected even if no Java-side references are active.

Weak references provided in JDK 1.2 can be used to avoid this problem.

All that remains is the minor matter of releasing the global reference. For that, the JNI provides `DeleteGlobalRef`. It is a very simple call.

```
env->DeleteGlobalRef(savedReference);
savedReference = NULL;
```

After this call, the value of `savedReference` is meaningless. If this is the last reference for the target object, the object becomes a candidate for garbage collection.

Releasing a Local Reference

Although local references are released upon return from the `native` method or local reference frame in which they were created, there are occasions when you may want to free them explicitly. There are two conditions under which a call to `DeleteLocalRef` may be in order: first, when the native code has allocated many local references, or second, when a local reference refers to a large Java object and you no longer need the reference.

In the first case, consider that local references require storage space. The more you create, the more space is required to keep track of them. This, of course, is obvious. However, what may not be obvious, or at least has not been said, is how and when local references are created. Knowing this can help you keep track of local references and allow you to make informed decisions about when to delete them.

Let's enumerate the actions which result in the creation of a local reference.

- Any object argument passed to a `native` method.
- A `native` method returning an object.
- Any call to `AllocObject` or `NewObject` within the native code. More on these JNI functions later.
- In general, any call to a JNI function that returns a `jobject` value.

The first three cases are straightforward. The last condition is sometimes subtle.

Consider iterating through a large object array in native code. Again, let's start with what NOT to do.

Listing 5.4 *Accumulating a Large Number of Local References*

```
JNIEXPORT void JNICALL Java_SomeClass_iterateArray(
    JNIEnv *env, jobject thisObj, jobjectArray arr) {
    jobject obj;
    jlong aBigNumber = env->GetArrayLength(arr);
    for (int i = 0; i < aBigNumber; i++) {
        obj = env->GetObjectArrayElement(arr, i);
        // Do something with obj
    }
}
```

(11)

Each pass through line [11] creates a new local reference. The above code will create `aBigNumber` of local references before `Java_SomeClass_iterateArray` returns. You can think of this condition as a short-term memory leak. If `aBigNumber` is large enough, you may reach the memory limits of your computing environment.

To prevent this, simply insert a call to `DeleteLocalRef` inside the loop [12].

Listing 5.5 *Deleting a Local Reference*

```
JNIEXPORT void JNICALL Java_SomeClass_iterateArray(
            JNIEnv *env, jobjectArray arr)
{
    jobject obj;
    jlong aBigNumber = env->GetArrayLength(arr);
    for (int i = 0; i < aBigNumber; i++) {
        obj = env->GetObjectArrayElement(arr, i);
        // Do something with obj...
        env->DeleteLocalRef(obj);
    }
}
```

(12)

The above example covers the first of the two scenarios wherein you may want to explicitly release local references within native code.

The second scenario has its subtleties also. Understanding this scenario depends on remembering that the JVM is still keeping an eye on memory even while executing a `native` method. Garbage collection can be triggered either asynchronously or in response to an allocation of more memory for an object.

Since an active local reference is bypassed by the garbage collector while native code is executing, it will not be reclaimed even if you are finished using it. So, if you have a fairly complex `native` method that uses a local reference to a large object early in the method execution, it is advisable to call `DeleteLocalRef` on that reference as soon as you are finished with the object. This will make available the object's memory without waiting until the `native` method returns.

This possibility can arise only when the local reference is created within the native method by `AllocObject` or one of the flavors of `NewObject`. Any reference passed as an argument or returned as a result of another JNI call will have at least one other reference to it that will prevent it from being garbage collected. Calling `DeleteLocalRef` within the native code will decrement the number of references but will not result in the object being available for garbage collection.

A Few More Facts About Native References

For completeness, a few more things need to be said about native references to Java objects.

- A JNI function which expects an object as an argument can be passed either a global or local reference.
- All references returned by JNI functions (e.g., `NewObject`) are local.
- A `native` method may return either a global or local reference.
- Local references may not be passed from one thread to another.

With the discussion of local and global references now behind us, we can now move on to the remaining JNI functions dealing with objects.

JNI Object Functions

Some of the preceding examples have hinted at how to create Java objects within native code with mention of `AllocObject` and `NewObject`. Both return a local object reference. They differ in that `AllocObject` does not call any of the constructors on the object is creates. It simply allocates memory for that object.

`NewObject`, in all its flavors, on the other hand, does a full-blown construction of a Java object. It allocates memory for an object and invokes one of its constructors. As its name suggests, it is the JNI equivalent to the Java `new` operator.

Besides these object creation functions, the JNI provides functions for testing if two references refer to the same object, and a native code equivalent to the Java `instanceof` operator.

Finally, `GetObjectClass` is a JNI function for determining the class of an object. Let's look at how this function works.

Determining an Object's Class

GetObjectClass is used to return a java.lang.Class object representing the class to which a particular object belongs. It takes a jobject value as an argument and returns a jclass reference. It is very useful in non-static native methods when a *this* object is always passed as an argument.

Listing 5.6 *Using* GetObjectClass *to Determine an Object's Class*

```
JNIEXPORT jobject JNICALL
Java_myClass_myNativeMethod(JNIEnv *env,
                            jobject thisObj)
{
    jclass clazz = env->GetObjectClass(thisObj);
    // Use clazz value...
}
```

GetObjectClass expects a valid Java object. If you mistakenly pass a NULL value to GetObjectClass it will throw a java.lang.NullException exception.

Creating a New Object Instance

The JNI provides three different functions for creating a new Java object: NewObject, NewObjectA, and NewObjectV. The functions differ only in how the constructor arguments are bundled as arguments to the JNI function.

All three of these functions take three arguments:

- A jclass value that identifies class from which an object instance is to be created
- A jmethodID value which is the method ID of the constructor to be invoked upon object creation
- A list of arguments that are to be passed to the constructor

The third bullet item is the area in which the object creation functions differ. The small examples below highlight this difference.

Using NewObject

NewObject simply takes a list of values immediately following the method ID argument.

Listing 5.7 *Creating an Object Using* NewObject

---

(13)
```
jmethodID mid = env->GetMethodID(clazz,
                    "<init>",
                    "(ILjava/lang/String;)V");
    jint ival = 10;
    jstring sval = env->NewStringUTF("A String");
```
(14)
```
    jobject obj = env->NewObject(clazz,
                            mid,
                            ival,
                            sval);
```

The number and types of the values listed in the call to NewObject [14] after the method ID argument must match the number and types of arguments as described in the signature string in the call to GetMethodID [13].

When retrieving the method ID of a constructor as in [13] above, the name of the method is always <init>. A constructor is considered to return void, hence the V in the method signature.

Using NewObjectA

NewObjectA takes an array of jvalue values as an argument. This array contains the arguments to the constructor of the class for which an instance is being created. Recall from page 54 in Chapter 4, the jvalue type is a union that can take as its value any of the JNI native types.

Listing 5.8 *Creating an Object With* NewObjectA

```
jvalue args[3];
// Set jvalue values in arg array
args[0].i = 100;
args[1].d = 100.0;
args[2].l = env->NewStringUTF("One Hundred");
//...
jobject obj = env->NewObjectA(clazz, mid, args);
```

Using NewObjectV

The third JNI function for object creation can take a variable number of arguments. After a jclass value and a jmethodID value, an arbitrary list of arguments is passed to a call to NewObjectV using the ANSI C variable arguments convention.

The following C function, itself capable of taking a variable number of arguments, illustrates the use of NewObjectV.

Listing 5.9 *Creating an Object With* NewObjectV

```
#include <stdarg.h>// In general, jni.h does this

jobject callNewObjectV(
JNIEnv* env, jclass clazz, jmethodID mid,...)
{
    va_list ap;
    va_start(ap, mid);
    jobject obj = env->NewObjectV(clazz, mid, ap);
    va_end(ap);
    return obj;
}
```

NewObjectV is most helpful when you, as above, want to create a helper function to do your object construction for you. The helper function is declared using the ellipsis syntax to denote a variable number of arguments. Within your helper function, va_start is used to set up the arguments for passing on to NewObjectV.

Example Object Creation

Let's look at a detailed example of calls to NewObject, NewObjectA and NewObjectV. Consider the following Java class ThreeConstructors consisting of, you guessed it, three constructors.

Listing 5.10 *Java Source for* ThreeConstructors

```
class ThreeConstructors {
public ThreeConstructors(String s0) {
    System.out.println("***\nString = " + s0);
}

public ThreeConstructors(String s0, int i0) {
    this(s0);
    System.out.println("int = " + i0);
}

public ThreeConstructors(
    String s0, int i0, boolean b0) {
    this(s0, i0);
    System.out.println("boolean = " + b0);
}
}
```

The following Java code declares the `native` methods, one for each flavor of JNI object creation function.

Listing 5.11 NewObjectEx1: *Java Class Initiating Native Object Creation*

```
public class NewObjectEx1 {
static {
    System.loadLibrary("Chap5example1");
}

public static native void createNewObjs();
public static native void createNewObjsA();
public static native void createNewObjsV();

public static void main(String[] args) {
    createNewObjs();
    createNewObjsA();
    createNewObjsV();
}
}
```

Each of class `ThreeConstructor`'s constructors will be called by each native method using `NewObject`, `NewObjectA` and `NewObjectV`, respectively. The calls to `NewObjectA` take an array of `jvalue` values. The number of values consumed by the constructor matches the number of arguments described by the signature.

Listing 5.12 *JNI Object Construction*

```
JNIEXPORT void JNICALL
Java_NewObjectEx1_createNewObjs
    (JNIEnv *env, jclass thisClass)
{
    jobject     newObj;
    jmethodID   mid;
    jclass      tcClz;
    jstring     helloStr;

    helloStr = env->NewStringUTF(
                        "NewObject says Hello");
    tcClz = env->FindClass("ThreeConstructors");
    mid = env->GetMethodID(tcClz,
                    "<init>",
                    "(Ljava/lang/String;)V");

    newObj = env->NewObject(tcClz, mid, helloStr);

    mid = env->GetMethodID(tcClz,
                        "<init>",
                        "(Ljava/lang/String;I)V");

    newObj = env->NewObject(tcClz, mid, helloStr, 1);

    mid = env->GetMethodID(tcClz,
                        "<init>",
                        "(Ljava/lang/String;IZ)V");

    newObj = env->NewObject(tcClz, mid,
                        helloStr, 2, JNI_TRUE);
}
```

Listing 5.12 (cont.) *JNI Object Construction*

```
JNIEXPORT void JNICALL
Java_NewObjectEx1_createNewObjsA
   (JNIEnv *env, jclass thisClass)
{
    jobject      newObj;
    jclass       tcClz;
    jvalue       args[3];
    jmethodID    mid;
    tcClz = env->FindClass("ThreeConstructors");
    // Get method ID for constructor
    // ThreeConstructors(String)
    mid = env->GetMethodID(tcClz,
                    "<init>",
                    "(Ljava/lang/String;)V");

    args[0].l =
    env->NewStringUTF("NewObjectA says Hello");
    args[1].i = 100;
    args[2].z = JNI_FALSE;
    newObj = env->NewObjectA(tcClz, mid, args);
    // Get method ID for constructor
    // ThreeConstructors(String, int)
    mid = env->GetMethodID(tcClz,
                    "<init>",
                    "(Ljava/lang/String;I)V");
    newObj = env->NewObjectA(tcClz, mid, args);

    // Get method ID for constructor
    // ThreeConstructors(String, int, boolean)
    mid = env->GetMethodID(tcClz,
                    "<init>",
                    "(Ljava/lang/String;IZ)V");
    newObj = env->NewObjectA(tcClz, mid, args);
}
```

Listing 5.12 (cont.) *JNI Object Construction*

```
JNIEXPORT void JNICALL
Java_NewObjectEx1_createNewObjsV
   (JNIEnv *env, jclass clazz)
{
    jobject      newObj;
    jmethodID    mid;
    jstring      helloStr;
    helloStr = env->NewStringUTF(
                  "NewObjectV says Hello ");
    jclass tcClz = env->FindClass(
                  "ThreeConstructors");
    mid = env->GetMethodID(tcClz,
                   "<init>",
                   "(Ljava/lang/String;)V");
    newObj = callNewObjectV(env, tcClz,
                    mid, helloStr);
    mid = env->GetMethodID(tcClz,
                   "<init>",
                   "(Ljava/lang/String;I)V");
    newObj = callNewObjectV(env, tcClz,
                    mid,
                    helloStr,10);
    mid = env->GetMethodID(tcClz,
                   "<init>",
                   "(Ljava/lang/String;IZ)V");
    newObj = callNewObjectV(env, tcClz,
                    mid, helloStr,
                    10, JNI_TRUE);
}
```

The pattern to note is that each call to an object construction function is preceded by a call to `FindClass` to get a class reference. Then the constructors method ID is retrieved with `GetMethodID`. Finally, the JNI object construction function is called.

The following program output should convince you that each of the calls does their job correctly. Each constructor simply prints its arguments, the first of which identifies how the constructor was called by naming the JNI object construction function. Each successive call to an object construction function is delimited by asterisks.

```
****
String = NewObject says Hello
****
String = NewObject says Hello
int = 1
****
String = NewObject says Hello
int = 2
boolean = true
****
String = NewObjectA says Hello
****
String = NewObjectA says Hello
int = 100
****
String = NewObjectA says Hello
int = 100
boolean = false
****
String = NewObjectV says Hello
****
String = NewObjectV says Hello
int = 10
****
String = NewObjectV says Hello
int = 10
boolean = true
```

Allocating Memory for an Object

As an alternative to the NewObject family of calls, there is the JNI function AllocObject. AllocObject allows you to allocate memory for an object and defer constructor invocation. The constructor is later called using the standard idiom of GetMethodID and CallVoidMethod.

A simple example will illustrate this operation. The following Java class simply calls a native method doIt. doIt will do all the work of allocating memory for an object and then calling the object's constructor. The class A is also defined and it will serve as the target class for the work of AllocObject.

Listing 5.13 `AllocObjectEx`: *Java Source for Native Object Allocation*

```java
public class AllocObjectEx {
    static {
       System.loadLibrary("Chap5example2");
    }
    public static native void doIt();
    public static void main(String[] args) {
       doIt();
    }
}

class A {
   public void msg() {
       System.out.println(
                  "Hello from a class A method");
    }
   public A() {
       System.out.println(
                  "Hello from A's constructor");
    }
}
```

The following implementation of `doIt` shows `AllocObject` in action. The invocation of the `A`'s constructor in line [16] after allocating an instance of `A` in [15] is intended to make explicit the fact that `AllocObject` does not invoke any constructors.

Listing 5.14 *Use of* `AllocObject`

```c
JNIEXPORT void JNICALL Java_AllocObjectEx_doIt
  (JNIEnv * env, jclass thisClass)
{
    jmethodID mid;
    jclass clazzA = env->FindClass("A");
(15)    jobject objA = env->AllocObject(clazzA);
    printf("After AllocObject...\n");
    mid = env->GetMethodID(clazzA, "<init>", "()V");
(16)    env->CallVoidMethod(objA, mid);
    printf("After CallVoidMethod...\n");}
}
```

The execution of this native code produces the following output. If we look at the output, we see that first `AllocObject` is called, and then, only after `CallVoidMethod` is executed, the output from `A`'s constructor, `Hello from A's constructor`, is printed.

> **Invocation of** `AllocObjectEx main` **Method**

```
After AllocObject...
Hello from A's constructor
After CallVoidMethod...
Hello from a class A method
```

After the allocation of an object using `AllocObject`, the methods and data fields of the new object instance are available for reference by subsequent JNI functions, as well as Java code. The only difference between an object created by `AllocObject` and `NewObject` is that any initialization performed by the class constructor is not done on the object created by `AllocObject`.

Warning:

Although `AllocObject` gives you the ability to create an object without initializing it, good programming practice dictates that the object is initialized before any other operations are performed on it.

Comparing Two References

If you ever need to compare two JNI object references to determine if they refer to the same object, the JNI provides the function `IsSameObject`.

`IsSameObject` takes two `jobject` values as arguments and returns `JNI_TRUE` if they point to the same object and `JNI_FALSE` otherwise.

This function is quite useful when you may be maintaining a table of global references in a native data structure. You can use `IsSameObject` to test for object identity between a table entry and a reference passed as an argument.

Using `IsSameObject` is straightforward.

Listing 5.15 *Use of* `IsSameObject`

```
jclass clazz = env->FindClass("java/lang/String");
// Create a local reference to a String object
jobject lref = env->AllocObject(clazz);
// Make a global reference from the local one

jobject gref = env->NewGlobalRef(lref);
if (env->IsSameObject(lref, gref) == JNI_TRUE) {
    printf("They are the same String object...");
}
```

The above code segment will always result in the message being printed. The point is that `IsSameObject` can be used to compare a global reference with a local reference, as well as two references of the same kind.

Since the reference is simply an index into a table of references, if you pass an invalid value, the behavior is unpredictable. That references are indices also explains why testing for equality of references does not tell you if you have the same object.

A Native instanceof

The JNI provides a native version to the Java `instanceof` operator. `IsInstanceOf` takes two arguments, an object reference and a class reference, and reports `JNI_TRUE` if the object can be cast to the named class. In other words, `IsInstanceOf` returns true exactly under the same conditions that `instanceof` would.

```
if (env->IsInstanceOf(anObj, aClazz) == JNI_TRUE) {
        // anObj can be cast to aClazz
}
```

`IsInstanceOf` can play an important role in native code where the native compiler cannot provide the checking of Java object types that the Java compiler does. Aside from the regular type checking done on C/C++ types, the native compiler's ability to check Java types is limited to the JNI native types. So, for example, although the C/C++ compiler will complain if you try to assign a `jobject` value to a `jint` or warn you when you assign a `jlongArray` to a `jintArray`, it has no capacity for discerning between Java objects of different types. Another way of looking at this is that the native code treats all Java objects as type `jobject`. All the type information is lost when the value is passed as an argument to a `native` method.

What this means is that type checking on Java objects is deferred until runtime. Unfortunately, the result of a type mismatch at runtime will often manifest itself as a JNI panic.

`IsInstanceOf` can be used to avoid these problems. Consider the following Java code wherein two classes B and C extend class A. Only B supports the method `doSomething`.

Listing 5.16 *Illegal Cast at Runtime*

```
class A {}
class B extends A {
   public void doSomething() {
      System.out.println("B is doing something...");
   }
}
class C extends A {}
public class Main {
   static {
      System.loadLibrary("Chap5example3");
   }
   public native static void doIt(A val);
   public static void main(String[] args) {
      B b = new B();
      C c = new C();
      doIt(b);
      doIt(c);
   }
}
```

The `native` method `doIt` takes an object of class A as an argument. That means objects of either class A, B or C may be sent as an argument to `doIt`. A Java implementation of `doIt` is shown in Listing 5.17.

Listing 5.17 `doIt` *Java Source*

```
public static void doIt(A val) {
   // val.doSomething() would cause compiler error
   if (val instanceof B) {
      B b = (B) val;
      b.doSomething();
   }
}
```

The Java compiler would catch any attempt to invoke the method `doSomething` before casting the input argument.

On the other hand, consider the following native code implementation of `doIt`.

Listing 5.18 *Native Code Lacking a Much Needed Call to* IsInstanceOf

```
// A poor implementation of Java_Main_doIt.
// There is no runtime check of to determine whether
// input argument can call "doSomething" method.
//

JNIEXPORT void JNICALL Java_Main_doNative(
    JNIEnv *env, jclass thisClass, jobject anAObject)
{
    // Do some stuff.
    // Invoke doSomething...
    jclass    clazz;
    jmethodID mid;

    clazz = env->GetObjectClass(anAObject);
    mid = env->GetMethodID(clazz,
                    "doSomething", "()V");
    env->CallVoidMethod(anAObject, mid);
    // Do some more stuff...
}
```

(17)

No C/C++ compiler will detect the problem within this native code. In fact, if the above Java class Main were compiled and run, it would crash the JVM. The first call to doIt would be successful but the second would cause the problem. The problem arises because the return value from the Get-MethodID in line [17] will be NULL since the class C does not implement a doSomething method. This NULL value, when then sent as a jmethodID to CallVoidMethod, makes for an unhappy JVM.

All of this argues for a liberal use of IsInstanceOf in native code. A better implementation of the doIt native method appears in Listing 5.19.

Listing 5.19 *Use of* IsInstanceOf *to Avoid Runtime Error*

```
JNIEXPORT void JNICALL Java_Main_doIt(
JNIEnv *env, jclass thisClass, jobject anAObject) {
    jclass clazz;
    jmethodID mid;

    // Do some stuff...
    // Invoke doSomething after ascertaining
    // we have correct class of object
    jclass clazzB = env->FindClass("B");

    if (env->IsInstanceOf(anAObject, clazzB)) {
        clazz = env->GetObjectClass(anAObject);
        mid = env->GetMethodID(clazz,
                    "doSomething",
                    "()V");
        env->CallVoidMethod(anAObject, mid);
    }
    // Do some more stuff...
}
```

In this case, we get the class reference for class B and then explicitly ask whether anAObject is an instance of that class.

Testing Class Inheritance Relationship

Whereas IsInstanceOf returns whether an object is an instance of, or can be cast to, a given class, IsAssignableFrom reports on the relationship between two classes. It takes two class references as arguments and returns JNI_TRUE if an object of the first class can be safely cast to the class designated by the second.

Speaking of classes, let's move on now and take a close look at the JNI class functions.

JNI Class Functions

Recall that a class object in JNI is identified by the JNI type jclass. The JNI provides a number of useful functions for getting a handle to a class object or testing the relationship between two classes. Just as the Java new operator requires a class name, the JNI functions that create new objects require a jclass value. In addition to GetObjectClass, there are three JNI functions that return a jclass value: FindClass, GetSuperclass and DefineClass. Let's look at FindClass and GetSuperclass here. DefineClass will be discussed in the next section.

From Class Name to Class

The most common means for getting hold of a `jclass` value—short of being passed one as an argument to a `static native` method—is the Find-Class function. `FindClass` takes as input a fully-qualified class name with package components separated by slashes. `FindClass` returns a reference to a `java.lang.Class` object that represents the class whose name was passed as an argument.

If you want a `jclass` value for the `java.lang.String` class, use `FindClass` as follows.

```
jclass clazz = env->FindClass("java/lang/String");
```

The same is true for a user-defined class.

```
jclass clazz =
       env->FindClass("theProject/myPkg/someClass");
```

Note that in both cases above, the slash character (/) is used regardless of the platform on which you are running.

It is important to observe that `FindClass` does not require a signature. Within a signature string, a class name would appear as

```
LtheProject/myPkg/someClass;
```

`FindClass` simply wants a fully-qualified class name whose components are separated by a slash character.

If you want the `java.lang.Class` object value for an array of a Java primitive type, prefix the JNI primitive type signature with a [as shown below.

```
jclass clazz = env->FindClass("[I");
```

Don't get carried away, though. You can NOT do the following.

```
jclass arrClazz =
       env->FindClass("[java/lang/Integer");
```

There is no such class that fills the description "array of `java.lang.Integer` objects." Attempting the above will return a NULL value into `arrClazz`. Any subsequent attempt to use `arrClazz` as a `jclass` argument to a JNI function will result in a JNI panic.

None of this is to say you cannot create an array of arrays of `java.lang.Integer` objects. That is possible using the JNI function `NewObjectArray`. We will look at this possibility in detail in Chapter 6.

In JDK 1.2, `FindClass` has been beefed up a bit. Previously, Find-Class was capable of only finding classes loaded by the null class loader, that is, those found in the class path. `FindClass` has been extended so that it finds classes loaded with a class loader. Specifically, the 1.2 `FindClass` will use the class loader associated with the `native` method from which it is called in its attempt to initialize a class.

From Class to Superclass

If you want to know the super class of a given class, use `GetSuperclass`. `GetSuperclass` simply takes a `jclass` value as an argument and returns a `jclass` value. The return value represents the super class of the input class.

```
jclass clazz = env->FindClass("java/lang/String");
jclass superClz = env->GetSuperclass(clazz);
```

The value of `superClz` is a class object for the `java.lang.Object` class. Easy enough. This JNI call function provides the exact functionality to native code as does the public method `getSuperClass` in `java.lang.Class`. Take a close look and you will see that `getSuperclass` is a `native` method!

From Bytes to Class

The final JNI function that returns a `jclass` value takes a `byte` array as its input argument. `DefineClass` provides a native mechanism for creating a class from any platform-specific source. Normally, the JVM loads classes from the local file system using the `CLASSPATH` environment variable.

It is not unusual for sophisticated Java applications to extend this capability by, for example, adding network loading functionality.

The purpose of both the `java.lang.Class` method `defineClass` and the JNI function `DefineClass` is to take a `byte` array as input and return a `java.lang.Class` object. Whence the raw class data originates is irrelevant.

The `java.lang.Class defineClass` method is mentioned because the best way to understand how to use the analogous JNI function is by starting with a pure Java class loader. When its operation is understood, it will be modified for use with the JNI function `DefineClass`.

A Simple Class Loader

The class `java.lang.ClassLoader` is an `abstract` class, so any building of a class loader begins by extending `ClassLoader`. Our loader, `SimpleLoader`, has a single constructor that takes a single argument. This argument represents the path name that is added to the front of a class file name. The resultant value is used to locate the class file to be loaded.

`SimpleLoader` is a caching loader. Before an attempt is made to load a class anew, the cache is checked to see if it contains the class. Every time a new class is loaded, it is added to the cache. The code follows.

Listing 5.20 *A Simple Classloader*

```
// SimpleLoader.java
import java.io.*;
import java.util.*;
```
(18)
```
public class SimpleLoader extends ClassLoader {
    private Hashtable _cache = new Hashtable();
    private String _pathBase;
    public SimpleLoader(String base) {
        _pathBase = base;
    }
```
(19)
```
protected Class loadClass(String name,
                        boolean resolve)
                    throws ClassNotFoundException {
    Class c;
    // Check class cache
```
(20)
```
    c = (Class) getCache().get(name);

    if (c == null) {
    try {
```
(21)
```
        c = findSystemClass(name);
        return c;
    } catch (ClassNotFoundException e) {
        try {
            String fileName = getPathBase() +
                System.properties("file.separator") +
                dotToSlash(name) +
                ".class";
```
(22)
```
            byte data[] = loadClassData(fileName);
            c = defineClass(name, data, 0,
                            data.length);
            // Cache it...
            getCache().put(name, c);
        } catch (ClassFormatError e) {
            throw new ClassNotFoundException(name);
        }
    }        }
```

Listing 5.20 (cont.) *A Simple Classloader*

```
// If we are going to use class, resolve it!
    if (resolve) {
        resolveClass(c);
    }
    return c;
}
private byte loadClassData(String name)[] {
    File file = new File(name);
    try {
        FileInputStream in =
                    new FileInputStream(file);
        byte[] buf = new byte[(int)file.length()];
        in.read(buf, 0, (int)file.length());
        return buf;
    } catch (Exception e) {
        e.printStackTrace();
        return null;
    }
}
public static String dotToSlash(String cname) {
    return cname.replace('.',
      System.properties("file.separator").charAt(0));
}

protected String getPathBase() {
    return _pathBase;
}

protected Hashtable getCache() {
    return _cache;
}
}
```

SimpleLoader follows the conventional structure for a class loader. It extends java.lang.ClassLoader [18] and implements the load-Class method [19]. loadClass looks for a class by first looking in the cache [20], then the system classes [21] and, finally, by calling loadClass-Data [22]. This order enforces the security measure that says local classes from the local file system should be loaded before looking elsewhere.

The loadClassData method is responsible for reading the class data for the class file. Keep in mind, this could just as well be a serial device. The point is, that for defineClass and DefineClass to do their work, all they need is an array of bytes. Notice that loadClassData returns a byte array in [22]. After `loadClassData` returns, the `byte` array is passed off to `defineClass`. In just a bit, we will see how we can replace `loadClass-Data` and `defineClass` with a `native` method that combines their work and uses the JNI function `DefineClass`. Before, we do that, though, let's look at how `SimpleLoader` works from the top down.

Using `SimpleLoader` requires that you first construct a `Simple-Loader` object and then invoke `loadClass`. The `loadClass` method returns a `Class` object. This class object is used to create an instance of itself using `newInstance`. The short example below illustrates this.

Listing 5.21 *Java Class Using a Simple Classloader*

```
import loaderClasses.*;
public class LoaderMain {
public static void main(String[] args) {
    LoadedClass      lc;
    Class            lcClass;
    SimpleLoader loader = new SimpleLoader(args[0]);
    try {
        lcClass = loader.loadClass(
                "SimplyLoadedClass", true);
        System.out.println("Loaded : " + lcClass);
        lc = (LoadedClass) lcClass.newInstance();
        lc.doIt();
    } catch (ClassNotFoundException e) {
        e.printStackTrace();
    } catch (InstantiationException e) {
        e.printStackTrace();
    } catch (IllegalAccessException iae) {
        iae.printStackTrace();
    }
}
}
```

(23)

Except for the creation of a different loader in line [23], this code will not change when we extend `SimpleLoader` to accommodate the use of `DefineClass`.

And it is now time to do just that.

A Loader Using `DefineClass`

Consider a subclass of `SimpleLoader`, `SpecialNativeLoader`. Only the `native` method declaration for `loadAndDefine` has been added. To use `loadAndDefine`, `loadClass` is over-ridden.

Listing 5.22 *A Classloader Using the JNI Function* DefineClass

```
// SpecialNativeLoader.java

import java.io.*;
import java.util.*;

public class SpecialNativeLoader
            extends SimpleLoader {

private native Class loadAndDefine(
            String base, String name);
public SpecialNativeLoader(String _path) {
 super(_path);
}

protected Class loadClass(
    String name, boolean resolve)
            throws ClassNotFoundException {
    Class c;
    // Check class cache
    c = (Class) getCache().get(name);
    if (c == null) {
        try {
            c = findSystemClass(name);
            return c;
        } catch (Exception ClassNotFoundException) {
            try {
                c = loadAndDefine(getPathBase(), name);
                // Cache it...
                getCache().put(name, c);
            } catch (ClassFormatError e) {
                throw new ClassNotFoundException(name);
            }
        }
    }
    // If we are to use class, resolve it!
    if (resolve) {
        resolveClass(c);
    }
    return c;
}
}
```

As promised, loadClassData and defineClass have been col-
lapsed into a single native method. One call will be made into native code,
the class data read or generated, and the class created.

The native method implementation appears below.

Listing 5.23 *A Classloader Using the JNI Function* DefineClass

```
static jlong readClass(
    const char*, const char*, const jbyte**);

JNIEXPORT jclass JNICALL
Java_SpecialNativeLoader_loadAndDefine(
        JNIEnv *env,
        jobject thisLoader,
        jstring base,
        jstring cname) {
    jboolean isCopy0, isCopy1;
    // Convert both jstrings to char*
    const char* basePath;
    const char* className;

    basePath = env->GetStringUTFChars(base,
&isCopy0);
    className = env->GetStringUTFChars(cname,
&isCopy1);

    const jbyte* buf;
    jlong sz = readClass(basePath, className, &buf);
    jclass newClz =
    env->DefineClass(className, thisLoader, buf, sz);
    // If we got copies of strings, we need release
them
    // now that we are finished with them.

    if (isCopy0)
        env->ReleaseStringUTFChars(base, basePath);

    if (isCopy1)
        env->ReleaseStringUTFChars(cname, className);

    return newClz;
}
```

Listing 5.23 (cont.) *A Classloader Using the JNI Function* DefineClass

```
static jlong readClass(const char* path,
               const char* fname,
               const jbyte** buf) {
// These details are very platform specific.
// A UNIX implementation is available
    // with the Example Set from the ftp site.
}
```

The rationale for putting the loadClassData and the defineClass functionality into a single native method is to reduce transitions into native code. The real 'native' work is the reading of the class data, wherever the source. If a separate native method were used for loadClassData to get the data, upon returning from this native call, another call into native code would be necessary to define, from the byte array, the class using Define-Class.

Summary

In this chapter we have taken a close look at all the JNI functions dealing with Java objects and classes.

With these functions, you can create Java objects and locate and define class information all within native code. As in Java code, you manipulate these objects with references. However, within native code, there is distinction between local and global references. The former are valid only for the duration of the local reference in which they were created. In JDK 1.1, this is the duration of the native method call in which they are created. In JDK 1.2, local references are valid while the local reference frame on which they were created is active. Global references exist until they are explicitly released by the programmer.

There are three ways to construct a Java object within native code. The three JNI object construction functions differ in how their arguments are packaged. NewObject lists a variable number of arguments in the call. NewObjectA sends a jvalue array and NewObjectV sends a va_list. In all cases, the number and type of arguments must match those described in the constructor method signature.

In the next chapter, you are going to learn about JNI functions for manipulating two special types of Java objects in native code: strings and arrays.

Chapter 6

ARRAYS AND STRINGS

Quote needed

Steve Talley

personal correspondence

Introduction

The JNI provides a specialized interface to two types of Java objects, arrays and strings. This interface is necessary because of the expectations native code has for the layout of arrays and strings in memory.

These expectations can be best seen with C strings. The *Java Language Specification* does not restrict how objects are laid out in memory. This applies to Java String objects as well. On the other hand, C/C++ code requires a string to occupy consecutive bytes in memory. To meet this requirement, the JNI provides a set of functions that allow native code to get access to contiguous memory when manipulating what the C/C++ language wants to treat as a null-terminated string of ASCII characters.

The same condition needs to be met for arrays of Java primitive types. For C/C++ code to iterate through an array of integers, the values need to occupy consecutive memory locations. Again, the JNI provides a set of functions for getting access to contiguous memory representing the elements of an array of Java primitive types.

Arrays of objects do not have the same contiguous memory requirements as strings and primitive arrays, but they are also covered in this chapter because they belong to the larger brotherhood of composite data types.

JNI Array Functions

The JNI provides a rich set of functions for manipulating arrays. There is one set of functions for object arrays and another for arrays of primitive types. In terms of Java syntax, this is the difference between:

```
Integer[]        IntegerArray;
```

and

```
int[]            intArray;
```

This is a very important distinction to keep in mind when writing native code using the JNI. Unlike Java syntax, which is the same for both primitive arrays and object arrays, the JNI array element accessor functions are different.

Support for object arrays includes a construction function and a set and get function for accessing array elements. The same functionality is available for primitive arrays, although there is the twist of additional set and get operations on regions within an array.

The `GetArrayLength` function operates on both object and primitive arrays.

Let's first take a look at object arrays.

Object Arrays

An object array contains Java objects as its elements. The Java Native Type for an object array is `jobjectArray`. The element objects may either be passed to native code or created within the native code. As is the case in general, if the object array is to persist across `native` method calls, it needs to be a global reference. However, the references maintained within the object array need not be explicitly made into global references. By virtue of being assigned to an array element, they function as global references in that they are maintained somewhere besides the local reference map and, therefore, not reclaimed by the JVM upon transition back to Java code. Object array elements will persist across `native` method calls even though these reference values were not set with global references. We will see this in the next example.

The following example illustrates the creation of an object array, the settings of its values and the retrieval of its values. The object array will be created in native code, returned to the Java side, printed, and passed back to the native side and printed again. Before looking at the native code, let's see the Java code which drives this example.

Listing 6.1 *Java Source for* ObjArrayEx

```
public class ObjArrayEx {
static {
    System.loadLibrary("Chap6example1");
}

public native static String[] newObjArray(int sz);
public native static void
                printObjArray(String[] objArr);

public static void main(String[] args)
{
    String[] arrOfStr = newObjArray(10);
    System.out.println("Printing from Java code:");
    for (int i - 0; i < arrOfStr.length; i++)
        System.out.println(arrOfStr[i]);
    printObjArray(arrOfStr);
}
}
```

(1)

(2)

The call to the native method newObjArray [1] creates an array of String objects in native code and returns this array to the Java world. The native method printObjArray [2] takes the array as an argument and prints it from native code. Below is the native code for the newObjArray method.

Listing 6.2 *Native Implementation of* newObjArray

```
JNIEXPORT jobjectArray JNICALL
Java_ObjArrayEx_newObjArray(
    JNIEnv *env, jclass thisClass, jint sz)
{
    char buf[16];
    jstring utf_str;
    jclass clazz;
    clazz = env->FindClass("java/lang/String");
    jobjectArray newArr;

    newArr = env->NewObjectArray(sz, clazz, NULL);
    printf(
        "Creating object array in native code.\n");
```

(3)

(4)

Listing 6.2 (cont.) *Native Implementation of* newObjArray

```
        for (int i = 0; i < sz; i++) {
            sprintf(buf, "elem%d", i);
            utf_str = env->NewStringUTF(buf);
(5)         env->SetObjectArrayElement(newArr,
                                        i, utf_str);
(6)         env->DeleteLocalRef(utf_str);
        }
        return newArr;
    }
```

The array is created with a call to the JNI function NewObjectArray in line [4]. This is possible, though, only after getting the jclass value for the element objects using FindClass [3]. The jclass value returned by FindClass is used as the second argument to NewObjectArray and determines the type of the array's element objects. The first argument to NewObjectArray is the number of elements to be created. The final argument is an initial value for the array elements.

NewStringUTF is used to create the jstring objects which will populate the object array while SetObjectArrayElement [5] assigns each element in the array.

Here the local reference utf_str is stored in the array. Following the guidelines laid out in the previous chapter, the local reference to utf_str is explicitly deleted in line [6] so as to not accumulate the storage associated with local references. When the newArr value is returned to Java, so are its reference elements.

The code for getting the elements and printing them is symmetrical to the above code. Instead of SetObjectArrayElement, the function Get-ObjectArrayElement [7] is used. DeleteLocalRef is again used to avoid filling memory with obsolete local references.

Listing 6.3 *Native Implementation of* printObjArray

```
JNIEXPORT void JNICALL
Java_ObjArrayEx_printObjArray(
    JNIEnv *env, jclass thisClass, jobjectArray arr)
{
    jboolean    isCopy;
    jstring     j_str;
    const char* c_str;
    jint sz = env->GetArrayLength(arr);
```

Listing 6.3 (cont.) *Native Implementation of* printObjArray

```
      printf("Printing from native code:\n");
      for (int i = 0; i < sz; i++) {
         j_str = (jstring)
(7)           env->GetObjectArrayElement(arr, i);
         c_str =
            env->GetStringUTFChars(j_str, &isCopy);
         printf("elem[%d] = %s\n",i, c_str);
         if (isCopy == JNI_TRUE)
(8)           env->ReleaseStringUTFChars(j_str, c_str);
         env->DeleteLocalRef(j_str);
      }
}
```

The call to ReleaseStringUTFChars is a newcomer. We will look at it in detail in the section on the JNI string functions.

The output of this code confirms that the object element references remain valid across native method calls.

• Program Output ⟩ **Printing Object Array for Java and Native Code**

```
Creating object array in native code.
Printing from Java code:
elem[0] = elem0
elem[1] = elem1
elem[2] = elem2
elem[3] = elem3
elem[4] = elem4
Printing from native code:
elem[0] = elem0
elem[1] = elem1
elem[2] = elem2
elem[3] = elem3
elem[4] = elem4
```

The values printed by the Java side are the same as those printed by the native code.

Array of Arrays

Notice the use of GetArrayLength in Listing 6.3. Its role is straightforward, yet indispensable.

We can take the current example a bit further to highlight the role of GetArrayLength and to illustrate the handling of arrays of arrays in native code.

Let's look at Java code that defines an array of object arrays and then populates each element of the array with an array of a different type of object. Often it is helpful to implement a prototype of native code using Java in order to understand the algorithmic issues before dealing with the JNI details.

In the example below, arrays of Integer, Float and Long objects are placed into various elements of the Java array of object arrays. The work of initializing the array will be done by the method initializeAofA. First, we will look at this initialization done by Java code, then we will look at an equivalent implementation using JNI functionality.

Listing 6.4 *Java Source for Manipulation of an Array of Arrays*

```
public class AofA {
public static void initializeAofA(Object[][] oArry)
{
      int el_sz;
      int sz = oArry.length;
      for (int i = 0; i < sz; i++) {
        switch (i) {
       case 0:
       case 2: {
          // Create an Integer array...
          oArry[i] = new Integer[3];
          el_sz - oArry[i].length;
          // ...and populate its elements
          for (int j = 0; j < el_sz; j++)
             oArry[i][j] = new Integer(j);
          }
          break;
```

(9)

Listing 6.4 (cont.) *Java Source for Manipulation of an Array of Arrays*

```
                case 1:
                case 3: {
                    // Create a Float array...
(10)                oArry[i] = new Float[5];
                    el_sz = oArry[i].length;
                    // ...and initialize its elements
                    for (int j = 0; j < el_sz; j++)
                        oArry[i][j] = new Float((j + 1)*10.0);
                    }
                    break;
                case 4: {
                    // Create a String array...
(11)                oArry[i] = new String[4];
                    el_sz = oArry[i].length;
                    // ...and initialize its elements
                    for (int j = 0; j < el_sz; j++)
                        oArry[i][j] = new String("string"+j);
                    }
                    break;
                }
            }
        }
        public static void printAofA(Object[][] ia) {
            for (int i = 0; i < ia.length; i++) {
                int sz = ia[i].length;
                System.out.println(
                    "Array length[" + i + "]= " + sz);
                for(int j = 0; j < sz; j++)
                    System.out.println(
                        "ia[" + i + "][" + j + "]= " + ia[i][j]);
            }
        }

        public static void main(String[] args) {
            Object[][] oArry = new Object[5][];
            initializeAofA(oArry);
            printAofA(oArry);
        }
    }
}
```

The method `initializeAofA` iterates over the array passed as an argument and allocates an object array for assignment to each of its elements. The element object arrays are allocated in lines [9]-[11]. For variety, and for the sake of illustration, different elements of the argument array get arrays of different types.

Before we look at the native code, let's look at how the JNI functions map into the Java code above. In Table 6.1 a representative line of Java code is matched with the corresponding JNI call.

Table 6.1 *Java/JNI Array Manipulation*

Java Code	JNI Call
oArry = new Integer[]	`NewObjectArray`
oArry.length	`GetArrayLength`
oArry[i][j] = new Integer()	`SetObjectElement`

Table 6.1 roughly says that to affect the Java operation on the left, the JNI function on the right must be called. This table just gives an overview. For example, it actually takes two JNI functions to achieve the equivalent of new Integer[]. First, the Integer class must be found using FindClass, and only then can NewObjectArray be called. Lines [12]-[14] make the necessary calls to FindClass.

Listing 6.5 *Native Implementation of* `initializeAofA`

```
JNIEXPORT void JNICALL
Java_NativeAofA_initializeAofA(
          JNIEnv * env,
          jclass thisClazz,
          jobjectArray oArry) {
     int i, j;
     jint el_sz;
     jclass iclazz, fclazz, sclazz;
     jmethodID imid, fmid,
     jint sz = env->GetArrayLength(oArry);
     // So that we do not have to do multiple times
     // in loop
(12) iclazz = env->FindClass("java/lang/Integer");
(13) fclazz = env->FindClass("java/lang/Float");
(14) sclazz = env->FindClass("java/lang/String");

     // Likewise, with the method IDs
     imid = env->GetMethodID(iclazz,
                          "<init>", "(I)V");
     fmid = env->GetMethodID(fclazz,
                          "<init>", "(F)V");
```

Listing 6.5 (cont.) *Native Implementation of* initializeAofA

```
for (i = 0; i < sz; i++) {
    switch (i) {
    case 0:
    case 2:
    {
        // Create an Integer array...
        // iarr[i] = new Integer[3];
(15)    jobjectArray iarr =
            env->NewObjectArray(3, iclazz, NULL);

(16)    env->SetObjectArrayElement(oArry, i, iarr);

(17)    el_sz = env->GetArrayLength(iarr);
        // ...and populate its elements
        //   iarr[i][j] = new Integer(j);
        jobject iob;
        for (j = 0; j < el_sz; j++) {
(18)        iob = env->NewObject(iclazz, imid, j);
(19)        env->SetObjectArrayElement(iarr, j, iob);
        }
    }
    break;
    case 1:
    case 3:
    {
    // Create a Float array...
    // oArry[i] = new Float[5];
    jobjectArray farr =
            env->NewObjectArray(5, fclazz, NULL);
    env->SetObjectArrayElement(oArry, i, farr);

    // el_sz = oArry[i].length;
    el_sz = env->GetArrayLength(farr);
    // ...and initialize its elements
    jobject fob;
    for (j = 0; j < el_sz; j++) {
        fob = env->NewObject(
                fclazz, fmid, (j+1)*10.0);
        env->SetObjectArrayElement(farr, j, fobj);
    }
    }
    break;
```

Listing 6.5 (cont.) *Native Implementation of* `initializeAofA`

```
case 4:
{
   // Create a String array...
   // oArry[i] = new String[4];
   jobjectArray sarr =
      env->NewObjectArray(4, sclazz, NULL);

   env->SetObjectArrayElement(oArry, i, sarr);

   // el_sz = oArry[i].length;
   el_sz = env->GetArrayLength(sarr);
   // ...and initialize its elements
   for (j = 0; j < el_sz; j++) {
      char  buf[8];
      sprintf(buf, "string%d", j);
      // oArry[i][j] = new String("string" + j);
      jstring jstr = env->NewStringUTF(buf);
      env->SetObjectArrayElement(sarr, j, jstr);
   }
   break;
} // case 4
} // switch
} // for
}
```

Interspersed throughout the JNI code, comments have been inserted that contain the Java code from the previous listing. These comments should make it clear what the JNI code is doing. Each branch of the switch statement does basically the same thing. Let's look at one of them.

- In line [15] an object array is created using `NewObjectArray`. This call uses the jclass reference from line [12].

- In line [16] that object array is assigned to an element in the input object array using `SetObjectArrayElement`.

- In line [17] the length of the element object array is retrieved using `GetArrayLength`.

- In the `for` loop new objects are created using `NewObject` at line [18].

- In line [19] `SetObjectArrayElement` is used to assign an object value to an entry in an array of objects.

Beyond the embedded commentary, there are a few other things worth mentioning. First, the calls to `FindClass` and `GetMethodID` are outside the main loop. There is no need to compute those values multiple times.

Second, although the construction

```
env->SetObjectArrayElement(iarr, i,
        env->NewObjectArray(iclazz, sz, NULL)));
```

is certainly possible, it is not amenable to exception checking. Ideally, one would want to ensure `NewObjectArray` was successful before using its return value. Exception checking and related topics will be discussed in the next chapter.

Some Output

Listing 6.5 contains a lot of code to look at without any output to convince you it works. If a picture is worth a thousand words, output from a thousand lines of code must be worth something.

The output below, produced by running the `main` method, is a modified version of the class `AofA` appearing in Listing 6.4. The class was modified by removing the Java source for the `initializeAofA` method, declaring it `native` [20], and implementing the `native` method code (Listing 6.5). These changes resulted in the class `NativeAofA` shown in the following listing.

Listing 6.6 *Java Source for* `NativeAofA`

```
public class NativeAofA {
static {
    System.loadLibrary("Chap6example2");
}
public static void printAofA(Object[][] oArry) {
    for (int i = 0; i < 5; i++) {
        int sz = oArry[i].length;
        System.out.println("
            Array length[" + i + "] = " + sz);
        for(int j = 0; j < sz; j++)
            System.out.println(
        "oArry[" + i + "][" + j + "]= " + oArry[i][j]);
    }
}
```

(20)
```
    public native static void
        initializeAofA(Object[][] oArry);
    public static void main(String[] args) {
        Object[][] oArry = new Object[5][];
        initializeAofA(oArry);
        printAofA(oArry);
    }
}
}
```

Invoking the `main` method of `NativeAofA` results in the following output.

• Program Output   **Invoking** `main` **Method of** `NativeAofA`

```
Array length[0]= 3
oArry[0][0]= 0
oArry[0][1]= 1
oArry[0][2]= 2
Array length[1]= 5
oArry[1][0]= 10.0
oArry[1][1]= 20.0
oArry[1][2]= 30.0
oArry[1][3]= 40.0
oArry[1][4]= 50.0
Array length[2]= 3
oArry[2][0]= 0
oArry[2][1]= 1
oArry[2][2]= 2
Array length[3]= 5
oArry[3][0]= 10.0
oArry[3][1]= 20.0
oArry[3][2]= 30.0
oArry[3][3]= 40.0
oArry[3][4]= 50.0
Array length[4]= 4
oArry[4][0]= string0
oArry[4][1]= string1
oArry[4][2]= string2
oArry[4][3]= string3
```

The lesson to learn from this voluminous output is that the JNI provides the full range of support for heterogeneous arrays of object arrays.

There is just one more thing to know about object arrays. We have seen the use of `NewObjectArray`, `GetArrayLength` and `SetObjectArrayElement`. All that is left is `GetObjectArrayElement`. `GetObjectArrayElement` takes an array object and index as arguments and returns a `jobject` as shown below.

```
jobject anObj;
anObj = env->GetObjectArrayElement(iarr, i);
```

Since it returns a `jobject` value, it may be necessary to test the returned value using `IsInstanceOf`.

Primitive Type Arrays

The JNI functions for manipulating arrays of primitive types follow a familiar pattern. There are functions for creating arrays, functions for setting element values and functions for getting element values. Each of these operations has multiple functions, one for each JNI native type.

Creating a Primitive Array

A family of JNI functions are provided for creating primitive array objects. All of these conform to the naming convention:

<pjniArrayType> New*<type>*Array

where the following table lists the correct combinations of *<pjniArrayType>* and *<type>*. *<pjniArrayType>* and *<type>* are placeholders that are replaced with corresponding entries in the following table. In the left column is the native type. The right column contains the name of the JNI function for constructing an array of this type.

Table 6.2 *JNI Primitive Array Constructors*

Native Array Type	JNI Array Constructor
jbooleanArray	NewBooleanArray
jbyteArray	NewByteArray
jcharArray	NewCharArray
jshortArray	NewShortArray
jintArray	NewIntArray
jlongArray	NewLongArray
jfloatArray	NewFloatArray
jdoubleArray	NewDoubleArray

All of these functions are invoked with two arguments in C, the JNI interface pointer and the desired array length. The following line of C code creates an integer array with ten elements.

```
jintArray intArray = (*env)->NewIntArray(env, 10);
```

creates an array of ten integers. The equivalent C++ call is shown below.

```
jintArray intArray = env->NewIntArray(10);
```

Getting Primitive Array Elements

Primitive array elements can be retrieved in two ways. One set of JNI functions returns a pointer to the entire array while another copies a region of the array into a user-supplied buffer. Both adhere to a naming convention similar to the one described above.

The two sets of functions will be discussed separately since the memory management issues are different.

Accessing the Entire Array Contents of a Primitive Array

To retrieve and modify the entire contents of a primitive array, use one of the Get<*type*>ArrayElements functions. These functions return a pointer to contiguous memory containing the elements of the array.

```
jboolean      isCopy;
jint*         intArrayPtr;
jintArray     intArray;

intArray = env->NewIntArray(10);
intArrayPtr =
   env->GetIntArrayElements(intArray, &isCopy);
```

After the call to GetIntArrayElements the value of isCopy will be either JNI_TRUE or JNI_FALSE. If the value of isCopy is JNI_TRUE, the memory pointed to by the return value is a copy of the Java object array. In this case, the contents of the Java object will not be updated until the appropriate release call is made.

If the value of isCopy is JNI_FALSE, the return value points directly into the Java array. In either case, the return value of GetIntArrayElements is guaranteed to point to contiguous memory.

If the value of isCopy is JNI_FALSE, the return value points directly into the Java array object, and the memory occupied by that object is guaranteed to be *pinned*. Pinning memory prevents it being moved during garbage collection. The memory occupied by the array values will not move during the execution of the native code.

If the Get<*type*>ArrayElements function returns a pointer to a copy of the array data, changes made to the values at this location will not be reflected in the original array until Release<*type*>ArrayElements is called. Release<*type*>ArrayElements does the job of copying the changed values back into the original Java array. If the native code that calls Get<*type*>ArrayElements changes values in the buffer pointed to by its return value, Release<*type*>ArrayElements must be called to update the original array. To test for this condition, check the value of isCopy.

It should also be noted that a primitive object array obtained as a result of a call to Get<*type*>ArrayElements call is capable of being changed by another Java thread. While one thread, say the thread in which the native code is executing, is writing into the copy returned by Get<*type*>ArrayElements, another Java thread may be writing the Java object directly. This, of course, is not desirable and care should be taken to prevent this condition using the proper locking techniques.

Let's look at an example that illustrates the operation of the JNI functions discussed above.

An Example: Accessing an Entire Array

We will first look at a Java class that contains a `native` method declaration. This `native` method, `zeroArray`, takes an `int[]` object as an argument and sets all of its elements to zero. The array is printed twice. It is printed first in line [22], before the call to `zeroArray`. The contents are printed a second time in line [23] after the call to `zeroArray`. This example illustrates the manipulation of a Java primitive array by native code.

Listing 6.7 *Java Source for* PArrayEx

```
public class PArrayEx {
static {
    System.loadLibrary("Chap6example3");
}
```

(21)
```
public static native void zeroArray(int[] intArray);

public static void printArray(int[] intArray) {
    int sz = intArray.length;
    for (int i = 0; i < sz; i++)
        System.out.print(intArray[i] + ":");
    System.out.println();
}

public static void main(String[] arg) {
    int[] intArray = new int[10];
    int sz = intArray.length;
    for (int i = 0; i < sz; i++)
        intArray[i] = i + 1;
```

(22)
```
    printArray(intArray);
    zeroArray(intArray);
```

(23)
```
    printArray(intArray);
}
}
```

The implementation of `zeroArray` appears below. The first thing it does is extract the elements of the array from the array object [24].

Listing 6.8 *Native Implementation of* zeroArray

```
JNIEXPORT void JNICALL Java_PArrayEx_zeroArray(
                JNIEnv * env,
                jclass thisClass,
                jintArray intArray)
{
    jboolean isCopy;
    jint* intArrayElems =
        env->GetIntArrayElements(intArray, &isCopy);

    jint sz = env->GetArrayLength(intArray);
    for (int i = 0; i < sz; i++)
        intArrayElems[i] = 0;
    if (isCopy == JNI_TRUE) {
        env->ReleaseIntArrayElements(intArray,
                                intArrayElems, 0);
    }
}
```

(24) appears beside the `jint* intArrayElems = env->GetIntArrayElements(intArray, &isCopy);` lines.
(25) appears beside the `for (int i = 0; i < sz; i++)` line.
(26) appears beside the `env->ReleaseIntArrayElements(intArray,` line.

The isCopy value is set by the call to the Get<*type*>ArrayElements. It is not an input value.

In the for loop at [25], the native code can iterates over the array elements as would any C/C++ program. Finally, in line [26], ReleaseIntArrayElements is called to, possibly, free the memory allocated for the array elements.

Whether the memory is freed depends on the value of the third argument to the release call. The Release<*type*>ArrayElements calls can take one of three values as its third argument. These values and their meaning are shown in the following table.

Table 6.3 *Release Modes*

Release Mode Value	Description
0	Copy the contents of the buffer back into array and free the buffer
JNI_ABORT	Free the buffer without copying back any changes
JNI_COMMIT	Copy the contents of the buffer back into array but do not free the buffer

Using 0 as the third argument to Release<*type*>ArrayElements will ensure consistent behavior for both pinned and copied arrays: any changes you make will show up in the Java object.

If JNI_COMMIT is used as the third argument to the release function, you are responsible for freeing the buffer that Get*<type>*ArrayElements allocated. Currently, the JNI specification describes neither how the memory is allocated nor how it should be freed.

In fact, the JNI specification says that 0 is the "preferred" value for the third argument to Release*<type>*ArrayElements calls. This is good advice given the lack of specifics regarding the JNI_COMMIT.

If a JVM implementation stores primitive arrays in contiguous memory within the Java objects, isCopy will always return JNI_FALSE and none of the above flags will have any affect. No additional memory is allocated beyond the Java array object and therefore all changes are made directly to that object and there is no additional buffer involved. This renders both JNI_COMMIT and JNI_ABORT meaningless.

In light of the lack of specifics provided in the JNI specification and the ability of a JVM implementation to make its own decision regarding whether it does memory copies in response to Get*<type>*ArrayElements calls, it is always good practice to call Release*<type>*ArrayElements.

Accessing a Region of a Primitive Array

This entire discussion of pinned versus copied memory can be avoided by using the JNI functions that perform region operations on the primitive arrays.

The JNI provides a family of functions, a pair for each Java primitive type, that copy elements into and out of a locally allocated buffer. When using these functions, you take full responsibility for the management of the memory which serves as a staging area for native data as it moves between a Java object and a native data buffer.

For each Java primitive type there is a JNI "get" operation that copies array element values from a Java object into a local buffer and a "set" operation that copies data from a local buffer into the array elements of a Java array object.

The prototypes for these functions look like this:

```
Get<type>ArrayRegion(<pjniArrayType> arry,
      jsize start,
      jsize count,
      <pjniType>* buf);

Set<type>ArrayRegion(<pjniArrayType> arry,
      jsize start,
      jsize count,
      <pjniType>* buf);
```

where the placeholders are replaced with values from Table 6.4.

Table 6.4 *Primitive Array Region Access Functions*

Type *<type>*	Array Type *<pjniArrayType>*	Primitive Native Type *<pjniType>*	Function Name
Boolean	jbooleanArray	jboolean	GetBooleanArrayRegion SetBooleanArrayRegion
Byte	jbyteArray	jbyte	GetByteArrayRegion SetByteArrayRegion
Char	jcharArray	jchar	GetCharArrayRegion SetCharArrayRegion
Short	jshortArray	jshort	GetShortArrayRegion SetShortArrayRegion
Int	jintArray	jint	GetIntArrayRegion SetIntArrayRegion
Long	jlongArray	jlong	GetLongArrayRegion SetLongArrayRegion
Float	jfloatArray	jfloat	GetFloatArrayRegion SetFloatArrayRegion
Double	jdoubleArray	jdouble	GetDoubleArrayRegion SetFloatArrayRegion

Each function starts its copy at the location in the array or buffer named by the `start` argument. The `count` argument determines the number of elements copied. In other words, `count * sizeof(<pjniType>)` bytes are copied.

There is one point that needs to be emphasized. This is an area where getting your conversion from Java types to native types is very important. If you are modeling a C array of `long`, for instance, be careful to use the correct JNI primitive array type to store the `long` values. This type will vary from platform to platform. On NT, a long is 32 bits, as well as on most SPARC systems. On these two platforms, you will want to use `SetIntArrayRegion` when copying longs.

A Java `long` and the JNI `jlong` are 64 bits. Trying to copy a native `long` array into a region of a `jlong` array using `SetLongArrayRegion` will result in junk in the array.

Specifically, the following code writes junk into the target array.

Listing 6.9 *A Bad Example Using* SetLongArrayRegion

```
long tenLongs[10] =
   {  100, 200, 300, 400, 500,
      600, 700, 800, 900, 1000 };

JNIEXPORT void JNICALL
Java_LongArr_populateLongArray(
               JNIEnv *env,
               jclass thisClz,
               jlongArray longArray)
{
   env->SetLongArrayRegion(
      (jlongArray)longArray, 0, 10,
      (jlong*)tenLongs);
}
```

As SetLongArrayRegion does its copying, it will copy two long values for each jlong in the array, leaving the upper elements in longArray with bad data and, possibly, causing a memory access violation. Attention to this potential problem is nothing more than good programming practice, however, it is easy to make the mistake of treating a long as being the same size as a jlong.

Let's look at an example of the use of JNI array region functions on an integer array. Below is a piece of Java code that relies on native methods to populate an integer array [28], and then print its values [30]. Between these two native method calls, the array is printed by Java code and has its values changed [29]. The Java code follows.

Listing 6.10 *Java Source for* ArrayRegionEx *Class*

```
public class ArrayRegionEx {
static {
   System.loadLibrary("Chap6example4");
}
public static native void printIntArrayRegion(
         int[] intArr, int start, int cnt);

public static native void populateIntArrayRegion(
         int[] intArr, int start, int cnt);
```

Listing 6.10 (cont.) *Java Source for* `ArrayRegionEx` *Class*

```
        public static void main(String[] args) {
(27)        int[] intArray = new int[10];
(28)        populateIntArrayRegion(intArray, 0, 10);
            for (int i = 0; i < 10; i++) {
                System.out.print(intArray[i] + ":");
(29)            intArray[i] = 999;
            }
            System.out.println();
(30)        printIntArrayRegion(intArray, 0, 10);
        }
    }
```

The implementation of the `native` method responsible for populating the array illustrates the use of the set region operation [32]. Keep in mind that the Java code that calls this method allocates the integer array.

Listing 6.11 *Setting a Region of a Primitive Array*

```
JNIEXPORT void JNICALL
Java_ArrayRegionEx_populateIntArrayRegion(
                JNIEnv *env,
                jclass thisClass,
                jintArray intArray,
                jint start,
                jint cnt)
{
        jint sz = env->GetArrayLength(intArray);
(31)    jint* p = (jint*) malloc(sz * sizeof(jint));
        for (int i = 0; i < sz; i++)
            p[i] = i;
(32)    env->SetIntArrayRegion(intArray, start, cnt, p);
(33)    free(p);
}
```

Note the calls to both `malloc` [31] and `free` [33]. The native code takes full responsibility for memory management of the copy buffer. Lest you worry about the array object being garbage collected before we copy the values back into it, keep in mind we have a local reference to it by virtue of it having been passed as an argument to the `native` method. This reference will prevent garbage collection of the array object.

The implementation for `printIntArrayRegion` illustrates the use of the `GetIntArrayRegion` function [34]. You will note again the use of `malloc` and `free` to take care of the native buffer which receives the data from the `jintArray`.

Listing 6.12 *Getting a Region of a Primitive Array*

```
JNIEXPORT void JNICALL
Java_ArrayRegionEx_printIntArrayRegion(
            JNIEnv *env,
            jclass thisClass,
            jintArray intArray,
            jint start,
            jint cnt)
{
    jint sz = env->GetArrayLength(intArray);
    jint* p = (jint*) malloc(sz * sizeof(jint));
    env->GetIntArrayRegion(intArray, start, cnt, p);
    for (int i = 0; i < sz; i++)
        printf("%d:", p[i]);
    printf("\n");
    free(p);
}
```

(34)

All that is left to do now is to convince you it all works as advertised. Hopefully, the following output will do that.

• Program Output Invoking `main` **Method of** `ArrayRegionEx`

```
0:1:2:3:4:5:6:7:8:9:
999:999:999:999:999:999:999:999:999:999:
```

The first line is printed by the Java code after the array was populated in native code. The second line is printed by native code after the Java code changed the values.

JNI String Functions

The JNI provides two parallel sets of functions for string manipulation. One set supports UTF-8 encoding and the other, Unicode characters.

The UTF-8 representation is the same as that used internally by the JVM. The UTF-8 encoding of a string allows sequences of non-null ASCII characters to be represented with one byte per character, but also is capable of representing characters that require sixteen bits. This means that C/C++ strings are a subset of the strings represented using UTF-8 encoding, since C/C++ strings are arrays of one-byte characters. Every C/C++ string of ASCII characters (ordinal value <= 127) is a UTF-8 string. Of course, this is handy when writing native code in C/C++. The JNI provides functions for creating java.lang.String objects from C/C++ strings as well as retrieving a C/C++ string representation of a java.lang.String.

The JNI also supports Unicode characters. The Unicode standard is a multi-byte character set important in the localization of text. Since many locales require more than one byte to represent a character, the Unicode standard is also supported by the JNI. This allows the reading and writing of sources that provide and expect Unicode character encoding. The JNI functions for Unicode character string handling map one for one to the UTF-8 functions.

We will take a close look at the UTF-8 JNI functions since they are most handy when manipulating C/C++ strings. We will follow with a brief look at the corresponding JNI functions for Unicode string handling.

UTF-8 String Handling

Java passes a java.lang.String object to a native method using a jstring reference. To make use of the ASCII string which the String object represents, the native code needs to get at the sequence of characters internal to that object.

The JNI function GetStringUTFChars does just that. It takes a jstring object as an input argument and returns a pointer to a sequence of bytes.

To illustrate the use of GetStringUTFChars, we will take a close look at an example we glossed over in earlier chapters. Let's look at a native method that prints out the java.lang.String object it receives as an argument.

Listing 6.13 *Conversion of* jstring *to C String*

```
JNIEXPORT void JNICALL Java_Native_printString(
JNIEnv *env, jobject this, jstring str)
{
    const char* utf_string;
    jboolean    isCopy;

    utf_string = env->GetStringUTFChars(str,
                                &isCopy);
    printf("%s\n", utf_string);
    if (isCopy == JNI_TRUE) {
        env->ReleaseStringUTFChars(str, utf_string);
    }
}
```

GetStringUTFChars returns a pointer to a C/C++ string: a null-terminated sequence of ASCII bytes. If that pointer points to a copy of the bytes maintained by the String object, the value of isCopy after the call returns will be JNI_TRUE. If this is so, then the memory containing the copied characters needs to be freed. This is done with a call to ReleaseStringUTF-Chars. If a copy of the string characters is returned by GetStringUTFChars, then ReleaseStringUTFChars *must* be called in order for any changes made by native code to be reflected in the java.lang.String object.

The use of the isCopy flag is very similar to the flag returned from the JNI functions for getting primitive array elements. Since there are no promises made about how a JVM stores a character sequence for a string and since C/C++ code expects those characters to be consecutive bytes in memory, the JVM may need to copy its non-consecutive representation of a java.lang.String object into contiguous memory. If this is required, the JVM signals this by returning JNI_TRUE in the second argument to Get-StringUTFChars.

Creating a New String Object

The JNI function NewStringUTF creates a new java.lang.String object returned as a jstring value. This is basically a conversion function that takes a UTF-8 string and creates the Java object. Such a value could be returned to the Java side into a String object reference.

Consider a short piece of Java code that relies on a native method to create a String object and return it.

Listing 6.14 *Java Source for* NewStringEx

```
public class NewStringEx {
static {
    System.loadLibrary("Chap6example6");
}
public static native String newStringUTF();
public static void main(String[] arg) {
    String s = newStringUTF();
    System.out.println(s);
}
}
```

The implementation of the native method newStringUTF appears below. The return value of NewStringUTF is returned directly to the Java code.

Listing 6.15 *Creating a Java String Object in Native Code*

```
JNIEXPORT jstring JNICALL
Java_NewStringEx_newStringUTF(
            JNIEnv *env, jclass clazz)
{
   const char* msg =
         "String constructed using NewStringUTF";
   return env->NewStringUTF(msg);
}
```

Before we move on to the Unicode analogs of these UTF-8 String functions, we will take a quick look at GetStringUTFLength. This function returns the number of bytes in the UTF-8 sequence of characters. It takes a jstring value as input argument. In the JNI GetStringUTFLength is to a java.lang.String object what the ANSI C function strlen is to a char* value. Its use is straightforward.

Listing 6.16 *Determining Length of a Java String Object*

```
JNIEXPORT void JNICALL Java_Native_printString(
         JNIEnv *env, jobject this, jstring str)
{
   jsize sz = env->GetStringUTFLength(str);
   // Do some stuff...
}
```

That's it for the JNI UTF-8 functions. Below we will see how the Unicode string functions are analogous to the UTF-8 functions.

Unicode String Functions

For each operation provided for UTF-8 character strings that we saw above, there is a corresponding JNI function for Unicode character strings. The related functions are listed below.

Table 6.5 *Unicode String Functions*

JNI UTF-8 String Functions	JNI Unicode String Functions
NewStringUTF	NewString
GetStringUTFLength	GetStringLength
GetStringUTFChars	GetStringChars
ReleaseStringUTFChars	ReleaseStringChars

Their use is equivalent to the UTF-8 counterparts. The only difference appears in the type used to represent strings. All the UTF-8 strings are of type `char*` whereas the Unicode functions handle sequences of `jchar` values.

All the previously mentioned guidelines for the use of the release function apply for Unicode strings as well. It is always good practice to use `ReleaseStringChars` after a call to `GetStringChars`.

Summary

That does it for arrays and strings. You have seen how the JNI has two different sets of functions for object arrays and arrays of primitive types. Object arrays are created with `NewObjectArray`, and primitive arrays are created by a type-safe function whose name includes the element type.

To get and set elements in an object array, the JNI functions `GetObjectArrayElement` and `SetObjectArrayElement` are used respectively.

You can access the elements of primitive arrays in either of two ways. In the first, `Get<type>ArrayElements` returns a pointer to contiguous memory containing the element values. Different implementations of the JVM may return a copy of the array elements or a pointer into the array object. In either case, it is good practice to call `Release<type>ArrayElements` to ensure any changes made by the native code are written to the object. Secondly, the JNI provides a collection of type-safe functions that explicitly copy a region of a primitive array into a local buffer. In this case, the user assumes responsibility for management of the buffer memory.

We also covered the JNI functions for manipulating Java String objects as C/C++ strings. As with primitive arrays, the JNI provides functions for getting a pointer to a buffer of contiguous bytes in memory. These functions also provide a return argument that informs the native code whether or not a copy of the string was received.

Finally, the JNI provides support for both UTF-8 strings and Unicode strings. With these functions, C strings and Unicode strings respectively can be converted to the native type `jstring` and vice-versa.

Chapter 7 ___ EXCEPTIONS

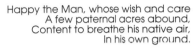

Happy the Man, whose wish and care
A few paternal acres abound,
Content to breathe his native air,
In his own ground.

Alexander Pope
Ode on Solitude

Introduction

The JNI provides support for throwing and handling exceptions. The treatment of exceptions in native code parallels closely their treatment in Java. Native code may raise arbitrary exceptions as well as handle exceptions raised by JNI functions when calling into the JVM.

All the discussion of exceptions in this chapter deals with JVM exceptions. There is no coverage of exceptions thrown and caught by the run-time environment of the native programming language, for example, C++'s `try`/`catch` facility. The two topics are orthogonal and both types of exception handling may be intermixed.

There are two JNI functions for throwing exceptions and three others that help with exception handling and reporting.

The native programmer needs to pay particular attention to handling exceptions since failure to do so can result in crashing the JVM, thereby complicating debugging.

121

Throwing Exceptions

Native code has at its disposal all of the Java language exceptions. A JNI exception can be thrown using either an object reference or a class reference. In the former case, the object must be an instance of a subclass of java.lang.Throwable. In the latter case, the class reference must be a subclass of java.lang.Throwable.

The JNI functions for throwing exceptions are Throw and ThrowNew. Two quick examples highlight the differences. Before we look at the native code, let's take a look at the Java code that declares and uses native methods that throw an exception.

Listing 7.1 *Java Source for Native Exception Throwing*

```
public class ExcEx {
static {
    System.loadLibrary("Chap7example1");
}
public static native void nativeThrow(String arg)
                        throws Exception;
public static native void nativeThrowNew()
                        throws Exception;

public static void hello() {
    System.out.println("hello");
}

public static void main(String[] args) {
    try {
        nativeThrow(null);
    } catch (Exception e) {
        e.printStackTrace();
    }
    try {
        nativeThrowNew();
    } catch (Exception e) {
        System.out.println("From getMessage() : " +
                        e.getMessage());
        e.printStackTrace();
    }
}
}
```

(1)

Two native methods are declared in the above code, nativeThrow and nativeThrowNew. Both declarations include a throws clause to identify the fact that they throw exceptions. That they do is neither a requirement of JNI nor a syntactical requirement of Java. Unlike non-native methods, the Java byte code compiler has no way to determine whether or not a `native` method throws an exception. If you fail to declare it as such, the Java compiler will not insist on a `catch` clause and it is likely that the exception will not be caught except by the `main` method, resulting in termination of your application. This is simply a case where writing `native` methods requires extra attention to detail normally checked by the Java byte code compiler.

Throwing an Exception

The implementation of the `native` method `nativeThrow` uses the JNI function `Throw` to throw an exception. `Throw` takes a single argument, an object reference. The object is created by calling `NewObject` with a `jclass` value. The `jclass` value must be a subclass of `java.lang.Throwable`.

NewObject called on a subclass of `java.lang.Throwable` returns a `jthrowable` object reference. `jthrowable` is a subclass of `jobject` for use with the JNI exception functions.

Listing 7.2 displays the native code for `nativeThrow`.

Listing 7.2 *Native Implementation of* `nativeThrow`

```
JNIEXPORT void JNICALL Java_ExcEx_nativeThrow(
        JNIEnv * env, jclass thisClass, jstring arg) {
    jclass clazz;
    jmethodID mid;
    jthrowable throwObj;

    if (arg == NULL) {
        clazz = env->FindClass(
            "java/lang/IllegalArgumentException");
        mid = env->GetMethodID(clazz,
                            "<init>", "()V");

        throwObj =
            (jthrowable)env->NewObject(clazz, mid);

        env->Throw(throwObj);
    }
    // Do something...
    fprintf(stderr,
            "nativeThrow: after exception\n");
}
```

(2)

(3)

(4)

In line [2] above, `FindClass` is used to return a `jclass` value for the class `java.lang.IllegalArgumentException`. This value is used by `NewObject` in line [3]. Finally, in line [4] the JNI `Throw` function raises an exception.

Before we look at the output for this code, let's look at `native` method `nativeThrowNew` and the JNI function `ThrowNew`.

Building and Throwing an Exception

An exception can also be thrown within native code using `ThrowNew`, a function that implicitly creates the `jthrowable` object. The implementation of `nativeThrowNew` illustrates the use of the JNI `ThrowNew` function.

Listing 7.3 *Native Implementation of* `nativeThrowNew`

```
JNIEXPORT void JNICALL Java_ExcEx_nativeThrowNew(
        JNIEnv *env, jclass thisClazz, jstring arg)
{
    jclass clazz;
    if (arg == NULL) {
        clazz   = env->FindClass(
            "java/lang/IllegalArgumentException");

        fprintf(stderr,
            "nativeThrowNew: before ThrowNew\n");

        env->ThrowNew(clazz,
                "\nArgument Type: ad hominem");
    }

    fprintf(stderr,
            "nativeThrowNew: after ThrowNew\n");
}
```

(5) and *(6)* mark the lines `clazz = env->FindClass(...)` and `env->ThrowNew(clazz, ...)` respectively.

As you can see from line [6], `ThrowNew` does not require the construction of a new object. Rather, it expects a reference to a class object that is a subclass of `java.lang.Throwable`. This reference is supplied by `FindClass` in line [5]. Additionally, a string argument to `ThrowNew` is provided for printing when the exception is caught by the JVM. Its `String` value can be accessed using the `getMessage` method of the `java.lang.Throwable` class. This is what the `ExcEx` class does at line [1] on page 122.

When Does an Exception Get Raised?

The fprintf statements are included in the above native method implementations to make a point. Looking at the output from these two native methods, you can see that native code is executed even after the calls to Throw and ThrowNew.

You will notice that the statements appear to be executed out of order. The output from the execution of nativeThrow below illustrates the printing of the message followed by the notification of the exception. The exception is not recognized and reported until after the native method completes and control is returned to the JVM.

• Program Output ⟩ nativeThrow **Native Method**

```
enter nativeThrow
nativeThrow: doing something after exception
java.lang.IllegalArgumentException
        at ExcEx.main(ExcEx.java:16)
```

We see the same behavior with ThrowNew as the following listing shows.

• Program Output ⟩ nativeThrowNew **Native Method**

```
nativeThrowNew: before ThrowNew
nativeThrowNew: after ThrowNew
From getMessage() :
Argument Type: ad hominem
java.lang.IllegalArgumentException:
Argument Type: ad hominem
        at ExcEx.main(ExcEx.java:21)
```

You can think of the Throw and ThrowNew functions as setting state which the JVM checks upon transition from native code to Java code. The implications of this for the native coder is that a return should be inserted immediately after the Throw or ThrowNew if you want the exception handled by the Java side without unwanted or unexpected side-effects.

There is a slight variation on this condition. Sometimes, an intervening JNI call can clear the exception state, thereby preventing the JVM and, consequently, your application, from seeing the exception at all.

This is illustrated in Listing 7.4. This listing shows slightly modified versions of nativeThrow and nativeThrowNew. The method nativeThrow has been modified to return immediately after the call to Throw in [7]. Additionally, the JNI code to call back into the Java method hello has been added in lines [8] and [9] after the ThrowNew call . The following code represents the modified implementations of nativeThrow and nativeThrowNew.

Listing 7.4 *Modified* nativeThrow *and* nativeThrowNew

```
JNIEXPORT void JNICALL Java_ExcEx_nativeThrow
  (JNIEnv * env, jclass thisClazz, jstring arg) {
   fprintf(stderr, "enter nativeThrow\n");
   if (arg == NULL) {
      jclass clazz = env->FindClass(
          "java/lang/IllegalArgumentException");
      jmethodID mid = env->GetMethodID(clazz,
                      "<init>", "()V");
      jthrowable throwObj =
      (jthrowable)env->NewObject(clazz, mid);
      env->Throw(throwObj);
      return;
   }
   // Do something...
   fprintf(stderr,"nativeThrow: after exception\n");
}

JNIEXPORT void JNICALL Java_ExcEx_nativeThrowNew
  (JNIEnv *env, jclass thisClazz)
{
   jclass clazz;
   jmethodID mid;
   clazz  = env->FindClass(
         "java/lang/IllegalArgumentException");
   fprintf(stderr,
      "nativeThrowNew: before throwNew\n");
   env->ThrowNew(clazz,
      "Argument Type: ad hominem");
   fprintf(stderr,
      "nativeThrowNew: after throwNew\n");
   mid = env->GetStaticMethodID(thisClazz,
                      "hello","()V");

   env->CallStaticVoidMethod(thisClazz, mid);

}
```

(7) appears to the left of `return;`

(8) appears to the left of `mid = env->GetStaticMethodID(thisClazz,`

(9) appears to the left of `env->CallStaticVoidMethod(thisClazz, mid);`

We will look at the output of running the ExcEx example separately so the impact of the two changes is clear. First, we will look at the output from invoking nativeThrow from the ExcEx main method.

• **Program Output** ⟩ **Invoking** `nativeThrow`

```
enter nativeThrow
java.lang.IllegalArgumentException
        at ExcEx.main(ExcEx.java:18)
```

The addition of the return in `nativeThrow` took care of the problem of executing native code after an exception in that `native` method. This much is obvious. Of course the code after the return will not get executed. What is important, though, is that we see the exception when it occurs and can handle it appropriately. No intervening code will get executed, possibly obscuring debugging efforts or, worse, producing unintended side-effects during operation.

The output from `nativeThrowNew` still is a bit puzzling. No exception is being reported!

• **Program Output** ⟩ **Invoking** `nativeThrowNew`

```
nativeThrowNew: before throwNew
nativeThrowNew: after throwNew
hello
```

A return after the `ThrowNew` was intentionally omitted to highlight a more pernicious effect of its absence. In this case, the call to `CallStaticVoid-Method` to invoke the `hello` method actually masks the exception thrown earlier. Upon entry to `CallStaticVoidMethod`, the exception state information is cleared and, since `CallStaticVoidMethod` did not throw any exceptions, once control is returned to the Java code, the exception thrown by `ThrowNew` has been lost. The same is true for all of the JNI method invocation routines.

If `hello` had thrown an exception, we would have seen that exception and not the one produced by the call to `ThrowNew` within `nativeThrowNew`.

The lesson here is worth stating in a JNI Rule To Remember.

JNI Rule To Remember 13:

If it is your intention that the Java code catch an exception thrown by native code, you should return immediately following the call to `Throw` or `ThrowNew`.

If you are using `Throw` and `ThrowNew` within native code, you most likely intend that your Java code catch the exceptions. On the other hand, many JNI functions can raise conditions that you may want to catch within the native code. The JNI provisions for this approach will be discussed in the next section.

Catching Exceptions

When an exception occurs in native code, native code execution can proceed in one of two ways. It can either:

- Handle the exception itself by calling `ExceptionClear` and then executing appropriate handling code, or
- Return immediately, passing the exception on to the Java code that called the `native` method.

The JNI provides three handling functions for use when implementing either of these schemes. Their use is quite straightforward, since none of them takes any arguments.

To check for an exception, the native code uses the `ExceptionOccurred` function. `ExceptionClear` clears any pending exception. `ExceptionDescribe` prints out a message that describes the exception and provides a stack trace.

The `ExceptionOccurred` function returns an object reference to a `throwable` object. You can query this object extract the message string if desired.

If the native code chooses to handle an exception, a typical use of these functions follows.

```
jthrowable obj;

if ((obj = env->ExceptionOccurred()) != NULL) {
        // Do something to handle exception
        env->ExceptionClear();
}
```

Often a JNI function is capable of generating more than one type of exception. In this case, the exception handling code may have to determine which exception occurred in order to proceed properly. Let's look at that scenario now.

A Native Try-Catch

A common Java construct is a `try` block followed by multiple `catch` clauses. It is not unusual for a Java method call or a sequence of method calls to generate one of possibly multiple exceptions. The conventional way of handling this situation in Java code is shown below.

```
try {
    // try some things...
} catch (OneTypeOfException e) {
    // handle OneTypeOfException...
} catch (AnotherTypeOfException e) {
    // handle AnotherTypeOfException...
} catch (Exception e) {
    // Generic exception handler...
}
```

One can do the same thing using JNI functions, albeit not as elegantly. You are responsible for your checking to determine the type of the exception. This is a good chance to put `IsInstanceOf` from Chapter 5 to work.

First, we will introduce a simple Java class that calls some `native` method code.

Listing 7.5 *A Java Class with Native Exception Handling*

```
public class ExcEx2 {
static {
    System.loadLibrary("Chap7example3");
}
public static native void catchException(int flg);
public static void main(String[] args) {
    catchException(0);
    System.out.println("***********");
    catchException(1);
}
}
```

A single `native` method is declared here and called twice. The input argument simply triggers the throwing of different exceptions. The `native` method declarations purposely do not contain a `throws` clause because it is the intent to catch and then clear the exceptions within the native code.

The following native code deliberately generates an exception and then handles the exception based on the type of exception. The type of exception generated is determined by the `flg` input argument. One of two helper functions, `throwInstantiationException` and `throwOutOfMemory-Exception`, is called based on the value of the `flg` argument. Their job is to generate an exception.

Listing 7.6 *Catching Exceptions in Native Code*

```
JNIEXPORT void JNICALL Java_ExcEx2_catchException
    (JNIEnv * env, jclass thisClz, jint flg)
{
    jboolean isCopy;
    jthrowable throwObj;
    jmethodID mid;

(10)    jclass instExcClass = env->FindClass(
            "java/lang/InstantiationException");
(11)    jclass memExcClass = env->FindClass(
            "java/lang/OutOfMemoryError");

        if (flg == 0)
(12)        throwInstantiationException(env);
        else
(13)        throwOutOfMemoryException(env);

(14)    if ((throwObj = env->ExceptionOccurred())
                    != NULL) {
(15)     if (env->IsInstanceOf(throwObj, instExcClass)
                    == JNI_TRUE) {
(16)        mid = env->GetMethodID(instExcClass,
                "getMessage", "()Ljava/lang/String;");

(17)        jstring msg =
                (jstring) env->CallObjectMethod(
                        throwObj, mid, NULL);
            const char* cmsg =
                env->GetStringUTFChars(msg,&isCopy);
            fprintf(stderr, "getMessage : %s\n", cmsg);
            env->ExceptionClear();
         }
(18)     else if (env->IsInstanceOf(throwObj,
                memExcClass) == JNI_TRUE) {
(19)        env->FatalError(
                    "Out of Memory. Goodbye!\n");
         } else {
            fprintf(stderr, "Spurious Exception\n");
            env->ExceptionClear();
         }
      }
}
```

Listing 7.6 (cont.) *Catching Exceptions in Native Code*

```
void throwInstantiationException(JNIEnv* env) {
    jclass tclazz;
    tclazz = env->FindClass(
            "java/lang/InstantiationException");
    env->ThrowNew(tclazz, "Instantiation exception");
}
void throwOutOfMemoryException(JNIEnv* env) {
    jclass tclazz;
    tclazz = env->FindClass(
            "java/lang/OutOfMemoryError");
    env->ThrowNew(tclazz, "Out of memory error");
}
}
```

(20) (aligned with line `env->ThrowNew(tclazz, "Instantiation exception");`)

(21) (aligned with line `env->ThrowNew(tclazz, "Out of memory error");`)

In either [12] or [13] one of the two helper functions is called which throw an exception in either [20] or [21]. Line [14] tests for an exception condition and stores the `Throwable` object associated with it.

The two calls to `IsInstanceOf` implement what amounts to multiple catch clauses. In line [15] the class of the exception is tested against `java.lang.InstantiationException`. In line [18] it is tested against `java.lang.OutOfMemoryError`.

Notice that in [16] the reference to `instExcClass`. Since the `getMessage` method resides in `java.lang.Throwable`, the method ID can be retrieved from any of its subclasses. Normally, one would call `GetObjectClass` to get the class of an object for use with `GetMethodID` but since `throwObj` here is an instance of `java.lang.Throwable`, as is `instExcClass`, you can get away with skipping the `GetObjectClass` call.

Line [19] introduces `FatalError` in all its simple elegance.

As an aside, note the use of JNI functions in [16] and [17] to call the `getMessage` method. As you can see from the output of executing ExcEx2 from Listing 7.5, this method returns the string set in the creation of a `throwable` object in either [12] or [13]. The "JNI panic" string in the following output is generated by `FatalError`.

• Program Output ⟩ **Invoking catchException** native **Method**

```
getMessage : Instantiation exception
* * * * * * * * * *
JNI panic: Out of Memory...goodbye!
        at ExcEx2.main(ExcEx2.java:13)
```

This may seem like a bit of work simply to test for a particular exception. This could be improved upon if native code expects to do a lot of exception handling. If so, it would be a good idea to cache the `jclass` references of the exceptions the native code intends to handle as `static` variables. This will save your native code from the overhead of repeated calls to `FindClass` as in [10] and [11]. However, if you are going to do this, these references must be made into global references using `NewGlobalRef`.

Passing Exceptions to Java

As mentioned earlier, if the native code wants to pass on the job of exception handling, this simple piece of code will do the trick.

```
if (env->ExceptionOccurred()) {
    return;
}
```

Of course, if the native code needs to do any exception handling of its own, say, freeing a `malloc`'d buffer, it would do this before the `return`.

A JNI Stack Trace

The final JNI exception function, `ExceptionDescribe`, is most useful for debugging and can be used as a JNI version of `printStackTrace()` method from the `java.lang.Throwable`. If the line

```
env->ExceptionDescribe()
```

were added to the `native` method `catchException` above, the following output would be printed when the `main` method from `ExcEx2` is invoked.

• Program Output **Invoking** `ExcEx2.main`

```
getMessage : Instantiation exception
Exception in thread "main"
        java.lang.InstantiationException:
        Instantiation exception
          at ExcEx2.main(ExcEx2.java:11)
* * * * * * * * * *
JNI panic: Out of Memory...goodbye!
          at ExcEx2.main(ExcEx2.java:13)
```

The text before the asterisks beginning with `Exception in thread` 'main' and ending with the line number at which the exception occurred was generated by `ExceptionDescribe`. One of the shortcomings of this line number is that, understandably, the JVM cannot do any better than report the Java source line at which the exception occurred.

General Exception Handling Guidelines

Many JNI functions report an error condition by returning an error code and throwing an exception. In these cases, it is best to proceed by:

- Checking the return value of the JNI call for a value indicating an error and, if an error has occurred,

- Calling `ExceptionOccurred` to get the exception object.

With a reference to an exception object, the code can check on the details of the exception as in Listing 7.6. The code for extracting the text associated with an exception object appears in lines [16]- on page 130.

Under some conditions, native code may have to check for exceptions without being able to count on the return value of the JNI function. The JNI functions that invoke a Java method will return the value returned by the Java method that was called. This may or may not signify an exception condition. The safe route is to call `ExceptionOccurred` in these cases.

Additionally, some JNI array functions do not return a value and instead throw either an `ArrayIndexOutOfBoundsException` or an `Array-StoreException`. After calls to `SetObjectArrayElement`, `Get<pType>ArrayRegion` and `Set<pType>ArrayRegion`, you should immediately check for exceptions.

The JNI supports two types of exceptions: synchronous and asynchronous. A synchronous exception occurs within a JNI function. An asynchronous exception may occur in another thread in a multi-threaded application.

An asynchronous thread is not immediately seen by an executing native thread until either:

- The native code calls a JNI function that itself raises exceptions, or

- The native code calls `ExceptionOccurred` to check for any exceptions.

Appendix A lists all the JNI functions and the exceptions they raise. Only those that raise exceptions will recognize the occurrence of an asynchronous exception within another thread.

When a `native` method in a multi-threaded application is doing compute-intensive work, say, in a tight loop, it is good practice to insert an `ExceptionOccurred` call to check for, and respond to, asynchronous exceptions.

Summary

In this chapter we have covered the JNI provisions for throwing and handling exceptions. Two JNI functions, `Throw` and `ThrowNew`, were introduced. These functions provide the ability to throw an exception based on either an object instance or a class value.

Exception handling in JNI consists of testing for the occurrence of an exception and taking the appropriate steps. These steps may consist of printing a stack trace or simply returning so that your Java code can handle the exception. The JNI function `IsInstanceOf` is helpful in mimicking the try-catch structure in native code.

It is good practice to test the return value of all JNI functions, and if the value signals that an error has occurred, to check for an exception.

We saw that a failure to return immediately after throwing an exception in native code may produce undesirable side-effects. If you explicitly throw an exception within native code and then continue executing within that native code, make sure that is what you intend.

Finally, you saw that one thread within a multi-threaded application can test for asynchronous occurrences of exception in other threads.

Speaking of multiple threads, let's take a look at a JNI mechanism to help them cooperate with one another.

Chapter 8   *MONITORS*

The language, and the processes which stem from it, merely
release the fundamental order which is native to us.

Christopher Alexander
The Timeless Way of Building

Introduction

Since Java supports multiple threads, the problems of resource contention and
critical sections will eventually arise. Two threads competing for a limited
resource need to communicate in some fashion if they are going to cooperate.

The Java language provides three mechanisms for coordinating the activity
of multiple threads. First, there is the synchronized keyword that can be
used as a modifier in a method declaration. This prevents two threads from
executing the same method on the same object at the same time. Another way
of looking at this is if multiple methods in the same class are marked as
synchronized, only one thread can be executing one of these methods at a
given time.

Secondly, and closely related, is the use of the synchronized statement
to introduce a block of code. The synchronized statement acquires a lock
associated with an object on behalf of the executing thread. The use of the
synchronized statement allows a finer granularity of control over a critical
section. Instead of an entire method, as little as a single line of code can be
protected from simultaneous use by multiple threads that are synchronized on
the same object.

Finally, there is the `wait`/`notify` pair of Object methods. When synchronization is not enough, `wait` and `notify` can be used by two cooperating threads to control access to a shared resource.

JNI Synchronization Support

The `synchronized` keyword is directly applicable to `native` methods. The `synchronized` keyword may be used to modify the declaration of a `native` method. The JVM ensures that only one thread will execute that method for a given object at a time.

The block synchronization facility is provided within the JNI by two functions, `MonitorEnter` and `MonitorExit`. `MonitorEnter` is placed at the start of a critical section. The critical section is terminated by `MonitorExit`. Both functions take a `jobject` value as an argument to signify the object on which they are locking. This object typically represents some resource that, if accessed by two threads simultaneously, would be left in an incorrect or indeterminate state.

The `wait`/`notify` methods are available to native code using the usual JNI calling sequence of `GetMethodID` and `CallVoidMethod`.

In the next section, we will look at native code that makes use of both the JNI monitor routines and the Java `wait`/`notify` methods for coordinating two threads implementing the classic producer-consumer problem.

The Producer-Consumer Problem

Every undergraduate computer science student eventually sees some version of the producer-consumer problem before he leaves the comforts of school life and enters the workaday world. Here is a Reader's Digest description to tweak your memory: Two threads. One buffer. One thread puts things into the buffer. The other thread takes things out of the buffer. Some mechanism to keep the two threads from stepping on each other.

The buffer that the two threads manipulate typically has a couple of indices associated with it that point into what location things are put and from what location things are taken.

The nut of the problem is that the operation on these indices by one thread must be atomic relative to the other thread. The producer thread, for example, must be able to complete its increment operation of the put index before the consumer attempts to test that value.

Pseudo-code for the producer thread appears below.

```
getLock
if (bufferIsFull)
        wait

putIntoBuffer
incrementNextPutLocation
setFullState
wakeUpWaiters
freeLock
```

The pseudo-code for the consumer thread looks like this:

```
getLock
if (bufferIsEmpty)
        wait
getFromBuffer
incrementNextGetLocation
setEmptyState
wakeUpWaiters
freeLock
```

There are two mechanisms for synchronization used by the above pseudo-code. First, there is the locking that surrounds access to the shared buffer. This is represented by the **getLock/freeLock** pair. Second, there is the **wait/wake-UpWaiters** pair that the threads use to communicate activity in the buffer as it fills and then empties.

A Java Implementation

It is helpful to look at some Java source before we plunge into native code. In the following code, a class `Product` represents the object which is shared. A `Product` instance maintains an array of integers that functions as a buffer for holding the "products."

Private data variables, `putIndex` and `takeIndex`, maintain indices used by the `produce` and `consume` methods for tracking at what location in the buffer they are to perform their operation.

Listing 8.1 *Java Source for* `Product` *Class*

```
public class Product {

final private static int DEFAULT_SIZE = 100;
private int    size;       // size of buffer
private int[]  buffer;     // the buffer
private int    putIndex;   // put next product here
private int    takeIndex;  // get next from here
```

Listing 8.1 (cont.) *Java Source for* Product *Class*

```
private boolean empty;      // buffer is empty
private boolean full;       // buffer is full

Product() {
   this(DEFAULT_SIZE);
}
Product(int sz) {
   buffer = new int[sz];
   putIndex = takeIndex = 0;
   full = false;
   empty = true;
   size = sz;
}
```
(1)
```
synchronized void produce(int val)
                    throws Exception {
   if (full)            // consume may be complete
      wait();           // but buffer may be full
   buffer[putIndex++] = val;
   if (putIndex == size)
      putIndex = 0;
   printBuffer("P:");
   empty = false;
   if (putIndex == takeIndex) // full
      full = true;
   notify();
}
```
(2)
```
synchronized int consume() throws Exception {
   int val;
   if (empty)        // producer finished
      wait();        // but buffer is empty
   val = buffer[takeIndex++];
   if (takeIndex == size)
      takeIndex = 0;
   printBuffer("C:");
   full = false;
   if (putIndex == takeIndex)
      empty = true;
   notify();
   return val;
}
}
```

Looking at the Java source you see the use of the synchronized keyword ([1] and [2]) to provide the lock which prevents both of produce and consume from being executed at the same time. When a synchronized instance method executes, it is said to own the monitor associated with its object. If another thread attempts to execute a method requesting the same monitor, that thread will block.

As seen in the pseudo-code, another level of protection is provided for by the wait/notify pair of methods. Even if, say, the produce code has the lock for the Product object, it still may find itself faced with a full buffer. Upon detecting this, it politely waits. This wait call causes the thread running the produce method to suspend execution, give up its hold on the object monitor, and allow some other thread to run. The consume thread can then run, freeing up a slot in the buffer.

The consume method behaves in a symmetrical fashion. It checks for an empty buffer and, if it finds one, calls the wait method.

In both cases, at the end of the two methods, the notify method is called to wake up any waiters. Which waiter runs is a JVM scheduling decision and is beyond the scope of this book. A good source for a comprehensive discussion on this topic is *Java Threads* by Scott Oaks and Henry Wong (O'Reilly & Associates, 1997).

That should be enough of the details of the algorithm so that we can now look at the translation of the Java code to native code.

A JNI Producer-Consumer Implementation

In the translation to a native implementation of the producer-consumer code, the Product class becomes a shell of its former self. All that remains are the constructors and a few native method declarations.

Listing 8.2 *Java Source for* Product *Class Using* native *Methods*

```
        public class Product {
        final private static int DEFAULT_SIZE = 100;
        Product() {
            this(DEFAULT_SIZE);
        }
        Product(int sz) {
            init(sz);
        }
(3)     private native void init(int size);
(4)     public native void produce(int val)
                                    throws Exception;
(5)     public native int consume()
                                    throws Exception;

        }
```

One thing to note about the Java `Product` class is the introduction of the `native` method `init` in [3] above. This method will be used to cross into native land and initialize state upon construction of a `Product` object.

All of the state information that was maintained in the `Product` instance is now maintained in the native code. Had the state variables been left in the Java object, the native code would have had to make a JNI call for each reference to state information.

The C++ `ProductInfo` Class

To avoid the overhead of a JNI call for every reference to state information, the C++ `ProductInfo` class is used to maintain state.

Listing 8.3 *C++ Class* `ProductInfo`

```
class ProductInfo {
private:
int          _size;
int*         _buffer;
int          _putIndex;
int          _takeIndex;
int          _empty;
int          _full;
protected:
~ProductInfo();
public:
    int size()            { return _size; };
    int isFull()          { return _full; };
    int isEmpty()         { return _empty; };
    void setFull(int flg)    { _full = flg; };
    void setEmpty(int flg)   { _empty = flg; };
    int takeIndex()          { return _takeIndex; };
    int putIndex()           { return _putIndex; };
    void incrementTakeIndex()   { _takeIndex++; };
    void incrementPutIndex()    { _putIndex++; };
    void resetTakeIndex()       { _takeIndex = 0; };
    void resetPutIndex()        { _putIndex = 0; };
    int getBuffer(int i)        { return _buffer[i]; };
    void setBuffer(int i, int val)
                        { _buffer[i] = val; };

    ProductInfo();
    ProductInfo(int sz);
};
```

The `ProductInfo` class defines a set of `private` member variables that correspond to the instance variables once stored in the `Produce` object. For convenience and efficiency these variables are accessed using in-lined method definitions. The initialization of this data, including the allocation of memory for the shared buffer, occurs upon the construction of the `Product-Info` object which, in turn, is a result of invoking the `init native` method of the new, native-ready `Product` class.

The `init` Method

Now that we have seen the `ProductInfo` class, we get a better idea of how `init` works. The `init` method code is shown below. First, the C++ `ProductInfo` object is built in line [6] and then it gets interesting.

Listing 8.4 *Native Implementation of* `init` *Method*

```
static hashCodeMID = NULL;

JNIEXPORT void JNICALL Java_Product_init(
        JNIEnv *env, jobject thisObj, jint sz)
{
    ProductInfo* pi = new ProductInfo(sz);
    jclass clazz = env->GetObjectClass(thisObj);
    hashCodeMID =
        env->GetMethodID(clazz, "hashCode", "()I");
    int hashCode = getHashCode(env, thisObj);
    env->MonitorEnter(thisObj);
    piMap.SetAt((void*)hashCode, (void*) pi);
    env->MonitorExit(thisObj);
}
```

(6)

(7)

In the pure Java example above, the state information was maintained in the `Product` object as instance data. With the movement to a native implementation and the decision to avoid the overhead of possibly multiple JNI calls per state variable reference, the state data lives in a C++ object in native code. It is in no way tied to the Java `Product` object whose state it represents. However, there does need to be a way to tie together the Java `Product` object and the C++ `ProductInfo` object.

C++/Java Object Correspondence

We have come upon a larger issue here of how to manage a correspondence between Java objects and native data. Clearly, there needs to be a one-to-one relationship between a Java `Product` object and a C++ `ProductInfo` object. For now, that mapping is going to be maintained by a C++ table object, piMap[1], using two methods, `SetAt` and `Lookup`.

```
int Lookup(void* key, void*& value) const;
void SetAt(void* key, void* value);
```

`SetAt` takes a key and a value and stores a correspondence between the two. `Lookup` takes a key argument and returns, into its second argument, the corresponding value. In our example, the key is a unique number associated with a `Product` object and the value is a pointer to a `ProductInfo` object.

The unique key is returned by the function `getHashCode` which actually calls back into Java and invokes the `hashCode` method on the object passed as its second argument. The following listing shows the implementation of `getHashCode`.

Listing 8.5 *Implementation of* `getHashCode`

```
static jmethodID hashCodeMID;

static int
getHashCode(JNIEnv* env, jobject obj) {
    jint hashCode;
    hashCode = env->CallIntMethod(obj,hashCodeMID);
    return hashCode;
}
```

Notice that `getHashCode` is not a `native` method. It is simply a helper function used by `native` methods to retrieve the object reference of the invoking object. If you look back at line [7] in the `init native` method in Listing 8.4 above, you will see where `hashCodeMID` is initialized. `getHashCode` is used frequently enough to warrant caching this method ID in a static variable.

When we look at the native implementation of `produce` and `consume`, you will see how `getHashCode` is used to retrieve the key, which is then used as an argument to the `Lookup` method. `Lookup` returns the `Product-Info` object that corresponds to the *this* `Product` object that comes to the

---

1. For the sake of this discussion, you can think of `piMap` as a hash table. Folks familiar with Microsoft's MFC will probably recognize this interface as that of a `CMapPtrToPtr`. The details, however, of `piMap`'s implementation will be omitted. Implementations using both Rogue Wave's `RWHashTable` and Microsoft's `CMapPtrToPtr` objects are available with the example code from the *Essential JNI* ftp site.

native method as an argument. The `ProductInfo` object pointer is then used to access all of the `Product`'s state information.

The use of `getHashCode` in this example works because the `Product` class does not override the `hashCode` method of the `java.lang.Object` class. If the `hashCode` method is overridden by a subclass, there is no explicit guarantee that it return a unique value. In the next chapter, we will take a closer look at this and other issues involved with integrating Java and C++ code. Until then, let's return to the native implementation of the producer-consumer solution.

Native Implementation of `produce` Method

The code for the `produce` method appears in Listing 8.6. Immediately upon entry to the `produce` method, the `MonitorEnter` function is called at [8]. This call acquires a lock on the `thisObj` object, namely, the `Product` object. So that no assumptions need be made about any lower-level locking on the mapping table, the `Lookup` call is included within the scope of the lock. This complements the use of the `MonitorEnter/MonitorExit` pair around `SetAt` in the `init` method in Listing 8.4 on page 141.

The `Lookup` call returns a pointer to a `ProductInfo` object corresponding to the Java `Product` on which the `produce` method was invoked. Once the `ProductInfo` that corresponds to the calling `Product` object is retrieved, all references to state variables occur through the in-lined methods defined by the class.

Listing 8.6 *Native Implementation of* produce *Thread*

```
JNIEXPORT void JNICALL Java_Product_produce(
        *env, jobject thisObj, jint val)
{
    ProductInfo* pi;
    int hashCode;
    env->MonitorEnter(thisObj);
    hashCode = getHashCode(env, thisObj);
    piMap.Lookup((void*)hashCode, (void*&) pi);

    // Must wait on a full buffer
    while (pi->isFull()) {
        if (invoke_wait(env, thisObj) == JNI_ERR) {
            env->MonitorExit(thisObj);
            return;
        }
    }
}
```
(8)
(9)
(10)

Listing 8.6 (cont.) *Native Implementation of* produce *Thread*

```
(11)        pi->setBuffer(pi->putIndex(), val);
(12)        pi->incrementPutIndex();

            // Wrap around to front of buffer
            if (pi->putIndex() == pi->size())
               pi->resetPutIndex();

(13)        printBuffer(pi, "P:");
            pi->setEmpty(JNI_FALSE);

            if (pi->putIndex() == pi->takeIndex()) /* full */
               pi->setFull(JNI_TRUE);

            // Tell waiting consumers buffer no longer empty
(14)        if (invoke_notify(env, thisObj) == JNI_ERR) {
               env->MonitorExit(thisObj);
               return;
            }
(15)        env->MonitorExit(thisObj);
            return;
            }
```

While the thread running the produce method holds this lock associated with thisObj, no other thread can gain access to it. Except under some error conditions, this lock is not given up until line [15]. This MonitorEnter/MonitorExit locks the entire duration of the call to the produce native method. The implication of this for the current example is that the consume thread cannot manipulate the state of the Product object while the produce method is doing so.

Having said that, it must also be known that the need for the MonitorEnter and MonitorExit pair could be obviated by simply declaring the produce and consume methods as synchronized in lines [4] and [5] on page 139. Their use here is merely a pedagogical device. Their intended purpose is not to lock out two methods from competing, as does the synchronized modifier, but to protect an arbitrary block of code like the synchronized statement. With that in mind, we will move on.

The wait/notify coordination is done with calls to a pair of helper functions, invoke_wait and invoke_notify. They are so named because they call back into Java code to invoke the wait and notify methods of java.lang.Object, respectively. When the wait method is called, the lock held due to MonitorEnter is temporarily relinquished.

This will allow the `consume` method access to the shared buffer undisturbed by the `produce` method.

The `produce` method does its actual production at lines [11] and [12]. A new value is placed in the buffer and the "put" index incremented. The `printBuffer` call at line [13] produces output so we are able to monitor the progress of the buffer. We will see it at work in a later section.

Native Implementation of `consume` Method

The `consume` code is symmetrical and follows the same locking strategy as the `produce` method.

Listing 8.7 *Native Implementation of* `consume` *Method*

```
JNIEXPORT jint JNICALL
Java_Product_consume( *env, jobject thisObj) {
   int val;
   ProductInfo* pi;
   env->MonitorEnter(thisObj);
   int hashCode = getHashCode(env, thisObj);
   piMap.Lookup((void*)hashCode, (void*&) pi);

   // Must wait on an empty buffer
   while (pi->isEmpty() == JNI_TRUE) {
      if (invoke_wait(env, thisObj) == JNI_ERR) {
         env->MonitorExit(thisObj);
         return JNI_ERR;
      }
   }
   val = pi->getBuffer(pi->takeIndex());

   pi->setBuffer(pi->takeIndex(), 0);
   pi->incrementTakeIndex();

   // If we are at the end of buffer, wrap around
   if (pi->takeIndex() == pi->size())
      pi->resetTakeIndex();

   printBuffer(pi, "C:");
   pi->setFull(JNI_FALSE);

   if (pi->putIndex() == pi->takeIndex())
      pi->setEmpty(JNI_TRUE);
```

Listing 8.7 (cont.) *Native Implementation of* consume *Method*

```
    // If any thread is waiting, wake'em up
    if (invoke_notify(env, thisObj) == JNI_ERR) {
        env->MonitorExit(thisObj);
        return JNI_ERR;
    }
    env->MonitorExit(thisObj);
    return val;
}
```

Both the produce and consume threads adhere to the wait/notify convention. If confronted with a buffer that is full, the producer thread will invoke the wait method. Likewise, the consumer thread will call wait if it finds the product buffer empty. Calling wait causes the executing thread to yield the processor and allows the JVM to schedule another thread to run. This way, deadlock is avoided.

A Native wait and notify

As mentioned earlier, the JNI has no analogue to wait and notify. For native code to use these functions, it must use the standard JNI technique of obtaining a method's ID and then calling the appropriate method invocation function.

Two functions, invoke_wait and invoke_notify, provide this functionality and appear below.

Listing 8.8 *Native Implementation of* wait *Semantics*

```
static jmethodID waitMID = NULL;
static jmethodID notifyMID = NULL;
static jboolean invoke_wait( *env, jobject thisObj){
    if (waitMID == NULL) {
        jclass clazz = env->GetObjectClass(thisObj);
        waitMID = env->GetMethodID(clazz,
                            "wait", "()V");
    }
    env->CallVoidMethod(thisObj, waitMID);
    // wait may raise either ThreadInterrupted or
    // IllegalMonitorException. In either case,
    // throw it and let caller handle it.
    if (env->ExceptionOccurred() != NULL) {
        return JNI_ERR;
    }
    return JNI_OK;
}
```

(16)
(17)

Listing 8.9 *Native Implementation of* notify *Semantics*

```
static jboolean
invoke_notify( *env, jobject thisObj) {
    if (notifyMID == NULL) {
        jclass clazz = env->GetObjectClass(thisObj);
        notifyMID = env->GetMethodID(
            clazz, "notify", "()V");
    }
    env->CallVoidMethod(thisObj, notifyMID);

    // notify may raise IllegalMonitorStateException
    // If so, return JNI_ERR and caller handles it.
    if (env->ExceptionOccurred() != NULL) {
        return JNI_ERR;
    }
    return JNI_OK;
}
```

(18)

(19)

Both functions employ a little optimization to reduce the overhead associated with frequent JNI calls. The GetObjectClass/GetMethodID sequence is only called once to get the method ID of the appropriate Java method. Subsequent calls to these routines check for a non-null method ID value (lines [16] and [18]). Recall that the method IDs of a class are fixed as long as the class stays loaded. They can be retrieved once, stored in a static variable, and re-used without multiple calls into the JNI.

There is an additional optimization available, however it comes at a loss of generality to invoke_notify and invoke_wait. Since these functions are always called with a Product object reference, the class reference in lines [17] and [19] could also be cached, *as long as they are first converted to global references.*

The invoke_wait and invoke_notify functions handle exceptions in a similar fashion. If either receives an exception resulting from the call to wait or notify, they simply return JNI_ERR. The produce and consume threads test for an error and immediately return. Handling of the exception is left to the Java code after the native code returns.

Native Producer-Consumer Output

A call to printBuffer appears in both the produce and consume native method definitions. The code has been omitted since it does not offer anything to the discussion of JNI programming but it does produce nice output. This snapshot was taken a after a few iterations through the buffer.

```
C:  [ 0  0  0  0  0  0  76 77 0  0  ]
C:  [ 0  0  0  0  0  0  0  77 0  0  ]
P:  [ 0  0  0  0  0  0  0  77 78 0  ]
C:  [ 0  0  0  0  0  0  0  0  78 0  ]
P:  [ 0  0  0  0  0  0  0  0  78 79 ]
P:  [ 80 0  0  0  0  0  0  0  78 79 ]
C:  [ 80 0  0  0  0  0  0  0  0  79 ]
C:  [ 80 0  0  0  0  0  0  0  0  0  ]
C:  [ 0  0  0  0  0  0  0  0  0  0  ]
P:  [ 0  81 0  0  0  0  0  0  0  0  ]
P:  [ 0  81 82 0  0  0  0  0  0  0  ]
C:  [ 0  0  82 0  0  0  0  0  0  0  ]
C:  [ 0  0  0  0  0  0  0  0  0  0  ]
P:  [ 0  0  0  83 0  0  0  0  0  0  ]
P:  [ 0  0  0  83 84 0  0  0  0  0  ]
P:  [ 0  0  0  83 84 85 0  0  0  0  ]
C:  [ 0  0  0  0  84 85 0  0  0  0  ]
```

This could on forever, but you get the point.

The bracketed values represent the contents of the buffer. Each line of output is prefixed by a letter designating the thread that generated it, P for produce and C for consume. The output is generated after the thread performs its operation.

A Reminder

The JNIEnv pointer is only valid in the current thread. Avoid the temptation to use a static variable to store a JNIEnv pointer for use as a global by other non-method C/C++ functions. Each thread passes a different JNIEnv value to the methods it invokes. This JNIEnv pointer will work only for that thread. Whenever you need to reference a JNIEnv pointer within a native method, it is best to use the JNIEnv value passed into that method as the first argument. This is seen above in calls to getHashCode, invoke_wait and invoke_notify.

A Global Reference as Lock

The above implementation of the produce and consume methods uses the lock associated with the Product object reference to synchronize their use of the product buffer. In this case, this is an appropriate approach since each Product object, in fact, represents a resource for which threads are competing.

If, on the other hand, you need only a single lock across many different objects, you would need only a single object, on whose lock you would synchronize. The question arises, from where does this object come? In the above example, each `native` method call passes in the object whose lock it uses. If you are not using a strategy that requires a single lock per object, there are a couple alternative strategies you can use to make the lock object available to all the required `native` methods.

The first, of course, is to simply add the lock object as an additional argument to all the `native` methods which need it. This is sometimes unworkable because it may do nothing more than push the problem up to the Java level.

The alternative solution, and one that localizes the lock object to the native code, is to use a global reference on an object created by some native initialization code. Your initialization code would create an arbitrary object:

```
static jobject globalLock;
// ...
jclass clazz = env->FindClass("java/lang/Object");
jobject obj = env->AllocObject(clazz);
globalLock = env->NewGlobalRef(obj);
```

With a global reference you do not have to worry about the reference being garbage collected between `native` method calls. Consequently, you could use this reference as your global locking object as shown below:

```
env->MonitorEnter(globalLock);
//...
env->MonitorExit(globalLock);
```

This approach frees you from the constraint of needing the object on which you want to lock as one of the arguments to the `native` method executing a critical section.

Summary

In this chapter we reviewed the thread synchronization and coordination facilities of Java and saw how they applied to `native` methods.

Using the `synchronized` keyword for a `native` method declaration means exactly what it means for a regular Java method.

Two JNI functions, `MonitorEnter` and `MonitorExit`, provide the functionality of the Java `synchronized` statement. In the native implementation of the producer-consumer solution above, `MonitorEnter` and `MonitorExit` were used to implement the equivalent functionality of the `synchronized` method declaration modifier. However, they could just as well be used on smaller blocks of code.

The `wait` and `notify` methods are not directly available to native code. To use these methods, the native code has to use the standard JNI method invocation calls, `GetMethodID` and `Call<type>Method`, for calling into Java. This was accomplished in this chapter by defining two helper functions, `invoke_notify` and `invoke_wait`.

Finally, in the translation of the Java producer-consumer solution to native code, we came up against some larger issues of integrating Java code with C/C++ data. In the next chapter, we will explore these issues in depth.

Chapter 9

JAVA AND C++

And now a quick glance at our time. We are shocked,
we fly back: whither is all clarity, all naturalness and purity
of that relation life and history, how confused,
how exaggerated, how troubled is this problem
which now surges before our eyes!

Friedrich Nietzcshe
On the Advantage and Disadvantage of History for Life

Introduction

What is the "problem which now surges before our eyes"? We have all this
existing code that we have written. Millions of dollars have been invested in
its development and testing. The code works and we are proud of it. Our man-
agers love us and the code we have written.

However, upper management has recently read something in the *Wall Street
Journal* about this hot, new thing called Java. They don't quite understand it,
but many important sounding people were quoted in the article as saying how
Java is The Next Big Thing.

The word comes down from on high, "Use Java!" This is a mixed blessing.
Being smart engineers, we understand that Java is neat stuff. We understand
that Java programmers will be able to command top salaries. We have been
dying to get a chance to use it on a project. Our prayers have been answered.

However, we wonder what is to be done with all our existing code. Being
smart engineers, we fear the worst and it happens.

We are told we have to use our existing C++ object library. We groan. We
try to convince management that we can rewrite 1.5 million lines of bug-free
C++ code in Java in just thirty days.

Management knows better. They know we are software engineers and prone to underestimating schedules. We are stuck with the C++ code whether we like it or not.

We get to use Java but we can't throw away all our existing code. "Whither is all clarity?"

This scene is being played out in many firms these days. Everyone is faced with the challenge of maintaining a mature code base while making it possible for their application to work with Java.

This chapter and the next provide general approaches for addressing the problem of integrating legacy code, specifically class libraries, with Java. This chapter deals with mirroring C++ classes in Java, and the next deals with creating Java classes and related native code from existing C structures.

C++ Legacy Code

The engineer faced with integrating a Java front-end with an existing C++ class library may be faced with one of two sets of constraints:

- The class library must be treated like a black box. Possibly, the source code is not available and the developer only has access to the header files. Alternatively, the source code exists, but the Java programmer may not modify it.

- The source code is available and it may be altered. If this is the scenario, the changes that will be allowed to the existing source are minimal.

This section discusses a simple manual approach that is certainly amenable to automation. It can be applied to both of the above scenarios.

More often than not, when faced with legacy code, you will not be able to make changes to it. You will be required to mirror existing C++ classes in Java without altering the C++ classes. Ideally, for every C++ class, a new Java class would be built that behaves exactly like the C++ class: it implements the same contract with its client classes. The Java method names would be the same and would have analogous signatures as their C++ counterparts. Achieving this ideal would preserve the investment in existing C++ classes while allowing the developer familiar with these classes to migrate to Java with little effort.

There are, however, some differences between the two languages which complicate matters. Before we take a closer look at some obstacles to integrating an existing C++ class library with a Java application, let's look at a general strategy for mirroring C++ classes.

The General Strategy

It is helpful to borrow from the lexicon of design patterns here to describe the general strategy for attacking the problem which surges before our eyes. This lexicon will come in handy as we flesh out this general description in later sections.

We start with a C++ class. This class will be mirrored in Java using a new Java class which will provide access to the C++ object. This is an example of the *proxy* pattern. The proxy pattern provides a surrogate or placeholder for another object, known as the *subject*, to control access to it. Technically a stretch, but appropriate for highlighting the special circumstances of leaving the JVM to get at C++ objects, the Java proxy can be thought of as a *remote proxy*. A remote proxy provides a local representative (within the JVM) for an object in a different address space (native code).[1]

Usually a proxy and its subject are written in the same language and their relationship is fairly straightforward. For example, a C++ proxy object may simply delegate operations to the C++ subject in response to a request from a client, another C++ object. The subject is often referenced in the proxy as an instance variable. In our case, and with remote proxies in general, the relationship between proxy and client is mediated by intervening code. And, of course, the intervening code we need to implement consists of `native` methods.

A `native` method within a proxy class performs two roles. First, its declaration reflects the signature of its analogue in the subject class. Second, it maps a Java proxy object into the corresponding C++ subject.

To perform this mapping, the `native` method relies on an object registry maintained by the native code. The goal of this chapter is to show how such a registry can be built and managed. Each entry in the registry is a pair of elements. One element is a unique identifier for a Java object retrieved using the `java.lang.Object getHashCode` method. The other element is a unique identifier for a C++ object, typically just a pointer to that object. There are operations on the registry to add new entries, find an entry based on a key and delete entries.

Depending on the features of the supporting C++ class library (e.g. Microsoft Foundation Classes, Rogue Wave's Tools.h++), two registries may be necessary. One registry would map Java objects to C++ objects and the other would map C++ objects to Java objects. Another approach would be to use just a single registry and create two entries for each Java object/C++ object pair. One entry would be keyed off the C++ object address, the other off the Java object hash code value. On the other hand, if the table used to implement the registry supports a method that turns a value into a key, all that would be necessary would be one table and one entry per object pair. In this chapter,

---

1.Gamma, Erich, et. al., *Design Patterns*, Addison-Wesley, 1995, p. 207-218.

we will look at an implementation that provides only one entry per object pair, with the Java object's hashCode value serving as a key.

In the following discussion, the native code assists in the mapping from Java object to C++ object. As provider of this mapping function, the native method implements the adapter pattern. An adapter pattern converts one class so that it can operate with another.[2] In this case, the native method converts a Java interface into a C++ interface and vice-versa.

The foregoing can be summarized with the following code snippets and pseudo-code. For the sake of this example, assume an existing C++ class CPerson and its Java proxy JPerson. CPerson defines a method setFirstName. A skeletal implementation of these two classes would look like the code segment appearing below.

```
// C++ skeleton for CPerson
class CPerson: public CObject {
//...
public:
void setFirstName(const char* name);
//...
}
```

```
// Java skeleton for JPerson
public class JPerson implements JObject {
//...
public native void setFirstName(String name);
}
```

When the Java method setFirstName is invoked on an object O_j, the native code needs to first map O_j into a C++ object, O_c. The method setFirstName of O_c then needs to be invoked. The following steps outline the operation of the native implementation of setFirstName.

1. Convert O_j reference to a unique ID.

2. Use unique ID as key to registry lookup yielding O_c.

3. Invoke O_c.setFirstName.

The native method will receive a JPerson object reference as an input argument. This reference is a local reference and therefore simply an index into the local reference table that the JVM maintains on each transition into native code. It does not uniquely identify a Java object and therefore is useless as a key in the object registry. This is an important point to note.

To convert this object reference into a unique identifier, we will call back into Java, invoking the object's hashCode method. We saw this in the last

---

2. See *Design Patterns*, p. 139-150.

chapter when we employed the `getHashCode` function in the producer-consumer example. In fact, the example in this chapter will use the same function.

Before we look at an example, one question has been left unanswered. How do objects get added to the registry? This is done at construction time. When the Java application creates an instance of a proxy, the proxy's constructor calls into native code and creates an entry in the object registry. Deletion of an entry from the registry can be handled by the proxy's `finalize` method.

To summarize this general approach:

- At object construction, a mapping between a Java proxy object and its C++ subject is made as an entry in an object registry.

- At method invocation on a Java proxy object, the object registry is referenced and the corresponding C++ subject method invoked.

- The proxy's `finalize` method is responsible for deleting the entry for its object from the registry and deleting the C++ subject.

The following diagram shows the relationship between the Java proxy object, the registry in native code, and the C++ object.

Figure 9-1 *The Registry in Pictures*

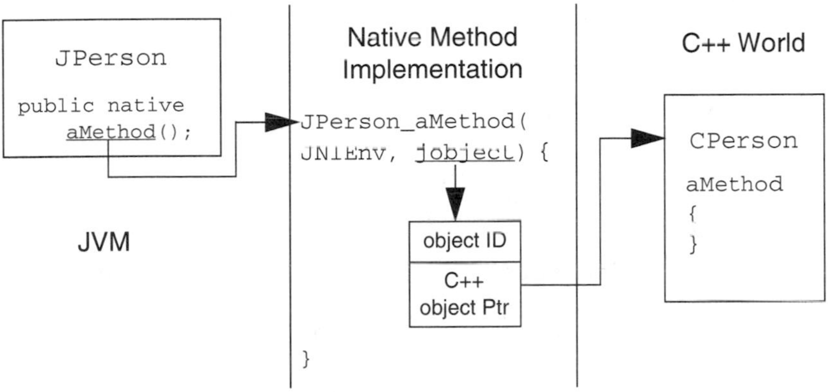

With this overview of a strategy behind us, let's look at an example.

Mirroring Example

For a complete example of C++ class mirroring, the `CPerson` and `JPerson` skeletal code snippets from above will be filled out.

For the sake of this discussion, we will assume that the C++ object for which a proxy will be built inherits from the Microsoft Foundation Class (MFC) class `CObject`. Application libraries which depend upon the MFC are certainly abundant. The desire and need to reuse this code in Java is equally abundant. It is important, however, not to get hung up on the detail that

CPerson inherits from MFC's CObject. It could just as well inherit from the RWCollectable class in Rogue Wave's Tools.h++ class library. In fact, we are going to look at the details of implementing the CPerson proxy in both cases.

It is also important not to focus on the simplicity of the CPerson object and ask "Why not just implement CPerson in Java?" For the purposes of implementing the strategy outlined above, a simple class like CPerson will suffice to illustrate the salient points of the approach. In real life, you probably would implement CPerson in Java. However, if CPerson were a very complex class, spanning many lines of code and many man-hours of development and test, you probably would not want to undertake porting CPerson to Java. It is in this context that CPerson should be considered.

The C++ Side

In the following code listing, some flesh has been put on the bones of the CPerson skeleton above. From this example, a Java proxy class will be constructed.

Listing 9.1 CPerson *C++ Header*

```
       #include <string.h>
       #ifdef WIN32
(1)    #include <afx.h>
       #else
       #include <rw/collect.h>
       #endif
       #ifdef WIN32
       class __declspec(dllexport) CPerson : public CObject
       #else
       class CPerson : public RWCollectable
       #endif
       {
       DECLARE_SERIAL(CPerson)

       private:
       static int_value;
       char*     _firstName;
       char*     _lastName;

       public:
       ~CPerson();
       CPerson() {};
       CPerson(CPerson&);
       void operator=(CPerson& pSrc);
```

Listing 9.1 (cont.) `CPerson` *C++ Header*

```
void Serialize(CArchive& archive);

static void setValue(int value);
int pField;

void setFirstName(char* first) {
    _firstName = strdup(first);
}

void setLastName(char* last) {
    _lastName = strdup(last);
}

char* getFirstName() {
return _firstName;
}

char* getLastName() {
    return _lastName;
}

};

#ifdef WIN32
BOOL AFXAPI CompareElements(const CPerson* p0,
                            const CPerson* p1);
#endif
```

There is nothing earth-shattering about this class, but before we proceed to the Java proxy code, it is worth making a few observations.

First, this class contains some compile-time directives [1] that determine whether it is being built on a Win32 machine or not. On Win32 machines, the `CPerson` class inherits from `CObject`, the root of the MFC class library. For other platforms, where "other" is defined by those platforms supporting Rogue Wave's Tools.h++ class library, the `CPerson` class inherits from `RWCollectable`.

Why is this relevant? Most commercial class libraries have the notion of a root class that implements some basic functionality, for example, serialization. If the classes for which you need to develop proxies all inherit from the same root class, it is easy to implement a single registry that holds all proxy/subject pairs. The registry's methods can be written to manipulate the root class and, therefore, are capable of handling any of its subclasses.

This is not an issue with MFC as it is with Rogue Wave. The MFC library has a CMapPtrToPtr class that handles void* arguments. As you can see from the method declarations below, CMapPtrToPtr does not provide type-safe operations.

```
BOOL CMapPtrToPtr::Lookup(void* key,
                              void*& rValue) const;
void SetAt(void* key, CObject* newValue);
```

Normally, you would want to stay away from such a wide open interface but given the purpose of the registry and the fact that the MFC CMapPtr-ToPtr uses void*, a map for all types of objects, it is reasonable to allow void* arguments. A bit less reasonable is the use of void* as a key. However, given the very constrained use of the registry within native code, this is not an unacceptable approach. In all cases, the key value will be generated by the getHashCode method.

The Rogue Wave library does a little better job of supplying a type-safe interface. The registry implementation using the Tools.h++ library uses an RWHashTable object. A RWHashTable stores a key/value pair. The class of both the key and value must be a subclass of RWCollectable. For that reason, CPerson subclasses from RWCollectable for non-Win32 compilations.

The final note concerning the CPerson class is that it defines a copy constructor. This is a hint that the Java proxy needs to support the Cloneable interface. We will see that this is so next.

The Java Side

Just as all the classes in MFC inherit from CObject and the classes in Rogue Wave inherit from RWCollectable, all the proxy classes will inherit from JObject. The definition of JObject is shown below.

Listing 9.2 JObject *Class*

```
import java.io.*;
public class JObject extends Object
                    implements Cloneable, Serializable
{
    public Object clone()
                throws CloneNotSupportedException {
        return super.clone();
    }
}
```

The JObject class supplies no functionality beyond implementing the Serializable and Cloneable interfaces. It is merely intended to serve as a root from which all proxy classes will be extended.

Corresponding to the C++ CPerson class is its Java proxy. For each of the public methods of CPerson, JPerson declares a method of the same name. Note, though, that the JPerson version of the method is declared as a native method. The purpose of this declaration is simply to maintain an interface defined by the C++ object and adhered to by the JPerson proxy.

Listing 9.3 *Java Proxy Class* JPerson

```
import java.io.*;

public class JPerson extends JObject
                     implements Serializable
{

    public native void setFirstName(String fName);
    public native void setLastName(String lName);
    public native String getFirstName();
    public native String getLastName();
    public static native void setValue(int value);

    public native void setPField(int val);
    public native int getPField();
    private native void _jni_initialize();

    JPerson() {
        _jni_initialize();
    }

    private native int _jni_delete();

    protected void finalize() {
        _jni_delete();
    }

    private native void _jni_clone(JPerson p);

    public Object clone()
            throws CloneNotSupportedException {
        JPerson p = (JPerson) super.clone();
        _jni_clone(p);
        return p;
    }
}
```

(2) — `private native void _jni_initialize();`

(3) — `_jni_initialize();`

(4) — `private native int _jni_delete();`

(5) — `_jni_delete();`

(6) — `private native void _jni_clone(JPerson p);`

(7) — `JPerson p = (JPerson) super.clone();`

(8) — `_jni_clone(p);`

Listing 9.3 (cont.) *Java Proxy Class* JPerson

```
(9)      private void writeObject(ObjectOutputStream out)
              throws IOException {

            out.writeUTF(getFirstName());
            out.writeUTF(getLastName());
         }


(10)     private void readObject(ObjectInputStream in)
              throws IOException, ClassNotFoundException
         {
            // Construct C++ object
(11)        _jni_initialize();

            String s = in.readUTF();
            setFirstName(s);
            s = in.readUTF();
            setLastName(s);
         }
         }
```

Beyond the fairly straightforward declaration of methods in the Java proxy, there are five other areas that require special attention: type mappings, construction, finalization, cloning and serialization. Each of these will be looked at in turn.

Type Mappings

When a proxy class is defined, the types of the method arguments may differ across the proxy and its subject. In the above example, java.lang.String is used in the Java class whereas char* is used in the C++ class CPerson. Type mapping is an area that requires some attention when defining a proxy class.

When selecting a primitive Java type for a C++ member variable, it is important to select one large enough to fit the C++ data type. Generally the mapping is straightforward but some thought must be given to the use of unsigned C++ types since Java does not have such a beast. A good strategy is to simply promote an unsigned C++ type to the next larger Java types. For example, an unsigned short can be implemented in a Java object as an int. Of course, it is then the responsibility of the Java application to treat the value appropriately.

Another common conversion decision is to translate char* and char buffers to either String or StringBuffer. This is the conversion JPerson makes of the char* member fields of CPerson.

Object Construction

Each constructor declared within the proxy class is responsible for creating its corresponding C++ object. This work is done in native code. In the JPerson example, the native method _jni_initialize [2] does the work of creating a C++ object and adding an entry to the registry that records the relationship between a JPerson object and a CPerson object. It is called each time a new object is constructed [3].

In general, you will need a separate _jni_initialize native method for each constructor the C++ class defines and the proxy object supports. The type and number of parameters defined by a _jni_initialize method will match the parameters for the constructor in which it is used.

Finalization

The C++ language depends upon manual memory management. It is the programmer's responsibility to free memory occupied by objects when those objects are no longer needed. Java, on the other hand, provides its own garbage collection and relieves the programmer of this burden.

The process by which garbage collection takes place is called finalization. When an object is no longer in use but before its memory is freed, its finalize method is called. The finalize method provides a means by which an application can associate some cleanup code with an object before it is garbage collected.

The finalize method as implemented by the java.lang.Object class is an empty method. If an application wants to perform cleanup prior to garbage collection, its classes must override the finalize method to do that work.

In light of a registry entry being created on its behalf, the JPerson class needs to include its own implementation of finalize. Before a JPerson object is garbage collected, its corresponding C++ object and its registry entry need to be deleted. If a customized finalize method is not defined, the Java garbage collector will take care of any JPerson proxy object but not the memory associated with its subject in the native code.

This is the role of the native method _jni_delete [4] in the preceding declaration of JPerson. When the finalize method of the JPerson object is called, it, in turn, calls _jni_delete [5]. As we will see, _jni_delete frees the C++ object and removes the entry from the registry.

Cloning

The clone operation, like construction and finalization, is an example of a Java operation that requires activity in the native world. If a JPerson object is cloned, so must its corresponding C++ object. Likewise, a new registry entry needs to be created to record this new relationship.

The clone method closely parallels the finalize method. When the clone method is invoked, the _jni_clone method [6] dives into native code and does the necessary work to make a copy of the C++ subject. Before doing this, however, the Java code clones an object from its superclass [7] to give the _jni_clone method a reference [8] to a JPerson object. The native code uses this reference as the target for copying the existing object's values. In the JPerson example, the _firstName and _lastName values needs to be copied.

Serialization

Serialization provides, among other things, the ability to write objects to and read objects from persistent storage. The basic idea of serialization is that an object should be able to write its current state, usually indicated by the value of its member variables, to persistent storage. Later, the object can be re-created by reading, or deserializing, the object's state from the storage.

The two classes java.io.ObjectOutputStream and java.io.ObjectInputStream provide default mechanisms for serializing and deserializing objects, respectively. The writeObject method of ObjectOutputStream writes the class of the object, the signature of the class, and the values of the non-transient and non-static fields of the class and all of its superclasses. The readObject method of ObjectInputStream reads these same values back into an object.

The default behavior for serialization is not going to do the trick for proxy objects. A proxy object's state is maintained within its C++ subject. For example, the _firstName and _lastName member fields are defined in CPerson, not JPerson. This means that to serialize a proxy object, the native methods that access the C++ subject need to be invoked to get the values. In order to serialize a proxy object, special handling is required.

Classes that require special handling during the serialization and deserialization process must implement special methods with these exact signatures:

```
private void
writeObject(java.io.ObjectOutputStream out)
        throws IOException
```

```
private void
readObject(java.io.ObjectInputStream in)
        throws IOException, ClassNotFoundException;
```

You can see that these methods are defined for JPerson in [9] and [10]. The writeObject method is straightforward. The native methods are called to get the field values and these values are written using the ObjectOutputStream method for writing out byte character sequences, writeUTF.

There is a little twist to `readObject`. Deserialization is initiated by a call to the `readObject` method of `ObjectInputStream`. This method returns an object which is then cast to the type expected from the input stream. `readObject` takes care of allocating the memory for the Java object whose fields it then populates from the input stream. What the default `readObject` method does not do is cross into native territory and create the C++ object. `JPerson`'s implementation of `readObject` must do this. This is taken care of by the call to `_jni_initialize` at line [11]. This guarantees that when `ObjectInputStream`'s `readObject` returns with a Java object reference there will be a corresponding entry in the registry.

The Native Methods

Now that we have seen the Java proxy class code and the corresponding C++ class code, it is time to look at the native code that connects the two. The native code consists of support functions for object construction, setters and getters for member data fields, support for cloning, and object deletion. All of these operations require access to the registry, so we will start with a look at the `Registry` class.

The Registry Interface

As mentioned earlier, the mapping between proxy and subject is kept in a registry maintained by the native code. This registry is accessed whenever a new proxy object is created, referenced, and destroyed.

First, let's look at the interface to the Registry.

Listing 9.4 *Native Registry Interface*

```
class ObjMap;

class Registry {
private:
    static ObjMap* _map;

protected:
    ~Registry();
    Registry() {};

public:
    static void add(void* key, void*& value);
    static int remove(void* key);
    static int lookup(void* key, void*& value);
};
```

The `Registry` class provides a generic interface to the `native` method code. The details of the registry itself are pushed down one level by declaring a pointer to an `ObjMap` object. The `Registry` class delegates all of its operations to the implementation of `ObjMap`. Two implementations of the `ObjMap` are provided with the *Essential JNI* example code. One implementation uses an MFC `CMapPtrToPtr` object as the map. The second uses Rogue Wave's Tools.h++ `RWHashTable` object. The following discussion will focus on the MFC implementation. This will be sufficient to highlight the principles involved in writing native code necessary to manipulate the registry.

Before we look at the implementation of the `Registry`, let's look at how it is used by the proxy's `native` methods.

Object Construction and the Registry

Addition of a new entry to the Registry occurs with each creation of a proxy object. To affect this addition, the proxy's constructor must call the `native` method `_jni_initialize`.

Recall that a non-static `native` method gets passed a reference to the object on which is invoked as its first argument. The role of `_jni_initialize` is to create a registry entry mapping this object reference to a C++ object. It does this by:

1. Mapping the proxy object reference to a unique identifier

2. Constructing a C++ object

3. Creating a registry entry using the proxy's unique identifier as a key and a pointer to the C++ object as the value

That said, the following code should make perfect sense.

Listing 9.5 *Native Code Object Construction*

```
JNIEXPORT void JNICALL
Java_JPerson__1jni_1initialize(
                JNIEnv *env, jobject thisJPerson)
{
    jint hashCode = getHashCode(env, thisJPerson);
    CPerson *cp = new CPerson();
    Registry::add((void*) hashCode, (void*&) cp);
}
```

(12)

The only part of this function that requires further explanation is the call to `getHashCode`. We first saw this function in the last chapter but it has now been modified a bit to generalize its use. In its previous incarnation, `getHashCode` was designed to handle objects from a single class by caching the method ID. The new version must call `GetObjectClass` each time it is called.

Listing 9.6 *Modified* `getHashCode`

```
jint getHashCode(JNIEnv* env, jobject anObj) {
   jclass clazz = env->GetObjectClass(anObj);
   jmethodID hcMID =
      env->GetMethodID(clazz, "hashCode", "()I");
   jint hashCode = env->CallIntMethod(anObj, hcMID);
   return hashCode;
}
```

Once the proxy object's unique identifier is retrieved and the C++ object constructed, the registry entry is made. With the registry entry in place, the mapping between the proxy and its subject is secure and operations on the proxy can be delegated to the subject.

Instance Data Access and the Registry

Implementation of the proxy's `native` methods is quite simple. In general, an implementation of a proxy method must perform the following tasks:

1. Retrieve the proxy object's unique identifier.
2. Use the identifier as a key for registry lookup, returning a pointer to a C++ object.
3. Convert the arguments to the `native` method to types appropriate for a C++ method call.
4. Invoke the C++ method that corresponds to the proxy method.

Only Step (3) above differs greatly across different `native` method implementations. In the following examples, all that is necessary is that `jstring` objects get converted to `char*` buffers and vice-versa.

Listing 9.7 *Native Implementation of* `JPerson` *Accessor Methods*

```
JNIEXPORT void JNICALL Java_JPerson_setFirstName(
               JNIEnv *env,
               jobject thisJPerson,
               jstring nameCString) {
   jboolean isCopy;
   CPerson *cp;
   char* name = (char*) env->GetStringUTFChars(
                        nameCString, &isCopy);
   jint hashCode = getHashCode(env, thisJPerson);
   Registry::lookup((void*)hashCode, (void*&) cp);
   cp->setFirstName(name);
   if (isCopy == JNI_TRUE)
      env->ReleaseStringUTFChars(nameCString, name);
}
```

Listing 9.7 (cont.) *Native Implementation of* JPerson *Accessor Methods*

```
JNIEXPORT jstring JNICALL Java_JPerson_getFirstName
  (JNIEnv *env, jobject thisJPerson)
{
    char* name;
    CPerson *cp;

    jint hashCode = getHashCode(env, thisJPerson);
    Registry::lookup((void*)hashCode, (void*&) cp);
    name = cp->getFirstName();
    if (name == NULL)
        return NULL;
    return env->NewStringUTF(name);
}
```

In general, argument conversion is straightforward. Table 4.2 on page 51 provides a guide to the size of Java data types. However, any jobject value passed to a proxy's native method must have an entry in the registry. The conversion of a jobject value, of course, involves finding its corresponding C++ object in the registry. The implication of this is that the class of any C++ object required as an argument to a C++ class that is mirrored must also be mirrored.

We have looked at the native code used by the proxy that constructs the C++ object. We have also seen how the proxy's methods access the C++ subject. Now let's look at proxy object finalization.

Object Finalization and the Registry

Recall from the Java source for JPerson that the finalize method was over-ridden. To simply rely on the default finalization would result in a memory leak due to lost C++ objects in the registry. The Java proxy object would get garbage collected, leaving no reason for the C++ object's existence and no way to access it.

The definition of JPerson's finalize method contains a single line, a call to _jni_delete. _jni_delete contains the necessary code to clean up the registry entry for the C++ object corresponding to the instance of JPerson that is being finalized.

Listing 9.8 *Object Deletion*

```
JNIEXPORT int JNICALL Java_JPerson__1jni_1delete(
                  JNIEnv *env, jobject thisJPerson){
    jint hashCode = getHashCode(env, thisJPerson);
    return Registry::remove((void*)hashCode);
}
```

The call to the remove method of the Registry class takes care of calling the destructor of the C++ object as well as removing the registry entry.

Deleting C++ objects can get present a problem with some applications. Consider the following relationships among proxy objects and C++ objects.

Figure 9-2 *Internal C++ Reference to a Mirrored Object*

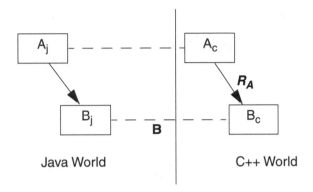

The reference A_c has to B_c can be obtained in one of two ways. Either A_c defines a public method that allows clients to set the reference or it is done privately. If the latter is the case, the above diagram would not be valid since the Java side does not mirror any private references that A_c maintains.

The former case is what interests us here. How does it lead to the object relationship depicted in Figure 9-2 ? Let's say A_c has a public method `setB` for setting its reference (R_A) to B_c. To mirror A_c properly, A_j would need to implement `setB` as a `native` method. Further, the C++ class B_c would need to be mirrored by the Java application. This native implementation of `setB` would take an input argument B_j and locate the corresponding B_c object in the registry. The native code would call A_c's C++ version of `setB` with B_c as the input argument. This method invocation establishes the reference depicted by line R_A in Figure 9-2 -2.

If A_j as its first argument becomes unreachable and A_j holds the only reference to B_j, B_j is also unreachable. In such a situation, the *Java Language Specification* does not specify in what order A_j and B_j will be finalized.

If A_j is finalized first and if, in its deletion of A_c, B_c gets deleted, this will cause a problem when B_j is finalized and attempts to delete B_c. Matters are no better if B_j is finalized first. In this case, the finalization of B_j deletes B_c and any subsequent attempt to delete B_c during the finalization of A_j will result in an error.

What this argues for is an extended registry implementation that maintains a reference count on each C++ in its map. If upon finalization of a proxy object, the object's _jni_delete detects that the C++ object that corresponds to the proxy is contained in the registry more than once, it will bypass calling the C++ object's destructor and, instead, decrement a reference count.

Object Cloning and the Registry

Cloning requires making an exact duplicate of an object. Making a duplicate, of course, requires creating a new object and a new object needs a registry entry.

From the code above (line [7] on page 159), the cloned Java object is created by calling the clone method of the proxy's super class. This assures all the super class information is correctly cloned. Additionally this new object is used to send to native code using the _jni_clone method. The _jni_clone method is responsible for:

1. Retrieving from the registry the C++ object corresponding to the incoming Java proxy object

2. Applying the copy constructor to this C++ object to create a new C++ object

3. Adding the cloned proxy object sent as an argument and the newly created C++ object into the registry

The code for this activity is shown below. Keep in mind that the first jobject argument to a non-static native method is a *this* reference to the object on which the method was invoked. In this case, *this* is the to-be-cloned object. The second jobject argument is the newly cloned Java object. The _jni_clone code needs to create a C++ object corresponding to this Java object.

Listing 9.9 *Native Code for Cloning*

```
JNIEXPORT void JNICALL Java_JPerson__1jni_1clone(
            JNIEnv *env,
            jobject thisJPerson,
            jobject newJPerson)
{
    CPerson* cp;
    jint hashCode = getHashCode(env, thisJPerson);
    Registry::lookup((void*) hashCode, (void*&) cp);
    CPerson* newCp = new CPerson(*cp);
    Registry::add((void*) hashCode, (void*&) newCp);
}
```

This function works as advertised. A lookup produces the C++ object corresponding to the proxy object passed as an argument. The copy constructor creates a clone of the C++ object. Finally, the add method of the Registry creates an entry mapping the new Java proxy to the new C++ object.

Serialization and the Registry

The only native code required in support of serialization is the call to _jni_initialize when deserializing an object. This is called by readObject to create a registry entry for receipt of the newly created C++ object and its proxy.

The Registry Implementation

As was previously mentioned, two example implementations of the registry are provided with the example code. We will first look at the MFC implementation followed by a discussion of the Rogue Wave implementation.

The interface to the registry is contained in Listing 9.4 on page 163. Note the use of an ObjMap pointer to maintain the actual entries. This has been done to push all the details of the implementation to the ObjMap class and preserve a consistent interface for the Registry class. Looking at the code for the implementation of the Registry class below, you will see that it delegates all operations to the ObjMap implementation.

Listing 9.10 *Registry Implementation Using MFC*

```
ObjMap* Registry::_map = NULL;

Registry::~Registry() {
    _map->free();
}
void
Registry::add(void* key, void*& value) {
    if (_map == NULL)
        _map = new ObjMap(10);
    _map->add(key, value);
}
int
Registry::remove(void* key) {
    if (_map == NULL)
        return FALSE;
    return _map->remove(key);
}
int
Registry::lookup(void* key, void*& value) {
    if (_map == NULL)
        return FALSE;
    return _map->lookup(key, value);
}
```

The implementation of `ObjMap` entry will differ based on the C++ class library you are using to implement it. Let's look at the MFC implementation.

MFC Implementation of `ObjMap`

An implementation of `ObjMap` will commit to a specific implementation of the _map instance variable. In the MFC case, the `ObjMap` class uses a `CMapPtrToPtr`.

Listing 9.11 `ObjMap` *MFC Interface Definition*

```
#include <afxcoll.h>

class ObjMap {
private:
    CMapPtrToPtr*               _map;
public:
    void           add(void* key, void*& value);
    int            remove(void* key);
    int            lookup(void* key, void*& value);
    void           free();
}
```

The `ObjMap` class also declares the `free` method for use by the `Registry` destructor. Otherwise, the `ObjMap` class is what you would expect from a class using the `CMapPtrToPtr` class to implement the registry. Each of the methods declared by the `ObjMap` interface map closely to the operations on the `CMapPtrToPtr` object.

The MFC implementation of the `ObjMap` follows.

Listing 9.12 *MFC* `ObjMap` *Implementation*

```
#include "ObjMap.h"

void
ObjMap::free() {
    delete _map;
}

ObjMap::ObjMap(int gran) {
    _map = new CMapPtrToPtr(gran);
}

void
ObjMap::add(void* key, void*& value) {
    _map->SetAt(key, value);
}

int
ObjMap::remove(void* key) {
    void* value;
    _map->Lookup(key, value);
    delete value;
    return _map->RemoveKey(key);
}

int
ObjMap::lookup(void* key, void*& value) {
    return (int)_map->Lookup(key, value);
}
```

The `CMapPtrToPtr` type provides, more or less, exactly the interface you need for the type of registry being constructed. The implementation for the Rogue Wave class library is a bit different. Let's take a look.

Tools.h++ Implementation of `ObjMap`

The interface to the Rogue Wave implementation of `ObjMap` differs only in its use of the `RWHashTable` as the map for relating Java objects to C++ objects.

Listing 9.13 *Tools.h++* ObjMap *Inteferface*

```
#include <rw/hashtab.h>
#include <rw/colldate.h>
#define BOOL int
#define FALSE 0
#define TRUE 1

class ObjMap {
private:
    RWHashTable*                _map;

public:
    void        add(void* key, void*& value);
    int         remove(void* key);
    int         lookup(void* key, void*& value);
    void        free();
    ObjMap(int gran);
};
```

The only difference between this code and the MFC ObjMap interface is the declaration of the _map member variable and the inclusion of files required by the Tools.h++ classes.

The implementation of the ObjMap class using the RWHashTable is a bit different in its details. Specifically, a new class ObjMapEntry is introduced. This class inherits from RWCollectable and describes what an entry in the RWHashTable looks like.

Listing 9.14 ObjMapEntry *Interface*

```
#include <rw/collect.h>

class ObjMapEntry: public RWCollectable
{
private:
    unsigned int        _hashCode;
    RWCollectable*      _objPtr;
public:
    RWBoolean isEqual(const RWCollectable*) const;
    unsigned hash() const;
    RWCollectable*getObject() { return _objPtr; };

    ObjMapEntry(unsigned key);
    ObjMapEntry(unsigned key, RWCollectable* p);
};
```

All entries in RWHashTable must inherit from RWCollectable. Instead of using the hashCode and object pointer values directly in the map, they are used to construct an ObjMapEntry. The ObjMapEntry is then inserted into the RWHashTable.

Before we look at the implementation of ObjMapEntry, let's see how this class is used by the ObjMap code. Following is the implementation of ObjMap using the Tools.h++ RWHashTable.

Listing 9.15 *Tools.h++* ObjMap *Implementation*

```
#include "ObjMapEntry.h"

ObjMap::ObjMap(int gran) {
        _map = new RWHashTable(gran);
}

void
ObjMap::add(void* key, void*& value) {
    ObjMapEntry* entry;

    entry = new ObjMapEntry((unsigned) key,
                   (RWCollectable*) value);
    _map->insert(entry);
}

int
ObjMap::remove(void* key) {
    ObjMapEntry* keyEntry;
    ObjMapEntry* match;

    keyEntry = new ObjMapEntry((unsigned) key);
    match = (ObjMapEntry*) _map->remove(keyEntry);
    if (match == NULL)
        return FALSE;
    delete match->getObject();
    delete match;
    return TRUE;
}
```

Every call to the add method results in the creation of an ObjMapEntry instance. The key and value sent as arguments to the method are packaged into an ObjMapEntry and inserted into the RWHashTable. Similarly, whenever a search or removal is done, an ObjMapEntry object is created using the single argument constructor, the key field of the ObjMapEntry. As you can see, the only methods from the ObjMapEntry used by the ObjMap code are the two constructors. The implementation of `ObjMapEntry` appears below and you can see the difference between the two constructors.

Listing 9.16 `ObjMapEntry` *Implementation*

```
#include "ObjMapEntry.h"

RWBoolean
ObjMapEntry::isEqual(const RWCollectable* c) const {
    ObjMapEntry* entry = (ObjMapEntry*) c;
    return (entry->_hashCode == _hashCode);
}

unsigned
ObjMapEntry::hash() const {
        return _hashCode;
}

ObjMapEntry::ObjMapEntry(unsigned key,
                         RWCollectable* p) {
    _hashCode = key;
    _objPtr = p;
}

// This constructor is used for creating a test
// for equivalence used by lookup
ObjMapEntry::ObjMapEntry(unsigned key) {
    _hashCode = key;
    _objPtr = NULL;
}
```

The other methods declared by the `ObjMapEntry` interface are required by the `RWHashTable` for managing its collection. The method `isEqual` reports whether elements are identical. The method `hash` returns a unique identifier for each element. Not surprisingly both of these methods make use of the hash code provided by the `getHashCode` function and stored in the `_hashCode` private member variable.

That wraps up the example for mirroring `CPerson` with a Java class. For completeness, a couple more topics need to be addressed. So far no mention has been made of either `static` methods or `public` data fields that have no setter or getter. Let's look at those issues now.

Static Variables and Methods

In the CPerson class in Listing 9.1 on page 156, neither class methods nor any publicly available data fields were declared. All the methods were instance methods so the mapping to a proxy method was straightforward. Similarly, the question of how to use the registry to access public data fields was not addressed. Although neither of these circumstances presents any special problems, they merit a few words for the sake of completeness.

C++ Class Methods

Static methods are easily invoked within a native method implementation by an explicit reference to the C++ class name. There is no harm in hardcoding the class reference within a native reference since the implementation for a native method is bound to a single class.

If the class method declaration

```
static void setValue(int value);
```

were added to the definition of CPerson, the corresponding declaration in the JPerson class would be

```
static native void setValue(int value);
```

The native implementation of setValue follows.

Listing 9.17 *Static Proxy Method*

```
JNIEXPORT void JNICALL Java_JPerson_setValue
   (JNIEnv *env, jclass thisClz, jint value)
{
   CPerson::setValue(value);
}
```

A static method does not require the use of the registry for mapping a proxy object to a C++ object. The class to class mapping is achieved by hardcoding the C++ class reference within a method generated specifically for the corresponding Java proxy class.

Public Data Field Access

If either class or instance variables are directly available within a C++ object, the proxy object will need to supply native setters and getters for these data fields. When accessing non-static data fields, the native setters and getters will use the registry as in all the preceding code samples. However, instead of invoking a C++ method, they will do a direct set or get of the appropriate C++ data field.

For a `public int` data field `pField` in the `CPerson` class, you will want to declare a pair of `native` methods

```
public native void setPField(int val);
public native int getPField();
```

The implementation of `setPField` appears in the following listing.

Listing 9.18 *Proxy* native *Method for Setting* public *Variables*

```
JNIEXPORT void JNICALL Java_JPerson_setPField
   (JNIEnv *env, jobject thisJPerson, jint val)
{
    CPerson *cp;
    jint hashCode = getHashCode(env, thisJPerson);
    Registry::lookup((void*)hashCode, (void*&) cp);
    cp->pField = val;
}
```

The `getPField` code is similar except, of course, the `pField` of the C++ object is returned rather than set.

For `static public` variables, you will still need to write native setters and getters in your proxy class but their implementation, like that for `static` methods, will not need to reference the registry.

Java Mirroring at Work

Much discussion and many code listings have been thrown at you without an example of some output. It it now time to put it all together and do what has been advertised.

What follows is a Java program that creates two `JPerson` objects, invokes their methods, clones them, and, finally, serializes and deserializes them. At each step it reports its progress. The `native` method code and registry code from the foregoing examples are all employed to make this happen.

Without further adieu, Listing 9.19 presents the Java source.

Listing 9.19 *Java Source for Mirror Example*

```java
import java.io.*;

public class Main {
static {
   System.loadLibrary("Chap9example2");
}
public static void main(String args[]) {
   JPerson jp = new JPerson();
   jp.setValue(10);
   jp.setPField(100);

   jp.setFirstName("Matthew");
   jp.setLastName("Gordon");

   System.out.println("First Name: " +
                   jp.getFirstName());
   System.out.println("Last Name: "+
                   jp.getLastName());

   JPerson jp1 = new JPerson();

   jp1.setFirstName("Kilian");
   jp1.setLastName("Gordon");

   System.out.println("First Name: "+
               jp1.gctFirstName());
   System.out.println("Last Name: "+
               jp1.getLastName());

   // Clone the proxy
   try {
      JPerson njp = (JPerson) jp.clone();
      System.out.println("Clone First Name: "
                   + njp.getFirstName());
      System.out.println("Clone Last Name: "
                   + njp.getLastName());
   }
   catch (Exception e) {
      e.printStackTrace();
```

Listing 9.19 (cont.) *Java Source for Mirror Example*

```java
try {
    JPerson njp = (JPerson) jp1.clone();

    System.out.println("Clone First Name: "
                    + njp.getFirstName());

    System.out.println("Clone Last Name: "
                    + njp.getLastName());
}
catch (Exception e) {
    e.printStackTrace();
}

// Serialize the proxy

try {
    FileOutputStream fOut =
        new FileOutputStream("serialProxy");
    ObjectOutputStream oOut =
        new ObjectOutputStream(fOut);
    oOut.writeObject(jp);
    oOut.writeObject(jp1);
    oOut.close();
    fOut.close();
} catch (Exception e) {
    e.printStackTrace();
}
```

Listing 9.19 (cont.) *Java Source for Mirror Example*

```
// de-Serialize proxy
try {
   FileInputStream fIn =
      new FileInputStream("serialProxy");
   ObjectInputStream oIn =
      new ObjectInputStream(fIn);
   JPerson sjp = (JPerson) oIn.readObject();
   JPerson sjp1 = (JPerson) oIn.readObject();

   System.out.println(
      "(de)Serialized First Name: " +
            sjp.getFirstName());
   System.out.println(
      "(de)Serialized Last Name: " +
      sjp.getLastName());
   System.out.println(
      "(de)Serialized First Name: " +
      sjp1.getFirstName());
   System.out.println(
      "(de)Serialized Last Name: " +
      sjp1.getLastName());
   } catch (Exception e) {
      e.printStackTrace();
   }
}
}
```

It looks just like nice, clean Java code. Two Java objects are created, cloned, serialized and then deserialized. The only indication that anything else is at work is the `static` initializer block to load a library.

The output from invoking the main method from Listing 9.19 follows.

```
First Name: Matthew
Last Name: Gordon
First Name: Kilian
Last Name: Gordon
Clone First Name: Matthew
Clone Last Name: Gordon
Clone First Name: Kilian
Clone Last Name: Gordon
(de)Serialized First Name: Matthew
(de)Serialized Last Name: Gordon
(de)Serialized First Name: Kilian
(de)Serialized Last Name: Gordon
```

After each object is created, its name fields are printed. They are printed again after the objects are cloned. Finally, a report of successful deserialization is printed.

An Alternative to the Registry

Alas, there is a slight problem with the use of the hashCode method of java.lang.Object as a means of uniquely identifying a Java object. It is not a deal breaker but it must be kept in mind. If any classes in your inheritance hierarchy that will be placed in the registry override either the hash-Code or equals methods, they must do so in such a way as to provide a unique return value from the hashCode method. The default implementation of hashCode and equals guarantees a unique integer value for each object. However, some classes override the default implementation defined by java.lang.Object. For example, java.awt.Color defines two instances to be equal if they have the same red, blue and green values. Therefore, two distinct color objects may produce the same hashCode value. Whether this is a problem will vary from application to application. However, it is worth mentioning.

As a workaround, you could store a pointer to your C++ object in the Java object. The Java object would contain an instance variable, say cObjectID. Two helper functions for setting and getting this field would replace getHashCode. These two functions would look something like the code snippet below.

Listing 9.20 *Accessing a C++ Pointer in a Java Object*

```
jlong
getCID(JNIEnv* env, jobject anObj) {
    jclass clazz = env->GetObjectClass(anObj);
    jfieldID fid =
        env->GetFieldID(clazz, "cObjectID", "J");
    jint id = env->GetLongField(anObj, fid);
    return id;
}

void
setCID(JNIEnv* env, jobject anObj, jint val) {
    jclass clazz = env->GetObjectClass(anObj);
    jfieldID fid =
        env->GetFieldID(clazz, "cObjectID", "J");
    env->SetLongField(anObj, fid, val);
}
```

The function `setCID` would be used when the C++ object was constructed as in `_jni_initialize` from Listing 9.5 on page 164. The call to `getHashCode` in [12] from Listing 9.5 would be removed and a call to `setCID` inserted after the construction of the C++ object. The registry would then disappear altogether. `getCID` would replace the need for maintaining a separate map of Java objects to C++ objects.

Of course, once you decide to store the C++ pointer in the Java object, you must commit to the size of the variable used to store that pointer. Your best bet is to choose a Java `long` (64 bits) and cast it down for platforms that use 32-bit pointers. This gives you room to grow without modifying your Java code.

Some Other Issues

There are other issues involved with the mapping of Java classes into C++ objects which do not involve `native` methods programming and JNI. Two are mentioned here for your consideration. This coverage is not intended to be exhaustive as many applications may impose special considerations.

Multiple Inheritance

Multiple inheritance is not possible in Java. The closest you can get is to extend from one class and implement multiple interfaces.

Consider a C++ class `CMultiple` that inherits from `CaClass`, `CxClass`, and `CyClass` that you want to mirror in Java. When mirroring those classes, a class `JMultiple` would need to extend one of the classes and define an `interface` for each of the other two.

The code segment below provides a sketch of how this is done. Assume a Java class `JaClass` intended to mirror `CaClass`, and two interfaces `JInterfaceX` and `JInterfaceY`, one each for `CxClass` and `CyClass`.

```
public class JMultiple extends JaClass
            implements JInterfaceX, JInterfaceY {
(13)    private JInterfaceX i1 = new anImplOfInterfaceX();
(14)    private JInterfaceY i2 = new anImplOfInterfaceY();

(15)    public void intfXmethod1(args ...) {
            i1.intfXmethod1(args ...);
        }

(16)    public foo intfYmethod1(args ...) {
            return i2.intfYmethod1(args ...);
        }
        }
```

Class `JMultiple` inherits from `JaClass` and therefore would mirror the `CMultiple` inheriting from `CaClass`. For each of the other classes from which `CMultiple` inherits, a Java interface would be defined that imposes the contract that the C++ classes impose.

Within `JMultiple`, references to concrete implementations of each interface would be maintained as in lines [13] and [14]. For each method declared by the interfaces, `JMultiple` would implement its own versions ([15] and [16]) which would delegate to the instances of the concrete implementation of each interface. This is the role of `intfXmethod1` and `intfYmethod1` above. They each represent a method defined in one of the interfaces that `JMultiple` implements.

For each class involved in the foregoing, `JMultiple`, `JaClass` and all the implementations of the interfaces used by `JMultiple`, you could use the registry approach to mirror their C++ counterparts.

C++ Templates

C++ templates also complicate the move to Java. Because a template class signals the compiler to generate multiple class definitions, there is no way to mimic this in Java.

However, you may certainly take advantage of an instantiation of a template class from within Java just like you would any class. Since the context of our discussion here is the use of existing library functionality within a Java application, the types for which a template class is to be used can be known beforehand. A Java class that supports each type can be built to mirror a particular instantiation of a template class. So what you have is a specific usage of a template class rather than general usage of the template mechanism.

Summary

In this chapter we looked at a general strategy for making use of existing C++ class libraries from Java code using `native` methods and JNI.

We saw how a registry written in C++ could be used by `native` methods to map the calling Java object onto a C++ object. We saw this relationship was best understood by the proxy pattern since the Java object acts as a stand-in for the C++ object.

The implementation of the registry is dependent on what C++ class library you have at your disposal. We looked at implementations for both the Microsoft Foundation Class library and the Tools.h++ class library from Rogue Wave. In general, a hash table is a good choice for implementing the registry. In fact, a user-defined hash table could have been used rather than one provided by the MFC or Tools.h++.

The registry approach is general enough to support object cloning and serialization. It is also amenable to automation but such a task is left, as they say, as an exercise to the reader. In the next chapter, we will look at an approach to converting C structures to Java code and JNI code that is automated.

Chapter 10

CONVERSION OF C STRUCTURES

> Give me convenience or give me death.
>
> Dead Kennedys

Introduction

Death would be a bit premature at this point, so I have opted for convenience.

Much legacy code requires the manipulation of C structures by Java code. This involves creating a Java class which corresponds to each C `struct` and the appropriate C code for copying data between the two data structures. The translation from a C `struct` is straightforward but, for a large application, time.consuming.

In this chapter we are going to take a look at a tool designed to make your life easier. The tool, `structConverter`, takes as input a C `struct` from your dusty, old C application and generates the source for a Java class and JNI functions for transferring data between the C `struct` and a Java object.

Let's see it in pictures.

Figure 10-1 *Operation of* structConverter

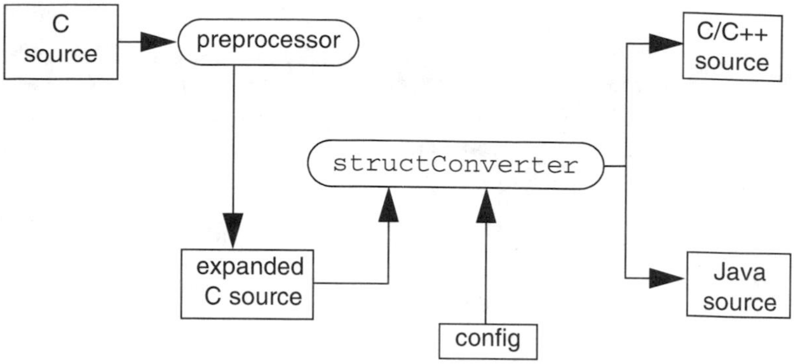

As you can see from Figure 10-1, structConverter relies on the C preprocessor for a little help. The actual input to structConverter is a file output by the C/C++ preprocessor. The output from structConverter consists of two files for each converted C structure. A Java source file contains the definition of a Java class corresponding to the original C structure. A second file, containing either C or C++ code, defines a collection of C/C++ *adapter* functions for the Java class. The language here is borrowed from the *Design Patterns* book. It is important to keep in mind throughout this discussion that the adapter functions are not native methods. They are intended for use by the native methods for copying data back and forth between a C struct and a Java object.

The structConverter tool uses information from a configuration file. The configuration file simply names which C structures should be converted and in which Java package they belong.

The Java Source

The first file output by structConverter is the Java source defining a class which serves as a proxy for the application's C structure. For each data field in the C structure, there is a corresponding private member variable generated in the Java proxy source file. For each member variable, a setter and getter is generated.

The Java proxy source file also contains a single native method declaration. This native method is responsible for initializing the field identifiers (jfieldID) for each member variable within the class. This initialization caches the field identifiers in static memory at class load time so that subsequent repeated references to these values do not require calling back into the JVM. The implementation for this native method is automatically generated and output to the adapter source file.

The C Adapter Code

The second output file generated by `structConverter` contains either C or C++ functions which copy data between the Java proxy object and a C structure. For each field in the C structure there is a pair of functions, or adapters, which, given a Java object and a pointer to a C `struct`, know how to copy data between the two.

As mentioned above, the implementation of the initialization method is also written to the adapter file.

It is important to note that although the adapter functions call JNI functions, they are not `native` methods. They are intended to be used by `native` methods for doing the low-level JNI calls necessary to transfer data between fields in a C structure and fields in a Java object.

An example will better explicate some of the mechanics.

POSIX User Database Access

For the sake of this discussion, we are going to look at the password file functionality defined by the POSIX standard (ISO Standard 9945-1 or, alternatively, ANSI/IEEE 1003.1). The purpose of the POSIX standard is to define a standard operating system interface and environment based on the UNIX Operating System.

One such interface the POSIX standard defines is access to a user database. The user database maintains general information on user accounts. An entry in the user database base is defined by the standard to include the following member fields:

Table 10.1   `passwd` *Structure Fields*

Type	Field Name	Description
char*	pw_name	User Name
uid_t	pw_uid	User ID
gid_t	pw_gid	Group ID
char*	pw_dir	Initial Working Directory
char*	pw_shell	Initial User Program

A database entry is represented by a data object of type `passwd`, a pointer to which is returned by the following two functions:

```
struct passwd*getpwnam(const char* name);
struct passwd*getpwuid(uid_t uid);
```

The POSIX standard also requires that `struct passwd` and the function prototypes for `getpwnam` and `getpwuid` be defined in a file `pwd.h` residing in the canonical include directory `/usr/include` and appearing in C source as `<pwd.h>`. This is the file we will use as input to `structConverter`.

Using `structConverter`

Let's look at the steps required for running the `structConverter` tool.

Running the C Preprocessor

The first step is to run the C preprocessor on the file `<pwd.h>`. On Solaris, and most UNIX compilers, the C preprocessor is invoked by using the `-E` command line option to the C compiler.

► **• User Input**   **Running Preprocessor on Solaris**

```
% cc -E /usr/include/pwd.h > pwd_e.h
```

The output of this step is captured in the file `pwd_e.h` which will be used as input to `structConverter`. Of course, the output file name is entirely your choice.

Platform Specific Note Win32

Although the above example does not apply to a Win32 machine, similar flags are available when converting application include files in the Win32 environment using Microsoft's compiler. In this case, the `/E` option directs the compiler, `cl`, to run the preprocessor. For example,

```
c:\projects> cl /E my_include.h > my_include_e.h
```

would leave the preprocessor output in the file `my_include_e.h`. This file would serve as input to `structConverter`.

Another possibility is the use of the `/P` option with the C/C++ source file. Unlike the `/E` option, the `/P` option requires that the input file have a `.c` or `.cpp` extension. However even this requirement can be circumvented with the `/Tc (Tp)` option which forces the compiler to treat a file as a C (C++) source file.

```
c:\projects> cl /P /Tcmy_include.h
```

Whenever the `/P` is used, the output file name is constructed from the input file name by stripping off the extension and replacing it with a `.i` suffix. In the above example, the preprocessor output will appear in `my_include.i`.

Microsoft Visual Studio does not provide a means to set the `/E` or `/P` flags, so you must run the compiler from the command line to generate the expanded file for input to `structConverter`. Other IDEs may support manipulating this flag and therefore, by customizing your build settings, you need not run the compiler by hand.

It should be noted that the `/EP` option should not be used to produce input to `structConverter`. This option suppresses the generation of `#line` directives. The `#line` directives are required by `structConverter` in order to identify which header files need be included in the adapter file.

Finally, to run Microsoft's `cl` from the command line, some environment has to be set up. The appropriate `PATH` environment settings for doing this are defined in the `vcvars32.bat` file. This file is installed in `VC\bin` under your Development Studio install directory.

The `structConverter` Configuration File

Before we run `structConverter`, we need to create a configuration file that tells `structConverter` the names of the C structures for which it should generate Java proxy class source and adapter code. Since our goal here is to generate a Java class for the `passwd` structure, we create a file `jclass.cfg` in the current directory and add a single line.

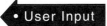 `structConverter` **Configuration File**

passwd

This entry tells `structConverter` that we are interested in only the C language `struct` with the structure tag or typedef name `passwd`. In this example, `passwd` happens to be the structure tag for the `passwd` structure.

In general, a configuration file entry can have two fields per line. The first field names the C type for which output is to be generated. The second field identifies the package in which the generated Java class is to reside. For example, if we were doing a complete POSIX package we may have an entry as shown below.

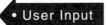 **Package Name in Configuration File**

passwd posix

This would cause the line

```
package posix;
```

to be generated at the front of the Java proxy class source file.

Running `structConverter`

To run `structConverter` on the preprocessed file, make sure your CLASSPATH environment variable includes the example classes directory and type:

◀ • User Input   **Running** `structConverter`

```
% java structConverter.structConverter -c pwd_e.h
```

The `-c` option instructs `structConverter` to generate C adapter code. If you wish to generate C++ output, use the -C option instead. The above command generates C or C++ files containing adapter code and Java source files for each `struct` named in the configuration file.

The Java Source File

The Java source file that mirrors the `passwd` structure contains the following:

- A `private` instance variable for each field of the `passwd` structure. The instance variable takes the same name as the field name.

- A `public` method for setting the value of each of the `private` instance variables. For a field named pw_name, the setter method is given the name `setPw_name`. The convention is to follow `set` with a version of the field name in which the first character is capitalized.

- A `public` method for getting the value of each of the `private` instance variables. For a field named pw_dir, the getter method is `getPw_dir`. A getter adapter is named by following `get` with a version of the field name in which the first character is capitalized.

- A declaration for the `private static native` method `initFIDs`.

- A `static` block which calls `initFIDs`.

Below is the Java source generated for the C `passwd` structure declaration. Per the Java requirement, `structConverter` generates a Java class named `passwd` declared in a file `passwd.java`.

Listing 10.1 *Java Output for* passwd

```java
public class passwd {

private String    pw_name; //Converted from char*
public void setPw_name(String _lcl_val_1){
    pw_name = _lcl_val_1;
}
public String getPw_name() {
    return pw_name;
}

private String    pw_passwd;//  Converted from char*
public void setPw_passwd(String _lcl_val_1) {
    pw_passwd = _lcl_val_1;
}
public String getPw_passwd() {
    return pw_passwd;
}

private long      pw_uid;
public void setPw_uid(long _lcl_val_1){
    pw_uid = _lcl_val_1;
}
public long getPw_uid(){
    return pw_uid;
}

private long      pw_gid;
public void setPw_gid(long _lcl_val_1) {
    pw_gid = _lcl_val_1;
}
public long getPw_gid(){
    return pw_gid;
}

private String    pw_dir;//   Converted from char*
public void setPw_dir(String _lcl_val_1) {
    pw_dir = _lcl_val_1;
}
public String getPw_dir() {
    return pw_dir;
}
```

Listing 10.1 (cont.) *Java Output for* passwd

```
private String     pw_shell;//    Converted from char*
public void setPw_shell(String _lcl_val_1) {
   pw_shell = _lcl_val_1;
}
public String getPw_shell() {
   return pw_shell;
}

private native static void initFIDs();
   static {
       initFIDs();
   }
}
```

The setters and getters defined in the passwd class are strictly for the Java world's manipulation of objects of this class. With the exception of the native method initFIDs, there is nothing within the Java code which accesses the native world. As this example is developed, a model for connecting data maintained within a Java object and data maintained within the corresponding C structure will be illustrated.

The comments in the above code hint at a reality of mapping a C structure into Java code. That is, data types differ across the two languages. Decisions have to be made as to how to map data types of one language onto the other. A word about how structConverter does this mapping is essential so that you can completely understand its operation.

structConverter Data Type Conversion

As we saw in Table 4.2 on page 51, the JNI defines a set of native types for use when referring to Java types in native code. We saw that JNI maps a Java int onto jint, a Java long onto jlong and so on. The motivation behind this is to make explicit how Java types are to be manipulated by native code or, more precisely, to ensure that a Java primitive type of a given size (i.e. number of bytes) maps to an equivalently sized data type on the native machine. In fact, we saw that the file $JDK_HOME/include/*platform*/jni_md.h guaranteed an appropriate mapping by providing typedefs for various native types on a platform-dependent basis.

The job of structConverter is to do a similar thing only in reverse. structConverter sees C types as input and must map them to the appropriate Java type. This mapping is a little more complex because the C language has a larger set of primitive (or scalar) types than does Java. The most obvious difference is the C language's support of unsigned types. Java does not support unsigned types and therefore a decision has to be made on how to handle unsigned types when they appear as input. Likewise, C supports pointers while Java does not. This is another type of mapping decision that `structConverter` must make. Regardless of whether or not you use `structConverter`, you will still be confronted by such decisions.

The following table makes explicit the type mapping performed by `structConverter`. You will note that in some cases, the mapping is controlled by a command line option.

Table 10.2   `structConverter` *C to Java Type Mappings*

C Type	Java Type	Command Line Options	Default
unsigned char	byte	none	
unsigned char[]	byte[]	none	
unsigned short	int	none	
unsigned int	long	none	
unsigned long	long	none	
char	byte	none	
char*	String	NoCharStarStrings	convert
char[]	String	NoCharArrayStrings	convert
pointer to scalar	primitive	none	
pointer to struct	reference		

Conversion of C strings to `java.lang.String` objects is controlled by two command line options. By default, all `char*` and `char[]` variables are treated as `java.lang.String` objects. If you want to turn off conversion of `char*` variables, use the `-NoCharStarStrings` option when invoking `structConverter`. Likewise, if you want a character array to remain a character array, use the `-NoCharArrayStrings` option. If neither conversion is desired, use the `-NoStrings` option.

Whenever a conversion is performed by `structConverter`, the generated Java source contains a comment informing you of that conversion. In Listing 10.1, all of the Java `java.lang.String` objects are reported as having been converted from C `char*` variables.

`initFIDs` and the `static` Block

Every Java class definition generated by `structConverter` will contain a `static` initialization block. Within this `static` block a call to the `native` method `initFIDs` is made. This method is responsible for initializing the field IDs for each of the Java member variables.

Both the `static` block and the `native` method declaration are generated by default. To suppress their generation and the caching of the field IDs, you can use the `-NoFIDCache` option. A significant speed-up is achieved when accessing Java member variables from native code if field IDs are maintained as `static` variables and initialized when the class is loaded.

By placing the initialization within a `static` block, we are guaranteed that the code is only executed once when the class is loaded. There is the added benefit that if the class gets unloaded and then reloaded, the `jfieldIDs` will be properly re-initialized. Recall that the `jfieldIDs` are only valid during the life of a class. If ever a class were to be unloaded and then referenced again, these values would change. By initializing the `jfieldID` variables in a `static` block executed during the loading of the class, their values are guaranteed to be correct.

Of course, the interesting part of all this is the native code which does the initialization. We will look at that now.

The Adapter Source File

The adapter code generated by `structConverter` is written to a file `jnipasswd.c`. The convention used by `structConverter` to name the output file is to add `jni` to the front of the class name for the adapter native code.

This file contains:

- The `static jfieldID` declarations
- The `native` method code which implements `initFIDs`
- The adapter code for each field member of the C `struct` for which it was generated or, equivalently, for each member variable in the Java class generated
- Two aggregate adapters for a bulk transfer of data, one from the C `struct` to the Java object and vice-versa
- `#include` directives for all relevant include files

As always, a few lines of code are worth a thousand lines of prose. Let's take a look at an excerpt from `jnipasswd.c`

Field ID Initialization

All the field IDs are stored as `static` variables. They are initialized by a function called by the implementation of the `initFIDs` native method. The code below shows the initialization code for the `passwd` class in the file `jnipasswd.c`.

Listing 10.2 *Adapter Initialization Code*

```
static jfieldID passwd_Pw_name_FID;
static jfieldID passwd_Pw_passwd_FID;
static jfieldID passwd_Pw_uid_FID;
static jfieldID passwd_Pw_gid_FID;
static jfieldID passwd_Pw_dir_FID;
static jfieldID passwd_Pw_shell_FID;

static void initpasswdFieldIDs(
JNIEnv* env, jclass clazz) {
   passwd_Pw_name_FID = (*env)->GetFieldID(
           env, clazz, "pw_name",
           "Ljava/lang/String;");
   passwd_Pw_passwd_FID = (*env)->GetFieldID(
           env, clazz, "pw_passwd",
           "Ljav a/lang/String;");
   passwd_Pw_uid_FID = (*env)->GetFieldID(
           env, clazz, "pw_uid", "J");
   passwd_Pw_gid_FID = (*env)->GetFieldID(
           env, clazz, "pw_gid", "J");
   passwd_Pw_dir_FID = (*env)->GetFieldID(
           env, clazz, "pw_dir",
           "Ljava/lang/String;");
   passwd_Pw_shell_FID = (*env)->GetFieldID(
           env, clazz, "pw_shell",
           "Ljava/lang/String;");
}

JNIEXPORT void JNICALL Java_passwd_initFIDs(
           JNIEnv *env, jclass clazz) {
   initpasswdFieldIDs(env, clazz);
}
```

There are two things worth noting. First, the naming of the `jfieldID` variables follows a convention that includes both the class name and the structure variable name.

classname_capitalized-field-name FID

This is helpful to keep in mind if you are going to be writing additional native code which needs to refer to the field IDs for the Java proxy class.

Secondly, all the work of initialization is actually done within the function `initpasswdFieldID` which is called by the `native` method `initFIDs`. Since this method was declared `static`, it receives the `jclass` value of the calling class as an argument. This value is then used by

GetFieldID to retrieve the Java member variable's field ID. There is nothing out of the ordinary involved with the GetFieldID calls.

That takes care of the field ID initialization. Let's move to the adapter code.

Adapter Code

As previously mentioned, a pair of adapter functions is generated for each Java member variable. One of these functions copies the Java member variable's value from the Java object into a C structure. This function is known as the getter adapter. The other adapter function copies a value from a C structure field into the corresponding Java object member variable. This function is known as the setter adapter. As you can see, the functions are named based on their treatment of the Java object, not the related C structure. The getter adapter "gets" data from the Java object. The setter adapter "sets" values in the Java object.

Continuing our password database example, a pair of adapter functions for the pw_name field of the passwd structure appear below.

Listing 10.3 *Adapter Functions for* pw_name

```
void jni_SetPw_name_in_passwd(
     struct passwd* __passwd_,
     JNIEnv *env,
     jobject thispasswd)
{
     jboolean isCopy;
     (*env)->SetObjectField(env,
         thispasswd,
           passwd_Pw_name_FID,
         (*env)->NewStringUTF(env, __passwd_->pw_name));
}
```
(1)

```
void jni_GetPw_name_from_passwd(
               struct passwd* __passwd_,
               JNIEnv *env, jobject thispasswd)
{
     jboolean     isCopy;
     int          ix0;
     char*        ch0;
     __passwd_->pw_name =
         (char*) (*env)->GetStringUTFChars(env,
                    (jstring) (*env)->GetObjectField(env,
                       thispasswd,
                       passwd_Pw_name_FID),
                       &isCopy);
     if (isCopy == JNI_TRUE)
         (*env)->ReleaseStringUTFChars(env, 0);
}
```
(2)

(3)

The argument list for an adapter follows a pattern. The first argument is always a pointer to the relevant C structure. The second is always a Java run-time environment pointer. The third argument is always a jobject reference to the corresponding Java object.

You can see that the above two functions take advantage of the fact that field IDs are cached. The JNI functions within the native adapters involved in setting Java object variables use, at lines [1] and [3], the static variables that cache the field IDs. Because of this, each adapter function gets right to the business of either setting or getting the Java data member for which it is responsible.

There are two more observations worth making. First, the adapter assumes that any object member variable has been previously allocated. In particular, the code in line [2] assumes the GetObjectField returns a valid object pointer. What this means is that the Java side is responsible for allocating all object references within a Java proxy object. This is important enough to make a big deal of.

Warning:

Any `structConverter`-generated Java object must initialize all object member variables before a call into a `native` method which uses native adapters.

Failure to honor the above warning will likely result in a `java.lang.NullPointerException`. It is worth pointing out, though, for graduates of 1.0 `native` method programming that the native code does not have to worry about pinning C memory for accommodating Java array and String objects. The JNI functions for accessing these objects now take care of that work for you.

The second observation of interest is the naming convention used by `structConverter` for the native adapter functions. From the above pair of adapters for `pw_name`, the convention should be clear. For the getter adapter, the function which copies a value from the Java object to the C structure, the name is constructed as follows:

`jni_Getupper-case-member-name_from_class-name`

The setter adapter follows the same pattern:

`jni_Setupper-case-member-name_in_class-name`

`structConverter` also generates aggregate setter and getter adapters. The naming convention for these functions is similar.

```
jni_SetAll_in_class-name
jni_GetAll_in_class-name
```

Understanding these naming conventions makes clear the operation of the aggregate adapters generated by `structConverter`. Below is the aggregate setter adapter for the `passwd` class.

Listing 10.4 *Aggregate Setter Adapter for the* passwd *Structure*

```
void jni_SetAll_in_passwd(
        struct passwd* __passwd_,
        JNIEnv* env,
        jobject thispasswd)
{
   jni_SetPw_shell_in_passwd(
      __passwd_, env, thispasswd);
   jni_SetPw_name_in_passwd(
      __passwd_, env, thispasswd);
   jni_SetPw_passwd_in_passwd(
      __passwd_, env, thispasswd);
   jni_SetPw_uid_in_passwd(
      __passwd_, env, thispasswd);
   jni_SetPw_gid_in_passwd(
      __passwd_, env, thispasswd);
   jni_SetPw_dir_in_passwd(
      __passwd_, env, thispasswd);
}
```

The aggregate setters and getters are written to the same source file as the individual field setters and getters.

Looking at the native adapter code leads one to ask: Where does the passwd structure come from? Where does the Java object come from? We have seen Java code and we have seen native code, but we have yet to see how the two work together. How is the Java proxy object connected to the native adapter code? We will look at a strategy for doing this in the next section.

Tying It All Together

All the code we have looked at in this chapter has been generated by structConverter. structConverter provides the lowest level building blocks for an application. As we continue with the POSIX passwd database example, we will see one way these pieces can be integrated into larger applications.

As a first step, we will look at a new class, `PasswdStruct`. `Passwd-Struct` is Java source that you need to write. The intent of `PasswdStruct` is to tie together the Java code in the `passwd` class and the C code of the native adapters. The `PasswdStruct` class has three roles:

1. It extends the `passwd` class to make available the Java setters and getters to the application.

2. It declares `native` methods that populate the member variables of the `passwd` class from a C `passwd` structure.

3. It ensures that all object member variables, including arrays and Strings, of the `passwd` class are initialized.

Let's look at how `PasswdStruct` meets the requirements outlined above. The class declaration extends `passwd` in line [4] to meet the first requirement. The two `native` method declarations in lines [5] and [6] will populate the Java fields with data from a `passwd` database entry. This meets the second requirements but, to be convinced, we will have to wait and see the native code.

Listing 10.5 *Java Source for* `PasswdStruct`

```
(4)    public class PasswdStruct extends passwd {
(5)        private native void posix_getpwnam(String name);
(6)        private native void posix_getpwuid(long uid);
(7)        private void _init() {
               setPw_name(new String());
               setPw_passwd(new String());
               setPw_shell(new String());
               setPw_dir(new String());
           }
           public PasswdStruct(String name) {
               _init();
               posix_getpwnam(name);
           }
           public PasswdStruct(long uid) {
               _init();
               posix_getpwuid(uid);
           }
       }
```

The third criterion above is met by the `_init` method at line [7]. `_init` is called in the constructors to ensure that all the necessary Java objects are created and available to the native code.

The larger purpose of `PasswdStruct` is to impose application semantics on the generated code. Depending on your application, your extending of the structConverter-generated Java class may look a little different. However, it still must perform the three roles outlined above.

Here is the `native` method implementation written to take advantage of the adapter functions. This is the first piece of C code written by hand.

Listing 10.6 *Native Implementation of* PasswdStruct *Methods*

```
#include "jniPasswdStruct.h"
#include <pwd.h>
#include <string.h>

JNIEXPORT void JNICALL
Java_PasswdStruct_posix_1getpwnam(
                JNIEnv * env,
                jobject thisPasswd,
                jstring name)
{
    jboolean isCopy;
    const char* nm;
    nm = (*env)->GetStringUTFChars(env,
                                   name,
                                   &isCopy);
    struct passwd *p = getpwnam(nm);
    jni_SetAll_in_passwd(p, env, thisPasswd);
}

JNIEXPORT void JNICALL
Java_PasswdStruct_posix_1getpwuid(
                JNIEnv *env,
                jobject thisPasswd,
                jlong uid)
{
    struct passwd *p = getpwuid(uid);
    jni_SetAll_in_passwd(p, env, thisPasswd);
}
```

The only difference between these two `native` method implementations is the manner in which they populate the passwd structure. The first uses getpwnam while the second uses getpwuid. This is really the central point of the PasswdStruct class: it uses the automatically generated native adapters to tie into platform-dependent code in an application-specific manner. The generated adapters act as helpers in the construction of `native` methods.

In the above example, the aggregate adapters are used to move data from a C structure in a Java object. Data from the Java object is not written into the C structure. The code could have been written using the individual field adapters. Instead, the aggregate function, `jni_SetAll_in_passwd`, was used as a convenience. In general, the application will drive how the adapters are used. In this simple example, a bulk transfer is desired from the C `struct` to the Java object so the aggregate adapters are used. The following example, modeling a legacy database, illustrates the use of the getter native adapters.

Another Database Example

A short, toy example will be developed to illustrate the use of getter adapters, as well as describing a slightly different approach to integrating the native adapters within a Java application. In the previous example, the constructor of the Java proxy class made a call that read data from a native C structure. This design modeled well the usage of `getpwnam` and `getpwuid`. There is a slightly different model which more closely resembles typical interaction with a legacy database.

In this example we will look at a toy hotel booking system. Our starting point is a C `struct` which we want to model in Java. The information recorded about a hotel reservation is stored in the `Booking` structure shown Listing 10.7.

Listing 10.7 Booking *Structure for Reservation Information*

```
typedef struct booking {
    long                reservationKey;
    char                lastName[16];
    char                firstName[16];
    char                street[31];
    char                city[19];
    char                state[3];
    char                zip[11];
    char                phone[13];
    unsigned long       adult;
    unsigned long       child;
    unsigned long       bed;
    unsigned long       bath;
    double              rent;
    short               arrivalDate;
    short               departureDate;
    unsigned char       checkedIn;
    unsigned char       checkedOut;
}Booking;
```

Pretty ugly, huh? Well, this example is based on a true story, as they say in Hollywood. This is the kind of work your Java Brethren are doing out there. Keep them in your prayers.

The Booking struct will be input to structConverter and will generate the lovely looking class, Booking. It will be shown here, if only partially, as a reminder of why we are moving our applications to Java.

Listing 10.8 *Java Source for* Booking *Class*

```java
public class Booking {
public long        reservationKey;
public void setReservationKey(long _lcl_val_1) {
   reservationKey = _lcl_val_1;
}
public long getReservationKey() {
   return reservationKey;
}
private String     lastName;
               /*Converted from char[16] */
public void setLastName(String _lcl_val_1){
   lastName = _lcl_val_1;
}
public String getLastName() {
   return lastName;
}
private String     firstName;
                  /*Converted from char[16] */
public void setFirstName(String _lcl_val_1) {
   firstName = _lcl_val_1;
}
public String getFirstName() {
   return firstName;
}
/* Details deleted... */
public long        adult;/*  unsigned long */
public void setAdult(long _lcl_val_1) {
   adult = _lcl_val_1;
}
public long getAdult() {
   return adult;
}
public long        child;/*  unsigned long */
public void setChild(long _lcl_val_1) {
   child = _lcl_val_1;
}
```

Listing 10.8 (cont.) *Java Source for* Booking *Class*

```
public long getChild() {
   return child;
}
public long        bed;/*  unsigned long */
public void setBed(long _lcl_val_1) {
   bed = _lcl_val_1;
}
public long getBed() {
   return bed;
}
/* Details deleted... */
private native static void initFIDs();
   static {
       initFIDs();
   }
}
```

There is nothing new here. The Java proxy class is generated as expected. The variation on the previous example is introduced with the subclass, dbBooking, which extends Booking.

Listing 10.9 *Java Source for* dbBooking

```
public class dbBooking extends Booking {
   private native void jni_commit();
   private native void jni_retrieve(long key);
   public void commit() {
       jni_commit();
   }
   public void retrieve(long key) {
       jni_retrieve(key);
   }
}
```

(8)
(9)

dbBooking defines two methods, retrieve and commit. These methods are indirectly responsible for reading and writing native data. Their job is to call native methods which, in turn, call the adapter routines. The adapter routines finally are responsible for doing the data transfer.

In Listing 10.10 we look at the implementation of the native methods jni_commit and jni_retrieve declared above. We can see they map straightforwardly onto (pretend) database lookup and store functions. For the sake of brevity, only a subset of dbBooking's fields are written/read in the following listing.

Listing 10.10 *Implementation of* jni_commit *and* jni_retrieve

```
JNIEXPORT void JNICALL Java_dbBooking_jni_1retrieve(
            JNIEnv* env,
            jobject thisBooking,
            jlong key) {
    /* Fake a lookup of a booking 'record' */
    Booking* res = lookup(key);

    /* Copy from 'record' into Java object */
    jni_SetReservationKey_in_Booking(
            res, env, thisBooking);
    jni_SetFirstName_in_Booking(
            res, env, thisBooking);
    jni_SetLastName_in_Booking(
            res, env, thisBooking);
}


JNIEXPORT void JNICALL Java_dbBooking_jni_1commit(
            JNIEnv* env, jobject thisBooking){
    Booking* res =
            (Booking*) malloc(sizeof(Booking));

    /* Copy from Java object ---> 'record' buffer */
    jni_GetReservationKey_from_Booking(
            res, env, thisBooking);
    jni_GetFirstName_from_Booking(
            res, env, thisBooking);
    jni_GetLastName_from_Booking(
            res, env, thisBooking);
    jni_GetAdult_from_Booking(
            res, env, thisBooking);
    jni_GetChild_from_Booking(res, env, thisBooking);
    jni_GetBed_from_Booking(res, env, thisBooking);
    /* write 'record' to db */
    store(res);
    free(res);
}
```

Now that we have seen the adapter functions, there is just one more piece of code needed to bring the machine-generated and the hand-generated code together.

Updating a Booking Record

What we have seen so far is a C struct that represents data in a reservation database, a Java class, Booking, that acts as a proxy for that data, and C adapter functions which move data between the C struct and a Java object.

We have also seen a subclass of Booking, dbBooking, that provides native methods that use the adapter functions. One question remains answered: What does the top-level application look like that uses this code? We won't answer that question completely but we will look at one example of how all the code we have seen so far can be used.

Consider a very simple application to look up a record in the reservation database, update some of the fields and then put the entry back to a database. Here is the Java code for performing those operations using the dbBooking class.

Listing 10.11 *Updating a* Booking *Record*

```
public class Main {
static {
    System.loadLibrary("Chap10example2");
}
public static void main(String[] args) {
(10)    dbBooking res = new dbBooking();
        // Fake a key
(11)    res.retrieve(1010);
        System.out.println("\nFound..." +
                "\nFirst Name: " + res.getFirstName() +
                "\nLast Name: " + res.getLastName());
(12)    res.setAdult(2);
        res.setChild(12);
(13)    res.setBed(1);
(14)    res.commit();
}
}
```

First, a dbBooking object is created [10]. This object gives us access to both the setter and getter that can retrieve record information from the fields caching the data, and the retrieve and commit methods which fill and flush the Java object cache.

The dbBooking object is filled with field values with a call to retrieve in line [11]. We fake the key and the database by simply maintaining some static data in the native code but that does not alter the essence of the example.

In lines [12]-[13] three of the fields in the database record are modified, and then in [14], the data is flushed from the Java object and written to the native database.

When we run this mini-application for updating a reservation database record, the following output is generated.

• Program Output ⟩ **Updating a** dbBooking **Record**

```
Retrieving record key 1010
Found...
First Name: Shawn
Last Name: Bertini
Adults: 0
Children: 0
Beds: 0
Updating booking record...
Key              : 1010
First Name       : Shawn
Last Name        : Bertini
No. of Adults    : 2
No. of Children  : 12
No. of Beds      : 1
```

After the `retrieve` call, the contents are printed and the `getAdult`, `getChild` and `getBed` methods all report zero. These are the values currently in the database.

After the Java setters update the values, the `commit` method is called to write the data back to the database. In the simulated `store` routine, the current values of the record are printed after the message "Updating booking record..." You can see from the output that the values have been updated.

In summary, the Java setters and getters operate on the Java Book object. The `dbBooking` methods, `commit` and `retrieve`, call the appropriate adapter functions for copying data between the Java object and the C struct.

In this and the previous example, the Java object effectively caches the values of the corresponding C structure for use by Java code. The native adapters put the values from the C structure into Java data fields, and the Java application uses the object setters and getters to set and retrieve these fields. One could just as well write `native` methods that do not use the Java object as a cache, accessing the data directly from the C structure. This approach bypasses native adapters altogether. However, by using the Java object to cache the values you are left in a better position for moving away from the C adapter functions toward a pure Java application.

In some cases, you may need to maintain a session mapping between a Java object and a C structure, much like we saw in Chapter 8 with the producer-consumer example. Each time you foray into native code with a given Java object, you may want to access the same C structure without, say, the luxury of a database that ensures persistence. In this case, you would want to replicate what we did in Chapter 9 and maintain a table that maps Java objects to C structures. Of course, with this approach you must be careful about memory leaks. You don't want your Java object to go away without freeing the corresponding native `struct`.

Some applications may require an immediate and direct correspondence between Java values and native values. In this case, the Java code will need to write-through values upon setting and read-through values upon getting. If that is what your application requires, `structConverter` can still provide help.

Generating Just Java

By default, `structConverter` generates Java code and C or C++ code. The Java class generated is intended to act as a cache for the C values. This approach is not always desirable or possible. Often, you will want to map each Java method directly to a `native` method.

If this is desired, the `-j` flag on `structConverter` causes output of only a Java source file. For each field in the input C structure, a setter/getter pair is generated. Both are declared native. It is up to you to write the entire `native` method implementation without the help of native adapters.

To put this prose into code, consider a C structure, `aDevice`, intended to provide an interface for a very, very simple device.

Listing 10.12 *Structure Definition for a Simple Device*

```
typedef struct device_s {
    long            reg0;
    long            reg1;
    unsigned char   buf;
} aDevice;
```

Running this file through the C preprocessor and then applying `struct-Converter` with the `-j` option produces the Java class shown below.

Listing 10.13 *Java Class for* aDevice

```
public class aDevice {
    native public void setReg0(long lcl_arg_0);
    native public long getReg0();
    native public void setReg1(long lcl_arg_0);
    native public long getReg1();
    native public void setBuf(byte lcl_arg_0);
    native public byte getBuf();
}
```

Not a big deal, but enough to get you started. If you are not interested in using the automatically generated native adapters, you can still use struct-Converter to generate Java source for a class that models a C structure you need to integrate with your Java application.

Some Design Considerations

Mirroring one piece of data with another always raises the issue of coherency. In the first two examples, we looked at the Java proxy object which effectively acted as a cache for the C passwd structure. In general, this approach raises the issue known as cache coherency. The fundamental problem is maintaining a correct representation of the underlying data in the cache, i.e. the Java proxy object.

In the third example, we avoided this problem by directly implementing the setters and getters of the Java object as native methods. Of course, the cost of this approach is the frequent excursions into native code and the overhead involved in the JVM setting up the reference table. On the other hand, one need not worry about any coherency issues.

A Bit More About structConverter

structConverter can do a bit more for you. The reference page in Appendix C has all the details, but a few of the more useful options are mentioned here to whet your appetite.

Making all those JNI calls, as in the above examples, without checking for exceptions is not ideal practice. There is a better way. Either of two options, -E or -e, can be used to generated exception checking code after every JNI function call.

The -f option allows you to use another configuration file other than jclass.cfg.

The -I option allows you to name the base include directory. This allows structConverter to identify when it is appropriate to use the angle bracket notation when laying down an #include directive.

For more information on these and other options, see Appendix C.

Summary

With the introduction of `structConverter`, I hope we have averted any premature deaths. If you are an erstwhile C programmer and an aspiring Java programmer, `structConverter` offers a good start for integrating, in a relatively painless way, your legacy C applications into your new and flashy Java applications.

By providing both the Java class to interface to your Java application and some C/C++ to copy data between the two worlds of native code and Java, you will be able to reduce your development time.

`structConverter` can be used in different ways depending on your application requirements. Either you can use the Java proxy class as a cache for your C structure data by generating both Java and C source or you can simply generate a Java class with setters and getters for the C fields.

This and the previous chapter discussed general techniques for integrating legacy code with Java applications. In the next chapter, we will apply the JNI to solve a specific, yet widespread, problem in search of a Java solution.

Chapter 11   *NATIVE SERIAL I/O*

Introduction

The Java language provides no direct means of talkng to physical devices connected to physical computers. That's okay. That is the way it should be. After all, it is a virtual machine and likes to think in abstractions. For engineers developing Java applications, thinking in abstractions is not always possible. Eventually, that I/O device has to be written to.

Don't despair, for when you are finished with this chapter you will say that I have found a good solution.

This chapter will cover two major topics. First, it will present an API for accessing serial and parallel ports from Java. The API is defined by Central Data's `portio` package and consists of high-level classes for a `Port-Driver` and a `Port`. Additionally, a `PortPrivate` class can be extended to add device specific behavior.

Implementing device-specific behavior requires native methods programming. This is the second major topic covered in this chapter. Java and native code supporting serial I/O for both POSIX (a standardized UNIX) and Win32 platforms will be presented. Using Central Data's `portio` package, and extending `PortDriver` and `PortPrivate`, we will see how a well-designed Java package simplifies the job of `native` methods programming.

213

The portio *Package*

The programming model presented by the portio package is one of a port driver that maintains state for any number of ports on a single device. To get access to these ports, the programmer first creates a port driver and then creates a port, associating it with a port driver.

A port has various attributes. These attributes may be manipulated by the programmer to alter the behavior of the port. A port also has status associated with it. The programmer may read and write this state data. Finally, a port has an input and an output stream associated with it.

With that model in mind, let's take a look at the classes contained within the portio package. The following description of the portio classes borrows heavily from Central Data's *portio User Guide*.

PortDriver

This is an abstract class that is extended to provide the functionality for a single device. A device consists of any number of serial and parallel ports. Ports may not be created until the PortDriver which controls the ports has been successfully instantiated. The PortDriver class ensures that each port is only opened once and can be used to regulate access to any resources shared by multiple ports on the device. PortDriver maintains a PortDriver-Info reference. Subclasses of PortDriver are responsible for populating the PortDriverInfo with information relevant to their device.

Port

This is the class from which different types of ports extend. Port's constructor associates the port with a driver and assigns itself a port number. Otherwise, most of the work asked of a Port object is delegated to the driver or to a port-specific object, PortPrivate.

SerialPort

This is an extension of the Port class. It is instantiated with a reference to the PortDriver and the port number which is to be opened. After successful instantiation, the getInputStream and getOutputStream methods can be used to provide normal Java InputStream and OutputStream access to the port. It also provides an interface for manipulating port parameters and status, although these operations are delegated to the Port's PortPrivate object.

ParallelPort

This is an extension of the Port class. It contains a constructor that calls Port's constructor and associates a ParallelPort with a PortDriver. It also assigns the ParallelPort a port number. The work of

`ParallelPort` is accomplished by the extensions to `PortPrivate` and `PortDriver` for devices serving parallel ports.

SerialPortParams

This class maintains a serial port's attributes or parameter values. A port's parameter settings can be changed by passing a `SerialPortParams` object to the `setParams` method of `SerialPort`. The `SerialPortParams` class maintains settings for such parameters as baud rate, character size, parity settings and flow control.

SerialPortStatus

This class maintains status values for a serial port's signal lines. A reference to a `SerialPortStatus` object is returned by `getStatus` method of `Port` and is expected as an argument to `setStatus` method of `Port`.

ParallelPortStatus

This class simply maintains instance variables that track the state of a parallel port.

PortDriverInfo

This class maintains information about a `PortDriver` including the number of serial and parallel ports. This information is read-only and is set by the `PortDriver` itself. It is available to the programmer with a call to the `getDriverInfo` method of a `PortDriver` instance.

PortIOException

This class extends `IOException` and provides a package-specific exception for easy identification of `portio` errors.

The above classes define the public `portio` API. There is one more class that needs to be metioned. The `PortPrivate` class is not exposed to the user but is central in targeting the `portio` package to a specific device and platform.

PortPrivate

This is an abstract class that must be extended when adding new ports to a device. Implementations are responsible for extending `PortPrivate` and implementing device-specific behavior. Classes extending `PortPrivate` are required to implement the abstract methods `open`, `close`, `read`, `write`, `purge`, `sendBreak`, `flush`, `available`, as well as methods for setting and getting the port parameters and status. The `PortPrivate` class is the last stop in Java code before diving into `native` method code. When a

Port is opened, an instance of a device-specific subclass of PortPrivate is created by the corresponding PortDriver.

Two more portio classes deserve mention simply to answer the question: What type of java.io object does portio use? The answer is a java.io.OutputStream for output and a java.lang.Input-Stream for input. PortOutputStream and PortInputStream extend OutputStream and InputStream, respectively. A user is given a reference to these objects by the getOutputStream and getInputStream methods defined by the Port class.

The complete documentation of the portio classes in javadoc format is included with the *Essential JNI* examples at the Prentice-Hall ftp site.

Using portio

We can now begin to explore the details of using the portio package. The following code sample illustrates how the portio classes fit together when writing to a Central Data EtherLite® device. The EtherLite device is a serial interface implemented on top of TCP/IP. The EtherLite driver is implemented without any use of native methods but nonetheless exhibits a working example of the portio package. After looking at this code, we will look under the covers of the portio package and see how it can be augmented for platform-specific serial I/O.

Listing 11.1 *Using* portio *for the EtherLite Device*

```
EtherLiteDriver driver = null;
    try {
        driver = new EtherLiteDriver("EtherLite1");
    } catch(PortIOException e) {
        System.out.println(
                    "Failed making driver: "+ e);
        System.exit(1);
    }

    // get information about the device
    PortDriverInfo info = driver.getDriverInfo();
    if(info.serialCount == 0) {
        System.out.println(
                "No serial ports on device");
        System.exit(1);
    }
```

(1)

(2)

Listing 11.1 (cont.) *Using* portio *for the EtherLite Device*

```
       // make some arrays to hold objects related
       // to each serial port
(3)    SerialPort port[] =
                    new SerialPort[info.serialCount];

(4)    InputStream in[] =
                    new InputStream[info.serialCount];
(5)    OutputStream out[] =
                    new OutputStream[info.serialCount];

       // open the first serial port
       try {
(6)       port[0] = new SerialPort(driver, 0);
       } catch(PortIOException e) {
          System.out.println(
                    "Failed opening port: " + e);
          System.exit(1);
       }

       in[0] = port[0].getInputStream();
(7)    out[0] = port[0].getOutputStream();

       // choose settings we want and then change
       // them at the port
(8)    SerialPortParams params = new SerialPortParams();
       params.inBaud = params.outBaud = 115200;
       params.charSize = 8;
       try {
(9)       port[0].setParams(params);
       } catch(PortIOException e) {
          System.out.println(
                    "Failed setting params: " + e);
          System.exit(1);
       }

       // create a block of data to send out
       // and then send it!
       byte outBuf[] = new byte[256];
       for (int i = 0; i < 256; i++ )
          outBuf[i] = (byte)i;
```

Listing 11.1 (cont.) *Using* `portio` *for the EtherLite Device*

```
       try {
(10)        out[0].write(outBuf);
       } catch(IOException e) {
         System.out.println(
               "Failed write to port: " + e);
         System.exit(1);
       }

       // close the port neat and clean after
       // releasing objects
       SerialPort thisPort = port[0];
       port[0] = null;
       in[0] = null;
       out[0] = null;
       try {
(11)        thisPort.close();
       } catch(PortIOException e) {
         System.out.println(
               "Failed closing port: " + e);
         System.exit(1);
       }
```

The above code represents the prototypical use of the `portio` package. It illustrates all the steps required in creating and using a port while adhering to the `portio` API. Let's take a close look at it.

In [1] above, a `PortDriver` is created. In this example, it happens to be a subclass of `PortDriver`, namely `EtherLiteDriver`. In [2] the `Port-DriverInfo` is retrieved. It is used to determine the number of serial ports the `EtherLiteDriver` supports. This value is then used in [3]-[5] to allocate memory resources for later use. In [6] the `SerialPort` is created. This action opens and initializes the port. Notice that ports are identified by an integer value. Line [7] records the `OutputStream` for the port in a user allocated object array. Using a `SerialPortParams` object created in [8], line [9] sets the baud rate and data bit parameters for the port. After a buffer is populated with some data, it is written to the port in [10]. Finally, the port is closed in [11].

As you will see when we look at how to augment the `portio` package to do serial I/O to a POSIX tty or a Win32 COM port, the above code will change only by the type of `PortDriver` that is created. Although the POSIX and Win32 implementations will rely on some `native` methods which the `EtherLite` driver does not, and which vary significantly from each other, the only change to the top-level code involves instantiating a different type of `PortDriver`. All this is the mark of a well designed Java package for which this author can take no credit. Instead, credit belongs to Dennis Cronin, formerly of Central Data.

The EtherLite driver is part of the `portio` release included with the *Essential JNI* examples.

`portio` *Template Class Files*

The `portio` package is shipped with two files that can be modified to target the `portio` package for a particular driver. These files contain Java source which partially defines two Java classes, `TemplatePortDriver` and `TemplatePortPrivate`. By modifying and augmenting these two files, the `portio` package can easily be made to support many different serial and parallel devices.

The `TemplatePortDriver` class extends the `abstract` class `Port-Driver` and can be used to implement the functionality of a platform-specific driver. The `TemplatePortPrivate` class extends `PortPrivate`. The modified version of `TemplatePortPrivate` for a specific implementation is as close as the Java code gets to device-specific code. In fact, as we will see, it is the class in which the `native` methods are declared.

TemplatePortDriver

This class extends `PortDriver` and implements the `Runnable` interface. In its unaltered state it performs four basic tasks:

- Sets debug flags
- Initializes device
- Allocates memory for `PortPrivate` object references
- Polls for incoming data, reads this data, and passes it back to its associated port, in its role as a `Runnable` object

Aside from the polling, all of this work is done within the template class constructor. Any or all of these steps may be modified to support a specific device.

Two of these tasks are explicitly marked as requiring device-specific modifications. First, the private method `initDevice`, at the very least, requires that the number of serial and parallel ports be initialized. Any device initialization and setup is also done within this method. Second, the `run` method needs to make a call to a `native` method that knows how to read the specific port. This call should populate a buffer with incoming data and report the length of the buffer. The buffer and its length are passed to the associated `PortPrivate` object and copied into its input buffer.

The `run` method of `TemplatePortDriver` is designed to multiplex input from a variety of sources. For example, on most UNIX systems a native method using a `select` call could be inserted within the while-read loop. Upon return from the `select` call, the reporting file descriptor could be mapped to a `portio` `Port` and the appropriate callback invoked when the `native` method returns.

Lacking a function like `select` to wait on input from multiple sources, another approach must be used. In this case, Java's multi-threading comes in handy. When we look at an extension of the `PortDriver` class for Solaris POSIX tty I/O, we will see the use of multiple threads to allow a single driver to manage multiple ports.

TemplatePortPrivate

This class extends `PortPrivate`. In its unaltered state it performs the following tasks:

- Initializes and manages both input and output buffers including full implementations of buffered `read` and `write` methods

- Provides skeletal implementations of the `open`, `close`, `sendBreak`, `purge`, and a timer-based `flush` methods

- Provides a simple implementation of the `available` method which simply returns the number of characters in the input buffer

- Maintains cached versions of the port parameters and status, and checks when these values have changed

- Implements skeletal versions of methods for setting and getting port parameters and status, including support for a "wait-for-change" mode when manipulating modem status lines

- Implements a `callback` method used by the `PortDriver` class to copy incoming data into its input buffer

- A skeletal implementation of a helper method for doing baud rate conversion from `portio` package values to port-specific values

The bulk of the work in targeting the `portio` package to a specific device is in fleshing out the details of the `TemplatePortPrivate` class. For example, in the `portio` implementation on Solaris, ten `native` methods were required to support a POSIX interface to a terminal device. These `native` methods correspond directly to the `abstract` methods declared in the `PortPrivate` abstract class, excepting `available` and `read`, which are fully implemented using Java code in `TemplatePortPrivate`.

In both template class definitions, comments clearly mark the areas which require consideration when implementing the `portio` package for a particular device.

Augmenting `portio`

The general strategy for bringing a new device under the `portio` API is to copy the template class files to appropriately named files. In the new file, change the class and constructor names to match the file name. Finally, insert `native` method calls where needed and then write the `native` methods.

It is important to note that it is not intended that you extend the `TemplatePortDriver` and `TemplatePortPrivate` classes. `PortDriver` is the base class from which your new driver extends and `PortPrivate` is the base class from which you extend a new class to encapsulate the device-specific details of your new port.

Let's see how this works with a couple of examples. In the remainder of this chapter, we will look at making changes to the `portio` template classes to support a POSIX tty device and a Win32 COM port. In each case, we will focus on the modifications necessary to the files `TemplatePortDriver.java` and `TemplatePortPrivate.java`.

`portio` *and POSIX tty*

In this first example, we will look at extending the `portio` package to support the POSIX tty interface on Solaris. We start by defining two classes, `PosixPortDriver` and `PosixPortPrivate`. These classes are modified versions of `TemplatePortDriver` and `TemplatePortPrivate`.

The `PosixPortDriver` Class

One significant change has been made to the `TemplatePortDriver` in the making of `PosixPortDriver`. Specifically, unlike `TemplatePortDriver`, `PosixPortDriver` does not implement the `Runnable` interface. Instead the `run` method has been removed and placed in a new class, `PosixPortReader`. `PosixPortReader` extends `Thread` and is responsible for reading from a port and passing the data on to the `PosixPortPrivate` object. This architecture avoids the possibility of a read blocking on a specific port and preventing the `PortDriver` from processing input from other ports.

Let's look at `PosixPortDriver`. The changes made to the `TemplatePortDriver` are numbered and discussed below.

Listing 11.2 PosixPortDriver *Source*

```
package portio;

import java.util.*;
import java.io.*;
import java.net.*;
public class
```
(12)
```
    PosixPortDriver extends PortDriver {
```
(13)
```
    String[] serialPortNames;

    public PosixPortDriver(int options)
            throws PortIOException{
        info.driverRev = "V1.0";
        messageLevel = options & 7;

        if (messageLevel >= DEVALL)
            System.out.println(
                "Opening POSIX serial device");

        initDevice();
```
(14)
```
        portPrivate = new PortPrivate[
        info.serialCount + info.parallelCount];
        portState = new int[info.serialCount +
                            info.parallelCount];

        if (messageLevel >= DEV)
            System.out.println(
                "Manufacturer: " + info.manufacturer +
                ", Device: " + info.deviceId +
                ", Revision: " + info.deviceRev );

        if (messageLevel >= DEVALL)
            System.out.println("Posix Port opened");
    }

    public PosixPortDriver()
        throws PortIOException{
        this(0);
    }
```

Listing 11.2 (cont.) `PosixPortDriver` *Source*

```
void open(Port port) throws PortIOException {
    int portNumber = port.portNumber;
     // see which port type they're opening
    if (port instanceof SerialPort) {
        if ((portNumber < 0) ||
            (portNumber >= info.serialCount))
                throw new PortIOException(
                    "Serial port " + portNumber +
                    " out of range");
    } else {
        if ((portNumber < 0) ||
            (portNumber >= info.parallelCount))
                throw new PortIOException(
                    "Parallel port " + portNumber +
                    " out of range");

        // convert to index into portPrivate array
        portNumber += info.serialCount;
    }

    if (messageLevel >= PORTALL)
        System.out.println(
            "Open for port " + portNumber);

    // make sure we exclusively have the port
    synchronized(this) {
      while(portState[portNumber] !=
                            PORT_UNOPENED){
        if (portState[portNumber] == PORT_CLOSING)
            try {
               wait();
            } catch(InterruptedException e) {}
        else
            throw new PortIOException(
                "Port already in use");
      }
      portState[portNumber] = PORT_OPENING;
    }
    PosixPortPrivate spp =
        new PosixPortPrivate(portNumber, port);

    // let the super class do most of the work
    super.open(port, spp);
```

(15)

Listing 11.2 (cont.) `PosixPortDriver` *Source*

```
(16)          PosixPortReader reader =
                  new PosixPortReader(this, port);
(17)          reader.start();
(18)          spp.portReader = reader;
          }

      private void initDevice()
          throws PortIOException {
(19)          info.serialCount = 2;
              info.parallelCount = 0;

(20)          serialPortNames =
                      new String[info.serialCount];
(21)          serialPortNames[0] = "/dev/ttya";
(22)          serialPortNames[1] = "/dev/ttyb";

              info.manufacturer = "Kieran Devices, Inc.";
              info.deviceId = "KooLamBa II";
              info.deviceRev = "1.0";
          }
      }
```

The first thing to note is that `PosixPortDriver` does not implement `java.lang.Runnable` but simply extends `PortDriver` [12]. With this change, the `run` method goes. It will reappear in the `PosixPortReader` class below.

In line [13] a `String` array is declared. This array holds the names of tty devices on Solaris. These values are set in lines [21]-[22] after the array is allocated in [20]. The number of `String` slots allocated is determined by the number of serial ports supported by the driver and recorded in the `serial-Count` variable of the `PortDriverInfo` object in [19].

In line [15] the `PosixPortDriver` gets its reference to a `Posix-PortPrivate` instance. It is not enough to keep a reference to a `Port-Private` object, as in `TemplatePortDriver`. A `PosixPortPrivate` instance is created since its `portReader` field will need to be referenced [18] by `PosixPortDriver`.

Finally, the most interesting modification to the template driver involved in building `PosixPortDriver` is the creation of a thread object for receipt of incoming data. In line [16] an instance of `PosixPortReader` is created and then started in [17]. Since this code is contained in the `open` method of `PosixPortDriver`, a new read thread is created for each port opened on the driver. This `open` method does not get called directly by the programmer but, rather, by the constructor of the `Port` class. A `Port` object is created when the user creates a `SerialPort` object. Considered from the user level, this sequence is kicked off when a `SerialPort` object is created as in [6] on page 217.

The `PosixPortReader` Class

The gist of the foregoing discussion is that whenever a `SerialPort` is created, a thread is started for reading from that port. That thread is implemented as a `PosixPortReader` object, which we will look at now.

Listing 11.3 `PosixPortReader` *Source*

```
package portio;

public class PosixPortReader extends Thread {
```
(23)
```
    private native int jni_read(
                PosixPortDriver driver,
        int portNumber,
        byte[] buffer);
```

(24)
```
    private PosixPortDriver driver;
```
(25)
```
    private PortportObj;

    public PosixPortReader(PosixPortDriver d, Port p)
    {
        driver = d;
        portObj = p;
    }

    public void run(){
```
(26)
```
        int port = portObj.portNumber;
        int length = 0;
        byte data[] = new byte[256];

        if(driver.messageLevel >= driver.DEVALL)
            System.out.println(
                    "Receiver thread started");
```

Listing 11.3 (cont.) PosixPortReader *Source*

```
        try {
          while(true) {
(27)           length = jni_read(driver, port, data);

              if(driver.messageLevel == driver.ALL)
                System.out.println(
                    "Receive for port " + port);

              if(driver.portPrivate[port] != null)
                ((PosixPortPrivate)
(28)                (driver.portPrivate[port])).callback(
                              data, length);
          }
        } catch(PortIOException e) {
          System.out.println(
                "Receiver thread: " + e);
        }
      }
    }
```

The PosixPortReader is the last stop in the read sequence before going native. It declares the native method jni_read in line [23] and invokes this method in the read while loop at [27].

A PosixPortReader instance maintains a reference to a Posix-PortDriver object [24] and a Port object [25]. Both of these values are passed to the constructor. The Port object is used to retrieve the port number [26] with which this reader is associated. The port number, along with the PosixPortDriver reference, is passed to the native code and then passed on to the jni_read method. As we will see below, the native method uses these values to access the appropriate PosixPortPrivate object and, ultimately, the POSIX file descriptor for the port.

Although this is not specific to the POSIX implementation of the portio package, line [28] is worth looking at because it is the mechanism by which the PosixPortReader gets data back to the PosixPortPrivate object. After the native read, the incoming data should reside in the data variable and the number of bytes read is placed in the length variable. The invocation of the callback method copies the bytes in the data buffer to the per port input buffer maintained by the PosixPortPrivate object. From there it is available to user-initiated reads on the SerialPort object.

There is one more class definition we need to look at before exploring the implementation of the native methods.

The `PosixPortPrivate` Class

There has been much mention of the `PosixPortPrivate` class. This class extends `PortPrivate`. The class which extends `PortPrivate` is the workhorse of any `portio` implementation targeted for a specific platform. As an indication of this, consider that `PosixPortPrivate` declares eight native methods. `PosixPortPrivate` is pretty much a copy of `TemplatePortPrivate` with a `native` method call inserted into each of the methods that `TemplatePortPrivate` defines. Most of the interesting work, of course, is done by those `native` methods.

Two of the `abstract` methods from `PortPrivate`, `available` and `read`, are completely defined by `TemplatePortPrivate` and are used unchanged by `PosixPortPrivate`. If you are satisfied with `TemplatePortPrivate`'s buffered read scheme, you can simply use these methods as is if you extend `PortPrivate` for some other device.

Let's look at the code for `PosixPortPrivate`, paying special attention to how it fills the holes in the `TemplatePortPrivate` class.

Listing 11.4 `PosixPortPrivate` *Instance Variable Declarations*

```
       package portio;
       class PosixPortPrivate extends PortPrivate {
(29)           private PosixPortDriver driver;
               private boolean typeSerialPort;
               private boolean eof;
(30)           private SerialPortParams params;
(31)           private PortStatus stat;
(32)           private PortStatus lastStat;
(33)           private boolean statChgPending;
                 // output stuff
(34)           private byte outputBuffer[];
               private int outBufSize;
               private int outputCount;
               private boolean writeWaiting;
               // input stuff
(35)           private byte inputBuffer[];
               private static final int IN_BUF_SIZE = 2048;
               private int inputCount;
               private int inputFill;
               private int inputEmpty;
               private boolean readWaiting;
(36)           int fd;       // EJNI Addition
(37)           PosixPortReader        portReader;
```

Each `PosixPortPrivate` object maintains a reference to the `Port-Driver` [29] with which it is associated. In addition it maintains references to `SerialPortParams` [30] and `PortStatus` [31] objects. Additionally, it caches the `PortStatus` object [32] and maintains a flag [33] to determine whether or not to push changes to the port. All of these declarations are part of the template provided for extensions of `PortPrivate`.

The `PosixPortPrivate` object also maintains an output buffer [34] and an input buffer [35] and the various flags needed to track their state. The input buffer is filled by the `callback` method. The output buffer is filled by the user's invocation of the `SerialPort.write` method and emptied by the `startSend` method's call to the `native` method `jni_write`.

Lines [36]-[37] introduce two new member variables specific to the POSIX implementation. The first [36] stores the value of the POSIX file descriptor needed by most of the `native` methods. Line [37]associates with this port a `PosixPortReader` for listening for input. This thread is created and started by the `PosixPortDriver` as we saw in lines [16] and [17] on page 224.

Now let's move on to the `native` method declarations.

Listing 11.5 `PosixPortPrivate` native *Method Declarations*

```
private native int jni_open(String name)
   throws PortIOException;
private native int jni_close(int fd)
   throws PortIOException;
private native int jni_getBaudCode(int baud)
   throws PortIOException;
private native void jni_setParams(
   int fd, SerialPortParams params)
            throws PortIOException;
private native void jni_write(
   int fd, byte[] outputBuffer, int outputCount)
            throws PortIOException;
private native void jni_purge(
   int fd, boolean write, boolean read)
            throws PortIOException;
private native void jni_sendBreak(
   int fd, int duration)
            throws PortIOException;
private native void jni_flush(int fd)
            throws PortIOException;
```

These declarations speak for themselves. For each operation that needs to interact with the platform-specific software, a `native` method has been declared to do this work. The mapping between `native` methods and POSIX system calls is straightforward, jni_open maps to open, jni_close maps to close, etc.

Moving on to the constructor for the PosixPortPrivate class, we see it is responsible for saving the associated port number and driver in instance variables and allocating the input [39] and output [40] buffers for the port.

Listing 11.6 *Java Source for* PosixPortPrivate **Constructor**

```
PosixPortPrivate(int portNumber, Port port){
    this.portNumber = (byte)portNumber;
(38)    this.driver = (PosixPortDriver)port.driver;
    typeSerialPort = port instanceof SerialPort;
(39)    inputBuffer - new byte[IN_BUF_SIZE];

    outBufSize = 256;
(40)    outputBuffer = new byte[outBufSize];
    statChgPending = false;
}
```

Except for the cast in line [38], the constructor is unchanged from the TemplatePortPrivate. The choice for buffer sizes is entirely application dependent.

We see the first appearance of a native method call in PosixPortPrivate's open method. In [42] below, a call is made into native code to perform the open on the terminal device. We will see that the POSIX open requires a port name argument, so a String from the serialPortNames array [41] containing a tty device name is passed to jni_open.

Listing 11.7 *Java Source for* PosixPortPrivate open **Method**

```
synchronized void open() throws PortIOException {
    SerialPortParams startingParams =
                    new SerialPortParams();

    if(driver.messageLevel >= PortDriver.PORTALL)
        System.out.println( "open()" );
(41)    String portName =
        driver.serialPortNames[portNumber];
(42)    fd = jni_open(portName);
    if (fd < 0) {
        throw new PortIOException(
                "Unable to open file");
    }
```

Listing 11.7 (cont.) *Java Source for* PosixPortPrivate open *Method*

```
        if(typeSerialPort) {
            params = new SerialPortParams();
            params.outBaud = 0;
(43)        setParams(startingParams);

            stat = new SerialPortStatus();
            lastStat = new SerialPortStatus();

            ((SerialPortStatus)lastStat).RTS = true;
            ((SerialPortStatus)lastStat).DTR = true;
(44)        setStatus((SerialPortStatus)lastStat);
        }
        // if it's a parallel port, just create the
        // status objects
        else {
            stat = new ParallelPortStatus();
            lastStat = new ParallelPortStatus();
        }
        // Put something in place here to check status
    }
```

The rest of the open method remains unchanged from the TemplatePortPrivate class. For serial ports only, after the native method call returns, the port parameters [43] and status [44] are set using the setParams and setStatus methods.

The close method closes the physical device by making a call to the native method jni_close in line [46] but not until the reader thread is stopped in [45].

Listing 11.8 *Java Source for* PosixPortPrivate close *Method*

```
synchronized void close() throws PortIOException
{
    // stop any more data flow that may sneak in
    eof = true;
    notifyAll();

    if(driver.messageLevel >= PortDriver.PORTALL)
        System.out.println("close()");

(45)    portReader.stop();
(46)    jni_close(fd);
}
```

Note the use of the instance variable `fd` to supply `jni_close` with a POSIX file descriptor.

The `read` and `write` operations provided by the `TemplatePortPrivate` need no modification for the POSIX implementation of `portio`. Both implement a loop, waiting for data if necessary, which copies data from one buffer to another. The `write` method initiates a write to the native port with a call to the `startSend` method.

Listing 11.9 *Java Source for* `PosixPortPrivate startSend` *Method*

```
private synchronized void startSend()
        throws PortIOException{
    if(driver.messageLevel >= PortDriver.PORTALL)
        System.out.println("startSend()");
    jni_write(fd, outputBuffer, outputCount);

    outputCount = 0;
    if(writeWaiting)
        notifyAll();
}
```

(47)

The `write` method moves data from the buffer sent as an argument to the `outputBuffer` array and then calls `startSend`. It is the role of `startSend` to put data from `outBuffer` out to a port using a native write routine. You can see this in line [47] of `startSend`.

Although `read` and `write` do not require direct access to the native port, there are other methods defined by `PosixPortPrivate` that, like `open`, `close` and `startSend`, directly call `native` methods to do their work. This can be seen in Listing 11.10. As you can see, there is a direct mapping between the `PortPrivate` methods and the `native` methods.

Listing 11.10 *Java Source for* PosixPortPrivate flush, purge, sendBreak
   Methods

```
synchronized void flush(int waitTime)
           throws PortIOException{
   jni_flush(fd);
}

synchronized void purge(boolean write, boolean read)
                  throws PortIOException{
   if(write) {
      outputCount = 0;
   }

   if(read) {
      inputCount = 0;
      inputEmpty = inputFill;
   }
   jni_purge(fd, write, read);
}

synchronized void sendBreak(int duration)
              throws PortIOException {
   jni_sendBreak(fd, duration);
}
```

Two of these methods get right down to the business of calling a native
method. The third, purge, resets some flags governing the use of the input
and output buffers before calling jni_purge.

There are two more methods from TemplatePortPrivate that need
some flesh on their bones. The helper method getBaudCode simply takes as
input a portio-defined baud value and converts it to a value that is meaningful to the real device.

Listing 11.11 *Java Source for* PosixPortPrivate getBaudCode **Method**

```
private int getBaudCode(int baud)
        throws PortIOException{
   int ret_baud;
   if ((ret_baud = jni_getBaudCode(baud)) < 0)
      throw new PortIOException(
         "Baud rate " + baud + " not supported");

   return ret_baud;
}
```

(48)

getBaudCode makes a call to jni_getBaudCode [48] to convert an integer baud value (e.g. 9600) to the appropriate value to configure the targeted port. In the case of a POSIX tty port, the integer 9600 is translated to B9600, a constant whose value is defined in <termios.h>. This kind of translation is best done in native code so the appropriate macros and constants can be used without reproducing them in the Java code.

Finally, setParams needs to go out to native code to configure the physical port. That magic is done by a call to jni_setParams in line [49] below.

Listing 11.12 *Java Source for* PosixPortPrivate setParams *Method*

```
synchronized void setParams(
        SerialPortParams newParams)
                throws PortIOException {
    int inBaud = getBaudCode(newParams.inBaud);
    int outBaud = getBaudCode(newParams.outBaud);
    if(driver.messageLevel >= PortDriver.PORT)
        System.out.println("Port " + portNumber +
            " Output baud=" + outBaud +
            ", Input baud=" + inBaud);

(49)    jni_setParams(newParams);

    // the params must be valid, so copy them over
    params = (SerialPortParams) newParams.clone();
}
```

We will look at the magic of jni_setParams and all the other native methods declared by PosixPortPrivate in the next section.

The POSIX Native Code

We have done as much as we can in Java code. It is time to kiss purity goodbye and delve into the details of the implementation of the native methods required for the serial I/O.

The good news is that we will not look at all the native code that is required to target the portio package for POSIX tty I/O. There are quite a few helper routines that are specific to a POSIX platform and that shed no light on JNI functionality or its application. We will not spend any time on the details of this code although mention will be made of them when necessary. The context of the discussion will make clear their purpose. The complete code for these routines is available along with the *Essential JNI* example source at the Prentice-Hall ftp site.

We will look at the implementation of nine `native` methods. Table 11.1 gives a quick overview of these `native` methods along with the specific POSIX system calls they use.

Table 11.1 `native` *Methods and POSIX System Calls*

Native Method	Called By	Java Class	POSIX call(s)
jni_open	open	PosixPortPrivate	open tcgetattr tcsetattr
jni_close	close	PosixPortPrivate	close
jni_read	run	PosixPortReader	read
jni_write	startSend	PosixPortPrivate	write
jni_flush	flush	PosixPortPrivate	tcdrain
jni_sendBreak	sendBreak	PosixPortPrivate	tcsendbreak
jni_purge	purge	PosixPortPrivate	tcflush
jni_setParams	setParams	PosixPortPrivate	tcgetattr tcsetattr cfsetospeed cfsetispeed
jni_getBaudCode	getBaudCode	PosixPortPrivate	<termios.h>

In the case of `jni_getBaudCode` instead of POSIX calls, the include which contains the required macros is listed.

Let's take a look at each of the `native` methods required for the POSIX implementation of the `portio` package. *Advanced Programming in the UNIX Environment* by W. Richard Stevens provides a good description of the calls used in the following `native` methods.

Opening and Closing a `Port` Using POSIX System Calls

The `jni_open` and `jni_close` methods are responsible for opening and closing the POSIX tty device. Their interfaces were designed to map straight-forwardly to the POSIX `open` and `close` routines.

The `portio` API does not specify any input processing discipline, so `jni_open` is implemented here to open the tty device in "raw" mode. No character or line processing will be done within the native code. Any special character processing is deferred to the user level.

Listing 11.13 *Native Implementation for* PosixPortPrivate jni_open

```
JNIEXPORT jint JNICALL
Java_portio_PosixPortPrivate_jni_1open(
                JNIEnv *env,
                jobject thisObject,
                jstring name)
{
    int fd;
    jboolean isCopy;
    const char* nm =
    env->GetStringUTFChars(name, &isCopy);
    struct termios portSettings;

(50)    fd = open(nm, O_RDWR | O_NONBLOCK);
        if (fd < 0) {
            char * s = strerror(errno);
            throwPortioException(env, s);
            return -1;
        }
(51)    if (tcgetattr(fd, &portSettings) < 0) {
            char * s = strerror(errno);
            throwPortioException(env, s);
            return -1;
        }
(52)    portSettings.c_lflag &= ~(ICANON | ECHO | ISIG);
(53)    portSettings.c_iflag &=
                ~(BRKINT | ICRNL | INPCK | ISTRIP);
(54)    portSettings.c_cc[VMIN] = 0;
(55)    portSettings.c_cc[VTIME] = 0;
(56)    if (tcsetattr(fd, TCSANOW, &portSettings) < 0) {
            char * s = strerror(errno);
            throwPortioException(env, s);
            return -1;
        }
        if (isCopy == JNI_TRUE)
            env->ReleaseStringUTFChars(name, 0);
        return fd;
    }
```

After the open call at [50], the port attributes are fetched using tcgetattr [51]. The flags set in [52] suppress canonical input processing, character echo and signal generation. Canonical input processing means that the device handles the erase and kill characters and assembles the input characters into lines delimited by newline, end-of-line and end-of-file characters. If ISIG is set, each input character is checked against special control characters (INTR, QUIT and SUSP) and a signal is generated if there is a match. Since the ISIG flag is turned off, this checking will not be done by the device.

The two lines [54]-[55] determine the blocking behavior when the port is read. For the details on the range of possible values, see Stevens' book. The two values used above mean that a read on the tty will not block and will return the minimum of the number of bytes requested and the number of bytes available, including, possibly, zero. These values optimize for latency at the cost to throughput. These settings will vary based on the needs of your application.

Finally, when the device attribute flags are set appropriately, a tcsetattr call at line [56] pushes those values out to the device.

The jni_close method is straightforward. Since the PosixPortPrivate object keeps the file descriptor of the open port around, it can pass it to the native method which simply calls the POSIX close routine.

Listing 11.14 *Native Implementation of* PosixPortPrivate jni_close

```
JNIEXPORT jint JNICALL
Java_portio_PosixPortPrivate_jni_1close(
        JNIEnv *env, jobject thisObject, jint fd)
{
    return (close(fd));
}
```

Reading and Writing a Port Using POSIX System Calls

Before we look at the code for the Solaris implementation of jni_read, a review of the workings of portio is in order. Recall that each port has a PortPrivate object associated with it and this object maintains a private instance variable that stores the POSIX file descriptor of a tty device. Since jni_read is a PosixPortReader method, it has to call back into Java to get at the PortPrivate object. From this object it can retrieve the correct POSIX file descriptor. Keep this in mind when studying the following code for jni_read.

Listing 11.15 *Native Implementation of* PosixPortReader jni_read

```
JNIEXPORT jint JNICALL
Java_portio_PosixPortReader_jni_1read(
    JNIEnv *env, jobject thisReader,
    jobject driver, jint portNumber,
    jbyteArray buffer)
{
    int fd;
    jboolean isCopy;
    jclass portPrivateClz;
    jobject portPrivateObj;
    jobjectArray portPrivateArr;
    jbyte* buf;
(57)    jint cnt = env->GetArrayLength(buffer);

        // Get portPrivate array from PortDriver object
(58)    jclass portClz = env->GetObjectClass(driver);
(59)    jfieldID fid =
            env->GetFieldID(portClz,
                    "portPrivate",
                    "[Lportio/PortPrivate;");

(60)    portPrivateArr =
            (jobjectArray)env->GetObjectField(driver,fid);

        // Get port'h element from array
(61)    portPrivateObj = env->GetObjectArrayElement(
                                    portPrivateArr,
                                    portNumber);

        if (portPrivateObj == NULL) {
            throwPortioException(env,
                    "Attempt to write to closed port");
            return -1;
        }

        // Get fd field from PortPrivate
(62)    portPrivateClz =
            env->FindClass("portio/PosixPortPrivate");
(63)    fid = env->GetFieldID(portPrivateClz, "fd", "I");
(64)    fd = env->GetIntField(portPrivateObj, fid);
```

Listing 11.15 (cont.) *Native Implementation of* PosixPortReader jni_read

```
// Extract buffer of bytes from array object
(65)    buf = env->GetByteArrayElements(buffer, &isCopy)
        // Do a POSIX read!!!
(66)    int n_read = read(fd, buf, cnt);
        if (n_read < 0) {
           char* s = strerror(errno);
           throwPortioException(env, s);
        }
        if (isCopy == JNI_TRUE)
           env->ReleaseByteArrayElements(buffer, buf, 0);

        return n_read;
}
```

There is a lot going on in this code but not much new from a JNI perspective. There are two examples of the standard means of getting a field value from a Java object. First, in lines [58]-[60] the portPrivate array object is retrieved from the PortDriver object passed as an argument. Then, after a call in line [61] to get a reference to a PortPrivate object from the object array portPrivate, the fd field is pulled from that object in lines [62]-[64]. At this point, the integer value for the POSIX file descriptor is at hand and the only thing that needs to be done before the actual POSIX read is to get a contiguous representation of the byte array intended as the destination for the incoming data. This is accomplished in line [65].

Finally, in line [66] the POSIX read is executed using the file descriptor retrieved at [64], the buffer retrieved at [65], and the buffer size retrieved way back at [57].

The write operation is a bit simpler since, as an instance method of PosixPortPrivate, the file descriptor of the terminal device is passed to it as an argument.

Listing 11.16 *Native Implementation of* PosixPortPrivate jni_write

```
JNIEXPORT void JNICALL
Java_portio_PosixPortPrivate_jni_1write(
        JNIEnv *env,
        jobject thisObject,
        jint fd,
        jbyteArray buffer,
        jint cnt) {
    jboolean isCopy;
    jbyte* buf = NULL;
    buf = env->GetByteArrayElements(buffer, &isCopy);

    if (write(fd, buf, cnt) < 0) {
        char * s = strerror(errno);
        if (isCopy == JNI_TRUE)
          env->ReleaseByteArrayElements(
                              buffer, buf, 0);
        throwPortioException(env, s);
    }
    if (isCopy == JNI_TRUE)
        env->ReleaseByteArrayElements(buffer, buf, 0);
}
```

(67)

(68)

The POSIX write [68] is laid down only after a contiguous array of bytes is retrieved in line [67] from the byte array object passed as an argument to the native method.

A few words need to be said about the mysterious function throwPortioException. Most of the above native methods were declared as throwing a PortIOException and, in fact, may generate conditions that need to be handled by the Java code. To standardize this operation, the function throwPortioException was defined. The definition for this function appears below.

Listing 11.17 throwPortioException *Function Definition*

```
static jclass excClz = NULL;

void
throwPortioException(JNIEnv* env, char* s) {
    if (excClz == 0) {
        jclass clazz =
            env->FindClass("portio/PortIOException");
        excClz = (jclass) env->NewGlobalRef(clazz);
    }
    env->ThrowNew(excClz, s);
}
```

(69) appears at the `if (excClz == 0) {` line and **(70)** at the `excClz = (jclass) env->NewGlobalRef(clazz);` line.

In line [69] the code tests for a zero value of the static variable excClz and, if it is zero, sets the value in line [70]. Note, however, that it is set only after a global reference is created. Since we are trying to avoid a call to FindClass each time an exception is generated, we save away a class reference for PortIOException once and use it many times subsequently. Unlike field and method IDs, this value is an object reference and therefore subject to garbage collection if we do not make it a global. Hence, the call to NewGlobalRef in [70].

Using POSIX System Calls flush, sendBreak and purge

The flush, sendBreak and purge methods of thePosixPortPrivate class map quite well to POSIX functionality. Each of jni_flush, jni_sendBreak and jni_purge call only one POSIX routine and require no massaging of the native method arguments.

Listing 11.18 *Native Implementation of* jni_flush, jni_sendBreak, jni_purge

```
JNIEXPORT void JNICALL
Java_portio_PosixPortPrivate_jni_1flush(
    JNIEnv *env, jobject thisObject, jint fd) {
    if (tcdrain(fd) < 0) {
        char * s = strerror(errno);
        throwPortioException(env, s);
    }
}
```

Listing 11.18 (cont.) *Native Implementation of* `jni_flush`, `jni_sendBreak, jni_purge`

```
JNIEXPORT void JNICALL
Java_portio_PosixPortPrivate_jni_1sendBreak(
        JNIEnv *env,
        jobject thisObject,
        jint fd,
        jint duration) {
    if (tcsendbreak(fd, duration) < 0) {
        char * s = strerror(errno);
        throwPortioException(env, s);
    }
}
JNIEXPORT void JNICALL
Java_portio_PosixPortPrivate_jni_1purge(
        JNIEnv *env,
        jobject thisObject,
        jint fd,
        jboolean wr,
        jboolean rd)
{
    if (wr == JNI_TRUE) {
        if (tcflush(fd, TCOFLUSH) < 0) {
            char* s = strerror(errno);
            throwPortioException(env, s);
            return;
        }
    }
    if (rd == JNI_TRUE) {
        if (tcflush(fd, TCIFLUSH) < 0) {
            char* s = strerror(errno);
            throwPortioException(env, s);
            return;
        }
    }
}
```

Setting POSIX Device Parameters

The largest of the `native` methods is `jni_setParams`. The role of this method is to extract parameter values from the `SerialPortParams` object, translate them into values that are device-specific, and call the appropriate POSIX routine for settings those parameters on the terminal device.

The first of these steps is accomplished by the JNI function `Get<type>Field`. The transformation from `portio` values to device-specific values is performed by a set of helper functions that do not contain any JNI code. Finally, to set the parameters on the POSIX tty device, a call is made to tcsetattr.

The first step in the jni_setParams method is to retrieve the current settings from the port [71]. Later, new values will be OR'd with the current settings of orthogonal attributes so as to not overwrite them. The local variable portSettings will hold the existing values.

Listing 11.19 *Native Implementation of* PosixPortPrivate jni_setParams

```
JNIEXPORT void JNICALL
 Java_portio_PosixPortPrivate_jni_1setParams(
    JNIEnv *env,
    jobject thisObject,
    jint fd,
    jobject params)
{
    struct termios portSettings;
    jclass         paramClz
    jfieldID       fid;
    int            n_parity;
    paramClz = env->GetObjectClass(params);
    // Get current termios settings
(71)    if (tcgetattr(fd, &portSettings) < 0) {
        char* s = strerror(errno);
        throwPortioException(env, s);
        return;
    }
    // Char data size
(72)    fid = env->GetFieldID(paramClz, "charSize", "I");
(73)    int charSize = env->GetIntField(params, fid);
(74)    int n_csize = csizeXform(charSize);
    if (n_csize < 0) {
        throwPortioException(env,
              "Illegal data size value");
        return;
    }
```

After retrieving the field ID of the charSize field [72] of the SerialPortParams, object this section of code extracts the value of this field from the object [73]. The helper function csizeXform then translates that value into a value understood by tcsetattr.

In the following code segments, you will see the same pattern. First, parity values are translated.

Listing 11.20 *Translating Parity Values*

```
// Set parity
fid = env->GetFieldID(paramClz, "parity", "I");
int parity = env->GetIntField(params, fid);
n_parity = parityXform(env, paramClz, parity);
if (n_parity < 0) {
   throwPortioException(env, "Illegal parity value");
      return;
}
```

Next, the `portio` encoding for designating stop bits is translated to a value `tcsetattr` will understand.

Listing 11.21 *Translating Number of Stop Bits*

```
// Stop bits
fid = env->GetFieldID(paramClz, "framing", "D");
double stop = env->GetDoubleField(params, fid);
int n_stop = stopXform(stop);
if (n_stop < 0) {
   throwPortioException(env,
         "Illegal number of stop bits");
   return;
}
```

The `portio` flow control values are now translated to legal POSIX values by the following code.

Listing 11.22 *Translating Flow Control Parameters*

```
tcflag_t n_flow_cflags;
tcflag_t n_flow_iflags;
fid = env->GetFieldID(paramClz,"inFlowControl","I");
int inFlow = env->GetIntField(params, fid);
fid = env->GetFieldID(paramClz,
                     "outFlowControl", "I");
int outFlow = env->GetIntField(params, fid);
flowXform(env, paramClz, params, inFlow, outFlow,
               &n_flow_cflags,
               &n_flow_iflags,
               portSettings.c_cc);
```

In the next section of code, the ability to receive characters is determined by the value of the `receiveEnable` field of the `SerialPortParams` object. Then in [75] and all the values translated so far are set in the `portS-ettings` variable in preparation for the `tcsetattr` call.

Listing 11.23 *Setting POSIX Control Flags*

```
// Receive Enable
fid = env->GetFieldID(paramClz,
                "receiveEnable", "Z");
jboolean rcvEnable =
    env->GetBooleanField(params, fid);
int n_rcvEnable = rcvEnable ? CREAD : 0;
portSettings.c_cflag |= n_csize |
                        n_parity |
                        n_stop |
                        n_rcvEnable |
                        HUPCL |
                        n_flow_cflags;
portSettings.c_iflag |= n_flow_iflags;
```

(75) appears beside `portSettings.c_cflag |= n_csize |`

The final translation converts the `portio` representation for baud values to legal POSIX values. This conversion is done in line [77] after retrieving the current setting value from the `SerialPortParams` object [76].

Listing 11.24 *Translating Baud Rate*

```
// Input baud rate
fid = env->GetFieldID(paramClz, "inBaud", "I");
int inBaud = env->GetIntField(params, fid);
int n_baud = baudXform(inBaud);
cfsetispeed(&portSettings, n_baud);
// Output baud rate
fid = env->GetFieldID(paramClz, "outBaud", "I");
int outBaud = env->GetIntField(params, fid);
n_baud = baudXform(outBaud);
cfsetospeed(&portSettings, n_baud);
if (tcsetattr(fd, TCSANOW, &portSettings) < 0) {
    char * s = strerror(errno);
    throwPortioException(env, s);
}
```

(76) beside `int inBaud = env->GetIntField(params, fid);`
(77) beside `int n_baud = baudXform(inBaud);`
(78) beside `if (tcsetattr(fd, TCSANOW, &portSettings) < 0) {`

Finally, in [78] the new settings are pushed out to the terminal device.

It is worth calling attention to the various routines used for translating `SerialPortParam` values to `tcsetattr` values. These do most of the work within `jni_setParams` and will require the most attention when porting the above code to another serial device. These functions are:

Table 11.2 *Transformation Functions*

Function	Description
baudXform	Baud rate translation
csizeXform	Data size translation
flowXform	Flow control translation
stopXform	Stop bits translation
parityXform	Parity translation

The source for these routines, for both the POSIX and Win32 implementation of the `portio` package, is available with the *Essential JNI* example source at the Prentice-Hall `ftp` site.

`portio` *and Win32 COM*

At the Java level, the Win32 implementation of `portio` is very similar to the POSIX implementation. Three Java classes are required for support of the Win32 code. These classes parallel the three classes used in the POSIX implementation.

- `Win32PortDriver`
- `Win32PortPrivate`
- `Win32PortReader`

The main difference in these classes when compared to the POSIX implementation is `Win32PortPrivate`'s use of a long variable to store the Win32 `HANDLE` returned by `CreateFile` when opening the COM port. This change trickles down to the `native` methods in that they all, other than `jni_open`, take a `long` value representing the `HANDLE` object rather than an `int` file descriptor as an argument. For its part, `jni_open` returns the `long` value that represents the Win32 file `HANDLE`.

The structure of the Win32 native code also parallels that of the POSIX implementation. Table 11.3 reflects these parallels. For each device operation provided `Win32PortPrivate`, there is a call to a `native` method.

Let's take a look at the Win32 functions needed to support `portio` on a Win32 platform.

Table 11.3   *Native methods and Win32 calls*

Native Method	Called By	Java Class	Win32 call(s)
jni_open	open	Win32PortPrivate	CreateFile GetCommState SetCommState SetupComm ClearCommError SetCommTimeouts
jni_close	close	Win32PortPrivate	CloseHandle
jni_read	run	Win32PortReader	ClearCommError ReadFile
jni_write	startSend	Win32PortPrivate	WriteFile
jni_flush	flush	Win32PortPrivate	FlushFile- Buffers
jni_sendBreak	sendBreak	Win32PortPrivate	SetCommBreak ClearCommBreak
jni_purge	purge	Win32PortPrivate	PurgeComm
jni_setParams	setParams	Win32PortPrivate	GetCommState SetCommState
jni_getBaudCode	getBaud- Code	Win32PortPrivate	<winbase.h>

In addition to these above `native` methods, there are helper functions for doing conversion of `portio SerialPortParams` values into values meaningful to the Win32 device. The functions are named as in Table 11.2 on page 245.

The complete source code for the Win32 serial I/O version of the `portio` package is included with the example source.

Summary

This chapter has described a Java package that provides a Java API for serial and parallel I/O. The package, Central Data's `portio` package, defines the notion of a driver that supports multiple ports. The ports may be either serial or parallel. Using this package allows a Java application to interface with devices on different platforms using a consistent API.

The `portio` package does not include any native code for targetting a particular platform-specific device. It does, however, provide two classes, `TemplatePortDriver` and `TemplatePortPrivate`, which provide a skeletal implementation of buffered I/O on serial ports. These classes are a good start toward a platform-specific driver. They provide the basis for the classes developed in this chapter that do contain `native` methods.

To target the classes derived from the template classes for a particular system, `native` methods have to be implemented. This was the second major topic of this chapter. We saw, in detail, a POSIX implementation of the `portio` package. Three classes were introduced to do this. First, `TemplatePortDriver` and `TemplatePortPrivate` were modified and renamed to `PosixPortDriver` and `PosixPortPrivate`. In addition to these classes, `PosixPortReader` defined a thread object for reading a single port.

After we saw all the details of the POSIX implementation, we got a peek at a Win32 implementation of the `portio` package.

The complete code for both of these port drivers, along with the complete `portio` package from Central Data, is available from the Prentice-Hall `ftp` site. The `portio` package can also be obtained from the Central Data web site at www.`cd.com`.

Chapter 12

RUNNING THE JVM FROM A C/C++ APPLICATION

Becoming Native To This Place

Wes Jackson

Introduction

Up to this point, our entire focus has been on accessing native functionality from within Java code. A Java class declares `native` methods that are called by Java and execute native code. These `native` methods are written in C/C++ and use JNI calls to call back into the JVM when necessary.

There is a flip-side to all of this that allows you to create a JVM from within a C/C++ program. The most obvious application of this functionality is a web browser that supports the execution of Java applets. In general, an application that creates a JVM and is capable of loading and executing Java classes is said to be Java-enabled.

The piece of the JNI that defines this ability is the *Invocation API*. The Invocation API is a collection of JNI functions that allow you to embed the JVM into an arbitrary native application. Once this is done, the native application has the full power of the JVM at its disposal using the JNI calls we have seen in previous chapters.

In this chapter we will look at the functions that make up the Invocation API. This will be followed by an example of a C++ program that loads the JVM and invokes a Java method. Although the C++ code introduced focuses on the Invocation API, this in no way prevents the same piece of native code

249

from using all the other calls from the JNI. In fact, we will build upon the simple code that invokes the JVM, incrementally enhancing it using the Java reflection package (java.lang.reflect) to build a simple C language Java method invocation tool. Finally, we will look at how a Java-enabled application can register native methods that exist in a static library.

Before we look at the functions that comprise the Invocation API, let's look at an important data structure needed to kick off a JVM from within a native application.

JVM Initialization

In addition to the functions that comprise the API, there is a structure for initializing the JVM when it is created. Among other things, this structure presents the same configuration options as the command line flags to the Java interpreter. Before a JVM can be created, this structure must be set up. The structure name is JDK1_1InitArgs. It is defined in <jni.h>.

The JDK1_1InitArgs structure we will look at below is specific to JDK 1.1. In fact, the version field [1] on page 251 was introduced in JDK 1.1.2 to identify what the initialization structure looks like. The folks at Sun did not want to force every JVM vendor to adhere to a standard layout so they added the version field to allow programs to distinguish between different structures.

Further improvements to JVM initialization were added in JDK 1.2. See Chapter 15 for complete coverage of these enhancements if you are using JDK 1.2.

Before setting any values in a JDK1_1InitArgs structure, you will want to populate the structure with default values. To do this, set the version field and then call JNI_GetDefaultJavaVMInitArgs as below.

```
JDK1_1InitArgs vm_args;
vm_args.version = 0x00010001;
JNI_GetDefaultJavaVMInitArgs(&vm_args);
```

The use of the version field ensures you get what you expect. For applications embedding a 1.1 version of the JVM equal to or greater than 1.1.2, the version value must be set to 0x00010001. This value encodes the major version number in the higher sixteen bits and the minor version number in the lower sixteen bits.

The following listing shows what you can expect in a JDK 1.1 initialization structure.

Listing 12.1 *The JVM Initialization Structure*

```
     typedef struct JDK1_1InitArgs {
(1)       jint version;
(2)       char **properties;
          jint checkSource;
          jint nativeStackSize;
          jint javaStackSize;
          jint minHeapSize;
          jint maxHeapSize;
          jint verifyMode;
          char *classpath;

(3)       jint (JNICALL *vfprintf)
              (FILE *fp, const char *format, va_list args);
(4)       void (JNICALL *exit)(jint code);
(5)       void (JNICALL *abort)();

          jint enableClassGC;
          jint enableVerboseGC;
          jint disableAsyncGC;
          jint verbose;
          jboolean debugging;
          jint debugPort;
     } JDK1_1InitArgs;
```

The best way to understand the meaning of the bulk of these fields is in the familiar context of the command line flags for the Java interpreter.

Table 12.1 displays the fields of the `JDK1_1InitArgs` structure side-by-side with the corresponding command line flags.

Table 12.1 `JDK1_1InitArgs` *Fields*

Field Name	java Flag	Description
nativeStackSize	-ss	Maximum stack size for native threads
javaStackSize	-oss	Maximum stack for any JVM thread
minHeapSize	-ms	Initial heap size
maxHeapSize	-mx	Maximum heap size
verifyMode=0	-noverify	Do not verify byte code when loading
verifyMode=1	-verifyremote	Verify byte code only on remote load
verifyMode=2	-verify	Verify loading of all byte code
classpath	-classpath	Local directories for loading classes
enableClassGC	-noclassgc	Enable/disable class garbage collection
enableVerboseGC	-verbosegc	Enables reporting of garbage collection activity
disableAsyncGC	-noasyncgc	Disable asynchronous garbage collection
verbose	-verbose or -v	Reports JVM information, including all class loads
debugging	-debug	Allow remote debugging of JVM

Stack and Heap Values

Both Solaris and Win32 versions of the JVM have the same default values for stack and heap memory.

Table 12.2 *JVM Memory Default Values*

Description	Size(bytes)
Maximum stack size for native threads	128K
Maximum stack for any JVM thread	400K
Initial heap size	1024K
Maximum heap size	16384K

Garbage Collection Settings

When the JVM is started the user has some control over the behavior of the garbage collector. Table 12.3 describes the aspects of garbage collection that can be manipulated via the JDK1_1InitArgs structure and lists default values.

Table 12.3 *Default GC Values*

Description	Value
Enable/disable class garbage collection	On
Enables reporting of gc activity	Off
Disable asynchronous garbage collection	Off

These settings apply to both Solaris and Win32 versions of the JDK JVM.

Load Verification Mode

By default, the JVM only verifies the byte code values of classes loaded from a remote source (verify=1).

The classpath Field

Care must be taken when setting the classpath field. Be sure to include the location of the class, zip, or jar files that come with the JDK distribution. Just like the classpath command flag, the location of *all* the necessary classes must appear in the classpath field. In versions of the JDK prior to 1.1.4, the default value of the classpath field was NULL. In 1.1 versions of the JDK later than 1.1.4, JNI_GetDefaultJavaVMInitArgs returns a value in the classpath field that contains the current CLASSPATH environment setting.

You need to be mindful of the correct string syntax for the classpath field. UNIX and Win32 systems require a different file name separator value as well as a different separator between directory or zip file names. The correct syntax for a Win32 JVM is shown below.

Listing 12.2 *Win32 Syntax for the* classpath *Field Value*

```
JDK1_1InitArgs vm_args;
vm_args.version = 0x00010001;
    JNI_GetDefaultJavaVMInitArgs(&vm_args);

vm_args.classpath =
        ".;\\jdk\\classes;\\jdk\\lib\\classes.zip"
```

Backslashes separate the components of a path name and semicolons separate each directory or zip file name.

The UNIX syntax follows.

Listing 12.3 *UNIX Syntax for* `classpath` *Field Value*

```
JDK1_1InitArgs vm_args;
vm_args.version = 0x00010001;
    JNI_GetDefaultJavaVMInitArgs(&vm_args);


vm_args.classpath =
            ".:/jdk/classes:/jdk/lib/classes.zip"
```

Under UNIX, the path will contain forward slashes and colons.

In all versions of the JDK prior to 1.1.4, the `classpath` value returned by `JNI_GetDefaultJavaVMInitArgs` was NULL. That meant, as in the examples above, you needed to hardcode all of the system class file locations in your application. In JDK 1.1.4, `JNI_GetDefaultJavaVMInitArgs` returns a string containing all the relevant system class directories and zip files. When linking with the JDK 1.1.4 `javai` library, you will want to catenate `classpath` with the value returned by `JNI_GetDefaultJavaVMInitArgs`. The following example offers one approach.

Listing 12.4 *Setting* `classpath` *Under JDK 1.1.4*

```
vm_args.version = 0x00010001;
JNI_GetDefaultJavaVMInitArgs(&vm_args);

int len = strlen(MY_CLASSPATH) +
        strlen(vm_args.classpath) + 1;
char * newcp = (char*) malloc(len * sizeof(char));
strcpy(newcp, MY_CLASSPATH);
strcat(newcp, vm_args.classpath);
vm_args.classpath = newcp;
// ...
free(newcp);
```

The `properties` Field (JDK 1.1.2 and Greater)

The `properties` field of the `JDK1_1InitArgs` structure ([2] on page 251) provides a mechanism by which the native application can set the property list of the JVM. The property list is maintained by the `java.lang.System` class.

The `properties` field is a pointer to a null-terminated list of character strings. Each string has the format

```
key=value
```

where `key` is a property name, either system-defined or user-defined, and `value` is the value for that property.

If you need to start the JVM at system boot, you could use the `proper-ties` field to specify a working directory since generally such system loaded services are run from some standard location that may not be convenient.

To do this you would define an array of strings, say:

```
char* properties[] = {
"  user.dir=c:\\home\\rgordon",
    NULL
};

//...
vm_args.properties = properties;
```

Note that the syntax of the `user.dir` string is platform-dependent. Also, the NULL entry at the end of the array is required.

For a list of the system-defined properties, see the `javadoc` documentation pages for the `getProperties` method of the `java.lang.System` class.

Application Hooks for the JVM

There are three fields within the initialization structure that can be used to provide a call back from the JVM into the native application. Each of these fields allows you to provide a function address to the JVM so that it can call back into native code for notification or output.

The `vfprintf` field ([3] on page 251) points to a function that the JVM is to use for printing its verbose output when loading classes. The function must adhere to the C library variable arguments format and return a `jint` value. Below is a possible implementation for a function to print on the JVM's behalf. We will see this code in action in the next section.

Listing 12.5 *A* `vfprintf` *Function for the JVM*

```
// <stdio.h> included above for vfprintf
static FILE * fp = NULL;
static jboolean triedOnce = JNI_FALSE;

jint
(JNICALL y_fprintf)(FILE *, const char *format,
                                va_list args)
{
    jint rc;

    if (fp == NULL) {
        if (triedOnce == JNI_TRUE)
            return -1;// fopen failed previously
        triedOnce = JNI_TRUE;
        if ((fp = fopen("vm.out", "w")) == NULL)
            return -1;
    }
    rc = vfprintf(fp, format, args);
    fflush(fp);
    return rc;
}
```

The lines `(6)` and `(7)` mark the two static declarations above.

When the value of the `vfprintf` field is set to the address of the `y_fprintf` function, the JVM will use `y_fprintf` for printing its verbose output. The above code will cause the JVM's verbose output to be written to the file `vm.out`. To elicit this behavior from the JVM, set the `vfprintf` and `verbose` fields as below.

Listing 12.6 *To Enable Printing on the JVM's Behalf*

```
JDK1_1InitArgsvm_args;
vm_args.version = 0x00010001;
    JNI_GetDefaultJavaVMInitArgs(&vm_args);

vm_args.verbose = JNI_TRUE;
vm_args.vprintf = y_fprintf;
```

The native application can also supply the JVM with functions to be called upon exit from the JVM and under unusual termination conditions. These fields are used just like the `vfprintf` field and appear in lines [4] and [5] on page 251. The exit handler will only be called if the JVM is exited with a call to `System.exit`. Listing 12.7 shows a simple implementation of an exit callback.

Listing 12.7 *An Exit Function for the JVM*

```
void (JNICALL y_exit)(jint code) {
// Do whatever cleanup may be need in app...
    if (fp == NULL) {
        if (triedOnce == JNI_TRUE)
            return;
        triedOnce = JNI_TRUE;
        fp = fopen("vm.out", "w");
        if (fp == NULL)
            return;
    }
    fprintf(fp, "Exiting JVM...%d\n\n", code);
}
```

This function relies on the `static` variables declared above ([6]-[7] on page 256) to determine if it has a open `FILE` pointer. If so, it reports the destruction of the JVM.

Invocation API Overview

The Invocation API consists of only a few function calls. It is a small interface that delivers the full power of the JVM. With the Invocation API you can:

- Initialize the JVM arguments.
- Load a JVM into your application.
- Attach/detach subsequently created native threads to the JVM. In JDK 1.2, there is the ability to test whether a native thread is attached to the JVM.
- Unload or destroy the JVM, properly cleaning up and freeing any system resources.

One of the side effects of creating the virtual machine is that you are provided with a `JNIEnv` pointer. With this pointer, you may access the entire suite of JNI functions.

InvokeMain: Creating a JVM

The best way to understand the workings of the Invocation API functions is to take a look at the canonical example for loading a JVM into a native application. Appendix A provides a complete description of the Invocation API functions. Here we will just see how they are used.

Listing 12.8 *Loading the JVM Into a Native Application*

```c
#include <stdlib.h>
#include <string.h>
#include <jni.h>

char* properties[] = {
    "user.dir=c:\\home\\rgordon",
    NULL
}

#define MY_CLASSPATH".;..\\..\\..\\classes;"

int main(int argc, char *argv[]) {
    JNIEnv *env;
    JavaVM *jvm;
    int i;
    JDK1_1InitArgs vm_args;
    jint ret;
    jmethodID mid;
    vm_args.version = 0x00010001;
    JNI_GetDefaultJavaVMInitArgs(&vm_args);

    // Combine my classpath with system's
    int len = strlen(MY_CLASSPATH) +
            strlen(vm_args.classpath) + 1;

    char * newcp = (char*) malloc(len * sizeof(char));

    strcpy(newcp, MY_CLASSPATH);
    strcat(newcp, vm_args.classpath);

    vm_args.classpath = newcp;
    vm_args.properties = properties;
    vm_args.vfprintf = y_fprintf;
    vm_args.exit = y_exit;
    ret = JNI_CreateJavaVM(&jvm, &env, &vm_args);
    if (ret < 0) {
        fprintf(stderr,
            "Can't create JVM. Error: %ld\n", ret);
        return(1);
    }
```

(8) — `JNI_GetDefaultJavaVMInitArgs(&vm_args);`

(9) — `vm_args.classpath = newcp;`

(10) — `vm_args.properties = properties;`

(11) — `vm_args.vfprintf = y_fprintf;`

(12) — `vm_args.exit = y_exit;`

(13) — `ret = JNI_CreateJavaVM(&jvm, &env, &vm_args);`

Listing 12.8 (cont.) *Loading the JVM Into a Native Application*

```
(14)        if (argc < 2) {
                printf("No class specified. Exiting...\n\n");
                return(-1);
            }

            jstring jstr = env->NewStringUTF("");
(15)        jobjectArray str_array =
                    env->NewObjectArray(argc-2,
                        env->FindClass("java/lang/String"),
                        jstr);
(16)        for (i - 2; i < argc; i++) {
                jstr = env->NewStringUTF(argv[i]);
                if (jstr == 0) {
                    fprintf(stderr, "Out of memory\n");
                    return(1);
                }
(17)            env->SetObjectArrayElement(str_array,
                                            i-2, jstr);
            }
(18)        jclass clazz =
                env->FindClass(dotsToSlashes(argv[1]));
            if (clazz == 0) {
                fprintf(stderr,
                    "Can't locate the %s class. Exiting...\n",
                    argv[1]);
                return(1);
            }
(19)        mid = env->GetStaticMethodID(clazz, "main",
                            "([Ljava/lang/String;)V");
            if (mid == 0) {
                fprintf(stderr,
                "Can't locate the main method. Exiting...\n");
                return(1);
            }
(20)        env->CallStaticVoidMethod(clazz, mid, str_array);
(21)        jvm->DestroyJavaVM();
            return(0);
        }
```

This code is meant to run from the shell on a UNIX system or as a console application on a Win32 system. It takes an arbitrary number of arguments but requires at least one [14]. Let's pause here for a platform-specific word of warning.

Platform Specific Note Solaris

When building a Java-enabled application on Solaris and linking against the green threads version of `libjava.so`, you must defer system calls until after the call to `JNI_CreateJavaVM`. This is because the user-level threads package in `libjava.so` (green threads) defines its own system calls, e.g. `open`, `close`. The table of pointers to the real system calls does not get initialized until after the call to `JNI_CreateJavaVM`.

To avoid this problem altogether requires the use of the native threads package on the Solaris 2.6 operating system.

See

`http://java.sun.com/products/jdk/1.2/docs/index.html`

for information on the Solaris native threads package.

We will now return to our regularly scheduled prose.

The required argument to `main` is expected to be a fully-qualified class name in dot notation. The helper function `dotsToSlashes` converts from the dot notation to the slash notation required by `FindClass` [18]. Any additional arguments are converted to Java `String` objects and passed as arguments to the `main` method using `str_array` in [20].

This application invokes the `static main` method of the class whose name is passed as an argument. Invoking a `static` method inside a Java class is old hat by now. The `FindClass`/`GetStaticMethodID`/`CallStatic<type>Method` triumvirate ([18], [19], [20]) have served us well in this role.

Before the `main` method is called in [20], any command line arguments are packaged in a Java object array allocated at [15] and populated in the following `for` loop at [16] using `SetObjectArrayElement` [17].

To call these familiar methods, we need a JNI interface pointer through which we can access the JNI function table. The call to `JNI_CreateJavaVM` [13] provides the `JNIEnv` pointer.

The `JNIEnv` pointer is only a side-effect of the real job of `JNI_CreateJavaVM`. As its name suggests, this function creates a Java Virtual Machine. Using the arguments initialized with default values in line [8] and customized in [9]-[12], `JNI_CreateJavaVM` creates a new native thread and loads the JVM into it. With the `JNIEnv` pointer provided by this call, access to all the JNI functions and, consequently, all the power of the JVM is available to the native application.

The call to JNI_CreateJavaVM also returns a JVM pointer into a user-supplied variable, jvm. This value can be used to attach and detach native threads to the JVM and, thereby, give them access to a JNI interface pointer. We will see more about this in Chapter 13.

Before we get ahead of ourselves, mention must be made of Destroy-JavaVM at line [21]. Only the main thread may call DestroyJavaVM. And, in JDK 1.1.1, the main thread must be the only thread running when it makes the call. JDK 1.1.2 loosens this restriction. If DestroyJavaVM is called when more than one user thread is running, the JVM waits until the calling thread is the only user thread and then destroys itself.

A Java-enabled Application in Action

To explicate the foregoing discussion, let's take a look at the actual behavior of a Java-enabled application and its JVM.

Consider the simple Java application shown in Listing 12.9.

Listing 12.9 *A Simple Java Application*

```
package test;
public class InvokeMain {
    public static void main(String[] args) {
        System.out.println("Hello from InvokeMain");
        String cwd = System.getProperty("user.dir");
        System.out.println("cwd = " + cwd);
        System.out.println("Arguments:");
        for (int i = 0; i < args.length; i++) {
            System.out.println(
                "arg[" + i + "]=" + args[i]);
        }
        System.exit(5);
    }
}
```

(22)

Assume the C code fromListing 12.9 was built as the executable invokeMain then executed from the command shell as shown below.

▸ **• User Input**   **Running a Java-Enabled Application**

% **invokeMain test.Main one two three**

This would result in the main method [22] of the InvokeMain class to run within the JVM. The following output to standard out would be generated.

> **• Program Output** **Running** invokeMain

```
Hello from InvokeMain
cwd = c:\home\rgordon
Arguments:
arg[0]=one
arg[1]=two
arg[2]=three
```

Two observations are worth making:

- The user.dir property was properly changed via the properties field in the JDK1_1InitArgs structure.

- The arguments are properly passed from the command line to the JVM and then to the Java method.

Finally, the file vm.out in the current directory contains the line:

```
Exiting JVM...5
```

This value is written to the output file by the y_exit routine in Listing 12.7.

Expanding the Java code a bit illustrates the behavior of Destroy-JavaVM using JDK 1.1.2. If a thread is started from the main method and continues executing after the main thread, DestroyJavaVM will not take down the JVM as long as the subordinate thread is running. Consider the Java class InvokeWithThread.

Listing 12.10 *A* main *Method That Creates a Thread*

```
package test;
import java.lang.Exception;

public class InvokeWithThread {
    public static void main(String[] args) {
        System.out.println(
                    "Hello from InvokeWithThread");
        sleepyThread s = new sleepyThread();
        s.start();
    }
}
class sleepyThread extends Thread {
    public void run() {
        int cnt = 0;
        try {
            while (cnt < 10) {
                sleep(1000, 0);
                System.out.println("sleepy running...");
                cnt++;
            }
        } catch (Exception e) {}
    }
}
```

(23)

(24)

The major difference between this class and the one from Listing 12.9 is that the main method here creates and starts a thread. Immediately after starting the thread, it terminates. Because of the delay loop at [24], the instance of sleepThread is still running when the main method completes. When main completes, the JNI call which invoked it (see [20] on page 259) returns and DestroyJavaVM is called ([21] on page 259).

However, the output below confirms that the sleepyThread completes its napping.

• Program Output InvokeWithThread **under JDK 1.1.2 or Later**

```
Hello from InvokeWithThread
sleepy running...
sleepy running...
sleepy running...
sleepy running...
sleepy running...
sleepy running...
```

As advertised, the `DestroyJavaVM` call does not terminate the JVM until all user threads complete. Again, this includes `native` methods that may have attached to the JVM using `AttachCurrentThread`. Note, however, that a `System.exit` does not appear in the `main` method of `InvokeWithThread`. If it did, `sleepyThread`'s nap would be truncated.

Building a Java-Enabled Application

When building a C/C++ application that loads the JVM, the executable must be linked with the JDK library that implements the Java interpreter. The details differ across platforms.

The important thing to keep in mind is that, in any case, the library that implements the JVM must be linked with your application. We will look at how that is done on Solaris and Win32 systems.

A Solaris Java-Enabled Build

Below is the compile and link line from a Solaris makefile. This command builds the source `invokeMain.c` and links it with the requisite JDK library.

Listing 12.11 *A Solaris makefile for a Java-Enabled Application*

```
.cc.o:
            ${CC} ${CCFLAGS} ${INCLUDES} -c $<

PROG=invokeMain
OS=solaris
PLATFORM=sparc
THREADS=green_threads
JDK_INCLUDES=-I${JDK_HOME}/include\
            -I${JDK_HOME}/include/${OS}
INCLUDES= ${JDK_INCLUDES}

JAVALIB=java
LIB_PATH=${JDK_HOME}/lib/${PLATFORM}/${THREADS}

OBJS= invokeMain.o
C_SRC= invokeMain.c

all: ${OBJS}
        ${CC} -g -o ${PROG} ${OBJS} -L${LIB_PATH} \
            -l${JAVALIB} \
            -R${LIB_PATH}
```

(25)

(26)

(27)

(28)

(29)

(30)

(31)

The relevant library on Solaris is `libjava.so` [28] which lives in the directory named by the value of `LIB_PATH` [29]. The `LIB_PATH` variable, as well as being defined by the `JDK_HOME` value, is dependent on both your platform, in this case `sparc` [25], and the type of threads the JVM employs, here `green_threads` [26].

The link command at line [30] names `LIB_PATH` as the directory to search for the library named by the `JAVALIB` variable. Since this is a shared object library, searched for and loaded at runtime, the `-R` flag at [31] also names `LIB_PATH`.

Also remember that the appropriate directories for picking up `<jni.h>` and `<jni_md.h>` need to be named when compiling. This is assured by definition of `JDK_INCLUDES` in line [27] and its use in the compile target.

A Win32 Java-Enabled Build

We will take a look at building a Java-enabled console application for a Win32 system within the context of Microsoft Developer Studio. Four steps are required to properly link the JVM to your console application.

1. Create your project as a Win32 Console Application.

2. In the Project->Settings dialog, select the General Category under the Link tab. Add `javai.lib` to the list of Object/Library modules.

3. In the Tools->Options dialog, select the Directories tabs. Choose "Library files" in the Show Directories ComboBox. Add the value `$JDK_HOME\lib` to the list of library search directories.

4. In the Project->Settings dialog, select the Preprocessor under the C/C++ tab. Add `$JDK_HOME\include` and `$JDK_HOME\include\win32` to the list of "Additional include directories."

Following these steps will take care of building your application properly. For it to run, you need the directory that contains the file `javai.dll` in your PATH environment variable.

The Invocation API and Reflection

The Java Core Reflection API can come in handy within a Java-enabled application. You may want more information about a class or object than is available from the JNI. By using the JNI to access the Java reflection (or introspection) classes, you can pull apart a Java class, learning the names and types of its data fields as well as the names, return types and parameter types of its methods.

An example of an application that may need access to this type of information is a debugger that provides a class inspector. If this debugger were written in Java, the `java.lang.reflect` package could be used directly. On the other hand, if the debugger were written in C/C++ and used the Invocation API to get and set values in Java objects and display information about a Java class, it would need to access the reflection package using the JNI.

We will take just a peek at how that could be done. To do so, we will start with the central example of this chapter, Listing 12.9 on page 261, and augment it.

Listing 12.9 presented a native application capable of invoking the static main method with a class whose name is passed as an argument. Any additional arguments passed on the command line were handed to main in a String array.

In this next example, we will extend the functionality of our Java-enabled application to allow invocation of any method, static or non-static, the types of whose arguments are limited to the Java primitive types and java.lang.String. Granted, this is not a generalized invocation that would be required by a debugger. It is, rather, an illustration of how to use the Core Reflection API together with the Invocation API and JNI.

Since the overall structure of using the Invocation API and the JNI to invoke a method is well-understood, we will look first at the use of the Core Reflection API and JNI. The purpose here is not a full discussion of the Core Reflection API. For that you can consult the javadoc delivered with the JDK. Rather, we will look at how a subset of the reflection package is made available to a native application and used to support the mini-invoker.

JNI and Reflection

To support the more general, not but completely general, invocation tool, some JNI code is needed which mimics the operations provided by the reflection API. Our mini-invoker will require at least two arguments, the name of a class and one of its methods. It will then need to map the method name onto an object that describes that method.

The reflection package provides a Class.getMethods method that returns an array of Method objects. This array can be searched, comparing the name passed as an argument to the invoker with Method.getName to determine which Method object describes the method named by the input to the mini-invoker.

We will look at these types of operations in detail here.

To support the mini-invoker, we will need functionality from three[1] java.lang.reflect classes. For convenience, we will provide that functionality in native code. This is done with three C++ classes whose names reflect their reflection package counterparts. The header files for these classes appear in Listing 12.12.

1.Since the Java Core Reflection documentation states that the class Class "properly belongs in the java.lang.reflect package," it will be treated as such for this discussion.

Listing 12.12 *Interface for C++ Reflection Classes*

```
class JClass {
public:
   static jobjectArray getMethods(JNIEnv*, jclass);
   static const char* toString(JNIEnv*, jclass);
   static char* typeToSig(JNIEnv*,
                          const char*, int*);
};

class Method {
public:
   static jobjectArray
      getParameterTypes(JNIEnv* env, jobject);
   static const char* getName(JNIEnv*, jobject);
   static int      getModifiers(JNIEnv*, jobject);
   static jclass   getReturnType(JNIEnv*, jobject);
};

class Modifier {
public:
   static jboolean isStatic(JNIEnv*, int);
};
```

With the exception of typeToSig, each method name is borrowed as is from the Core Reflection API. Ignoring the JNIEnv pointer, and translating to JNI native types, the C++ methods above also have the same signature as their counterparts in the Core Reflection API.

typeToSig is a helper function whose implementation we will not see. It merely does the translation from Java type to signature as described in Table 4.7 on page 59.

The implementation of these classes offers further proof of their direct relationship to the Core Reflection API. Take a look.

Listing 12.13 *Implementation of C++ Reflection Classes*

```
// Class JClass
jobjectArray
JClass::getMethods(JNIEnv* env, jclass clzObject) {
   jclass classClz = env->GetObjectClass(clzObject);
   jmethodID mid = env->GetMethodID(classClz,
            "getMethods",
            "()[Ljava/lang/reflect/Method;");
   return (jobjectArray) env->CallObjectMethod(
                         clzObject, mid, NULL);
}
```

Listing 12.13 (cont.) *Implementation of C++ Reflection Classes*

```cpp
const char*
JClass::toString(JNIEnv* env, jclass clazz) {
   jboolean isCopy;
   jstring jstr;
   jclass classClz = env->GetObjectClass(clazz);
   jmethodID mid = env->GetMethodID(classClz,
            "toString", "()Ljava/lang/String;");
   str= (jstring)env->CallObjectMethod(
                  clazz, mid, 0);
   return env->GetStringUTFChars(str, &isCopy);
}
// Method Class
jobjectArray
Method::getParameterTypes(
        JNIEnv* env, jobject method) {
   jclass clazz = env->GetObjectClass(method);
   jmethodID mid = env->GetMethodID(clazz,
                  "getParameterTypes",
                  "()[Ljava/lang/Class;");
   return (jobjectArray) env->CallObjectMethod(
                           method, mid, NULL);
}

const char*
Method::getName(JNIEnv* env, jobject method) {
   jboolean isCopy;
   jstring name;
   jclass clazz = env->GetObjectClass(method);
   jmethodID mid = env->GetMethodID(clazz,
                  "getName",
                  "()Ljava/lang/String;");
   name = (jstring) env->CallObjectMethod(
                           method, mid, NULL);
   return env->GetStringUTFChars(name, &isCopy);
}
```

Listing 12.13 (cont.) *Implementation of C++ Reflection Classes*

```
int
Method::getModifiers(JNIEnv* env, jobject method) {
    jclass clazz = env->GetObjectClass(method);
    jmethodID mid =
        env->GetMethodID(clazz,
                         "getModifiers", "()I");
    return env->CallIntMethod(method, mid, NULL);
}


jclass
Method::getReturnType(JNIEnv* env, jobject method) {
    jclass clazz = env->GetObjectClass(method);
    jmethodID mid = env->GetMethodID(clazz,
                        "getReturnType",
                        "()Ljava/lang/Class;");
    return (jclass) env->CallObjectMethod(method,
                        mid, NULL);
}
// Modifier Class
jboolean
Modifier::isStatic(JNIEnv* env, int mods) {
    jclass clazz = env->FindClass(
                        "java/lang/reflect/Modifier");
    jmethodID mid = env->GetStaticMethodID(
                        clazz, "isStatic", "(I)Z");
    return env->CallStaticBooleanMethod(
                        clazz, mid, mods);
}
```

In each of these methods, the "get class reference, get method ID, invoke method" idiom is employed. What is of interest is how these C++ functions bring introspection capabilities to a native application. Now we can look at our mini-invoker and begin to make sense of it. There are still some stones to turn over but we will do that after we step back and look at the big picture.

Before we jump into the code, a summary of how reflection is used is presented.

- `JClass::getMethods` is used to return an array of `Method` objects from the `Class` object whose method we will invoke.

- `Method::getName` is used when iterating through the list of method objects to look for a match against the requested method.

- `Method::getParameterTypes` is used to retrieve from a `Method` object an array of `Class` objects describing its parameter types and a single `Class` object describing its return type. Both reference types and primitive types are defined by a `Class` object.

- `Method::getReturnType` is used to return a `Class` object describing the return type of a method. Both reference types and primitive types are defined by a `Class` object.

- `Method::getModifiers` returns the access modifiers of a `Method` object.

- `Modifier::isStatic` reports whether a `Method` object is `static` on not.

These are the central pieces of the reflection interface. There is also a significant routine, `buildArgs`, which constructs a `jvalue` array for handing off to a call to a JNI method invocation function. Recall that this array is one of the ways in which a JNI method invocation function can pass arguments to a Java method.

One of the arguments to `buildArgs` is the `Method` object array returned by `Class::getMethods`. Another is the `char**` array passed in on the command line. The strings in this array will be used to build the `jvalue` array that will be passed to the Java method. In addition to building the `jvalue` array, `buildArgs` also constructs a signature string for subsequent use by either `GetMethodID` or `GetStaticMethodID`. The source for `buildArgs` appears below.

Listing 12.14 *Building* `jvalue` *Argument Array*

```
char*
buildArgs(JNIEnv *env,
```
(32)
```
        jobjectArray params, jint nParams,
```
(33)
```
        jvalue* argValues, char** argv) {
        char* typeSig =
                (char*) malloc(sizeof(char) * 128);
        int strCnt = 0;
        int reAllocCnt = 2;
        int i;
        char* val;
```

Listing 12.14 (cont.) *Building* jvalue *Argument Array*

```
        if (typeSig == NULL)
           return NULL;

        memset((void*) typeSig, 0, sizeof(char) * 128);
        for (i = 0; i < nParams; i++) {
           jclass pClz =
           (jclass)env->GetObjectArrayElement(params, i);

           const char* tName = JClass::toString(env,
                                                pClz);

        if (strCnt > 100) {
               int sz = reAllocCnt * 128;
               typeSig = (char*) realloc((void^)typeSig,
                                         sz);
               reAllocCnt++;
               if (typeSig == NULL)return NULL;
        }
        if (strncmp(tName, "class", 5) == 0) {
           argValues[i].l =
               (jobject) env->NewStringUTF(argv[i]);
           strcat(typeSig,
               val = JClass::typeToSig(env, tName, NULL));
        }
        if (strcmp(tName, "boolean") == 0) {
               char* b = argv[i];
               if (strcmp(b, "true") == 0 ||
                   strcmp(b, "TRUE") == 0 ||
                   strcmp(b, "True") == 0 ||
                   atoi(b) > 0)
                   argValues[i].z = JNI_TRUE;
               else
                   argValues[i].z = JNI_FALSE;
               strcat(typeSig,
                       val = JClass::typeToSig(
                               env, tName, NULL));
        }
        if (strcmp(tName, "byte") == 0) {
               argValues[i].b = (jbyte) atoi(argv[i]);
               strcat(typeSig,
                       val = JClass::typeToSig(
                               env, tName, NULL));
        }
```

(34)

Listing 12.14 (cont.) *Building* jvalue *Argument Array*

```
      if (strcmp(tName, "char") == 0) {
         argValues[i].c = (jchar) atoi(argv[i]);
         strcat(typeSig,
               val = JClass::typeToSig(
                          env, tName, NULL));
      }
      if (strcmp(tName, "short") == 0) {
         argValues[i].s = (jshort) atoi(argv[i]);
         strcat(typeSig,
               val = JClass::typeToSig(
                          env, tName, NULL));
      }
      if (strcmp(tName, "int") == 0) {
         argValues[i].i = (jint) atoi(argv[i]);
         strcat(typeSig,
               val = JClass::typeToSig(
                          env, tName, NULL));
      }
      if (strcmp(tName, "long") == 0) {
         argValues[i].j = (jlong) atol(argv[i]);
         strcat(typeSig,
               val = JClass::typeToSig(
                          env, tName, NULL));
      }
      if (strcmp(tName, "float") == 0) {
         argValues[i].f = (jfloat) atof(argv[i]);
         strcat(typeSig,
               val = JClass::typeToSig(
                          env, tName, NULL));
      }
      if (strcmp(tName, "double") == 0) {
         argValues[i].d = (jdouble) atof(argv[i]);
         strcat(typeSig,
               val = JClass::typeToSig(
                          env, tName, NULL));
      }
      strCnt += strlen(val);
   }
   return typeSig;
}
```

First, consider the arguments to `buildArgs`. The first argument is the ubiquitous `JNIEnv` pointer. The second argument, `params [32]`, is an array of `Class` objects of length `nParams`, each of which describes a parameter to the method in which we are interested. `buildArgs` simply iterates through each element in the `jobjectArray` of `Class` objects. For each entry it asks "What type is this?" with a call to `Class::toString` in line [34] on page 271. For primitive types, the type is simply stored as a string: "int", "short", "long", etc. In the case of a class, say, the `java.lang.String` class, the type string looks like "class Ljava/lang/String;".

As `buildArgs` processes each element of the `params` array, it uses the type string returned by `Class::toString` to determine the appropriate conversion to apply to the corresponding string in the `argv` parameter [33]. The steps for each parameter are the same:

1. Test for type.

2. Convert corresponding value in `argv` array and assign to the `jvalue` array, `argValues`.

3. Convert the type name into an appropriate signature value and append to the `typeSig` string.

When returned, the `typeSig` string contains the signature, sans parentheses, that corresponds to the types of the parameters passed in the `params` array.

We now have enough to dive into the code for our mini-invoker. We will look at it in pieces since it spans a few pages.

First, note from [35] on page 274 that `miniInvoker` takes any number of arguments. The first of these arguments is a fully-qualified class name, and the second, the name of a method from that class. The remaining arguments will be passed to the Java method being invoked.

Listing 12.15 *The* miniInvoker: *Creating the JVM*

```
int main(int argc, char *argv[]) {
    int j;
    JNIEnv *env;
    JavaVM *jvm;
    JDK1_1InitArgs vm_args;
    jint ret;
    jclass clazz;
    jmethodID mid;
    vm_args.version = 0x00010001;
    JNI_GetDefaultJavaVMInitArgs(&vm_args);
    int len = strlen(MY_CLASSPATH) +
        strlen(vm_args.classpath) + 1;

    char * newcp = (char*) malloc(len * sizeof(char));
    strcpy(newcp, MY_CLASSPATH);
    strcat(newcp, vm_args.classpath);
    vm_args.classpath = newcp;

    ret = JNI_CreateJavaVM(&jvm, &env, &vm_args);
    if (ret < 0) {
        fprintf(stderr,
            "Can't create JVM. Error: %ld\n", ret);
        return(1);
    }
    if (argc < 3) {
        printf("usage: miniInvoker className \
                        methodName [args...]\n");
        return(-1);
    }
```

(35)

The above prefatory code declares some familiar local variables, including a JVM pointer and the JDK1_1InitArgs structure. It then creates the JVM and we are on our way.

The first thing that needs to be done is to figure out what method is to be invoked. We have the name from the command line, but it must be mapped to a Method object. To do this, the first argument is passed to FindClass in line [37] on page 275 and converted to a jclass reference maintained in the clazz variable. This value is used in line [38] to get an array of all the methods in the class referenced by clazz.

Listing 12.16 *The* `miniInvoker`: *Determining Method Object*

```
(36)        initCallTables(env);

(37)        clazz = env->FindClass(argv[1]);
            if (clazz == 0) {
                fprintf(stderr,
        "Can't locate the %s class. Exiting...\n", argv[1]);
                return(-1);
            }
(38)        jobjectArray clazzMethods =
                        JClass::getMethods(env, clazz);
(39)        char* methodToInvoke = argv[2];
            int nMethods = env->GetArrayLength(clazzMethods);

            jobject methodObj = NULL;
(40)        for (j = 0; j < nMethods; j++) {
                jobject method =
                env->GetObjectArrayElement(clazzMethods, j);
                if (strcmp(methodToInvoke,
                    Method::getName(env, method)) == 0) {
                    methodObj = method;
                    break;
                }
            }
            if (methodObj == NULL) {
                fprintf(stderr,
                    "Bad method name: %s\n", methodToInvoke);
                return(-1);
            }
```

In [39] the name of the method we are to invoke gets recorded in a local variable and used as a search key as the array of methods is iterated over in the while loop beginning at line [40]. When the loop completes and the methodObj value is non-null, we set out to construct a signature for that method and build a jvalue array.

This task is started in line [41] with a call to Method::getParameterTypes and, after some error checking and allocation of memory for the jvalue argument arrays, a call is made to buildArgs [42].

Listing 12.17 *The* `miniInvoker`: *Building Arguments and Signature*

(41)
```
jobjectArray mParams =
    Method::getParameterTypes(env, methodObj);
int mParamsCnt = env->GetArrayLength(mParams);
if (mParamsCnt != (argc - 3)) {
    fprintf(stderr,
        "Number of arguments [%d] does not match \
         parameters for method [%d].\n",
        argc-3, mParamsCnt);
    return(-1);
}
jvalue* argVals = (jvalue *) malloc(
                    sizeof(jvalue) * mParamsCnt);
if (argVals == NULL) {
    fprintf(stderr,
"Insufficient memory for method arguments\n.");
    return(-1);
}
const char * paramSig =
```
(42)
```
buildArgs(env, mParams, mParamsCnt,
                    argVals, &argv[3]);
if (paramSig == NULL) {
    fprintf(stderr,
"Insufficient memory for parameter signature.\n");
    return(-1);
}
```

Upon successful return of `buildArgs`, `paramSig` contains the input parameter portion of the method's signature and `argVals` contains all the arguments cast to their proper JNI types.

Before we can invoke the method we need its complete signature. As it stands, we are short a return type. The following code puts the complete method signature together.

Listing 12.18 *The* `miniInvoker`: *Setting Return Type*

```
        int mIndex;
        jclass mReturn =
(43)        Method::getReturnType(env, methodObj);
(44)    const char* clType = JClass::toString(
(45)                            env, mReturn);
        const char* retSig =
(46)        JClass::typeToSig(env, clType, &mIndex);

        // ( paramSig ) retSig + newline
        int sigSize = strlen(paramSig) +
                    strlen(retSig) + 3;
        char* methodSig = (char*) malloc(sigSize);
(47)    sprintf(methodSig, "(%s)%s", paramSig, retSig);

        free((void*)paramSig);
```

The method return type class is retrieved in [43] and the type name extracted in [44]. All the pieces are then put together in line [47].

Look closely at line [46]. The call to `JClass::typeToSig` is passed a pointer to an `int` as the last argument. This will be populated with an index into a table of JNI method invocation methods arranged according to their return type. More on this later.

One more thing must be learned about the method before it can be called. In [48] below, the method access modifier flags are retrieved. In [49], it is determined whether a `static` or non-static method is to be invoked.

Listing 12.19 *The* `miniInvoker`: *Calling the Method*

```
(48)    int mods = Method::getModifiers(env, methodObj);
(49)    if (Modifier::isStatic(env, mods)) {
            mid = env->GetStaticMethodID(clazz,
                            methodToInvoke, methodSig);
            if (mid == 0) {
            fprintf(stderr,
                "Can't locate static method: %s.\n",
                                methodToInvoke);
            return(-1);
            }
```

Listing 12.19 (cont.) *The* miniInvoker: *Calling the Method*

(50)
```
            (staticCallTable[mIndex])
                     (env, clazz, mid, argVals);
        } else {
          mid = env->GetMethodID(clazz,
                                   "<init>", "()V");
```
(51)
```
          jobject obj = env->NewObject(clazz,
                                    mid, NULL);
          mid = env->GetMethodID(clazz,
                 methodToInvoke, methodSig);
          if (mid == 0) {
             fprintf(stderr,
               "Can't locate non-static method: %s.\n",
                  methodToInvoke);
             return(-1);
          }
```
(52)
```
          (nonStaticCallTable[mIndex])
                  (env, obj, mid, argVals);
        }
        jvm->DestroyJavaVM();
        return(0);
    }
```

Whether a method is static or not will determine both how the method ID is retrieved and what flavor of JNI method invocation function is used. Class methods will be invoked using Call<*type*>StaticMethodA, whereas non-static methods will be invoked using Call<*type*>MethodA.

Two tables have been set up with the addresses of the appropriate JNI Call<*type*>MethodA and Call<*type*>StaticMethodA functions. One of the tables contains the address of the static invokers and the other, non-static invokers. These two tables are referenced in lines [50] and [52], respectively. They were initialized way back at line [36] on page 275 with a call to initCallTables. It is at line [50] that the static methods are actually invoked using an entry into staticCallTable. At line [52], non-static methods are invoked using nonStaticCallTable. In both cases, the index retrieved back in line [46] on page 277 is used to locate and call the correctly typed JNI method invocation function.

The code for initCallTables is shown below in an abbreviated form. Each entry gets set to the address of a JNI method invocation function of a different return type. Both tables are global.

Listing 12.20 *Initializing the JNI Invoker Table*

```
#ifndef _CALLTABLE_H_
#define _CALLTABLE_H_
#include <jni.h>
#include "callTable.h"
CMA        nonStaticCallTable[10];
CSMA       staticCallTable[10];
void
initCallTables(JNIEnv* env) {
staticCallTable[0] =
          (*env)->CallStaticObjectMethodA;
staticCallTable[1] =
          (*env)->CallStaticBooleanMethodA;
//...
nonStaticCallTable[0] = (*env)->CallObjectMethodA;
nonStaticCallTable[1] = (*env)->CallBooleanMethodA;
//...
}
```

It is worth looking at the header file that is associated with the init-CallTables code so that you can see how all the C type checking is finessed to make this happen.

Listing 12.21 *Header File* callTable.h

```
#ifdef __cplusplus
    extern "C" {
#endif
#ifdef WIN32
    typedef __int64   EIGHTBYTES;
#else
    typedef long long EIGHTBYTES;
#endif
typedef EIGHTBYTES (JNICALL *CSMA)(
          JNIEnv*, jclass, jmethodID, jvalue*);
typedef EIGHTBYTES (JNICALL *CMA)(
          JNIEnv*, jobject, jmethodID, jvalue*);
extern CSMA    staticCallTable[];
extern CMA     nonStaticCallTable[];
void initCallTables(JNIEnv*);
#ifdef __cplusplus
}
#endif
#endif
```

(53)

First notice that C language naming is imposed using the `extern C` convention [53]. This is necessary so that the names match how they are defined in `<jni.h>` and so that the linker is able to resolve them correctly.

Secondly, two interesting `typedefs` have been defined so that all the entries in the table return eight bytes. This will accommodate all the JNI native types. It will, however, force the user to appropriately cast the return from a call into this table. It should also be noted that these are non-standard types and not supported on all platforms.

Running `miniInvoker`

At this point, the attentive reader deserves an example—and the inattentive reader probably needs one.

Consider the following Java class that defines both a `static` and non-static method.

Listing 12.22 *Java Class for Use With* `miniInvoker`

```
package test;
public class InvokeMainWithArgs {
    public static void aMethod(String aString,
                        int anint,
                        long along,
                        double adouble,
                        boolean abool,
                        byte abyte) {
        System.out.println("Hello from aMethod");
        System.out.println("aString = " + aString);
        System.out.println("anint = " + anint);
        System.out.println("along = " + along);
        System.out.println("adouble = " + adouble);
        System.out.println("abool = " + abool);
        System.out.println("abyte = " + abyte);
    }

    public int aNonStaticMethod(
        String aString, short ashort) {
        System.out.println(
            "Hello from aNonStaticMethod");
        System.out.println("aString = " + aString);
        System.out.println("ashort = " + ashort);
    }
}
```

The two methods simply print their arguments with a tag identifying their values. We will use miniInvoker to invoke each of the methods.

First we will call aMethod. aMethod takes six arguments of different types.

• User Input Using miniInvoker **to Call a** static **Method**

```
% miniInvoker test.InvokeMainWithArgs \
              aMethod hello 10 100 200.0 true 2
```

The job of miniInvoker is to invoke aMethod getting it all the right arguments of the right type. The output is shown below.

• Program Output **Calling** aMethod **Using** miniInvoker

```
Hello from aMethod
aString = hello
anint = 10
along = 100
adouble = 200.0
abool = true
abyte = 2
```

Next we will call a non-static method. This method, aNonStatic-Method, takes two arguments.

• User Input Using miniInvoker **to Call a Non-Static Method**

```
% miniInvoker test.InvokeMainWithArgs \
              aNonStaticMethod hello 10
```

The output is nothing special, just proof it all works.

• Program Output **Calling** aNonStaticMethod **With** miniInvoker

```
Hello from aNonStaticMethod
aString = hello
ashort = 10
```

A Small Disclaimer

This, of course, is not a complete solution to a native based invocation of Java methods. Besides, there is already one of those. It is available for free from the

Sun's Java web site and it is called the Java Virtual Machine. Our `miniIn-voker` is limited in a couple of ways. First, when invoking an instance method, the constructor used to create an object cannot take any arguments. We saw this at line [51] on page 278. Second, the types of the arguments passed to methods called by the miniInvoker are limited to Java primitive types. The `miniInvoker` does not support any mechanism for passing Java reference types other than `java.lang.String` references to the methods it invokes.

Registering Native Methods

The JNI provides a means by which `native` methods can be registered programmatically. Registering `native` methods with the JVM is done with the JNI function `RegisterNatives`. This call can be used to programmatically register `native` methods.

Use the code from Listing 12.8 on page 258 as a starting point. In this example, we invoked the main method from a Java class that loaded its own `native` methods using `System.loadLibrary`. In the modified example, `invokeMain` will invoke the `main` method of a Java class `MainWithNatives`. What is interesting about `MainWithNatives` is that it does not load its own `native` methods. Instead, its `native` methods will be registered by the native code before calling the `main` method of `MainWithNatives`.

However, before we look at the modified `invokeMain` and the new Java source, let's understand the basics of registering `native` methods from C/C++ code.

The JNINativeMethod Structure

Native methods are described to the JVM using the `JNINativeMethod` structure. The declaration of this structure appears below.

Listing 12.23 *The* `JNINativeMethod` *Structure*

```
typedef struct {
    char *name;        // Name of native method
    char *signature;   // JNI method signature
    void *fnPtr;       // Addr. of native method impl.
} JNINativeMethod;
```

The `name` field is the name of the method as it appears in the declaration. The `signature` field contains the method signature of the `native` method. This can be lifted right from the `javah`-generated header file. Finally, the `fnPtr` field contains the address of the function implementing the `native` method. In C this is just the function name. In C++, this may be a method name. These names are generated using javah. For the remainder of this section, we will use the class MainWithNatives as the Java class whose native methods are registered programmatically.

Listing 12.24 *Java Class* MainWithNatives *and no* System.loadLibrary

```
package test;
public class MainWithNatives {
    // No System.loadLibrary
    public static native void native0(String msg);
    public static native String native1();
    public static void main(String args[]) {
        System.out.println(
      "Hello from MainWithNatives");
        native0("Hello from registered native");
        System.out.println(native1());
    }
}
```

Using javah to generate function prototypes results in two C function prototypes whose entry point names and signatures appear below.

Listing 12.25 *Function Prototypes for* MainWithNatives *Methods*

```
/*
 * Class:      MainWithNatives
 * Method:     native0
 * Signature: (Ljava/lang/String;)V
 */
JNIEXPORT void JNICALL Java_MainWithNatives_native0
  (JNIEnv *, jclass, jstring);
/*
 * Class:      MainWithNatives
 * Method:     native1
 * Signature: ()Ljava/lang/String;
 */
JNIEXPORT jstring JNICALL
Java_MainWithNatives_native1
  (JNIEnv *, jclass);
```

With this listing, we now have enough information to populate a
JNINativeMethod structure.

Listing 12.26 *Setting Up the* JNINativeMethod *Structure*

```
JNINativeMethod methods[] = {
{ "native0", "(Ljava/lang/String;)V",
Java_MainWithNatives_native0},
{ "native1", "()Ljava/lang/String;",
      Java_MainWithNatives_native1}
};
```

The setup is now complete. The next step is to make the JNI call do the
actual registration of the methods with the JVM.

Using RegisterNatives

After the set up of the JNINativeMethod structure, the call to register the
native methods may be made. However, this function, RegisterNatives, requires a jclass reference as an argument. This value identifies
the class for which the methods are being registered. This value is retrieved in
line [18] on page 259.

Continuing with our modifications to Listing 12.8 on page 258, the call to
RegisterNatives is added immediately before line [19] on page 259.

```
env->RegisterNatives(clazz, methods, 2);
```

When the application calls CallStaticVoidMethod in [20] on page
259, the native methods will be ready and waiting in the JVM.

For the Thomases among us, there exists with the Chapter 12 examples a
modified invokeMain built from Listing 12.8. This modified invoke-
Main contains the changes necessary for registering native methods as
described above. In addition, the implementation of the native methods that
appear below is available.

Listing 12.27 *Implementation for* MainWithNatives native *Methods*

```
JNIEXPORT void JNICALL Java_MainWithNatives_native0
  (JNIEnv *env, jclass thisClz, jstring jstr) {
  jboolean isCopy;
  const char* msg =
     env->GetStringUTFChars(jstr, &isCopy);
  fprintf(stderr, "%s\n", msg);
  if (isCopy)
     env->ReleaseStringUTFChars(jstr, 0);
}

JNIEXPORT jstring JNICALL
Java_MainWithNatives_native1(JNIEnv *env,
                             jclass thisClz) {
  return env->NewStringUTF(
     "Native code reporting in");
}
```

The output from the native methods is not very interesting. native0 prints a String passed in as an argument, and native1 returns a String for printing by the main method of MainWithNatives. That these native methods were registered with the JVM programmatically is quite interesting. When the JVM finds its way into embedded systems running only lean supporting operating systems that do not support the dynamic loading of libraries, this will become an important feature.

If we were to launch the Java application defined in Listing 12.24 from our canonical invoker, invokeMain, augmented with the registration of native methods, we would see the accompanying output.

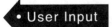 **Launching** MainWithNatives **from a C/++ Application**

% invokeMain test.MainWithNatives

• Program Output MainWithNatives **With Registered Methods**

```
Hello from MainWithNatives
Hello from registered native
Native code reporting in
```

All this with nary a System.loadLibrary. However, much has been left unsaid regarding the building of an application that registers native methods. We will look at this next.

Building for Native Method Registration

Building a Java-enabled application that registers native methods is similar to the procedures discussed in "Building a Java-Enabled Application" on page 264. One complication may arise, depending on where the code for your native methods lives. The above discussion assumed the implementation of your native methods lives in a static library. After all, the entire point of RegisterNatives is to overcome the inability to dynamically load a library. Substituting a statically linked library for a dynamically linked library means a little extra work at build time.

Linking With a Static Library on Solaris

On page 264 a Solaris makefile for building a Java-enabled application was discussed. That makefile links a Shared Object Library for both the user's native library and the Java library. In this section, a modified makefile for building a Java-enabled application that links with a static library containing native methods is shown.

The major difference between the two makefiles is the use of Solaris archive libraries, identified with a .a suffix, rather than Solaris Shared Object Libraries. This difference manifests itself in two places. First, there is a static library that contains the native methods. In the makefile below, this library is libStaticLib.a and is built using the ar command in line [54].

The second place a static library is used is when linking with the JVM itself. In line [55], the final link-edit step, libjava.a is linked with the native library and the main executable.

Listing 12.28 *A makefile for Building a Static Library*

```
AR= /bin/ar
STATIC_NATIVELIB = libStaticLib.a
STATIC_JAVALIB=libjava.a

LIB_PATH= ${JDK_HOME}/lib/sparc/green_threads

PROG= invokeMain
PROG_OBJS= invokeMain.o

OBJS= jniMainWithNatives.o

C_SRC= invokeMain.cpp jniMainWithNatives.cpp

lib: ${OBJS}
    ${AR} ${STATIC_NATIVELIB} ${OBJS}

all: ${PROG_OBJS} lib
    ${CC} -g -o ${PROG} ${PROG_OBJS} \
        ${STATIC_NATIVELIB}   \
        -L${LIB_PATH} -l${STATIC_JAVALIB}
```

(54)

(55)

The use of the static library for linking with the JVM is, of course, optional. On the other hand, if a system limitation, such as the lack of support for run-time loading of libraries, forces the use of a static native library, the same constraint will force the use of the static JVM library.

Linking With a Static Library on Win32

Again, the problem of building a static library will be considered within the context of the Microsoft Developer Studio. There are two main steps. First, a Win32 Static Library is built. This is done by selecting the appropriate project type when creating your project. The C/C++ source files containing the implementation of your native methods would be added to this project.

Second, from within the Win32 Console Application project that builds the Java enabled application, you must change two configuration values.

1. In the Project->Settings dialog, select the General Category under the Link tab. Assuming the name of your library is StaticNative.lib, add this value to the list of Object/Library modules.

2. In the Tools->Options dialog, select the Directories tabs. Choose "Library files" in the Show Directories ComboBox. Add the directory name in which your static library resides.

Avoiding Static Libraries

There are two ways you can avoid using static libraries to hold your native code. First, you can simply create a separate object module containing the implementation of your `native` methods. This object module could then be linked directly with your main program. Alternatively, you could include the implementation in the same source file as your main program.

Assume that you have a Java class that declares a `native` method as follows.

```
public native void foo();
```

In the same source file that creates the JVM and calls `RegisterNatives`, say a modified version of Listing 12.8 on page 258, you could define the function

```
void foo(JNIEnv* env, jobject obj) {
    fprintf(stderr, "A worthless function\n");
}
```

and name the C function `foo` in a `JNINativeMethod` structure that is passed to `RegisterNatives`. The following code segment illustrates how this is done.

```
JNINativeMethod methods[] = {
    { "foo", "()V", foo }
}
// ...
env->RegisterNatives(clazz, methods, 1);
```

The point of this little digression is that when registering native methods explicitly, you are not required to use the names generated by `javah`. They are only to allow a run-time binding of `native` method names to a C library entry point. When you are using `RegisterNatives`, you are binding at compile-time and so you can bind to whatever name you would like.

Summary

You can do it all now. You are finally becoming native to this interface. From within that once feeble little C program you can now unleash the power of the Java Virtual Machine. That is a lot of power. Use it wisely.

In this chapter you turned your JNI knowledge on its head and learned about the Invocation API. You learned how to embed a JVM in your application.

You first saw how to initialize the JVM using the `JDK1_1InitArgs` structure. This structure has a couple subtleties associated with it, depending on the revision of JDK 1.1 version you are using.

You then looked at the canonical way to use the Invocation API to write a C program that invokes the `static main` method of a Java class.

Not being satisfied with canonical uses, the little invoker-of-main application was spiced up and, using the `java.lang.reflect` package, extended it to invoke a method whose arguments were either Java primitive types or of type `java.lang.String`.

This chapter also covered a function that is properly part of the JNI. The `RegisterNatives` function can be used to register C/C++ functions as `native` methods. These functions can live in a static library that is linked with the program that loads the JVM, or they may exist directly within the main-line source for your program. The `RegisterNatives` function is necessary on platforms that do not support the dynamic loading of libraries at run-time.

That leaves two functions defined by the Invocation API to discuss. `AttachCurrentThread` and `DetachCurrentThread` were left for the next chapter, in which we will look at launching a JVM within an NT service.

Chapter 13

AN NT SERVICE APPLICATION

A man, though wise, should never be ashamed
of learning more, and must unbend his mind.

Sophocles
Antigone

Introduction

The last chapter looked at how to embed the Java Virtual Machine in a C/C++ application. Specifically, an executable was built that ran from a UNIX shell or as a Win32 Console Application.

In the real world, it is not reasonable to assume that all Java applications will be started by a user from the command line. Given Java's usefulness and popularity as a language for web-based applications and, particularly, web-based services, it is often the case that you will want your application to be started automatically by some system service, possibly at boot time. Throughout this chapter, such an application is called an *agent*.

That is the consideration of this chapter. We will look at how to start the JVM from Sun's JDK as an NT service under control of the Service Control Manager (SCM). Generally speaking, a *service* is an application that runs indefinitely and responds to requests from users or other applications.

The reason the focus is on the NT is twofold. First, in spite of available examples, the process of building a service can be tricky. Even experienced programmers have been known to pull their hair trying to get the examples to work. Second, if this book is going to be of use for Win32 developers, their

Java applications must run under a JVM that supports JNI. At this writing, the twain of JNI and Microsoft do not appear ready to meet.

In this chapter we will look at an NT service that creates a JVM and then starts a Java agent by invoking its `main` method. In a sense, then, this service is a "JVM creation service." Yet, it is also a "Java agent creation" service because the singular role of the service code is to invoke the `main` method of the Java agent.

Before we look at the details of the service code, let's learn a little about the SCM.

The Service Control Manager

The Service Control Manager (SCM) is an NT facility for launching, interrogating, and stopping services. The SCM is available from the Services Control Panel and provides a user interface for managing services. Within that interface, each system service that has been installed in the SCM database is displayed along with its current status. Once installed, it can be started and stopped via the SCM.

Registering a Service With the SCM

The Win32 API provides a straightforward way to install a service programmatically. The following code is often integrated with your mainline service code to facilitate testing and debugging of a new service.

Listing 13.1 *Installing a Service*

```
#include <windows.h>
#include <stdio.h>
#include <tchar.h>
#include "jservice.h"

void installService(){
    SC_HANDLE    serviceHandle;
    SC_HANDLE    scmHandle;
    TCHAR path[512];
    if (GetModuleFileName(NULL, path, 512) == 0) {
        _tprintf(TEXT("Can't install %s Error %s\n"),
            TEXT(SZSERVICEDISPLAYNAME),
            getErrorText(errString, 256));
    return;
    }
```

(1)

Listing 13.1 (cont.) *Installing a Service*

```
(2)         scmHandle = OpenSCManager(
                            NULL, NULL,
                            SC_MANAGER_ALL_ACCESS);
            if (scmHandle){
(3)             serviceHandle = CreateService(
                            scmHandle,
(4)                         TEXT(SZSERVICENAME),
(5)                         TEXT(SZSERVICEDISPLAYNAME),
                            SERVICE_ALL_ACCESS,
(6)                         SERVICE_WIN32_OWN_PROCESS |
(7)                         SERVICE_INTERACTIVE_PROCESS,
                            SERVICE_DEMAND_START,
                            SERVICE_ERROR_NORMAL,
(8)                         path,
                            NULL, NULL,
                            TEXT(SZDEPENDENCIES),
                            NULL, NULL);

            if (serviceHandle) {
               _tprintf(TEXT("%s installed.\n"*),
                        TEXT(SZSERVICEDISPLAYNAME));
               CloseServiceHandle(serviceHandle);
            } else {
               _tprintf(
                        TEXT("CreateService failed - %s\n"),
                        getErrorText(errString, 256));
            }
(9)         CloseServiceHandle(scmHandle);
            }
            else
               _tprintf(TEXT("OpenSCManager failed - %s\n"),
                        getErrorText(errString,256));
}
```

As you can see, it only requires three NT system calls to install a service. In line [2] OpenSCManager returns a handle to the SCM. The arguments to OpenSCManager specify that the default database on the local machine be opened, permitting all operations. The SCM handle is used in line [3] by CreateService to create an entry for a service. Finally, in [9] the connection with the SCM is closed.

Although the call to `CreateService` takes many arguments, there are two that really define the service. The first is the service name as identified in line [4]. The second value is the path to an executable returned by `GetModuleFileName` in line [1]. The path value tells the SCM where to find the service when it is asked to start it. These two values are enough to identify the service to the SCM. The actual implementation of the service needs to meet certain criteria but we will leave those details for later.

For complete details regarding these calls, refer to the Microsoft Developer's Studio Help subsystem. The following discussion will elaborate only on the details germaine to this specific example.

The strings `SZSERVICENAME` in line [4] and `SZSERVICEDISPLAYNAME` in line [5] are defined in `jservice.h`. We will see these macros often enough that it is worth making their definitions explicit. Here are the relevant definitions from `jservice.h`.

```
#define SZSERVICENAME        "ExampleJavaService"
#define SZSERVICEDISPLAYNAME "Example Java Server"
```

These strings define the service name for internal SCM use and the display name for the user interface, respectively. The `TEXT` macro that surrounds both is defined in `<tchar.h>`. Depending on compilation flags, it will cause the wrapped string to be represented as either single-byte, multi-byte or Unicode characters.

The other detail from Listing 13.1 of potential interest is line [6]. This argument tells the SCM that the process in which this service will run will not be shared with other services. Another possible value, `SERVICE_WIN32_SHARE_PROCESS`, informs the SCM that the process it starts may host multiple services. The current implementation of the JVM service could be modified to operate in this manner. Instead of launching just a single agent, it could serve as a generalized Java agent launcher.

The `SERVICE_INTERACTIVE_PROCESS` flag in line [7] allows the service to interact with the Win32 desktop. This flag is set because our Java agent is going to put up a window. As a rule, services do not get created with the ability to interact with the desktop. Rather, if the user wants to set this mode, it is done through the Service Configuration Dialog in the SCM.

The Service Process

Enough has been said about installing a service. It is time to look at the code for a service. A service is an executable that the SCM starts as a process. According to the flags to `CreateService`, the service running in that process may run by itself or share its process with other services. The services that run in a process are defined in the *dispatch table*. The dispatch table maps service names to addresses. Each service name must correspond to an installed service. Each address is a function within the service process called by the SCM when it wants to start a service. In the unfolding JVM server example, the service process will register only a single service with the SCM.

The only job of the main function in a service process is to call `Start-ServiceCtrlDispatcher`, passing the dispatch table as an argument. This tells the SCM at what address to start executing a service. However, in order for a service to be considered well-behaved, there are other constraints imposed upon it. Here is a brief overview of what a service needs to do to be considered well-behaved. A service must be written so that it:

- Registers itself with the SCM by providing an address of a function to call when starting the service (per above discussion)
- Registers a control handler routine with the SCM by providing the address of a function to call in response to SCM control commands
- Responds to the SCM when it inquires of its state

Only the first of these steps is done in the main routine of the service process. The latter two steps are the responsibility of the code that executes after the service has been started by the SCM.

Let's look at a canonical `main` routine of an NT service process. After that we will look at the code which actually implements the service proper.

Listing 13.2 *The* `main` *Routine for a Service Process*

```
#include <windows.h>
#include <stdio.h>
#include <tchar.h>
#include "service.h"
```

(10)
```
SERVICE_STATUS                servStat;
SERVICE_STATUS_HANDLE    statusHandle;
DWORD                         errCode = 0;
BOOL                          debug = FALSE;
TCHAR                         errString[256];

void _CRTAPI1 main(int argc, char **argv)
{
    BOOL doDispatch = TRUE;
```
(11)
```
    SERVICE_TABLE_ENTRY dispatchTable[] = {
        { TEXT(SZSERVICENAME),
            (LPSERVICE_MAIN_FUNCTION)service_main },
        { NULL, NULL }
    };
```

Listing 13.2 (cont.) *The* main *Routine for a Service Process*

```
        if (  (argc > 1) &&
              ((*argv[1] == '-') || (*argv[1] == '/')) ) {
            if ( _stricmp( "i", argv[1]+1 ) == 0 ) {
(12)            installService();
                doDispatch = FALSE;
            }
            else if ( _stricmp( "r", argv[1]+1 ) == 0 ) {
(13)            removeService();
                doDispatch = FALSE;
            }
            else if ( _stricmp( "d", argv[1]+1 ) == 0 ) {
                debug = TRUE;
(14)            debugService(argc, argv);
                doDispatch = FALSE;
            }
            else {
                doDispatch = TRUE;
            }
        }
        if (doDispatch) {
          printf( "Wait while service is started...\n" );
(15)      if (!StartServiceCtrlDispatcher(dispatchTable))
              AddToMessageLog(TEXT(
                  "StartServiceCtrlDispatcher failed."));
        }
        else
            exit(0);
}
```

This main routine is written to run either under control of the SCM or from the system console command line. As you see from line [12] it is capable of installing itself by calling the installService function that appeared in Listing 13.1 on page 292. Likewise, it is able to remove itself by calling the removeService routine in line [13].

Aside from the conveniences of self-installation and self-removal, the main routine in the above service process does the real work of defining the dispatch table in line [11] and calling StartServiceCtrlDispatcher in line [15] to inform the SCM of the services that will be running in this process. Our example service process contains only one service and its entry point, as defined in the dispatch table is, service_main.

One more handy feature is provided by the canonical example. The −d flag will run the service process from the command line [14] without any intervention from the SCM. This is helpful for debugging the behavior of the service process and does not exercise any code necessary for interacting with the SCM.

The Executing Service

Once the call to StartServiceCtrlDispatcher is made, the SCM has all it needs to start a service executing. The SCM does this by starting a thread that begins execution at the address associated with the service in the dispatch table.

In this example, the service_main routine represents the entry point for our service. Although we do not use them here, two arguments are passed to a service when it is started. The first is a count of the number of elements in an array of strings (i.e. LPTSTR*), which is the second argument. This is the standard call convention when a service is started.

The service_main routine represents the first code executed by the service proper as distinct from the service process. Above we saw that the service is responsible for three things, the first of which is handing off the dispatch table to the SCM. The other two are repeated here:

- Registers a control handler routine with the SCM by providing the address of a function to call in response to SCM control commands
- Responds to the SCM when it inquires of its state

We can see both of these responsibilities undertaken by service_main in the following listing. First, in line [16], RegisterServiceCtrlHandler is called to inform the SCM of the address of the function that will handle control requests from the SCM. This particular call instructs the SCM to call the function service_controller whenever it has a control request for the service SZSERVICENAME.

Listing 13.3 *The* `service_main` *routine*

```
void WINAPI service_main(
        DWORD dwArgc, LPTSTR *lpszArgv)
{
    BOOL startIt = TRUE;
(16)    statusHandle = RegisterServiceCtrlHandler(
        TEXT(SZSERVICENAME),
        service_controller);
    if (!statusHandle)
        startIt = FALSE;
    // These values don't change in example
    servStat.dwServiceType =
            SERVICE_WIN32_OWN_PROCESS;
    servStat.dwServiceSpecificExitCode = 0;
    if (statusHandle &&
(17)            !reportStatus(SERVICE_START_PENDING,
                    NO_ERROR,
                    3000))
        startIt = FALSE;

    if (startIt)
(18)        serviceStart( dwArgc, lpszArgv );

    if (statusHandle)
(19)        (VOID)reportStatus(SERVICE_STOPPED,
                        errCode,0);
    return;
}
```

Two other lines in the `service_main` call illustrate how the service fulfills its responsibility of informing the SCM of its status. In line the service calls `reportStatus` to inform the SCM it is about to start. That is the meaning of the SERVICE_START_PENDING flag. Combined with the "wait hint" value of 3000 milliseconds, this flag means that the service is on its way up and expects to report back with a new status in three seconds.

Line [19] reports that the service is stopped but, in this context, that report will only be sent due to some error condition.

In between the two calls into the SCM to report status, the real service code begins executing [18]. In fact, line [19] will not execute until `serviceStart` returns. Up to this point we have been discussing infrastructure code that is useful for starting any NT service. Inside of `serviceStart`, we will begin to see some code that looks a bit more like what we have been used to seeing in this book. We will look at `serviceStart` in just a bit, but first, in order to complete our understanding of the interaction between the service and the SCM, we need to look at how to report status to the SCM as well as how to respond to commands from the SCM.

Reporting Service Status

The reportStatus routine is little more than a wrapper around the Win32 call to SetServiceStatus. This is actually the call that informs the SCM of the service's status. The other work of reportStatus is to store state information locally so that the service knows its own state. The code for reportStatus appears below.

Listing 13.4 *The* reportStatus *Routine*

```
BOOL reportStatus(DWORD currState,
                  DWORD exitCode,
                  DWORD wHint)
{
    static DWORD checkPoint = 1;
    BOOL result = TRUE;
    if (!debug) {
        if (currState == SERVICE_START_PENDING)
(20)        servStat.dwControlsAccepted = 0;
        else
(21)        servStat.dwControlsAccepted =
                        SERVICE_ACCEPT_STOP;
        servStat.dwCurrentState = currState;
        servStat.dwWin32ExitCode = exitCode;
        servStat.dwWaitHint = wHint;
        if ((currState == SERVICE_RUNNING ) ||
                (currState == SERVICE_STOPPED ))
            servStat.dwCheckPoint = 0;
        else
            servStat.dwCheckPoint = checkPoint++;
(22)    if (!(result = SetServiceStatus(statusHandle,
                    &servStat))) {
            AddToMessageLog(TEXT("SetServiceStatus"));
        }
    }
    return result;
}
```

As you can see, most of the work in `reportStatus` is updating the global `SERVICE_STATUS` structure declared in [10] on page 295. Finally, though, in all cases when the `debug` flag is not set, it calls `SetServiceStatus` [22] to update the SCM. Each time `reportStatus` is called, it updates the service state according to the input arguments. If the input state is `SERVICE_START_PENDING`, it informs the SCM it will not accept any control commands by setting the `dwControlsAccepted` field of the `SERVICE_STATUS` structure, `servStat`, to zero in line [20]. This is only a temporary condition because if the input state is other than start pending, this control field is set so that service accepts the stop control [21].

The code which manipulates the `dwCheckPoint` field of the `servStat` structure does this so that other programs are able to monitor its status according to some service-defined meanings for the checkpoint values. Our JVM server under development does not assign any meaning to these values.

There is one more piece of the service infrastructure code we need to look at before getting to the Java agent code.

The `service_controller` Routine

The `service_controller` routine is part of the infrastructure necessary for building a well-behaved service. Its jobs is to respond to control requests sent by the SCM. At the very least, the handler must call the Win32 function `SetServiceStatus` (in our case, via `reportStatus`) to update the service's status.

There are four possible control codes the SCM can send to the control handler function:

```
SERVICE_CONTROL_INTERROGATE
SERVICE_CONTROL_PAUSE
SERVICE_CONTROL_CONTINUE
SERVICE_CONTROL_STOP
```

By default, all services accept the `SERVICE_CONTROL_INTERROGATE` value. Any or all of the other flags need to be specified to enable the other control codes.

When a service receives a control request, the service's handler function must call `SetServiceStatus`. This is so even if the service's status did not change. The handler code below meets this requirement, as all paths lead through `reportStatus`.

If you look at the source for `reportStatus`, you will see that the JVM service we are building only accepts the stop message when it is in the running state. Hence, in the following code, you will see no support of the pause and continue requests.

Listing 13.5 *The* `service_controller` *Routine*

```
VOID WINAPI service_controller(DWORD dwCtrlCode)
{
    switch(dwCtrlCode){
    case SERVICE_CONTROL_STOP:
        reportStatus(SERVICE_STOP_PENDING,
                NO_ERROR, 0);
(23)        serviceStop();
        return;
    case SERVICE_CONTROL_INTERROGATE:
        break;
    default:                // Bad code, bad SCM!!
        break;
    }
    reportStatus(servStat.dwCurrentState, NO_ERROR,
0);
}
```

At line [23], we see another, along with `serviceStart`, hook into the meat of the service code. The `serviceStop` routine is meant to do what it takes to gracefully end service activity. In our case, that means terminate the JVM.

We have now seen all the code that makes up a generic service. We have also seen the glint of the two hooks that connect the JVM to the generic service code, `serviceStart` and `serviceStop`. Let's look at those routines now.

The Java Agent Server

The role of the Java agent server is to start a Java application from the service process. To start a Java agent, one needs a JVM. To start a JVM within a C/C++ program requires the Invocation API.

Starting the Java Agent Server

In a nutshell, the job of `serviceStart` is to start the JVM and then start the Java agent. This is exactly the work of `invokeMain` from Chapter 12. However, for this discussion and to generalize the use of the Invocation API within an NT service, access to the Invocation API has been wrapped in a C++ class, `JvmServices`. We will look at this class in detail later. For now, we will rely on the method names from the `JvmServices` class to convey their purpose.

In addition to the JvmServices class, the JvmAppArgs class has also been provided to facilitate passing information to the NT thread in which the Java agent will run.

The serviceStart code that appears below is written to launch the Java agent defined by the main method of the class ServiceDisplayFrame.

Listing 13.6 *The* serviceStart *Routine*

```
         #include <windows.h>
         #include <stdio.h>
         #include "jservice.h"
         #include "JvmServices.h"
         #include "JvmAppArgs.h"


(24)     JvmServices*           jvmProvider;
(25)     static HANDLE          jThreadHandle;


         #define CLASSNAME "ServiceDisplayFrame"


         VOID serviceStart(DWORD dwArgc, LPSTR *lpszArgv) {
             JvmAppArgs*svc_args;


(26)         reportStatus (SERVICE_START_PENDING,0,0);


(27)         jvmProvider = new JvmServices();
(28)         jvmProvider->startJvm();


             svc_args = new JvmAppArgs();
(29)         svc_args->setClass(CLASSNAME);
(30)         svc_args->setJvmService(jvmProvider);


             reportStatus(SERVICE_RUNNING,0,0);
(31)         jThreadHandle =
                 (HANDLE)jvmProvider->startApp(svc_args);


             // Wait for thread to exit
(32)         WaitForSingleObject(jThreadHandle,  INFINITE);
             reportStatus(SERVICE_STOPPED,0,0);
         }
```

The first thing `serviceStart` does, being the good NT citizen that it is, is to report to the SCM that it is about to start [26]. From there it gets to its real work. As mentioned above, the role of `serviceStart` is to start the JVM and then start the Java agent. At the top level, these two steps are performed at line [28] and [31]. Both of these depend on the construction of the `JvmSer-vices` object at line [27]. The object returned by this constructor is stored in the global `jvmProvider` [24] which, as we shall see, is needed by `ser-viceStop`.

Lines [29] and [30] set up arguments that will be sent to the `startApp` method. The class argument is bound for a call to `FindClass` so it must use a slash (/) to separate components of its package name. The `startApp` method will start the NT thread in which the Java agent will run. The handle to this thread is returned and stored in the global variable `jThreadHandle` [25]. The arguments to `startApp` are passed right through to this thread, giving it all the information it needs to attach to the JVM.

Another thing to notice about `serviceStart` is the call to `WaitForS-ingleObject` [32]. This prevents `serviceStop` from returning until the NT thread identified by `jThreadHandle` exits. When this thread exits, `WaitForSingleObject` will return and `reportStatus` will inform the SCM that the service has stopped.

Stopping the Java Agent Server

The Java agent server is stopped by a call to `serviceStop`. `service-Stop` gets called by the control handler function as we saw at line [23] on page 301.

`serviceStop`'s primary job is to stop the NT thread in which the Java agent is running. We will look at a couple of different paths through `ser-viceStop` for terminating the agent before the service stops.

Listing 13.7 *The* serviceStop *Routine*

```
VOID serviceStop(){
        reportStatus (SERVICE_STOP_PENDING,0,0);
(33)    JavaVM*            jvm = jvmProvider->getJvm();
        JNIEnv*            env;
        JDK1_1AttachArgs* t_args;

(34)    jvm->AttachCurrentThread(&env, &t_args);

        jclass jserviceClz = env->FindClass(CLASSNAME);

        jmethodID mid = env->GetStaticMethodID(
                    jserviceClz, "cleanup", "()V");

        if (mid != 0)
           env->CallStaticVoidMethod(
                            jserviceClz, mid, NULL);

(35)    jvm->DetachCurrentThread();
(36)    CloseHandle(jThreadHandle);
        reportStatus(SERVICE_STOPPED,0,0);
}
```

The brute force mechanism for closing down the Java agent is to simply call CloseHandle [36] on the thread in which it is executing. This path is always taken by serviceStop. A call to CloseHandle will terminate the main thread in the Java agent. The termination of the main thread in this fashion will also terminate all of its subsidiary threads.

Although this is the most general solution for terminating an application, an alternative can be used for a Java agent written to conform to the expectations of serviceStop. Specifically, if the class whose main is executing contains a static method cleanup, serviceStop will invoke this method, providing an opportunity for the agent to shut down a little more elegantly.

The call to invoke cleanup is sandwiched between a couple of new entries in the Invocation API discussion. The call to AttachCurrent-Thread in line [34] provides the JNIEnv necessary to call the JNI routines needed to invoke cleanup. In general, if you need to get a JNIEnv pointer to access some JVM functionality via the JNI, call AttachCurrent-Thread. It has been said before, but it is worth saying again: do not pass the JNIEnv pointer returned by AttachCurrentThread from one thread to another.

The call to `AttachCurrentThread` needs a pointer to a `JavaVM` structure. That is provided at line [33] by a call into the `jvmProvider` object. In JDK 1.1 releases, the `JDK1_1AttachArgs` structure returned does not contain anything meaningful. In JDK 1.2, the specification calls for a version number to be returned which reflects the version of the JNI function table pointed to by the value returned in the first argument.

When finished with your `JNIEnv` pointer, a call to `DetachCurrentThead` disassociates the native thread from the JVM.

Whether or not the Java agent supplies the cleanup method, the `serviceStop` routine must complete in under three seconds. This is a constraint placed upon it by the SCM. If it is anticipated that `serviceStop` will take longer than three seconds, the service must inform the SCM of this by frequent (less than three second intervals) status reports that the service is still in the `SERVICE_STOP_PENDING` state. Generally, this is accomplished by starting a new thread that repeatedly calls `SetServiceStatus`. The mainline of `serviceStop`, after it is finished with shutdown, then kills this thread and reports `SERVICE_STOPPED`.

That wraps up the discussion of `serviceStop` and `serviceStart`. As you see, they rely heavily on `JvmServices` and `JvmAppArgs`. Let's look at those supporting players now.

Support for Java Agent Creation

The `JvmServices` class provides an interface to the C++ application that hides the details of the Invocation API. It also provides the ability, though not used here, to start multiple Java applications within the same JVM on different native threads. This capability is relevant for an NT service process that hosts multiple services, i.e. services created with a service type of `SERVICE_WIN32_SHARE_PROCESS`.

The `JvmServices` class provides a JVM to a C++ application (`startJvm`, `getJvm`) and the ability to start an agent (`startApp`). These three methods define its complete public interface. Most of the interesting work, however, is done by the private methods of the class. The following listing contains the entire class header file.

Listing 13.8 JvmServices *Header File*

```
#include <jni.h>
#include <windows.h>
class JvmAppArgs;

class JvmServices
{
private:
JavaVM*_jvm;

public:
    JvmServices() {};
    ~JvmServices();
    int           startJvm();
    JavaVM*       getJvm();
    virtual  DWORD startApp(JvmAppArgs*);

private:
    void          invokeMain(
                        JNIEnv*,char*,jobjectArray);

    jobjectArray  makeArgsArray(
                        JNIEnv*, int, char**);

    static DWORD WINAPIserviceThread(void*);
};
```

Prose descriptions of startJvm and getJvm will suffice. getJvm returns the private data member pointer to a JavaVM structure. startJvm is nothing more than a call JNI_CreateJavaVM and some error checking.

We won't reproduce here the code to the private method invokeMain either. We saw it in the last chapter and it is nothing more than a call to Call-StaticVoidMethod preceded by calls to the usual suspects, FindClass and GetStaticMethodID.

startApp and serviceThread, on the other hand, are worth looking at. They make JvmServices more than simply a wrapper around Invocation API calls. The JvmServices class also provides a mechanism for starting a Java agent within an NT thread.

startApp is a simple function that kicks off an NT thread.

Listing 13.9 *The* startApp *Method*

```
DWORD
JvmServices::startApp(JvmAppArgs* args)
{
    return (unsigned long)CreateThread(NULL,
                         4096,
                         serviceThread,
                         (void*) args,
                         0,
                         NULL);
}
```

CreateThread creates a new NT thread to run the function service-Thread. The thread is created with 4K of stack, and is passed the arguments pointed to by the args argument. We will see that this argument is meaningful to the thread that is being created. The fifth argument, 0, says the thread is created in ready-to-run mode and executes as soon as it is scheduled. It does not wait for some other thread to resume it.

This code merely creates the thread. What code does the thread run? The static serviceThread method provides that answer.

Listing 13.10 *The* serviceThread *Method*

```
DWORD
JvmServices::serviceThread(void* args)
{
    jint                 rc;
    jobjectArray         ja;
    JNIEnv*              t_env;
    JDK1_1AttachArgs*    t_args;
    JvmServices*         svc;
    JavaVM*              jvm;
    JvmAppArgs* appArgs = (JvmAppArgs*) args;

(37)    svc = appArgs->getJvmService();
(38)    jvm = svc->getJvm();

(39)    rc = jvm->AttachCurrentThread(&t_env, &t_args);
```

Listing 13.10 (cont.) *The* `serviceThread` *Method*

```
        if (rc < 0) {
            fprintf(stderr,
                "Attach of %s thread failed\n",
                appArgs->getClass());
            return(rc);
        }
(40)    ja = svc->makeArgsArray(t_env,
                            appArgs->getArgListSize(),
                            appArgs->getArgList());
        svc->invokeMain(t_env, appArgs->getClass(), ja);
        jvm->DetachCurrentThread();
        return(0);
    }
```

Since `serviceThread` is a `static` method of `JvmServices`, it needs the current JVM passed to it as an argument. In line [37] the `JvmServices` object is extracted from the `JvmAppArgs` object. Then in line [38] a pointer to a `JavaVM` structure is pulled from the `JvmServices` object. `AttachCurrentThread` [39] returns a `JNIEnv` pointer, and this value is passed to the C++ method version of our friend, `invokeMain`.

The `makeArgsArray` call [40] uses the `JvmAppArgs` object to convert an array of strings into a `jobjectArray` as is appropriate for passing to the JVM when invoking `main`.

The result of this is that an NT thread is used to launch a Java agent within a JVM. This NT thread will not exit until the main method in the JVM terminates. It is this thread that `serviceStart` waits on back at line [32] on page 302.

The JVM as Service: Some Considerations

This section outlines a few issues to keep in mind when running the JVM as an NT service.

The JVM's Current Working Directory

The service process executes in the `\winnt\services32`. Keep this in mind when setting the `classpath` field of the JVM in the `JDK1_1InitArgs` structure. Either your classpath will need to include absolute path names to the relevant class files or be relative to `\winnt\services32`.

If you want to change the working directory for the JVM, but not the service process, this must be done when calling `JNI_CreateJavaVM`. If you are coding to JDK 1.1.2 and later 1.1 revisions of the JDK, the `properties` field must be set in the JDK1_1InitArgs structure as described in Chapter 12 under "The properties Field (JDK 1.1.2 and Greater)" on page 254. If you are coding to the JDK 1.2 specification, you must set the properties option in a JavaVMOption structure as described in Chapter 15.

In either case, the properties value is an array of strings. Each string represents a key/value pair separated by an equal sign (=). The key that is relevant is user.dir. The value of this property sets the JVMs notion of current working directory. Setting this, however, is not quite enough. To use it correctly within your Java agent to, say, open a file, you need to create a java.io.File object. This object can be used to get an absolute path name which uses the setting of user.dir. The following code snippet illustrates this.

```
File file = new File("someFileName");
PrintWriter pWriter =
    new PrintWriter(file.getAbsolutePath());
```

Displaying a Frame

If your Java application brings up a window, you will need to set the "Allow Service to Interact with Desktop" check box from within Service Configuration Dialog of the SCM. As its name suggests, it allows a service to put up windows and get input from the desktop. In our call to CreateService at [3] on page 293, this flag is set so our service will be installed to interact with the desktop by default.

Some Common Errors

There are three common errors which can cause the SCM to complain during the start-up or shutdown of a service. These will be discussed in the context of starting a Java agent.

Error 109 The pipe has been ended

Grammatical weaknesses notwithstanding, this error most likely occurs because the main Java thread terminated with System.exit before the cleanup method has completed. The exit from the JVM takes the cleanup method with it and disrupts the connection the serviceStop routine has with the JVM as a result of its AttachCurrentThread call.

Error 1053 Service did not respond

The complete error message associated with this error is "The service did not respond to the start or control request in a timely fashion." This is usually a failure to report a SERVICE_STOPPED in a timely fashion. This may result from the cleanup code taking too long to exit. If this error occurs, the SCM will lock for what is supposed to be two minutes but seems like an eternity when you are trying to get your code to work correctly.

Error 1063 Service process could not connect

This error generally signals a failure in the start-up of the service. In our context, a likely cause is the failure of the JVM to load the class containing the Java agent and named in line [29] on page 302. If this occurs check the `classpath` field value you are sending to the JVM in the `JDK1_1InitArgs` structure or, if using JDK 1.2, the `classpath` option value sent in the `JavaVMInitArgs` array. In either case, be mindful of the directory in which your service is running.

A more general cause of this error is the `serviceStart` exiting without sending `SERVICE_STOP_PENDING` and `SERVICE_STOPPED` notification to the SCM.

The code included in the service example in this chapter is written to avoid errors 109 and 1063. Error 1053 can often be caused by a poorly-behaved Java agent. What follows is a discussion of what constitutes a well-behaved Java agent when launched from a JVM service.

A Java Agent Service

Let's start with a sketch of what it means to be a service. We will start with a very general idea and then refine it. The purpose of refining the general definition of a service is to bring it in line with the combined requirements of the NT Service Control Manager and the JVM. The above discussion on errors is an indication that there is some discipline required in terminating both the service code and the agent code.

For this reason, there are some guidelines to follow when building your agent. These guidelines are not hard and fast but failure to adhere to them will result in undesirable behavior. However, they are not so strict as to immediately preclude existing Java applications from being brought under the control of the NT Service Control Manager.

Before we look at any special considerations for the JVM, let's look at a general definition of a Java agent. A Java agent has the following characteristics:

- It defines a static `main` method that represents the main thread of the agent.
- It defines any number of subsidiary threads.
- It has some thread, possibly the main thread, that stays around "forever" and provides the service interface to clients.
- It starts at boot time and runs "forever" or until there is a specific request to shut it down.

What is described here is intended to be very general. This definition fits well with the conventional definition of a service as well as how we think of Java applications.

If the idea is extended to include in the definition of a service a `cleanup` method to avoid stopping an agent by simply terminating its JVM, we need to impose one more constraint on the Java agent:

- An agent may not call `System.exit` outside of `cleanup` method

Ignoring this constraint can lead to `Error 109` as described previously.

With this in mind, let's look at a very simple example of a Java agent. This code provides a skeleton for a well-behaved Java agent under control of an NT service as implemented in the code in the previous sections of this chapter.

Before we look at the code, an overview of the code will be presented in which its major components are discussed.

Overview of a Java Logging Agent

The Java agent we will look at has the following components:

- A `main` method which creates and displays a new `java.awt.Frame` containing a `java.awt.TextArea`
- Within the `main` method, a `while` loop which logs messages to the `TextArea` as long as the `Frame` is active
- A `static cleanup` method which sets the `Frame` to inactive, terminating the `while` loop in the `main` method
- Code in the `main` method after the loop exit to release all the resources that the agent holds

What this describes is a simple logging service. But what is more important is the general structure of the agent: the main loop and its termination via a `static` variable by the `cleanup` method. Designing the agent in this fashion will minimize the time spent in the `serviceStop` routine and avoid violating the three second limit on the SCM's patience.

With this overview, let's look at the source code for our logging agent.

Source for a Java Logging Agent

Below is the source for the `ServiceDisplayFrame` class which performs as a simple agent launched by the JVM service.

The main `Frame` object is maintained in a `static` variable [41] so that the cleanup method can access it.

Listing 13.11 `ServiceDisplayFrame` *Agent*

```
public class ServiceDisplayFrame extends Frame {
    protected static ServiceDisplayFrame mainFrame;
    protected TextArea messageArea;
    protected boolean active = true;

    public ServiceDisplayFrame () {
        super();
        this.setLayout ( new BorderLayout() );
        messageArea = new TextArea();
        this.add ( "Center", messageArea );
        this.setBackground ( Color.gray );
        this.setSize ( 200, 400 );
    }
    public synchronized boolean isActive () {
        return active;
    }
    public synchronized void setActive(boolean aBool)
    {
        active = aBool;
    }

    public synchronized void addMessage(
                        String aMessage){
        if (active)
            messageArea.append ( aMessage );
    }
```

(41)

Listing 13.11 (cont.) `SimpleDisplayFrame` *Agent*

```
       public static void main (String args[]) {
(42)       mainFrame = new ServiceDisplayFrame();
           mainFrame.show();
           int count = 0;
(43)       while (mainFrame.isActive()) {
               count++;
           try {
(44)       mainFrame.addMessage(
               "Message number " + count + "\n");
           } catch (Exception e) {
                   e.printStackTrace();
                   mainFrame.setActive ( false );
               }
           }
(45)       mainFrame.dispose();
           }
(46)   public static void cleanup () {
           mainFrame.setActive ( false );
           }
       }
```

The main `Frame` is created in line [42] before entering the `while` loop at [43]. You can think of this as the agent initialization code. Once all the setup is complete, the agent enters its work loop. It continues in this loop, logging messages [44] as long as `isActive` tests true.

The `isActive` test will fail only after the `cleanup` method is called [46] and resets the `active` variable. When the loop exits, the `main` method takes care of all agent-wide resource deallocation. In this case, that is simply disposing of `mainFrame` [45].

For a real world application, some sort of blocking loop would be appropriate. It is not uncommon for an agent or daemon to listen on a socket awaiting incoming requests.

Making It Happen

In the example source available from the *Essential JNI* ftp site, there is a Visual C++ Project file that contains all of:

- The service infrastructure code
- The JVM service start and stop code
- The C++ classes for agent support

This project builds a Win32 Console Application named `jservice.exe`. To install this service, from a DOS prompt, type:

Installing JVM Agent Service

`c:\myproject>` **jservice -i**

After this step, you should see a listing for the Example Java Server in the SCM display window.

To start the service, select the line of text containing Example Java Server and click on the Start button. Since we set the `SERVICE_INTERACTIVE_PROCESS` flag at service creation, the `Frame` created by `ServiceDisplayFrame` should appear as below. If it does not, check the setting in the Service Configuration Dialog.

Figure 1.1 *A Java Agent Logging Service Display Frame*

After you tire of watching the insipid message scroll across the `ServiceDisplayFrame` window, press the Stop button in the SCM and watch everything quietly go away and the status of the service in the SCM display revert to stopped.

Summary

This chapter set out to achieve a very specific goal: provide a means by which a Java application can be started at system start-up in an NT environment. This requires implementing what is known as an NT service. An NT service is a process that is built to be started and stopped under control of the Service Control Manager (SCM).

We saw the infrastructure code required of all NT services. This code can install itself and then respond to SCM control commands. That generic service code was augmented to launch a Java Virtual Machine using the Invocation API. Once the JVM is up and running, a Java application or agent is started on an NT thread using JNI calls provided by two supporting C++ classes: `Jvm-Services` and `JvmAppArgs`.

Care is required to properly start the JVM. The class path of the JVM must take into account that an NT service runs in the `\winnt\services32` directory. However, the JVM's properties can be set so as to redefine the notion of current directory for the purposes of file I/O.

The service process built in this chapter was an NT process capable of supporting only one service. However, with the support of the `JvmServices` class, an expansion of the dispatch table, and modification to the `Create-Service` call, the code could support the launching of multiple VMs. This way you could provide a generalized JVM service on NT.

Chapter 14

DEBUGGING NATIVE METHODS

Until the heart has found
Its native piece of ground

The day withholds its light,
The eye must stray unlit.

Wendell Berry
The Clear Days

Introduction

Debugging in a hybrid environment presents a special challenge. If you think of the Java bytecode as one instruction set and the host machine's object code as another instruction set, debugging a Java application with native methods is a special case of debugging in a heterogeneous environment. As such, IDE technology does not provide a seamless solution for debugging hybrid Java/C applications.

If the absence of a technological solution, we are left with our wits. With the right state of mind and a few tweaks of the proper settings on your favorite IDE, you can bring the full power of the debugger to bear on successfully debugging your `native` methods.

Outside of an IDE, you can still debug `native` methods. The trick is understanding exactly what it is you are debugging.

What Is It You Are Debugging?

It is important to understand what it is you are debugging when you are debugging native code and, for that matter, Java code. You must think of the JVM,

317

your Java application and the native code as one big happy executable. What executes when you run a Java application is the Java interpreter. As the interpreter runs, it executes the byte code representation of your application, that is, your class files. It may be that while it is interpreting your byte code, it does a `native` method call.

When a `native` method is running, native machine code is executing. The Java interpreter cannot run this code—it interprets Java byte codes—but it does arrange for it to be run, as if it were part of the interpreter itself. That is to say it correctly sets up its own stack and calls the `native` method as if it were one of its own function calls.

This is a bit of a simplification but it will suffice for our purposes. The point is to get you thinking in terms of debugging the interpreter. When debugging native code, you will run a debugger on the Java interpreter.

The only catch to this approach, in some environments, is that the symbols associated with your `native` methods are not available when you first load the Java interpreter into the debugger. Absent any special debugger support, they are not available until a `System.loadLibrary` call loads them. This may be done in a `static` block, in which case the symbols become available when the class containing the static block is loaded. Alternatively, the symbols may be loaded by a `System.loadLibrary` call in the main-line code. In either case, source files cannot be read and breakpoints cannot be set until the symbols from the native library are loaded.

Fortunately, IDEs such as Microsoft's Visual Studio provide a means for loading symbols from a dynamic library at the beginning of a debug session. Likewise, Sun's dbx provides a mechanism for setting a breakpoint whenever a shared library is loaded. Once the library is loaded, the symbols from the native code are available and you can then debug using all your ordinary tricks.

Before the specifics on debugging native code on different platforms and IDEs are discussed, a few general words about debugging the JNI API are in order.

JNI Debugging Tips

Listed below are a few sanity checks to apply while you are debugging native code. Since many JNI types are opaque to us mere mortals, you can't expect to know whether you have correct values. The following heuristics are helpful in gaining insight into what is and what is not working in your native code.

- Object references are indices into the local reference registry that the JVM maintains. These tend to be small values. As you step through native code creating more references, you will see their values increment.

- Global references have negative values.

- Don't be alarmed by a lot of unfamiliar names on the bottom of the call stack. The interpreter is very deep into its own stack by the time it calls a `native` method.

- `jmethodID`s are opaque pointers and so will have "big" values. Their value should look like whatever pointer values look like on your platform.

- If a `jfieldID` return value is zero, you most likely have given the `GetStatic<type>Field` or `Get<type>Field` call a bad type signature. The same is true if `GetMethodID` and `GetStatic-MethodID` return a zero value.

Microsoft Visual Studio

A few tweaks of the default settings is all that it takes to get Visual C++ to debug your native code. The changes that need to be made are enumerated below with accompanying shots of the relevant screens from Microsoft Visual Studio.

The steps enumerated below apply to the project that builds the DLL containing the `native` methods you wish to debug.

Within the Project->Settings dialog, select the Debug tab. Under the Debug form, select "General" category. Fill in the fields with the appropriate values as described below:

- Specify the path to the executable for the Java interpreter as the "Executable for debug session," e.g. `c:\jdk\bin\java.exe`.

- Specify the directory in which the main class for your Java application exists in the "Working Directory" field.

- Specify a classpath value followed by the name of the class file whose main method is to be run. The classpath value must include all relevant system class locations as well as directories containing classes required by your application.

In the following screen display, the full path name of the Java interpreter is named as the executable that is to be debugged. Two things should be noted.

- The -classpath flag is necessary as an argument to the executable.

- The inclusion of \jdk\bin\classes.zip in the value of the -classpath option is also necessary. This file contains the JDK system classes. The directory name should reflect the location of the class files for your JDK environment.

The current directory is also named in the classpath value since that is where the class to be debugged, NewObjectEx1, resides. Finally, as an additional argument to the executable under debug is the name of your application's main class, in this case, NewObjectEx1. Any arguments to the main method would then follow.

Figure 14-1 *Setting Execution Parameters for Visual C++ Debugging*

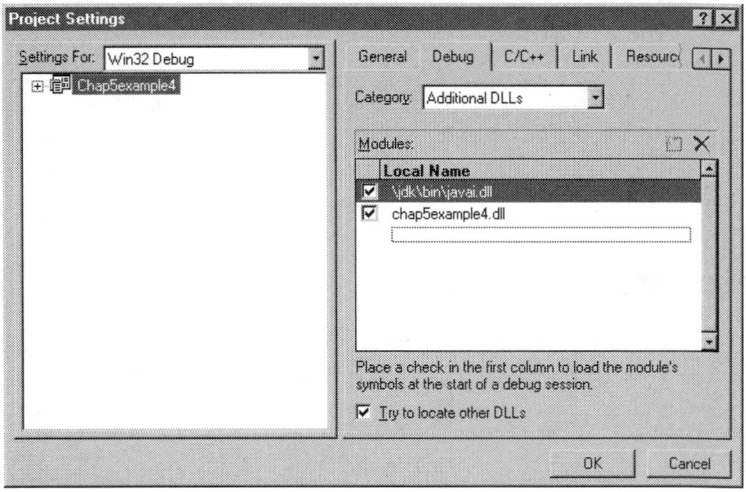

Within the Project->Settings dialog, select the Debug tab. Under the Debug tab, select the "Additional DLLs" category. Fill in the fields with the appropriate values as described below:

- Specify the Java interpreter's DLL, e.g. c:\jdk\bin\javai.dll.

- Specify the name of DLL which contains the implementation of your native methods. If multiple DLLs are loaded by your application, they all should be named.

In the following screen display, two additional DLLs are named. The first is the DLL required by the Java interpreter. The second is the library which contains the native methods needed by the class we are to debug, NewObjectEx1.

Figure 14-2 *Specifying Additional DLLs for Visual C++ Debugging*

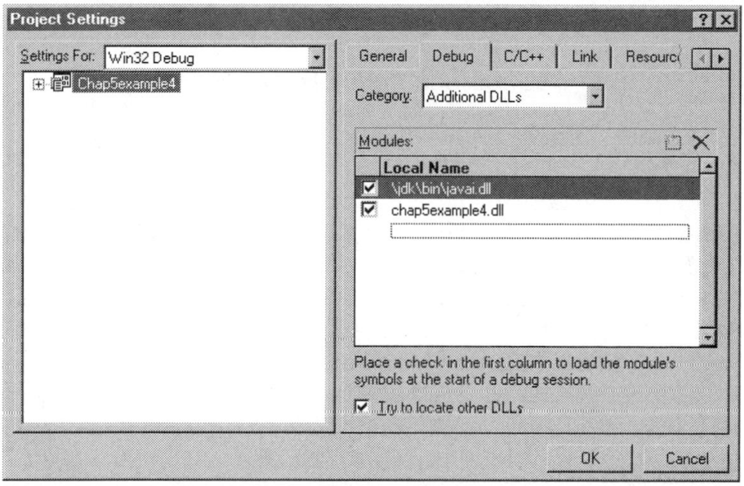

When supplying the names of the DLLs, you may either specify a complete path name or simply the name of the DLL. If you supply only the library name, you will need to specify the directories in which these DLLs reside. This is done under the Directories tab of the Tools->Options dialog.

If you specify the debug version of the interpreter, `java_g`, as the executable to debug, the JVM will attempt to load DLLs with a `_g` suffix.

Now that the configuration is complete, you can debug as usual. Select a line in your `native` method source, select the "Run to Cursor" feature under Build->Start Debug pull-down menu (Control-F10). The Java interpreter will stop when it arrives at the line of native code you selected.

The JVM: Starting a Debug Session

On UNIX machines, Sun provides some help in getting you started debugging.

To run Java on UNIX machines, you actually run a wrapper script. You may either run `$JDK_HOME/bin/java` or `$JDK_HOME/bin/java_g`. `java_g` starts the debug version of the interpreter.

If you take a close look at either of these scripts, you will see that the command executed to run the Java interpreter is:

```
exec $DEBUG_PROG $prog $opts "$@"
```

where `prog` is the full path name of the Java interpreter. On a SPARC machine using the green threads implementation, this is `$JDK_HOME/bin/sparc/green_threads/java`.

By default, the variable `DEBUG_PROG` is null so what gets executed is the Java interpreter. However, if you set `DEBUG_PROG` in your environment to, say, dbx, then this script will execute dbx with the full path name of the Java interpreter as its first argument. For example:

◄ ● User Input   dbx **Session Started From** java **Script**

```
% setenv DEBUG_PROG dbx
% java
Reading symbolic information for java
Reading symbolic information for rtld /usr/lib/
ld.so.1 Reading symbolic information for libjava.so
Reading symbolic information for libm.so.1
Reading symbolic information for libdl.so.1
Reading symbolic information for libX11.so.4
Reading symbolic information for libsocket.so.1
Reading symbolic information for libnsl.so.1
Reading symbolic information for libc.so.1
Reading symbolic information for libXext.so.0
Reading symbolic information for libw.so.1
Reading symbolic information for libintl.so.1
Reading symbolic information for libmp.so.1
(dbx)
```

Simply typing java puts you into the debugger. All the shared libraries that the interpreter needs are loaded at this point. Notice there is no mention of any of your native libraries. They have yet to be loaded. They await a System.loadLibrary call.

The advantage of this approach is that the wrapper script provided by Sun sets up all the environment for successful debugging. Specifically, it sets the CLASSPATH environment variable to include all the directories, zip, and jar files that the JVM needs. This script also set the correct value for the LD_LIBRARY_PATH environment variable.

If you choose not to use this wrapper script, you will have to set up these environment variables on your own. The following tables list the directories and zip and jar files that are set in your environment by the wrapper script. As always, JDK_HOME refers to the root of your JDK installation.

Of course, you would need to add any class directories, zip, or jar files required by your application. One way of doing this is by setting these environment variables in your .dbxrc file.

With this information in mind, let's look at a brief debugging example of a native method using dbx on Solaris.

Table 14.1 *Default Environment Set by* `java` *Script*

Environment Variable	Contains...
CLASSPATH	$JDK_HOME/classes $JDK_HOME/lib/classes.jar $JDK_HOME/lib/rt.jar $JDK_HOME/lib/i18n.jar $JDK_HOME/lib/classes.zip
LD_LIBRARY_PATH	$JDK_HOME/lib/sparc/green_threads

Debugging on Solaris

Using dbx

Stand-alone debuggers like Sun's dbx don't provide the same nice integration as Microsoft's Visual C++ environment but, nonetheless, provide sufficient support to debug native code in a straightforward fashion.

One command, `stop dlopen`, is all you have to add to your standard repertoire. This command sets a breakpoint when a shared library is loaded. When the native library in which you are interested is loaded, you have available to you all the symbols in your `native` methods. With this information you can look at source files and set breakpoints as you normally would.

Continuing with the dbx session above will illustrate the role of `stop dlopen` in helping you access the symbols within a shared object library. Before the `stop dlopen` command, an attempt is made to reference a C source file which was compiled into the native library.

 **• User Input**   dbx file **Command**

(dbx) **file jniDebugEx.c**

• Program Output   **Failure to Find Source File**

dbx: no such source file: "jniDebugEx.c"

This results in an error message. dbx does not yet know anything about this source file. This problem is avoided by setting a breakpoint with `stop dlopen`. The `run` command causes the Java interpreter to run until a library is loaded.

● User Input   dbx stop dlopen **Command**

```
(dbx) stop dlopen
(2) stop dlopen
(dbx) run
```

● Program Output   **Running Until Break at** dlopen

```
running: java DebugEx (process id 18639)
Reading symbolic information for
 libChapA2example1.so Reading symbolic information
 for libNativeUtil.so stopped in r_debug_state at
 0xdf7d8a5c 0xdf7d8a5c: r_debug_state :jmp %o7 + 0x8
```

From the output above, you can see that dbx reports that it is about to read the necessary symbols from two shared libraries and then hits the breakpoint.

A stack trace reveals where the interpreter has stopped. The function arguments have been removed from the dbx output to eliminate clutter but the function names remain. Notice the call to invokeNativeMethod. This signals the JVM has called out into native code.

 **User Input**   dbx where **Command to Produce Stack Trace**

(dbx) **where**

• Program Output   **Stack Trace at dlopen Breakpoint**

```
=>[1] r_debug_state(), at 0xdf7d8a5c
  [2] dl_new_so(), at 0xdf7da6c4
  [3] __dlopen(), at 0xdf7da3d0
  [4] dlopen(), at 0xdf7da1ac
  [5] sysAddDLSegment(), at 0xdf744464
  [6] java_lang_Runtime_loadFileInternal(),
   at 0xdf739150
  [7]Java_java_lang_Runtime_loadFileInternal_stub(),
   at 0xdf714a9c
  [8] invokeNativeMethod(), at 0xdf712504
  [9] finish_invokevirtual(), at 0xdf750060
 [10] do_execute_java_method_vararg(), at 0xdf7228ec
 [11] do_execute_java_method(), at 0xdf72229c
 [12] RunStaticInitializers(), at 0xdf71334c
 [13] RuntimeInitClass(), at 0xdf709bec
 [14] Locked_ResolveClass(), at 0xdf710e1c
 [15] FindClassFromClass(), at 0xdf71159c
 [16] java_main(), at 0xdf743100
```

At this point, the `file` command will be successful. You can view your native source code, set breakpoints, and debug away.

► **• User Input**   **Successful** `dbx` `file` **Command**

```
(dbx) file jniDebugEx.c
(dbx) list
```

• Program Output   **Source Listing After** *file* **Command**

```
1    #include "jniDebugEx.h"
2    #include <stdio.h>
3
4    JNIEXPORT void JNICALL Java_DebugEx_nativeHello
5      (JNIEnv *env, jclass thisClass)
6    {
7        jclass clazz = env->FindClass(
                         "java/lang/String");
8        printf("Hello from Native\n");
9
10   }
```

At this point, you can apply your best debugging skills to learn there is nothing wrong with the example code!

Debugging With Sun Workshop

Sun Workshop is, among other things, a front-end to dbx. Everything we learned in the previous section about debugging native code still applies in the Sun Workshop environment. You even employ the strategy of invoking Workshop by setting DEBUG_PROG environment variable to the name of the Workshop executable if you can tolerate the message that the file containing the Java interpreter is not a Workshop workset.

If you set the DEBUG_PROG environment variable to invoke Workshop, the correct CLASSPATH and LD_LIBRARY_PATH values will be set when you enter Workshop. You will still have to start a debug session. You do this by selecting Debug->New Program from the Workshop title bar menu.

This brings up the Debug New Program dialog that allows you to specify the name of the program to debug. This dialog is shown in Figure 14-3.

Figure 14-3 *Workshop Debug New Program Dialog*

In the Name text field, you should type the full path name of the Java inter-preter executable—not the wrapper script. If you specify the debug version of the interpreter, `java_g`, your library names should all contain the `_g` suffix. In the Arguments text field, you should type the name of the class you want to load.

A Debugging window will open. Select Windows->DBX Commands to display a `dbx` window. Figure 14-4 shows this step.

Figure 14-4 *Displaying a* dbx *Commands Window in Workshop*

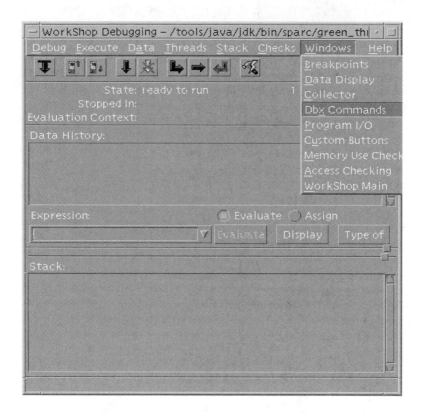

Selecting the "Dbx Commands" item will cause a window to be opened displaying a dbx command prompt. You can follow the instructions above to set a breakpoint using the stop dlopen command.

An alternative to launching Workshop via the Java wrapper script is to launch it directly. If you choose this route, you need to initialize the CLASSPATH and LD_LIBRARY_PATH environment variables as described Table 14.1. This can be done by either placing the appropriate export commands in your dbx start-up file, $HOME/.dbxrc, or selecting the Environment Variables button in the Debug New Program dialog when identifying the full path name of the Java interpreter.

When All Else Fails

If your debugger does not have a command similar to `stop dlopen` then you will need another way of stopping execution after your native library code is loaded, but before your native code is executed. The stack trace from the dbx session above gives us a clue.

With Sun's JVM, you can see that a function `invokeJNINative-Method` is called on the way toward executing a `native` method. This is as good a place as any to set a breakpoint.

Below is the output from a dbx session in which the `stop dlopen` command is not used.

▶ **• User Input**   Setting a Breakpoint at `native` **Method Invocation**

```
(dbx) stop in invokeJNINativeMethod
dbx: warning: 'invokeJNINativeMethod' has no
debugger info -- will trigger on first instruction
(2) stop in invokeJNINativeMethod
(dbx) run DebugEx
```

• Program Output   **Breakpoint When** `native` **Method Is Invoked**

```
Running: java DebugEx (process id 23727)
Reading symbolic information
 for libChapA2example1.so
Reading symbolic information for libNativeUtil.so
hello world stopped in invokeJNINativeMethod at
 0xdf712638 0xdf712638: invokeJNINativeMethod:
save     %sp, -0x60, %sp
```

• User Input   Using `file` **Command to View Source**

```
(dbx) file jniDebugEx.c
(dbx) list
```

• Program Output   **Listing of Source File**

```
1    #include "jniDebugEx.h"
2    #include <stdio.h>
3
4    JNIEXPORT void JNICALL Java_DebugEx_nativeHello
5      (JNIEnv *env, jclass thisClass)
6    {
7         jclass clazz = env->FindClass(
                        "java/lang/String");
8         printf("Hello from Native\n");
9
10   }
(dbx)
```

Once the breakpoint is reached, the source file that contains your `native` methods can be viewed. The full functionality of the debugger can now be used to find those pesky bugs.

The foregoing applies only to the Sun JVM in that it relies on a name of an internal function when setting the breakpoint. This name will be different for different JVMs. However, with a little patience and investigation using tools such as nm or dump on UNIX machines and `dumpbin` on Win32 machines, you will probably be able to figure out what function a given JVM uses to call into native code.

Summary

This chapter provided an overview of an approach to debugging in both a UNIX environment and within an Integrated Development Environment on a Win32 platform. The key notion to keep in mind is that it is the Java interpreter that is being debugged when you try to debug `native` methods. Remembering this one point should allow you to take the techniques discussed in this chapter and apply them to environments not addressed in this chapter.

Chapter 15   *JDK 1.2 ENHANCEMENTS TO JNI*

> You could not step twice into the same river; for other
> waters are ever flowing on to you.
>
> Heraclitus
> *On the Universe*

Introduction

The only APIs the ancient Greek Heraclitus ever saw were those involving nature. He watched the river waters flow, the skies change and the seasons pass. No humble observer, he took as his subject the universe and spoke to the universal. He could not have foreseen Java, but had he, he would have warned of many revisions.

This appendix summarizes changes introduced to the JNI in JDK 1.2.

The changes include both enhancements to existing JDK 1.1 functions and the addition of new functionality.

A summary of the new functionality appears below.

Summary of Enhancements

- A more robust means of passing arguments to the JNI_CreateJavaVM function
- Minor improvements to some of the Invocation API functions
- Extensions to the JNI function FindClass so that it can find classes loaded by a class loader. In JDK 1.1, FindClass was able to locate only system-loaded classes.

Summary of Additional Functionality

- Functions to take advantage of the weak reference facility of JDK 1.2.
- String and array functions that may return a pointer to object data even if the JVM does not support the pinning of memory.
- Functions that allow a user finer control over the allocation of memory for local references within native code.
- Functions that interact with the Java Core Reflection API.
- Functions that allow the extraction of a region of a java.lang.String object into a user-supplied buffer.
- An Invocation API function to test whether a native thread is attached to the JVM.
- JVM recognition of two user-supplied functions within a native library. These functions are exported by the native library and are invoked when the library is loaded and unloaded.
- Class loader support of native libraries.

JDK 1.2 JNI Enhancements

JVM Initialization

In JDK 1.2, a new JVM initialization structure is introduced to address portability issues surrounding the JDK1_1InitArgs structure. This new structure, JavaVMInitArgs, uses symbolic name/value pairs to encode arbitrary JVM start up options. Each name/value pair is represented by the JavaVMOption structure. Being able to supply a list of values provides a flexibility when configuring the JVM not available in JDK 1.1 where the configuration options were defined by the JDK1_1InitArgs structure.

The proposed JavaVMInitArgs and JavaVMOption structures are presented below.

```
typedef struct JavaVMInitArgs {
    jint version;
    jint nOptions;
    JavaVMOption *options;
    jint *result;
} JavaVMInitArgs;

typedef struct JavaVMOption {
    char *name;
    union {
        jint i;
        jdouble d;
        void *p;
    } value;
} JavaVMOption;
```

The JDK 1.2 introduces a set of standard options that all JVMs must recognize. You will recognize them from Chapter 12.

Table 15.1 *Standard JVM Arguments*

Name	Value
classpath	System class path
properties	An array of strings, each string of the form key=value
verbose	A string composed of names (gc, class, jni) separated by commas. The names indicate the types of messages reported by the JVM.
vfprintf	Address of vfprintf callback
exit	Address of exit callback
abort	Address of abort callback

In addition to the standard arguments, a JVM implementation may support its own options. The names of these options must start with an underscore (_). For example, JDK 1.2 support for the initial and maximum heap size options supplied by JDK 1.1 is available using the _ms and _mx options. Each JVM vendor is responsible for documenting what other options it supports.

The version field of the JavaVMInitArgs must be set to 0x00010002 to use the new options format. The nOptions value must be set to the number of JavaVMOption values specified in the array pointed to by the options field.

Like the JDK1_1InitArgs structure, the JavaVMInitArgs structure is passed to JNI_CreateJavaVM. As each option is processed, a result is placed in the corresponding slot in the result array.

JNI_CreateJavaVM returns a negative value as soon as it encounters an illegal option. There are three possible values that may be placed in the result array.

Table 15.2 *Option Result Values*

Name	Description
JNI_OK	Valid option
JNI_UNRECOGNIZED	Unrecognized option
JNI_ILLEGAL	Recognized, but illegal value

One important side-effect of the new JDK 1.2 JVM initialization structure is that a call to JNI_GetDefaultJavaVMInitArgs is no longer neces-sary before calling JNI_CreateJavaVM.

Improvements to Invocation API Functions

Some minor changes were made to three of the Invocation API functions. Some of these simply had to do with fleshing out details not completely spec-ified in JDK 1.1.

In the function

```
jint AttachCurrentThread(
        JavaVM *vm, void **penv, jint version);
```

the third argument, previously unspecified, now specifies the version of JNI function table to be returned in the second argument. The valid versions in JDK 1.2 are 0x00010001 or 0x00010002.

In JDK 1.1,

```
jint DetachCurrentThread(JavaVM *vm);
```

may not be used to detach the main thread from the JVM. That restriction will be relaxed in JDK 1.2. There is a similar relaxation on the use of

```
jint DestroyJavaVM(JavaVM *vm);
```

Although JDK 1.2 still does not support JVM unloading, any thread may call DestroyJavaVM. The JVM waits until the current thread is the only user thread before it returns an error code. This differs from JDK 1.1 in that only the main thread was allowed to call DestroyJavaVM, and the JVM waits until the main thread is the only user thread and then returns.

FindClass Enhancements

In JDK 1.1, FindClass searched only local classes in CLASSPATH. The resulting classes did not have a class loader. The Java security model has been extended to allow non-system classes to load and call native methods. In

JDK 1.2, FindClass locates the class loader associated with the current native method. If the native code belongs to a system class, no class loader will be involved. Otherwise, the proper class loader will be invoked to load and link the named class.

For details on the JDK 1.2 security model see http://www.java-soft.com/products/jdk/1.2/docs/guide/security/.

New JDK 1.2 JNI Functions

A synopsis of the new JNI functions follows.

Weak References

Weak references can be created and destroyed using the JNI functions:

```
jweak NewWeakGlobalRef(JNIEnv *env, jobject obj);
void DeleteWeakGlobalRef(JNIEnv *env, jweak obj);
```

A new JNI native type jweak to be used with these functions has been introduced. See

```
http://java.sun.com/products/jdk/1.2/docs/guide/
                  weakrefs/index.html
```

for a complete description of JDK 1.2 weak references. In short, weak references are a way to hold a reference to an object that the garbage collector will ignore when determining whether memory for an object can be reclaimed.

"Critical Region" String and Array Manipulation

In JDK 1.1 the JNI string and primitive array manipulation functions return a pointer to contiguous memory containing the data represented by a java.lang.String or a primitive array object. If a 1.1 JVM supports pinned memory, the functions can return a pointer directly into object memory while guaranteeing that memory will not move.

New 1.2 JNI functions allow native code to obtain a direct pointer to strings and primitive array elements even if the JVM does not support pinning. They do this by introducing the notion of a "critical region" in native code.

The following functions mark the start of a critical region in native code, as well as implement the semantics of their JDK 1.1 analogues.

```
jbyte * GetPrimitiveArrayCritical(
    JNIEnv *env, jarray arry, jboolean *isCopy);

jchar * GetStringCritical(
    JNIEnv *env, jstring string, jboolean *isCopy);
```

The counterparts to these functions are used to mark the end of a critical section.

```
void ReleaseStringCritical(
    JNIEnv *env, jstring string, const jchar *carry);

void ReleasePrimitiveArrayCritical(
    JNIEnv *env, jarray arry,
    void *carry, jint mode);
```

The critical region these functions define is self-imposed. Calling the `Get` functions is a signal to the JVM that the native programmer will adhere to the following restrictions:

1. No JNI functions will be called before the corresponding `Release` function is called. The only exception to this is that `Get` calls may be nested.

2. No system calls will be made that would cause the current thread to block and wait on another thread.

By adhering to these constraints, it is, and here the Sun documentation is quoted, "more likely that the native code will obtain an uncopied version of the array, even if the JVM does not support pinning." What we have here is that much is left to the JVM implementation. One possibility upon servicing a critical function is that the JVM may disable garbage collection. With garbage collection disabled, a direct pointer to object memory may be returned without concern that that memory will be moved out from under it.

If the JVM internally represents a string or an array in a non-contiguous manner, the `Get` functions will still make a copy of the data. Therefore, it is possible that the `Get` functions will return a NULL value. This should be tested for upon return of the `Get` function.

Similarly, the `isCopy` value set by the 'get' function will need to be tested. Introducing a critical section does not guarantee that memory is not copied. For portability across various JVMs, it is best to test `isCopy`.

Local Reference Management

Recall from page 70 in Chapter 5 the discussion on "Releasing a Local Reference." Therein possible memory allocation problems regarding the allocation of local references was touched upon, mostly in the form of a warning to be careful about injudicious use of local references. Excessive allocation of local references may exhaust memory during the execution of native code. The JDK 1.2 provides four additional functions for lifetime management of local references.

The first function allows the user to tell the JVM how many local references it needs. The function

```
jint EnsureLocalCapacity(

        JNIEnv *env, jint capacity);
```

ensures that at least a given number of local references can be created in the current thread. Upon entering a `native` method, the JVM automatically provides for the creation of at least sixteen local references.

Two additional functions give the JNI programmer finer control over the allocation of local references. The JDK 1.2 proposal introduces the notion of a local reference frame. While native code is executing, local references can be allocated and deallocated in groups using `PushLocalFrame` and `PopLocalFrame`.

```
jint PushLocalFrame(JNIEnv *env, jint capacity);

jobject PopLocalFrame(JNIEnv *env, jobject result);
```

When pushing a local reference frame, you can specify the number of references needed. When popping a frame, a value which represents a reference to an object in the previous frame can be returned.

Finally, `NewLocalRef` creates a new local reference. The input argument may either be a global or local reference.

```
jobject NewLocalRef(JNIEnv *env, jobject ref);
```

Core Reflection Support

The JDK 1.2 provides JNI functions that translate between JNI `jmethodID` and `jfieldID` values to field and method objects defined by the Java Core Reflection API.

The Java Core Reflection API defines, among others, two classes, `java.lang.reflect.Method` and `java.lang.reflect.Field`.

The new JNI functions convert objects from these classes to jmethodID and jfieldID values, respectively. Likewise, jmethodID and jfieldID values can be converted to objects of type java.lang.reflect.Method and java.lang.reflect.Field, respectively.

```
jmethodID FromReflectedMethod(
    JNIEnv *env, jobject method);

jfieldID FromReflectedField(
    JNIEnv *env, jobject field);

jobject ToReflectedMethod(
    JNIEnv *env, jclass cls, jmethodID methodID);

jobject ToReflectedField(
    JNIEnv *env, jclass cls, jfieldID fieldID);
```

The miniInvoker example from Chapter 12 could benefit from these calls. In that example, there were many instances of having to take a jobject representing a java.lang.reflect.Method and invoke it. Consider the code that returned an array of objects describing the parameters to a method.

Listing 15.1 getParameterTypes *Function From* miniInvoker *Example*

```
jobjectArray
Method::getParameterTypes(
              JNIEnv* env, jobject method) {
(1)      jclass clazz = env->GetObjectClass(method);
(2)      jmethodID mid = env->GetMethodID(clazz,
                  "getParameterTypes",
                  "()[Ljava/lang/Class;");

    return (jobjectArray) env->CallObjectMethod(
        method, mid, NULL);
}
```

This code could be simplified by the use of FromReflectedMethod. The two JNI calls in [1] and [2] could be replaced with a single call to FromReflectedMethod as in line [3] from Listing 15. 2.

Listing 15. 2 *Modified* `getParameterTypes` *Using JDK 1.2 JNI Function*

```
jobjectArray
Method::getParameterTypes(
            JNIEnv* env, jobject method) {
    jmethodID mid = FromReflectedMethod(env, method);
    return (jobjectArray) env->CallObjectMethod(
            method, mid, NULL);
}
```

(3)

String Character Extraction

Using the JDK 1.1 JNI you can extract a region of a primitive array into a buffer you supplied. JDK 1.2 gives you the same functionality for strings. Two new functions are proposed to provide this support.

```
void GetStringRegion(JNIEnv *env,
            jstring str, jsize start,
            jsize len, jchar *buf);
```

```
void GetStringUTFRegion(JNIEnv *env,
            jstring str, jsize start,
            jsize len, char *buf);
```

The first of these functions operate on Unicode strings, the second on UTF-8 strings. The arguments are as described for primitive arrays in Chapter 6.

New Invocation API Functionality

A single function to test whether a native thread is attached to the JVM is proposed for JDK 1.2.

```
jboolean IsAttached(JavaVM *vm);
```

Loading and Unloading Notification

In JDK 1.2 the JNI supports two user-defined functions, `JNI_OnLoad` and `JNI_OnUnLoad`. These two functions are supplied by the user as exported entry points from the native library code. The user defines these functions and the JVM invokes them at the appropriate time.

```
jint JNI_OnLoad(JavaVM *vm, void *reserved);
```

```
void JNI_OnUnload(JavaVM *vm, void *reserved);
```

When a native library is loaded, `JNI_OnLoad` is called. You may use this function, for example, to do any initialization required by the native library.

JNI_OnLoad is roughly equivalent to the DLL_ATTACH_PROCESS branch in an exported DllMain in a Win32 DLL. Likewise, exporting JNI_OnUnload is roughly equivalent to the DLL_DETACH_PROCESS branch in an exported DllMain function.

The return value of the JNI_OnLoad is important. This function must return a JNI version number. If a native library expects to use JDK 1.2 functionality, the JNI_OnLoad function must return 0x00010002. If the native library does not export JNI_OnLoad, the JVM assumes that the native library requires version 1.1 of the JNI.

JNI_OnUnload is called when the class loader that loaded the native library is garbage collected.

Native Library Management Via Class Loaders

A class loaded by a JVM is uniquely identified by its fully-qualified class name, a class loader, and a Class object. In JDK 1.1, when a native library is loaded it is not associated with a particular class loader. As a result, a class may mistakenly link with native libraries loaded by a class with the same name but loaded by a different class loader. This violates the requirement that each class loader have its own name space. To fix this problem, JDK 1.2 associates each native library with a class loader. In JDK 1.2 the same JNI native library cannot be loaded into more than one class loader.

A useful side-effect of properly associating a native library with a class loader is that native libraries can be unloaded when their corresponding class loaders are garbage collected.

Summary

This appendix summarized the enhancements and additions to the JNI for JDK 1.2. All code based on JDK 1.1 JNI will still operate under JDK 1.2.

Most of the changes involve the addition of new functionality. If you need finer control over local reference allocation, the new functions PushLocal-Frame and PopLocalFrame are useful. To avoid copying of string and array data, use GetStringCritical or GetPrimitiveArray-Critical. If the JVM with which your code is running supports "critical sections," you can access the Java object data without worrying about the memory moving out from under you due to garbage collection.

If you are starting the JVM from a C/C++ application and want to maximize portability across JVMs that support JNI, you may want to consider converting your JDK1_1InitArgs structure into a JavaVMInitArgs structure.

Appendix A JNI REFERENCE

The Java Native Interface?
Sounds like a National Geographic Special.

Bob Senese
ND'80

Introduction

This section serves as a quick reference guide for every JNI function. The functions are arranged alphabetically. The Invocation API functions appear herein as well. Collections of functions that perform a similar operation are discussed together in this appendix.

Notation

Collections of functions that perform a similar operation appear under a special parametric function name. For example, the JNI method calling routines that operate on non-static methods all appear on a page with the heading Call<*type*>Method. The <*type*> tag is just one of six tags used in this appendix to parameterize a JNI function name, return type or argument. These labels, and their possible replacement values, are described in following paragraphs.

<*type*> – Represents the Java types and may be replaced with Boolean, Byte, Char, Short, Int, Long, Double, Float, Object or Void.

<pType> – Represents the Java primitive types and may be replaced with any value from the above list except `Object`.

<jniType> – Represents the Java Native Types and may be replaced with `jboolean`, `jbyte`, `jchar`, `jshort`, `jint`, `jlong`, `jdouble`, `jfloat`, `void`, `jobject`.

<pjniType> – Represents the primitive Java Native Types and may be replaced with any value from the above list except `jobject`. No native array types may be used to replace this label.

<pjniArrayType> – Represents the Java Native primitive array types: `jbooleanArray`, `jbyteArray`, `jcharArray`, `jshortArray`, `jintArray`, `jlongArray`, `jdoubleArray`, `jfloatArray`.

With the exception of the Invocation API functions, all the functions described in this appendix include the JNIEnv pointer as their first argument. This is the C language convention for calling JNI functions. For example, a C language call to the JNI function `AllocObject` looks like:

```
JNIEnv*   env;
jclass    clazz;
/* ... */
(*env)->AllocObject(env, clazz);
```

When called from a C++ program, the equivalent call would appear as:

```
JNIEnv*   env;
jclass    clazz;
// ...
env->AllocObject(clazz);
```

The Invocation API

The Invocation API functions are not accessed through the JNI function table. The call syntax of three of the Invocation API functions require no special consideration. They are called as any C/C++ function. These functions are:

```
JNI_GetDefaultJavaVMInitArgs
JNI_CreateJavaVM
JNI_GetCreatedJavaVMs
```

However, the four other functions that make up the Invocation API are called through the JNIInvokeInterface function table. This structure is defined in <jni.h> and is shown below.

```
typedef const struct JNIInvokeInterface *JavaVM;

const struct JNIInvokeInterface ... = {
        NULL,
        NULL,
        NULL,
        DestroyJavaVM,
        AttachCurrentThread,
        DetachCurrentThread,
};
```

For JDK 1.2, the call `IsAttached` is also contained in the `JNIInvokeInterface`.

The `JavaVM` type is also defined in `<jni.h>`. This type contains a pointer to a `JNIInvokeInterface` structure. A call to `JNI_CreateJavaVM` returns such a pointer. This pointer can then be used to call the functions defined in the `JNIInvokeInterface` table. How the pointer is used depends on whether you are writing C or C++ code and is similar to the convention for using the `JNIEnv` pointer. To call a function in the `JNIInvokeInterface` table from C use the following syntax:

```
JavaVM              *jvm;
JNIEnv              *env;
JDK1_1AttachArgs    *targs;
/* ... */
(*jvm)->AttachCurrentThread(jvm, &env, &targs);
```

The analogous call within a C++ program looks like:

```
JavaVM              *jvm;
JNIEnv              *env;
JDK1_1AttachArgs    *targs;
/* ... */
jvm->AttachCurrentThread(&env, &targs);
```

In this appendix all the `JNIInvokeInterface` functions are shown with the `JavaVM` pointer as the first argument.

AllocObject

NAME

AllocObject

SYNTAX

jobject AllocObject(JNIEnv*env,
                    jclass   clazz);

DESCRIPTION

Allocates a new Java object without invoking any of the constructors for the object.

Note: This function cannot be used to allocate memory for an array object.

ARGUMENTS

env   The JNI interface pointer

clazz   A Java class object reference

RETURNS

Returns a Java object, or NULL if the object cannot be allocated.

THROWS

java.lang.InstantiationException: if the clazz argument is an interface or an abstract class.

java.lang.OutOfMemoryError: if there is not sufficient memory available to allocate the object.

Invocation API	AttachCurrentThread

NAME   AttachCurrentThread

SYNTAX
```
jint AttachCurrentThread(
               JavaVM      *vm,
               JNIEnv      **env,
               void        *thr_args);
```

DESCRIPTION   Attaches the current thread to a JVM. The second argument
                  is an address of a pointer to a JNIEnv struct that is
                  filled in by a call to AttachCurrentThread. JDK 1.1
                  assigns no meaning to the last argument. In JDK 1.2, the
                  third argument specifies the version of JNI function table
                  that is returned in the second argument. The valid versions
                  in JDK 1.2 are 0x00010001 (for 1.1) and 0x00010002
                  (for 1.2).

                  Trying to attach a thread that is already attached has no
                  effect. A native thread cannot be attached simultaneously to
                  two JVMs.

ARGUMENTS

vm	A pointer to a JavaVM struct
env	A pointer to a JNI interface pointer
thr_args	A pointer to JVM specific attachment args

RETURNS   Returns 0 on success or a negative value on failure.

Call<type>Method

NAME Call<*type*>Method

SYNTAX <*jniType*> Call<*type*>Method(

JNIEnv	*env,
jobject	obj,
jmethodID	methodID,
...);	

DESCRIPTION This template function is a placeholder for a family of functions that invoke a Java method. The actual function names are parameterized by the type of the return value of the method being invoked.

Methods from this family of functions are used to call a Java instance method from a native method. Arguments to be passed to the Java method are listed following the methodID argument. The Call<*type*>Method routine accepts these arguments and passes them to the Java method that is invoked. They must match the Java method signature in number and type.

A function from this group is used to invoke an instance (non-static) method specified by methodID on a Java object. The methodID argument is obtained by calling GetMethodID.

When these functions are used to call a private method or a constructor, the methodID must be derived from the actual class of obj, not from one of its superclasses.

The following table describes each of the method calling routines according to their result type.

Call<type>Method

<jniType>	Call*<type>*Method Function Name
void	CallVoidMethod
jobject	CallObjectMethod
jboolean	CallBooleanMethod
jbyte	CallByteMethod
jchar	CallCharMethod
jshort	CallShortMethod
jint	CallIntMethod
jlong	CallLongMethod
jfloat	CallFloatMethod
jdouble	CallDoubleMethod

ARGUMENTS

env	The JNI interface pointer
obj	A Java object
methodID	A method ID
. . .	List of arguments to the Java method

RETURNS

The value returned by the invocation of the Java method.

THROWS

The exceptions raised by the invocation of the Java method may be raised by a call to any of the Call*<type>*Method functions.

Call<type>MethodA

NAME   Call<*type*>MethodA

SYNTAX   <*jniType*> Call<*type*>MethodA(
                                    JNIEnv   *env,
                                    jobject   obj,
                                    jmethodID   methodID,
                                    jvalue   *args);

DESCRIPTION   This template function is a placeholder for a family of functions that invoke a Java method. The actual function names are parameterized by the type of the return value of the method being invoked.

Methods from this family of functions are used to call a Java instance method from a `native` method. Arguments to be passed to the Java method are supplied in a `jvalue` array immediately following the `methodID` argument. The Call<*type*>MethodA routine accepts these arguments and passes them to the Java method that is invoked. The elements of the `jvalue` array must match the Java method signature in number and type.

A function from this group is used to invoke an instance (non-static) method on a Java object, according to the specified method ID. The `methodID` argument is obtained by calling `GetMethodID`.

When these functions are used to call a `private` method or a constructor, the `methodID` must be derived from the actual class of `obj`, not from one of its superclasses.

The following table describes each of the method calling routines according to their result type. The proper JNI function name is determined by the return type of the Java method that is to be invoked.

Call<type>MethodA

<jniType>	Cal*l<type>*MethodA Function Name
void	CallVoidMethodA
jobject	CallObjectMethodA
jboolean	CallBooleanMethodA
jbyte	CallByteMethodA
jchar	CallCharMethodA
jshort	CallShortMethodA
jint	CallIntMethodA
jlong	CallLongMethodA
jfloat	CallFloatMethodA
jdouble	CallDoubleMethodA

ARGUMENTS

env	The JNI interface pointer
obj	A Java object
methodID	A method ID
args	A jvalue array of arguments

RETURNS

The value returned by the invocation of the Java method.

THROWS

The exceptions raised by the invocation of the Java method may be raised by a call to any of the Call<type>MethodA functions.

Call<type>MethodV

NAME   Call<*type*>MethodV

SYNTAX   <*jniType*> Call<*type*>MethodV(
                                    JNIEnv   *env,
                                    jobject   obj,
                                    jmethodID   methodID,
                                    va_list   args);

DESCRIPTION   This template function is a placeholder for a family of functions that invoke a Java method. The actual function names are parameterized by the type of the return value of the method being invoked.

Members of this family of functions are used to call a Java instance method from a native method. Arguments to be passed to the Java method are supplied in a variable argument list described by the type va_list immediately following the methodID argument. The Call<*type*>MethodV routine accepts these arguments and passes them to the Java method that is invoked. The number and type of elements in the va_list must match the Java method signature in number and type.

For a description of va_list see the <stdargs.h> include file accompanying the ANSI C compiler for your system.

A function from this group is used to invoke an instance (non-static) method on a Java object, according to the specified method ID. The methodID argument is obtained by calling GetMethodID.

When these functions are used to call private methods and constructors, the methodID must be derived from the actual class of obj, not from one of its superclasses.

The following table describes each of the method calling routines according to their result type. The proper JNI function name is determined by the return type of the Java method that is to be invoked.

Call<type>MethodV

<jniType>	Call*<type>*MethodV Function Name
void	CallVoidMethodV
jobject	CallObjectMethodV
jboolean	CallBooleanMethodV
jbyte	CallByteMethodV
jchar	CallCharMethodV
jshort	CallShortMethodV
jint	CallIntMethodV
jlong	CallLongMethodV
jfloat	CallFloatMethodV
jdouble	CallDoubleMethodV

ARGUMENTS

env	The JNI interface pointer
obj	A Java object
methodID	A method ID
args	A va_list of arguments

RETURNS

The value returned by the invocation of the Java method.

THROWS

The exceptions raised by the invocation of the Java method may be raised by a call to any of the Call*<type>*MethodV functions.

CallNonvirtual<type>Method

NAME   CallNonvirtual<*type*>Method

SYNTAX   <*jniType*> CallNonvirtual<*type*>Method(
                          JNIEnv *env,
                          jobject   obj,
                          jclass   clazz,
                          jmethodID   methodID,
                          ...);

DESCRIPTION   This template function is a placeholder for a family of functions
                  that invoke a Java method. The actual function names are
                  parameterized by the type of the return value of the method being
                  invoked.

                  A function from this family is used to invoke an instance
                  (non-static) method on a Java object according to the speci-
                  fied class and method ID. The methodID argument must
                  be obtained by calling GetMethodID on the class clazz.

                  The CallNonvirtual<*type*>Method functions allow a
                  method to be invoked from a superclass of an object even if
                  that method is defined for that object's actual class.
                  Whereas the Call<*type*>Method routines invoke a Java
                  method based on the class of the jobject reference, the
                  CallNonvirtual<*type*>Method routines invoke the
                  method based on the class, designated by the clazz
                  parameter, from which the method ID is obtained. The
                  method ID must be obtained from the actual class of the
                  object or from one of its superclasses.

                  All arguments that are to be passed to the method should be
                  listed immediately following the methodID argument. The
                  CallNonvirtual<*type*>Method routine accepts these
                  arguments and passes them to the Java method that is to be
                  invoked.

                  The following table describes each of the method calling
                  routines according to their result type. The proper JNI func-
                  tion name is determined by the return type of the Java
                  method that is to be invoked.

CallNonvirtual<type>Method

<jniType>	CallNonvirtual*<type>*Method Function Name
void	`CallNonvirtualVoidMethod`
jobject	`CallNonvirtualObjectMethod`
jboolean	`CallNonvirtualBooleanMethod`
jbyte	`CallNonvirtualByteMethod`
jchar	`CallNonvirtualCharMethod`
jshort	`CallNonvirtualShortMethod`
jint	`CallNonvirtualIntMethod`
jlong	`CallNonvirtualLongMethod`
jfloat	`CallNonvirtualFloatMethod`
jdouble	`CallNonvirtualDoubleMethod`

ARGUMENTS

env	the JNI interface pointer
clazz	A Java class
obj	A Java object
methodID	A method ID
. . .	Arguments to the Java method

RETURNS

Returns the result of calling the Java method.

THROWS

The exceptions raised by the invocation of the Java method may be raised by a call to any of the `CallNonvirtual`*<type>*`Method` functions.

CallNonvirtual<type>MethodA

NAME　　　　　　CallNonvirtual<*type*>MethodA

SYNTAX　　　　　<*jniType*> CallNonvirtual<*type*>MethodA(
　　　　　　　　　　　JNIEnv　　　　*env,
　　　　　　　　　　　jobject　　　　obj,
　　　　　　　　　　　jclass　　　　clazz,
　　　　　　　　　　　jmethodID　　　methodID,
　　　　　　　　　　　jvalue　　　　*args);

DESCRIPTION　　This template function is a placeholder for a family of functions that invoke a Java method. The actual function names are parameterized by the type of the return value of the method being invoked

A function from this family is used to invoke an instance (non-static) method on a Java object, according to the specified class and method ID. The methodID argument must be obtained by calling GetMethodID on the class clazz.

The CallNonvirtual<*type*>MethodA functions allow a method to be invoked from a superclass of an object even if that method is defined for that object's actual class. Whereas the Call<*type*>MethodA routines invoke the method based on the class of the object, the CallNonvirtual<*type*>MethodA routines invoke the method based on the class, designated by the clazz parameter, from which the method ID is obtained. The method ID must be obtained from the real class of the object or from one of its superclasses.

All arguments to the method should be placed in an array of jvalues immediately following the methodID argument. The CallNonvirtual<*type*>MethodA function accepts the arguments in this array, and, in turn, passes them to the Java method that is to be invoked.

The following table describes each of the method calling routines according to their result type. The proper JNI function name is determined by the return type of the Java method that is to be invoked.

CallNonvirtual<type>MethodA

<jniType>	CallNonvirtual<*type*>MethodA Function Name
void	CallNonvirtualVoidMethodA
jobject	CallNonvirtualObjectMethodA
jboolean	CallNonvirtualBooleanMethodA
jbyte	CallNonvirtualByteMethodA
jchar	CallNonvirtualCharMethodA
jshort	CallNonvirtualShortMethodA
jint	CallNonvirtualIntMethodA
jlong	CallNonvirtualLongMethodA
jfloat	CallNonvirtualFloatMethodA
jdouble	CallNonvirtualDoubleMethodA

ARGUMENTS

env	The JNI interface pointer
clazz	A Java class
obj	A Java object
methodID	A method ID
args	A jvalue array of arguments

RETURNS

Returns the result of calling the Java method.

THROWS

The exceptions raised by the invocation of the Java method may be raised by a call to any of the CallNonvirtual<*type*>MethodA functions.

CallNonvirtual<type>MethodV

NAME   CallNonvirtual<*type*>MethodV

SYNTAX

```
<jniType> CallNonvirtual<type>MethodV(
                JNIEnv      *env,
                jobject     obj,
                jclass      clazz,
                jmethodID   methodID,
                va_list     args);
```

DESCRIPTION

This template function is a placeholder for a family of functions that invoke a Java method. The actual function names are parameterized by the type of the return value of the method being invoked.

A function from this family is used to invoke an instance (non-static) method on a Java object, according to the specified class and method ID. The methodID argument must be obtained by calling GetMethodID on the class clazz.

The CallNonvirtual<*type*>MethodV functions allow a method to be invoked from a superclass of an object even if that method is defined for that object's actual class. Whereas the Call<*type*>MethodV routines invoke the method based on the class of the object, the CallNonvirtual<*type*>MethodV routines invoke the method based on the class, designated by the clazz parameter, from which the method ID is obtained. The method ID must be obtained from the real class of the object or from one of its superclasses.

All arguments to the method should be placed in an argument of type va_list immediately following the methodID argument. The CallNonvirtual<*type*>-MethodV routine accepts the arguments, and, in turn, passes them to the Java method that is to be invoked.

The following table describes each of the method calling routines according to their result type. The proper JNI function name is determined by the return type of the Java method that is to be invoked.

CallNonvirtual<type>MethodV

<jniType>	CallNonvirtual*<type>*MethodV Function Name
void	CallNonvirtualVoidMethodV
jobject	CallNonvirtualObjectMethodV
jboolean	CallNonvirtualBooleanMethodV
jbyte	CallNonvirtualByteMethodV
jchar	CallNonvirtualCharMethodV
jshort	CallNonvirtualShortMethodV
jint	CallNonvirtualIntMethodV
jlong	CallNonvirtualLongMethodV
jfloat	CallNonvirtualFloatMethodV
jdouble	CallNonvirtualDoubleMethodV

ARGUMENTS

env	The JNI interface pointer
clazz	A Java class
obj	A Java object
methodID	A method ID
args	A va_list of arguments

RETURNS

Returns the result of calling the Java method.

THROWS

The exceptions raised by the invocation of the Java method may be raised by a call to any of the CallNonvirtual*<type>*MethodV functions.

CallStatic<type>Method

NAME   CallStatic<*type*>Method

SYNTAX   <*jniType*> CallStatic<*type*>Method(
                    JNIEnv   *env,
                    jclass   clazz,
                    jmethodID   methodID,
                    ...);

DESCRIPTION   This template function is a placeholder for a family of functions that invoke a Java method. The actual function names are parameterized by the type of the return value of the method being invoked.

This family of operations invokes a static method on a Java class object, according to the specified method ID. The methodID argument must be obtained by calling Get-StaticMethodID.

The method ID must be derived from clazz, not from one of its superclasses.

All arguments that are to be passed to the method should immediately follow the methodID argument. The Call-Static<*type*>Method routine accepts these arguments and passes them to the Java method that is to be invoked.

The following table describes each of the method calling routines according to their result type. The proper JNI function name is determined by the return type of the Java method that is to be invoked.

CallStatic<type>Method

<jniType>	CallStatic*<type>*Method Function Name
void	CallStaticVoidMethod
jobject	CallStaticObjectMethod
jboolean	CallStaticBooleanMethod
jbyte	CallStaticByteMethod
jchar	CallStaticCharMethod
jshort	CallStaticShortMethod
jint	CallStaticIntMethod
jlong	CallStaticLongMethod
jfloat	CallStaticFloatMethod
jdouble	CallStaticDoubleMethod

ARGUMENTS

env	The JNI interface pointer
clazz	A Java class object
methodID	A static method ID
args	Arguments to the static method

RETURNS

Returns the result of calling the static Java method.

THROWS

The exceptions raised by the invocation of the Java method may be raised by a call to any of the CallStatic*<type>*Method functions.

CallStatic<type>MethodA

NAME   CallStatic*<type>*MethodA

SYNTAX   *<jniType>* CallStatic*<type>*MethodA(
                        JNIEnv   *env,
                        jclass   clazz,
                        jmethodID   methodID,
                        jvalue   *args);

DESCRIPTION   This template function is a placeholder for a family of functions that invoke a Java method. The actual function names are parameterized by the type of the return value of the method being invoked.

This family of operations invokes a `static` method on a Java object, according to the specified method ID. The `methodID` argument must be obtained by calling `GetStaticMethodID`.

The method ID must be derived from `clazz`, not from one of its superclasses.

All arguments to the Java method should be placed in an array of `jvalue` values that immediately follows the `methodID` argument. The `CallStaticMethodA` routine accepts the arguments in this array, and, in turn, passes them to the Java method that is to be invoked.

The following table describes each of the method calling routines according to their result type. The proper JNI function name is determined by the return type of the Java method that is to be invoked.

CallStatic<type>MethodA

<jniType>	CallStatic*<type>*MethodA Function Name
void	CallStaticVoidMethodA
jobject	CallStaticObjectMethodA
jboolean	CallStaticBooleanMethodA
jbyte	CallStaticByteMethodA
jchar	CallStaticCharMethodA
jshort	CallStaticShortMethodA
jint	CallStaticIntMethodA
jlong	CallStaticLongMethodA
jfloat	CallStaticFloatMethodA
jdouble	CallStaticDoubleMethodA

ARGUMENTS

env	The JNI interface pointer
clazz	A Java class object
methodID	A static method ID
args	A jvalue array of arguments

RETURNS

Returns the result of calling the Java method.

THROWS

The exceptions raised by the invocation of the Java method may be raised by a call to any of the CallStatic*<type>*MethodA functions.

CallStatic<type>MethodV

NAME   CallStatic<*type*>MethodV

SYNTAX   <*jniType*> CallStatic<*type*>MethodV(
                JNIEnv   *env,
                jclass   clazz,
                jmethodID   methodID,
                va_list   args);

DESCRIPTION   This template function is a placeholder for a family of functions that invoke a Java method. The actual function names are parameterized by the type of the return value of the method being invoked.

This family of operations invokes a static method on a Java class object according to the specified method ID. The methodID argument must be obtained by calling Get-StaticMethodID.

The method ID must be derived from clazz, not from one of its superclasses.

All arguments to the method should be placed in an argument of type va_list immediately following the methodID argument. The CallStatic<*type*>MethodV routine accepts the arguments, and, in turn, passes them to the Java method that is to be invoked.

The following table describes each of the method calling routines according to their result type. The proper JNI function name is determined by the return type of the Java method that is to be invoked.

CallStatic<type>MethodV

<jniType>	Call*type*MethodV Function Name
void	CallStaticVoidMethodV
jobject	CallStaticObjectMethodV
jboolean	CallStaticBooleanMethodV
jbyte	CallStaticByteMethodV
jchar	CallStaticCharMethodV
jshort	CallStaticShortMethodV
jint	CallStaticIntMethodV
jlong	CallStaticLongMethodV
jfloat	CallStaticFloatMethodV
jdouble	CallStaticDoubleMethodV

ARGUMENTS

env	The JNI interface pointer
clazz	A Java class object
methodID	A static method ID
args	A va_list of arguments

RETURNS

Returns the result of calling the static Java method.

THROWS

The exceptions raised by the invocation of the Java method may be raised by a call to any of the CallStatic<*type*>MethodV functions.

DefineClass

NAME   DefineClass

SYNTAX
```
jclass DefineClass(JNIEnv *env,
                   const char   *name,
                   jobject      loader,
                   const jbyte  *buf,
                   jsize        bufLen);
```

DESCRIPTION   Loads a class from a buffer of raw class data. The class data can either be read from an input source or constructed programmatically.

ARGUMENTS

env	The JNI interface pointer
name	Class name relative to CLASSPATH
loader	A class loader assigned to the defined class
buf	Buffer containing the .class file data
bufLen	Buffer length

RETURNS   Returns a Java class object or NULL if an error occurs.

THROWS   java.lang.ClassFormatError: if the class data does not specify a valid class.

java.lang.ClassCircularityError: if a class or interface would be its own superclass or superinterface.

DeleteGlobalRef

NAME   DeleteGlobalRef

SYNTAX   void DeleteGlobalRef(JNIEnv*env,
                                jobject   globalRef);

DESCRIPTION   Deletes the global reference pointed to by the object reference
                passed as an argument.

ARGUMENTS

env   The JNI interface pointer

globalRef   A global reference

DeleteLocalRef

NAME   DeleteLocalRef

SYNTAX   void DeleteLocalRef(JNIEnv*env,
                                        jobject   localRef);

DESCRIPTION   Deletes the local reference pointed to by the object reference
                           passed as an argument.

ARGUMENTS

                           env   The JNI interface pointer

                           localRef   A local reference

DeleteWeakGlobalRef (1.2)

NAME   DeleteWeakGlobalRef

SYNTAX   void DeleteWeakGlobalRef(
                              JNIEnv   *env,
                              jweak   gWeakRef);

DESCRIPTION   Deletes the JVM resources needed for the weak global
                  reference passed as the gWeakRef argument.

ARGUMENTS

                  env   The JNI interface pointer

                  gWeakRef   A global weak reference

DestroyJavaVM

NAME

DestroyJavaVM

SYNTAX

`jint DestroyJavaVM(JavaVM *vm);`

DESCRIPTION

In JDK 1.1 only the main thread may call `DestroyJavaVM`. The JVM waits until the main thread is the only user-level thread and returns an error code.

In JDK 1.2, any thread may call `DestroyJavaVM`. The JVM waits until the current thread is the only user thread before it returns an error code.

In either case, `DestroyJavaVM` does *not* unload the JVM. This is an acknowledged problem with this function.

ARGUMENTS

vm   A `JavaVM` pointer

RETURNS

Returns 0 on success or a negative value on failure.

Invocation API	DetachCurrentThread

NAME

DetachCurrentThread

SYNTAX

jint DetachCurrentThread(JavaVM *vm);

DESCRIPTION

Detaches the current thread from a JVM. All Java monitors held by this thread are released. All Java threads waiting for this thread to die are notified.

In JDK 1.1 the main thread, the one that created the JVM, should not call DetachCurrentThread to detach from the JVM. Instead, it should use DestroyJavaVM.

In JDK 1.2, the main thread can be detached from the JVM.

ARGUMENTS

vm   a JavaVM pointer

RETURNS

Returns 0 on success and a negative value on failure.

EnsureLocalCapacity (1.2)

NAME EnsureLocalCapacity

SYNTAX
```
jint EnsureLocalCapacity(
                JNIEnv      *env,
                jint        capacity);
```

DESCRIPTION The JNI programmer may call this function upon entry to native code to ensure that at least *capacity* local references can be created in the current thread.

Before the JVM enters a `native` method, it guarantees that at least 16 local references can be created. For backward compatibility, the JVM allocates local references beyond the ensured capacity.

As a debugging support, the JVM may give the user warnings that too many local references are being created. To view these warning use the `-verbose:jni` command line when starting the JVM. This option is only available in JDK 1.2.

The JVM calls `FatalError` if the native code attempts to create a local reference beyond the ensured capacity.

ARGUMENTS

env   The JNI interface pointer

capacity Minimum number of local references

RETURNS Returns 0 on success. On failure a negative number is returned and `java.lang.OutOfMemoryError` is thrown.

THROWS `java.lang.OutOfMemoryError`: if the JVM can not allocate sufficient resources for local references.

ExceptionClear

NAME   ExceptionClear

SYNTAX   void ExceptionClear(JNIEnv *env);

DESCRIPTION   Clears any exception that is currently thrown. If no exception is currently thrown, this call has no effect.

ARGUMENTS

env   The JNI interface pointer

ExceptionDescribe

NAME   ExceptionDescribe

SYNTAX   void ExceptionDescribe(JNIEnv *env);

DESCRIPTION   Prints the description of an exception equivalent to the getMessage method of the java.lang.Throwable class and a stack trace. This is a convenience routine provided for debugging.

ARGUMENTS

env   The JNI interface pointer

ExceptionOccurred

NAME   ExceptionOccurred

SYNTAX   jthrowable ExceptionOccurred(JNIEnv *env);

DESCRIPTION   Determines if an exception has occurred. The exception remains thrown until either the native code calls ExceptionClear, or until the Java code handles the exception.

ARGUMENTS

env   The JNI interface pointer

RETURNS   Returns the exception object that is being thrown, or NULL if no exception is currently being thrown.

FatalError

NAME　　　　　　FatalError

SYNTAX
```
void FatalError(JNIEnv *env,
                const char *msg);
```

DESCRIPTION　　Raises a fatal error and does not expect the JVM to recover. This function does not return and causes the JVM to print a "JNI Panic" message followed by the contents of the msg argument.

ARGUMENTS

env	The JNI interface pointer
msg	An error message

NAME   FindClass

SYNTAX
```
jclass FindClass(JNIEnv    *env,
                 const char    *name);
```

DESCRIPTION   This function loads a locally-defined class. In JDK 1.1,
FindClass searches the directories and zip files specified by
the CLASSPATH environment variable for the class with the
specified name. In JDK 1.2, FindClass locates the class loader
associated with the current native method. If the native code
belongs to a system class, no class loader will be involved.
Otherwise, the proper class loader will be invoked to load and link
the named class. FindClass has been enhanced in JDK 1.2 in
order to support the new security model that associates a class
loader with each native library.

The name argument should be a fully-qualified class name
with each component separated by slash (/) character. A
fully-qualified class name is a package name followed by a
class name. If the name begins with an open square bracket
([), FindClass returns an array class.

ARGUMENTS

env   The JNI interface pointer

name   A fully-qualified class name

RETURNS   Returns a class object from a fully-qualified name, or NULL if the
class cannot be found.

THROWS   java.lang.ClassFormatError: if the class data does
not specify a valid class.

java.lang.ClassCircularityError: if a class or
interface would be its own superclass or superinterface.

java.lang.NoClassDefFoundError: if no definition for a requested class or interface can be found.

java.lang.OutOfMemoryError: if the system runs
out of memory.

FromReflectedField (1.2)

NAME   FromReflectedField

SYNTAX   jfieldID FromReflectedField(
                                       JNIEnv   *env,
                                       jobject   field);

DESCRIPTION   Converts a reference to java.lang.reflect.Field
                            object to a JNI jfieldID value. If the field argument
                            does not represent a legal value, the result of a call to
                            FromReflectedField is undefined.

                            For the opposite conversion, see ToReflectedField on
                            page 438.

                            A java.lang.reflect.Field object may be
                            acquired using one of:

                            • getField
                            • getFields
                            • getDeclaredField
                            • getDeclaredFields

                            from java.lang.Class.

ARGUMENTS

                            env   The JNI interface pointer

                            field   A java.lang.reflect.Field object reference

RETURNS   A JNI jfieldID value that corresponds to the field object
                            passed as an argument.

FromReflectedMethod (1.2)

NAME FromReflectedMethod

SYNTAX

```
jmethodID FromReflectedMethod(
                    JNIEnv      *env,
                    jobject     method);
```

DESCRIPTION Converts a reference to `java.lang.reflect.Method`
or `java.lang.reflect.Constructor` object to a
JNI `jmethodID` value. If the `method` argument does not
represent a legal value, the result of a call to
`FromReflectedMethod` is undefined.

For the opposite conversion, see `ToReflectedMethod`
on page 439.

A `java.lang.reflect.Method` object may be
acquired using one of:

- `getMethod`
- `getMethods`
- `getDeclaredMethod`
- `getDeclaredMethods`

from `java.lang.Class`.

ARGUMENTS

env   The JNI interface pointer

method   A `java.lang.reflect.Method` object reference

RETURNS A JNI `jmethodID` value that corresponds to the method object
passed as an argument.

Get<pType>ArrayElements

NAME   Get<*pType*>ArrayElements

SYNTAX   <*jniType*> *Get<*pType*>ArrayElements(
                                   JNIEnv   *env,
                                   <*pjniArrayType*> array,
                                   jboolean   *isCopy);

DESCRIPTION   A family of functions that returns the body of the primitive
                    array. The result is valid until the corresponding
                    Release<*pType*>ArrayElements function is called.
                    Since the returned array may be a copy of the Java array,
                    changes made to the returned array will not necessarily be
                    reflected in the original array until
                    Release<*pType*>ArrayElements is called.

                    If isCopy is not NULL, then *isCopy is set to
                    JNI_TRUE if a copy is made; or it is set to JNI_FALSE if
                    no copy is made. This value should be tested to determine if
                    a call to Release<*pType*>ArrayElements needs to be
                    called. If a copy is made, Release<*pType*>Array-
                    Elements must be called for any changes to be written to
                    the Java array object.

                    Regardless of how boolean arrays are represented in the
                    JVM, GetBooleanArrayElements always returns a
                    pointer to memory, with each byte denoting a jboolean
                    element. All arrays of other types are guaranteed to be con-
                    tiguous in memory.

                    The following table describes the specific primitive array
                    element accessor functions. When substitutions from the
                    first two columns are applied, the third column represents
                    the proper function for those types.

Get\<pType\>ArrayElements

\<jniType\>	\<pjniArrayType\>	Get\<pType\>ArrayElements Function Name
jboolean	jbooleanArray	GetBooleanArrayElements
jbyte	jbyteArray	GetByteArrayElements
jchar	jcharArray	GetCharArrayElements
jshort	jshortArray	GetShortArrayElements
jint	jintArray	GetIntArrayElements
jlong	jlongArray	GetLongArrayElements
jfloat	jfloatArray	GetFloatArrayElements
jdouble	jdoubleArray	GetDoubleArrayElements

ARGUMENTS

env	The JNI interface pointer
array	A Java array object
isCopy	A pointer to a boolean

RETURNS

Returns a pointer to the array elements, or NULL if the operation fails.

Get<pType>ArrayRegion

NAME   Get<*pType*>ArrayRegion

SYNTAX   void Get<*pType*>ArrayRegion(

JNIEnv	*env,
<*pjniArrayType*>	array,
jsize	start,
jsize	len,
<*pjniType*>	*buf);

DESCRIPTION   A family of functions for copying a region of a primitive array into a user-supplied buffer.

The following table describes the specific primitive array element accessor functions. When substitutions from the first two columns are applied, the third column represents the proper function to use for those types.

<*pjniType*>	<*pjniArrayType*>	Get<pType>ArrayRegion Function Name
jboolean	jbooleanArray	GetBooleanArrayRegion
jbyte	jbyteArray	GetByteArrayRegion
jchar	jcharArray	GetCharArrayRegion
jshort	jshortArray	GetShortArrayRegion
jint	jintArray	GetIntArrayRegion
jlong	jlongArray	GetLongArrayRegion
jfloat	jfloatArray	GetFloatArrayRegion
jdouble	jdoubleArray	GetDoubleArrayRegion

ARGUMENTS

env	The JNI interface pointer
array	A Java array
start	The starting index
len	The number of elements to be copied
buf	The destination buffer

THROWS   java.lang.ArrayIndexOutOfBoundsException: if one of the indices in the region is not valid.

Get<type>Field

NAME

Get<*type*>Field

SYNTAX

```
<jniType> Get<type>Field(
                        JNIEnv    *env,
                        jobject   obj,
                        jfieldID  fieldID);
```

DESCRIPTION

This family of accessor routines returns the value of an instance (non-static) field of an object. The field to access is specified by a field ID obtained by calling GetFieldID.

The following table describes the different flavors of Get<*type*>Field based on the type of the Java field you are fetching. To fetch a Java field with type <*type*>, use the function Get<*type*>Field from the right column. The left column identifies the Java Native type that is returned. For example, if you want to fetch a Java array object, you use GetObjectField.

<*jniType*>	Get<*type*>Field Function Name
jobject	GetObjectField
jboolean	GetBooleanField
jbyte	GetByteField
jchar	GetCharField
jshort	GetShortField
jint	GetIntField
jlong	GetLongField
jfloat	GetFloatField
jdouble	GetDoubleField

ARGUMENTS

env	The JNI interface pointer
obj	A non-NULL Java object reference
fieldID	A valid field ID

RETURNS

Returns the value from the field in the Java object.

GetArrayLength

NAME   GetArrayLength

SYNTAX   jsize GetArrayLength(JNIEnv *env,
                                  jarray   array);

DESCRIPTION   Returns the number of elements in the array for arrays of either
                    primitive elements or object elements.

ARGUMENTS

                    env   The JNI interface pointer

                    array   A Java array object reference

RETURNS   Returns the number of elements in the array.

GetFieldID

NAME

GetFieldID

SYNTAX

```
jfieldID GetFieldID(JNIEnv    *env,
                    jclass     clazz,
                    const char *name,
                    const char *sig);
```

DESCRIPTION

Returns the field ID for an instance (non-static) field of a class. The field is specified by its name and signature. The Get<*type*>Field and Set<*type*>Field families of accessor functions use field IDs to retrieve object fields.

GetFieldID causes an uninitialized class to be initialized. Initialization of a class consists of executing its static initializers and the initializers for the static fields (class variables) declared in the class.

GetFieldID cannot be used to obtain the length field of an array. Use GetArrayLength instead.

ARGUMENTS

env	The JNI interface pointer
clazz	A Java class object reference
name	The field name in a 0-terminated UTF-8 string
sig	The field signature in a 0-terminated UTF-8 string

RETURNS

Returns a field ID, or NULL if the operation fails.

THROWS

java.lang.NoSuchFieldError: if the specified field cannot be found.

java.lang.ExceptionInInitializerError: if the class initializer fails due to an exception.

java.lang.OutOfMemoryError: if the system runs out of memory.

GetJavaVM

NAME

GetJavaVM

SYNTAX

jint GetJavaVM(JNIEnv *env, JavaVM **vm);

DESCRIPTION

Returns the JavaVM interface (used by the Invocation API) associated with the current thread. The result is placed at the location pointed to by the second argument, vm.

ARGUMENTS

env   The Java interface pointer

vm   A pointer to where the JavaVM
          pointer should be returned

RETURNS

Returns 0 on success or a negative value on failure.

GetMethodID

NAME GetMethodID

SYNTAX
```
jmethodID GetMethodID(JNIEnv    *env,
                      jclass     clazz,
                      const char *name,
                      const char *sig)
```

DESCRIPTION Returns the method ID for an instance (non-static) method of a class or interface. The method may be defined in the class object referenced by the `clazz` argument or inherited from one of its superclasses. The method is determined by its name and signature.

GetMethodID causes an uninitialized class to be initialized. Initialization of a class consists of executing its `static` initializers and the initializers for the `static` fields (class variables) declared in the class.

To obtain the method ID of a constructor, supply <init> as the method name and void (V) as the return type.

ARGUMENTS

env   The JNI interface pointer

clazz   A Java class object

name   The method name in a 0-terminated UTF-8 string

sig   The method signature in 0-terminated UTF-8 string

RETURNS Returns a method ID, or NULL if the specified method cannot be found.

THROWS `java.lang.NoSuchMethodError`: if the specified method cannot be found.

`java.lang.ExceptionInitializerError`: if the class initializer fails due to an exception.

`java.lang.OutOfMemoryError`: if the system runs out of memory.

GetObjectArrayElement

NAME GetObjectArrayElement

SYNTAX
```
jobject GetObjectArrayElement(
                JNIEnv        *env,
                jobjectArray  array,
                jsize         index);
```

DESCRIPTION Returns the element at offset `index` into the Java array object `array`.

ARGUMENTS

env	The JNI interface pointer
array	A Java array object reference
index	Array index

RETURNS Returns a reference to a Java object.

THROWS `java.lang.ArrayIndexOutOfBoundsException`: if `index` does not specify a valid index in the array.

GetObjectClass

NAME   GetObjectClass

SYNTAX   jclass GetObjectClass(JNIEnv *env,
                                          jobject   obj);

DESCRIPTION   Given a Java object reference, returns a reference to the class of
                    which that object is an instance.

ARGUMENTS

                    env   The JNI interface pointer
                    obj   A non-NULL Java object reference

RETURNS   Returns a Java class object reference.

GetPrimitiveArrayCritical (1.2)

NAME GetPrimitiveArrayCritical

SYNTAX

```
jbyte * GetPrimitiveArrayCritical(
                    JNIEnv      *env,
                    jarray      array,
                    jboolean    *isCopy);
```

DESCRIPTION GetPrimitiveArrayCritical allows native code to obtain a direct pointer to array elements within a Java array object even if the JVM does not support pinning. This call can be thought of as a notice to the JVM that the native code is entering a "critical section." Within this critical section, the native code expects that the JVM not move the memory associated with the Java object array. The critical section is exited by issuing a call to ReleasePrimitiveArrayCritical.

Inside a critical region, native code must not issue calls to either other JNI functions or any system call that may cause the current thread to block and wait for another Java thread. For example, the current thread must not call read on a stream being written by another Java thread.

Pairs of GetPrimtiveArrayCritical and ReleasePrimitiveArrayCritical may be nested.

This function imposes no requirement that a JVM internally represent a primitive array in contiguous memory. Therefore, it is still possible that isCopy returns JNI_TRUE. If the JVM does need to make a copy of the array data, lack of sufficient memory may cause GetPrimitiveArray-Critical to return NULL. It is best to code for the most general case and check the return value for NULL.

GetPrimitiveArrayCritical (1.2)

ARGUMENTS

env	The JNI interface pointer
array	A reference to a primitive array object
isCopy	The address of a jboolean variable that returns JNI_TRUE if the JVM returns a copy of the array data

RETURNS

Returns a jbyte to the primitive array data. If the JVM needed to make a copy and failed, NULL is returned.

GetStatic<type>Field

NAME

GetStatic<*type*>Field

SYNTAX

<*jniType*> GetStatic<*type*>Field(
        JNIEnv *env,
        jclass clazz,
        jfieldID fieldID);

DESCRIPTION

This family of accessor routines returns the value of a static field of an object. The field to access is specified by a field ID, which is obtained by calling GetStaticFieldID.

The following table describes the different flavors of GetStatic<*type*>Field based on the type of the Java field you are fetching. To fetch a Java field with type <*type*>, use the function GetStatic<*type*>Field from the right column. The left column identifies the Java Native type that is returned. If you want to fetch a Java array object, you GetStaticObjectField.

<jniType>	GetStatic<*type*>Field Routine Name
jobject	GetStaticObjectField
jboolean	GetStaticBooleanField
jbyte	GetStaticByteField
jchar	GetStaticCharField
jshort	GetStaticShortField
jint	GetStaticIntField
jlong	GetStaticLongField
jfloat	GetStaticFloatField
jdouble	GetStaticDoubleField

ARGUMENTS

env	The JNI interface pointer
clazz	A Java class object
fieldID	A static field ID

RETURNS

Returns the contents of the static field in the Java object.

GetStaticFieldID

NAME   GetStaticFieldID

SYNTAX
```
jfieldID GetStaticFieldID(
                    JNIEnv      *env,
                    jclass      clazz,
                    const char  *name,
                    const char  *sig);
```

DESCRIPTION   Returns the field ID for a `static` field of a class. The field is specified by its name and signature. The field ID returned can be used by the `GetStatic<`*type*`>Field` and `SetStatic<`*type*`>Field` families of accessor functions to retrieve `static` fields.

GetStaticFieldID causes an uninitialized class to be initialized. Initialization of a class consists of executing its `static` initializers and the initializers for the `static` fields (class variables) declared in the class.

ARGUMENTS

env	The JNI interface pointer
clazz	A Java class object
name	The `static` field name in a 0-terminated UTF-8 string
sig	The field signature in a 0-terminated UTF-8 string

RETURNS   Returns a field ID, or NULL if the specified `static` field cannot be found.

THROWS   `java.lang.NoSuchFieldError`: if the specified `static` field cannot be found.

`java.lang.ExceptionInInitializerError`: if the class initializer fails due to an exception.

`java.lang.OutOfMemoryError`: if the system runs out of memory.

GetStaticMethodID

NAME   GetStaticMethodID

SYNTAX   jmethodID GetStaticMethodID(
                            JNIEnv   *env,
                            jclass   clazz,
                            const char *name,
                            const char *sig);

DESCRIPTION   Returns the method ID for a static method of a class. The
                           method is specified by its name and signature. The class reference
                           is often returned by FindClass or GetObjectClass.

ARGUMENTS

                           env   The JNI interface pointer

                           clazz   A Java class object

                           name   The static method name in a 0-terminated
                                     UTF-8 string

                           sig   The method signature in a 0-terminated UTF-8
                                     string

RETURNS   Returns a method ID, or NULL if the operation fails.

THROWS   java.lang.NoSuchMethodError: if the specified
                           static method cannot be found.

                           java.lang.ExceptionInInitializerError: if
                           the class initializer fails due to an exception.

                           java.lang.OutOfMemoryError: if the system runs
                           out of memory.

GetStringChars

NAME   GetStringChars

SYNTAX
```
const jchar * GetStringChars(
                  JNIEnv      *env,
                  jstring     string,
                  jboolean    *isCopy);
```

DESCRIPTION   Returns a pointer to the array of Unicode characters of the string. This pointer is valid until `ReleaseStringchars` is called.

If `isCopy` is not NULL, then `*isCopy` is set to JNI_TRUE if a copy is made, or it is set to JNI_FALSE if no copy is made.

ARGUMENTS

env   The JNI interface pointer

string   A Java string object

isCopy   A pointer to a boolean

RETURNS   Returns a pointer to a Unicode string, or NULL if the operation fails.

GetStringCritical (1.2)

NAME   GetStringCritical

SYNTAX
```
const jchar* GetStringCritical(
                    JNIEnv      *env,
                    jstring     string,
                    jboolean*   isCopy);
```

DESCRIPTION   The semantics of GetStringCritical are similar to GetStringChars. This function is a means for the JVM to provide a pointer to string data even if it does not support pinning. Use of GetStringCritical imposes the same "critical section" restrictions as described under GetPrimitiveArrayCritical on page 388.

This function returns a jchar pointer to memory comprising the java.lang.String referenced by string.

The isCopy value will be JNI_TRUE on return if the JVM needed to make a copy of the string memory. Since there is no guarantee the JVM will be able to allocate memory in the case it does have to made a copy of the String data, it is good practice to check the return value of GetStringCritical.

ARGUMENTS

env   The JNI interface pointer

string   A Java string object

isCopy   A pointer to a jboolean

RETURNS   A jchar pointer to memory containing the characters of a java.lang.String object. This may be NULL if the JVM needed to acquire memory for the characters but could not.

GetStringLength

NAME   GetStringLength

SYNTAX   jsize GetStringLength(JNIEnv   *env,
                                          jstring   string);

DESCRIPTION   Returns the number of Unicode characters in the
                    java.lang.String object referenced by the string
                    argument.

ARGUMENTS

                    env   The JNI interface pointer
                    string   A Java string object

RETURNS   Returns the number of Unicode characters in a
                    java.lang.String object.

GetStringRegion (1.2)

NAME GetStringRegion

SYNTAX

```
void GetStringRegion(JNIEnv    *env,
                     jstring    string,
                     jsize      start,
                     jsize      len,
                     jchar      *buf);
```

DESCRIPTION

Copies len number of Unicode characters from the java.lang.String object to the user-supplied buffer buf. The copy begins at an offset start characters in the string.

This function is a Unicode string analogue to the Get<*pType*>ArrayRegion functions.

ARGUMENTS

env	The JNI interface pointer
string	A Java string
start	The starting index
len	The number of characters to be copied
buf	The destination buffer

THROWS

java.lang.StringIndexOutOfBoundsException: if copy is attempted beyond either end of the string.

GetStringUTFChars

NAME GetStringUTFChars

SYNTAX
```
const char* GetStringUTFChars(
                    JNIEnv      *env,
                    jstring     string,
                    jboolean    *isCopy);
```

DESCRIPTION Returns a pointer to an array of UTF-8 characters of the string. This array is valid until it is released by ReleaseStringUTFChars.

If isCopy is not NULL, then *isCopy is set to JNI_TRUE if a copy is made. It is set to JNI_FALSE if no copy is made.

ARGUMENTS

env	The JNI interface pointer
string	A Java string object
isCopy	A pointer to a boolean

RETURNS Returns a pointer to a UTF-8 string, or NULL if the operation fails.

GetStringUTFLength

NAME   GetStringUTFLength

SYNTAX   jsize GetStringUTFLength(JNIEnv *env,
                                             jstring   string);

DESCRIPTION   Returns the UTF-8 length of a java.lang.String object in
                     bytes. This functionis analogous to the ANSI C library routine
                     strlen.

ARGUMENTS

                     env   The JNI interface pointer
                     string   A Java string object

RETURNS   Returns the UTF-8 length of a java.lang.String object in
                     bytes.

GetStringUTFRegion (1.2)

NAME   GetStringUTFRegion

SYNTAX
```
void GetStringUTFRegion(JNIEnv *env,
                        jstring    string,
                        jsize      start,
                        jsize      len,
                        char       *buf);
```

DESCRIPTION   Converts `len` number of Unicode characters beginning at
offset `start` into UTF-8 format and copies the result in the
user-supplied buffer `buf`.

ARGUMENTS

env	The JNI interface pointer
string	A Java string
start	The starting index
len	The number of characters to be copied
buf	The destination buffer

THROWS   `java.lang.StringIndexOutOfBoundsException`:
if copy is attempted beyond either end of the string.

GetSuperclass

NAME   GetSuperclass

SYNTAX   jclass GetSuperclass(JNIEnv *env,
                                jclass   clazz);

DESCRIPTION   Returns a reference to the superclass of the clazz argument. If
                     clazz specifies the class Object, or clazz represents an
                     interface, this function returns NULL.

ARGUMENTS

                     env   The JNI interface pointer
                     clazz   A Java class object

RETURNS   Returns the superclass of the class represented by clazz, or
                     NULL.

GetVersion

NAME   GetVersion

SYNTAX   jint GetVersion(JNIEnv *env);

DESCRIPTION   Returns the version of the native method interface

ARGUMENTS

env   The JNI interface pointer

RETURNS   Returns the major version number in the higher 16 bits and the minor version number in the lower 16 bits. In JDK1.1, GetVersion returns 0x00010001. In JDK 1.2, GetVersion returns 0x00010002.

IsAssignableFrom

NAME   IsAssignableFrom

SYNTAX
```
jboolean IsAssignableFrom(JNIEnv *env,
                          jclass      clazz1,
                          jclass      clazz2);
```

DESCRIPTION   Determines whether an object of clazz1 can be safely cast to clazz2.

ARGUMENTS

env	The JNI interface pointer
clazz1	The first class argument
clazz2	The second class argument

RETURNS   Returns JNI_TRUE if either of the following is true:

- The first and second class argument are from the same Java class.
- The first class is a subclass of the second class.
- The first class has the second class as one of its interfaces.

Invocation API	IsAttached (1.2)

NAME IsAttached

SYNTAX jboolean IsAttached(JavaVM *vm);

DESCRIPTION Reports whether or not the thread from which it is called is attached to a JVM.

ARGUMENTS

vm a JavaVM pointer

RETURNS JNI_TRUE if the current thread is attached to the JVM, otherwise, returns JNI_FALSE.

IsInstanceOf

NAME   IsInstanceOf

SYNTAX
```
jboolean IsInstanceOf(JNIEnv *env,
                      jobject    obj,
                      jclass     clazz);
```

DESCRIPTION   Tests whether an object is an instance of a class.

ARGUMENTS

env   The JNI interface pointer

obj   A Java object

clazz   A Java class object

RETURNS   Returns JNI_TRUE if obj can be cast to clazz; otherwise, returns JNI_FALSE. A NULL object can be cast to any class.

IsSameObject

NAME　　　　　IsSameObject

SYNTAX

```
jboolean IsSameObject(JNIEnv *env,
                      jobject    ref1,
                      jobject    ref2);
```

DESCRIPTION　　Tests whether two object references refer to the same Java object.

ARGUMENTS

env	A JNI interface pointer
ref1	A Java object
ref2	A Java object

RETURNS　　　Returns JNI_TRUE if ref1 and ref2 refer to the same Java object, or are both NULL; otherwise, returns JNI_FALSE.

JNI_CreateJavaVM *Invocation API*

NAME   JNI_CreateJavaVM

SYNTAX

```
jint JNI_CreateJavaVM(JavaVM **vm,
              JNIEnv     **env,
              void       *vm_args);
```

DESCRIPTION   Loads and initializes a JVM. The current thread becomes the main thread. Sets the env argument to the JNI interface pointer of the main thread. The JNI does not support creating more than one JVM in a single process. The version field in vm_args must be set to 0x00010001 for JDK 1.1 and 0x00010002 for JDK 1.2. The version setting will determine the structure of the vm_args argument.

The JDK 1.1 expects a pointer to a JDK1_1InitArgs structure as the third argument. The JDK 1.2 expects a pointer to a JavaVMInitArgs structure.

ARGUMENTS

vm	An address to a JavaVM pointer
env	An address to a JNI interface pointer
vm_args	JVM specific argument structure

RETURNS   Returns 0 on success or a negative number on failure.

       JNI_GetCreatedJavaVMs

NAME   JNI_GetCreatedJavaVMs

SYNTAX

```
jint JNI_GetCreatedJavaVMs(
                JavaVM      **vmBuf,
                jsize       bufLen,
                jsize       *nVMs);
```

DESCRIPTION   Reports on all JVMs that have been created within the running process. Pointers to JavaVM structures are written in the buffer vmBuf in the order in which they were created. At most, bufLen number of entries will be written. The total number of created VMs is returned in *nVMs.

The JDK does not support creating more than one JVM in a single process.

ARGUMENTS

vmBuf   The address of a JavaVM pointer array

bufLen   The number of elements in the vmBuf array

nVMs   A pointer to a jsize value that is filled with the number of JVMs created

RETURNS   Returns 0 on success and a negative number on failure.

JNI_GetDefaultJavaVMInitArgs   *Invocation API*

NAME   JNI_GetDefaultJavaVMInitArgs

SYNTAX   jint JNI_GetDefaultJavaVMInitArgs(
                                            void   *vm_args);

DESCRIPTION   Returns a default configuration for the JVM. Before calling
                           this function, native code must set the
                           vm_args->version field to the JNI version it expects
                           the JVM to support. In JDK 1.1.2 and later 1.1 versions,
                           vm_args->version must be set to 0x00010001.
                           Previous versions of the JDK did not require the native code
                           to set the version field. For backward compatibility, JDK
                           1.1.2 assumes that the requested version is 0x00010001 if
                           the version field is not set. After this function returns,
                           vm_args->version will be set to the actual JNI version
                           the JVM supports.

                           This call is unnecessary in JDK 1.2.

                           The vm_args structure for JDK 1.1 is
                           JDK1_1InitArgs. See Chapter 12 for details on using
                           this structure.

ARGUMENTS

                           vm_args   A pointer to JDK1_1InitArgs structure

RETURNS   Returns 0 if the version requested is supported, otherwise it returns
                           a negative number.

Version Management   JNI_OnLoad (1.2)

NAME   JNI_OnLoad

SYNTAX
```
jint JNI_OnLoad(JavaVM    *vm,
                void      *reserved);
```

DESCRIPTION   The JVM calls JNI_OnLoad is an optional, user-supplied
                     function within a native library. It is called by the JVM
                     when the native library is loaded, for example, using
                     System.loadLibrary. JNI_OnLoad must return the
                     JNI version needed by the native library.

                     In order to use any of the new 1.2 JNI functions, a native
                     library must export a JNI_OnLoad function that returns
                     0x00010002. If the native library does not export a
                     JNI_OnLoad function, the JVM assumes that the library
                     only requires JNI version 0x00010001. If the JVM does
                     not recognize the version number returned by
                     JNI_OnLoad, the native library cannot be loaded.

                     Initialization of native library internal data may also be
                     accomplished within JNI_OnLoad much like the use of
                     DllMain on Win32 systems.

ARGUMENTS

                     env   The JNI interface pointer
                     reserved   For future use

RETURNS   A JNI version number. Legal values are 0x00010001 for JNI
                     version 1.1 and 0x00010002 for JNI version. This function
                     must return 0x00010002 if the native library uses the functions
                     introduced in JNI 1.2.

JNI_OnUnload (1.2)   *Version Management*

NAME   JNI_OnUnload

SYNTAX   void JNI_OnUnload(JavaVM *vm,
                                    void   *reserved);

DESCRIPTION   JNI_OnUnload is an optional user-supplied function
                   within a native library. When the class loader containing the
                   native library is garbage collected, the JVM calls
                   JNI_OnUnload.

                   This function can be used to perform cleanup operations.
                   Because JNI_OnUnload is called in an unknown context
                   (such as from a finalizer), programmers should be careful in
                   their use of JVM services and refrain from arbitrary Java
                   call-backs.

ARGUMENTS

                   env   The JNI interface pointer
                   reserved   For future use

MonitorEnter

NAME   MonitorEnter

SYNTAX
```
jint MonitorEnter(JNIEnv  *env,
                  jobject      obj);
```

DESCRIPTION   Enters the monitor associated with the underlying Java object referred to by `obj`.

Each Java object has a monitor associated with it. If the current thread already owns the monitor associated with `obj`, it increments a counter in the monitor indicating the number of times this thread has entered the monitor. If the monitor associated with `obj` is not owned by any thread, the current thread becomes the owner of the monitor, setting the entry count of this monitor to 1. If another thread already owns the monitor associated with `obj`, the current thread waits until the monitor is released, then tries again to gain ownership.

ARGUMENTS

    env   The JNI interface pointer
    obj   A Java object or class object

RETURNS   Returns 0 on success or a negative value on failure.

MonitorExit

NAME   MonitorExit

SYNTAX
```
jint MonitorExit(JNIEnv   *env,
                 jobject   obj);
```

DESCRIPTION   The current thread must be the owner of the monitor associated
                    with the underlying Java object referred to by obj. The thread
                    decrements the counter indicating the number of times it has
                    entered this monitor. If the value of the counter becomes zero, the
                    current thread releases the monitor.

ARGUMENTS

env	The JNI interface pointer
obj	A Java object or class object

RETURNS   Returns 0 on success or a negative value on failure.

New<pType>Array

NAME   New<pType>Array

SYNTAX   *<pjniArrayType>* New<*pType*>Array(
                                    JNIEnv *env,
                                    jsize length);

DESCRIPTION   A family of functions used to construct a new primitive array object. The table below describes the specific primitive array constructors. You should replace New<*pType*>Array with one of the actual primitive array constructor routine names from the following table, and replace *<pjniArrayType>* with the corresponding array type for that routine.

<pjniArrayType>	**New<*pType*>Array Function Name**
jbooleanArray	NewBooleanArray
jbyteArray	NewByteArray
jcharArray	NewCharArray
jshortArray	NewShortArray
jintArray	NewIntArray
jlongArray	NewLongArray
jfloatArray	NewFloatArray
jdoubleArray	NewDoubleArray

ARGUMENTS

env	The JNI interface pointer
length	The number of elements in the array

RETURNS   Returns a Java array, or NULL if the array cannot be constructed.

NewGlobalRef

NAME
NewGlobalRef

SYNTAX
```
jobject NewGlobalRef(JNIEnv *env,
                     jobject    obj);
```

DESCRIPTION
Creates a new global reference to the object referred to by the obj argument. The obj argument may be a global or local reference. Global references must be explicitly disposed of by calling DeleteGlobalRef.

This function is useful for creating an object reference in native code that will persist across native method calls.

ARGUMENTS

env	The JNI interface pointer
obj	A global or local reference

RETURNS
Returns a global jobject reference, or NULL if the system runs out of memory.

NewLocalRef (1.2)

NAME   NewLocalRef

SYNTAX   ```
jobject NewLocalRef(JNIEnv*env,
                    jobject   obj);
```

**DESCRIPTION**     Creates a new local reference that refers to the same object
                    as the obj argument. The reference passed as an argument
                    may be either a global or local reference.

**ARGUMENTS**

                    env         The JNI interface pointer
                    obj         A global or local reference

**RETURNS**         Returns NULL if obj refers to a null reference.
```

NewObject

NAME   NewObject

SYNTAX
```
jobject NewObject(JNIEnv  *env,
              jclass      clazz,
              jmethodID   methodID,
              ...);
```

DESCRIPTION   Constructs a new Java object. The method ID indicates which constructor method to invoke. This ID must be obtained by calling GetMethodID with <init> as the method name and void (V) as the return type.

NewObject can not be used to create new array objects, therefore the clazz argument must not refer to an array class. Use NewObjectArray or one of the New<pType>Array family to construct array objects.

All arguments that are to be passed to the constructor should be listed immediately following the methodID argument. NewObject accepts these arguments and passes them to the Java method that is to be invoked.

ARGUMENTS

env	The JNI interface pointer
clazz	A Java class object
methodID	The method ID of the constructor
...	Arguments to the constructor

RETURNS   Returns a Java object reference, or NULL if the object cannot be constructed.

THROWS   java.lang.InstantiationException: if the class is an interface or an abstract class.

java.lang.OutOfMemoryError: if the system runs out of memory.

Additionally, a call to NewObject may throw any exceptions thrown by the constructor.

NewObjectA

NAME   NewObjectA

SYNTAX
```
jobject NewObjectA(JNIEnv   *env,
                   jclass     clazz,
                   jmethodID  methodID,
                   jvalue     *args);
```

DESCRIPTION   Constructs a new Java object. The method ID indicates which constructor method to invoke. This ID must be obtained by calling GetMethodID with <init> as the method name and void (V) as the return type.

NewObjectA cannot be used to created arrays, therefore the clazz argument must not refer to an array class. Use NewObjectArray or one of the New<*pType*>Array family to construct array objects.

All arguments that are to be passed to the constructor should be placed in an array of jvalues immediately following the methodID argument. NewObjectA accepts the arguments in this array, and, in turn, passes them to the Java method that is to be invoked.

ARGUMENTS

env	The JNI interface pointer
clazz	A Java class object
methodID	The method ID of the constructor
args	A jvalue array of arguments to the constructor

RETURNS   Returns a Java array object reference, or NULL if the object cannot be constructed.

THROWS   java.lang.InstantiationException: if the class is an interface or an abstract class.

java.lang.OutOfMemoryError: if the system runs out of memory.

Additionally, a call to NewObjectA may throw any exceptions thrown by the constructor.

NewObjectArray

NAME   NewObjectArray

SYNTAX   jarray NewObjectArray(
                            JNIEnv   *env,
                            jsize   length,
                            jclass   elementClass,
                            jobject   initialElement);

DESCRIPTION   Constructs a new array containing objects from class
                    elementClass. All elements are initially set to
                    initialElement.

ARGUMENTS

                    env   The JNI interface pointer
                    length   Array size
                    elementClass   Array element class
                    initialElement   Initialization value

RETURNS   Returns a Java array object reference, or NULL if the array cannot
                    be constructed.

THROWS   java.lang.OutOfMemoryError: if the system runs out of
                    memory.

NewObjectV

NAME　　　　　　NewObjectV

SYNTAX

```
jobject NewObjectV(JNIEnv *env,
                jclass      clazz,
                jmethodID   methodID,
                va_list     args);
```

DESCRIPTION　　Constructs a new Java object. The method ID indicates which constructor method to invoke. This ID must be obtained by calling GetMethodID with <init> as the method name and void (V) as the return type.

NewObjectV cannot be used to create new array objects, therefore the clazz argument must not refer to an array class. Use NewObjectArray or one of the New<*pType*>Array family to construct array objects

All arguments that are to be passed to the constructor should be placed in an argument of type va_list immediately following the methodID argument. NewObjectV accepts these arguments, and, in turn, passes them to the Java method that is to be invoked.

ARGUMENTS

env	The JNI interface pointer
clazz	A Java class object
methodID	The method ID of the constructor
args	A va_list of arguments to the constructor

RETURNS　　　　Returns a Java object, or NULL if the object cannot be constructed.

THROWS　　　　java.lang.InstantiationException: if the class is an interface or an abstract class.

java.lang.OutOfMemoryError: if the system runs out of memory.

Additionally, a call to NewObjectV may throw any exceptions thrown by the constructor.

NewString

NAME   NewString

SYNTAX
```
jstring NewString(
        JNIEnv      *env,
        const jchar *unicodeChars,
        jsize       len);
```

DESCRIPTION   Constructs a new java.lang.String object from an array
                    of Unicode characters.

ARGUMENTS

env	The JNI interface pointer
unicodeChars	Pointer to a Unicode string
len	Length of the Unicode string

RETURNS   Returns a Java string object, or NULL if the string cannot be
                    constructed.

THROWS   java.lang.OutOfMemoryError: if the system runs out of
                    memory.

NewStringUTF

NAME NewStringUTF

SYNTAX
```
jstring NewStringUTF(JNIEnv *env,
                     const char   *bytes);
```

DESCRIPTION Constructs a new java.lang.String object from an array of UTF-8 characters.

ARGUMENTS

env   The JNI interface pointer

bytes   The pointer to a UTF-8 string

RETURNS Returns a Java string object, or NULL if the string cannot be constructed.

THROWS java.lang.OutOfMemoryError: if the system runs out of memory.

NewWeakGlobalRef (1.2)

NAME   NewWeakGlobalRef

SYNTAX   jweak NewWeakGlobalRef(JNIEnv*env,
                                   jobject   obj);

DESCRIPTION   Creates a new weak global reference from the reference
                  obj passed as an argument. Returns NULL if obj refers to
                  null, or if the JVM runs out of memory.

                  Generally obj is either a global reference that the native
                  programmer deletes after a call to NewWeakGlobalRef
                  or a local reference that will disappear when the current
                  local reference frame is popped.

ARGUMENTS

                  env   The JNI interface pointer
                  obj   An object reference

RETURNS   On success, returns a weak reference for the reference obj passed
                  as an argument. Otherwise, NULL is returned.

PopLocalFrame (1.2)

NAME   PopLocalFrame

SYNTAX
```
jobject PopLocalFrame(JNIEnv *env,
                 jobject      result);
```

DESCRIPTION   Pops the current local reference frame, freeing all the local references. The `result` argument contains a local reference from the calling frame that is made available as a return value to the previous frame in the stack.

If no local reference from the current frame needs to be passed to previous frame, pass NULL as the `result` argument.

The combination of `PushLocalFrame` and `PopLocalFrame` gives the native code finer control over the allocation of local references. For instance, if a block of native code requires a large number of local references for a short period of time, `PushLocalFrame` can be called to do a wholesale allocation. When finished with the local references, `PopLocalFrame` does a wholesale deallocation of the resources required for maintaining local references.

ARGUMENTS

env   The JNI interface pointer

result   A local reference from current frame returned to previous frame

RETURNS   A local referance in the current frame to the object passed as the `result` argument.

PushLocalFrame (1.2)

NAME   PushLocalFrame

SYNTAX   jint PushLocalFrame(JNIEnv *env,
                                      jint   capacity);

DESCRIPTION   Creates a new local reference frame in which at least the
number of local references as specified by capacity can
be created.

ARGUMENTS

                env   The JNI interface pointer

                capacity A local reference from current frame returned to
previous frame

RETURNS   Returns 0 on success. If the requested number of local references
can not be allocated, a negative number is returned and
java.lang.OutOfMemoryError is thrown.

THROWS   java.lang.OutOfMemoryError: if the JVM is unable to
allocate the resources for the requested number of local
references.

RegisterNatives

NAME   RegisterNatives

SYNTAX
```
jint RegisterNatives(JNIEnv        *env,
        jclass                      clazz,
        const JNINativeMethod       *methods,
        jint                        nMethods);
```

DESCRIPTION   Registers native methods with the JVM and associates them with the class specified by the `clazz` argument. The `methods` parameter specifies an array of `JNINativeMethod` structures that contain the names, signatures, and function pointers of the native methods. The `nMethods` parameter specifies the number of native methods in the array. The `JNINativeMethod` structure is defined as follows:

```
typedef struct {
    char *name;
    char *signature;
    void *fnPtr;
} JNINativeMethod;
```

The function pointers nominally must have the following signature:

```
<jniType> (*fnPtr)(JNIEnv *env,
            jobject objOrClass,
            ...);
```

ARGUMENTS

env	The JNI interface pointer
clazz	A Java class object
methods	The native methods in the class
nMethods	The number of native methods in the class

RETURNS   Returns 0 on success or a negative value on failure.

THROWS   `java.lang.NoSuchMethodError`: if a method named in the `JNINativeMethod` array cannot be found or is not declared as `native` in the class named by the `clazz` argument.

ReleasePrimitiveArrayCritical (1.2)

NAME

ReleasePrimitiveArrayCritical

SYNTAX

```
void ReleasePrimitiveArrayCritical(
                    JNIEnv      *env,
                    jarray      array,
                    void        *carray,
                    jint        mode);
```

DESCRIPTION

ReleasePrimitiveArrayCritical informs the JVM that the native code is finished with the primitive array data pointed to by carray and that it may resume normal memory management activity. A call to this function exits the "critical section" entered by a corresponding call to GetPrimitiveArrayCritical. See the description of GetPrimitiveArrayCritical on page 388 for a discussion of "critical section" in this context.

The array argument is a primitive array reference named in an earlier call to GetPrimitiveArrayCritical. The carray pointer is a pointer to primitive array data returned by the same call to GetPrimitiveArray-Critical.

The mode argument should have one of three values:

Release Mode	Action
0	Copy the elements into the array object and free the carray buffer
JNI_COMMIT	Copy the elements into the array object but do not free the elems buffer
JNI_ABORT	Free the buffer without copying the elements into the array object

For a JVM that does not copy the array data, the first two values are meaningless.

ARGUMENTS

env	The JNI interface pointer
array	A primitive array reference
carray	Pointer to array data
mode	Release mode

Release\<pType\>ArrayElements

NAME   Release\<*pType*\>ArrayElements

SYNTAX

```
void Release<pType>ArrayElements(
              JNIEnv               *env,
              <pjniArrayType>      array,
              <pjniType>           *elems,
              jint                 mode);
```

DESCRIPTION   A family of functions that informs the JVM that the native code no longer needs access to the elements in a primitive array. If necessary, this function copies the array data back into the array object from the address pointed to by the elems argument. The elems argument is a pointer returned by the corresponding Get\<*pType*\>ArrayElements function.

The mode argument instructs the JVM on how the array buffer should be released. The mode argument has no effect if elems does not point to a copy of the elements in array. The mode argument should have one of three values:

Release Mode	Action
0	Copy the elements into the array object and free the elems buffer
JNI_COMMIT	Copy the elements into the array object but do not free the elems buffer
JNI_ABORT	Free the buffer without copying the elements into the array object

In most cases, zero is passed as the mode argument to ensure consistent behavior for both pinned and copied arrays. The other options give the programmer more control over memory management and should be used with extreme care.

The following table describes the specific primitive array element accessor functions. When substitutions from the first two columns are applied, the third column represents the proper function for those types.

Release<pType>ArrayElements

<jniType>	*<pjniArrayType>*	**Release<pType>ArrayElements Function Name**
jboolean	jbooleanArray	ReleaseBooleanArrayElements
jbyte	jbyteArray	ReleaseByteArrayElements
jchar	jcharArray	ReleaseCharArrayElements
jshort	jshortArray	ReleaseShortArrayElements
jint	jintArray	ReleaseIntArrayElements
jlong	jlongArray	ReleaseLongArrayElements
jfloat	jfloatArray	ReleaseFloatArrayElements
jdouble	jdoubleArray	ReleaseDoubleArrayElements

ARGUMENTS

env	The JNI interface pointer
array	A Java array object
elems	A pointer to array elements
mode	Release mode

ReleaseStringChars

NAME   ReleaseStringChars

SYNTAX
```
void ReleaseStringChars(JNIEnv*env,
                 jstring      string,
                 const jchar  *chars);
```

DESCRIPTION   Informs the JVM that the native code no longer needs access to the Unicode characters associated with a java.lang.String object. The chars argument is a pointer to a user-supplied buffer previously obtained from string using GetStringChars.

ARGUMENTS

env	The JNI interface pointer
string	A Java string object
chars	A pointer to a Unicode string

ReleaseStringCritical (1.2)

NAME   ReleaseStringCritical

SYNTAX
```
void ReleaseStringCritical(
                    JNIEnv      *env,
                    jstring     string,
                    const jchar *carray);
```

DESCRIPTION   ReleaseStringCritical informs the JVM that the native code is finished with the character data pointed to by carray and that it may resume normal memory management activity. A call to this function exits the "critical section" entered by a corresponding call to GetStringCritical. See the description of GetPrimitiveArrayCritical on page 388 for a discussion of "critical section" in this context.

ARGUMENTS

env   The JNI interface pointer

string   A Java string object

carray   A pointer to a Unicode string

ReleaseStringUTFChars

NAME   ReleaseStringUTFChars

SYNTAX   void ReleaseStringUTFChars
                          JNIEnv   *env,
                          jstring   string,
                          const char *utf);

DESCRIPTION   Informs the JVM that the native code no longer needs access to the
                  UTF-8 characters associated with a java.lang.String
                  object. The utf argument is a pointer to a native buffer
                  previously obtained from string using
                  GetStringUTFChars.

ARGUMENTS

                  env   The JNI interface pointer
                  string   A Java string object
                  utf   A pointer to a UTF-8 string

Set<pType>ArrayRegion

NAME Set<*pType*>ArrayRegion

SYNTAX
```
void Set<pType>ArrayRegion(
        JNIEnv              *env,
        <pjniArrayType>     array,
        jsize               start,
        jsize               len,
        <pjniType>          *buf);
```

DESCRIPTION A family of functions that copies from a user-supplied buffer into a primitive array object.

The following table describes the specific primitive array element accessor functions. When substitutions from the first two columns are applied, the third column represents the proper function for use with those types.

<pjniType>	*<pjniArrayType>*	Set<pType>ArrayRegion Function Name
jboolean	jbooleanArray	SetBooleanArrayRegion
jbyte	jbyteArray	SetByteArrayRegion
jchar	jcharArray	SetCharArrayRegion
jshort	jshortArray	SetShortArrayRegion
jint	jintArray	SetIntArrayRegion
jlong	jlongArray	SetLongArrayRegion
jfloat	jfloatArray	SetFloatArrayRegion
jdouble	jdoubleArray	SetDoubleArrayRegion

ARGUMENTS

env	The JNI interface pointer
array	A Java array
start	The starting index
len	The number of elements to be copied
buf	The destination buffer

THROWS java.lang.ArrayIndexOutOfBoundsException: if one of the indices into the region is not valid.

Set\<type\>Field

NAME Set\<*type*\>Field

SYNTAX
```
void Set<type>Field(JNIEnv *env,
                    jobject      obj,
                    jfieldID     fieldID,
                    <jniType>    value);
```

DESCRIPTION This family of accessor routines sets the value of an instance (non-static) field of an object. The field to access is specified by a field ID obtained by calling GetFieldID.

Set\<*type*\>Field can not be used to set a data field of a primitive type that is declared final.

The following table expands the Set\<*type*\>Field routine names with the appropriate substitutions for \<*type*\> and \<*jniType*\>.

\<*jniType*\>	Set\<*type*\>Field Function Name
jobject	SetObjectField
jboolean	SetBooleanField
jbyte	SetByteField
jchar	SetCharField
jshort	SetShortField
jint	SetIntField
jlong	SetLongField
jfloat	SetFloatField
jdouble	SetDoubleField

ARGUMENTS

env	The JNI interface pointer
obj	A non-NULL Java object reference
fieldID	A valid field ID
value	The new value of the field

SetObjectArrayElement

NAME   SetObjectArrayElement

SYNTAX
```
void SetObjectArrayElement(
          JNIEnv       *env,
          jobjectArray array,
          jsize        index,
          jobject      value);
```

DESCRIPTION   Sets an element within an object array.

ARGUMENTS

env	The JNI interface pointer
array	A Java array
index	Array index
value	An object reference

THROWS   `java.lang.ArrayIndexOutOfBoundsException`
: if index does not specify a valid index in the array.

`java.lang.ArrayStoreException`: if the class of value is not a subclass of the element class of the array.

SetStatic<type>Field

NAME　　　　　SetStatic<*type*>Field

SYNTAX
```
void SetStatic<type>Field(
                JNIEnv      *env,
                jclass      clazz,
                jfieldID    fieldID,
                <jniType>   value);
```

DESCRIPTION　This family of accessor routines sets the value of a `static` field of a class. The field to access is specified by a field ID, which is obtained by calling `GetStaticFieldID`.

The following table expands the `Set-Static<type>Field` routine names with the appropriate substitutions for *<type>* and *<jniType>*.

<jniType>	SetStatic*<type>*Field Function Name
jobject	SetStaticObjectField
jboolean	SetStaticBooleanField
jbyte	SetStaticByteField
jchar	SetStaticCharField
jshort	SetStaticShortField
jint	SetStaticIntField
jlong	SetStaticLongField
jfloat	SetStaticFloatField
jdouble	SetStaticDoubleField

ARGUMENTS

env	The JNI interface pointer
clazz	A Java class object
fieldID	A static field ID
value	The new value of the field

Throw

NAME   Throw

SYNTAX   `jint Throw(JNIEnv *env, jthrowable obj);`

DESCRIPTION   Causes the `java.lang.Throwable` object named by
                  the `obj` argument to be thrown.

ARGUMENTS

env	The JNI interface pointer
obj	A `java.lang.Throwable` object

RETURNS   Returns 0 on success or a negative value on failure.

THROWS   The `java.lang.Throwable` object referenced by its
                  second argument.

ThrowNew

NAME

ThrowNew

SYNTAX

```
jint ThrowNew(JNIEnv *env,
        jclass      clazz,
        const char  *message);
```

DESCRIPTION

Constructs a `java.lang.Throwable` object from the specified class. The message specified by `message` can be retrieved by the code that catches the thrown object with the `getMessage` method.

ARGUMENTS

env	The JNI interface pointer
clazz	A subclass of `java.lang.Throwable`
message	The message used to construct the `java.lang.Throwable` object

RETURNS

Returns 0 on success or a negative value on failure.

THROWS

The newly constructed `java.lang.Throwable` object.

ToReflectedField (1.2)

NAME   ToReflectedField

SYNTAX   jobject ToReflectedField(
                                        JNIEnv   *env,
                                        jclass   clazz,
                                        jfieldID   fieldID);

DESCRIPTION   Converts a JNI jfieldID value derived from the class
                    clazz and passed as fieldID to a
                    java.lang.reflect.Field object.

                    Since the JVM needs to allocate resources for the returned
                    jobject value, a zero value may be returned if sufficient
                    memory is not available. In this case, a
                    java.lang.OutOfMemoryError is thrown.

ARGUMENTS

                    env   The JNI interface pointer
                    clazz   A java.lang.Class object reference
                    fieldID   A JNI field ID from the class referenced by
                              clazz

RETURNS   Returns a reference to a java.lang.reflect.Field upon
                    success. Otherwise, it returns zero.

THROWS   java.lang.OutOfMemoryError: if the conversion fails.

ToReflectedMethod (1.2)

NAME
      ToReflectedMethod

SYNTAX

```
jobject ToReflectedMethod(
                    JNIEnv      *env,
                    jclass      clazz,
                    jmethodID   methodID);
```

DESCRIPTION
Converts a JNI `jmethodID` value derived from the class `clazz` and passed as `methodID` to one of the following types:

- `java.lang.reflect.Method`
- `java.lang.reflect.Constructor`

If `methodID` identifies a constructor then a `Constructor` object reference is returned.

Since the JVM needs to allocate resources for the returned `jobject` value, a zero value may be returned if sufficient memory is not available. In this case, a `java.lang.OutOfMemoryError` is thrown.

ARGUMENTS

env	The JNI interface pointer
clazz	A `java.lang.Class` object reference
methodID	A JNI method ID from the class referenced by `clazz`

RETURNS
Returns a reference to either a `Method` or `Constructor` object upon success. Otherwise, it returns zero.

THROWS
`java.lang.OutOfMemoryError`: if the conversion fails.

UnregisterNatives

NAME   UnregisterNatives

SYNTAX
```
jint UnregisterNatives(JNIEnv*env,
                 jclass      clazz);
```

DESCRIPTION   Unregisters `native` methods of a class. The class goes back to the state before it was linked or registered with its `native` method functions.

This function should not be used in normal native code. Instead, it provides applications using the Invocation API a way to unload and relink native libraries.

ARGUMENTS

env   The JNI interface pointer

clazz   A Java class object

RETURNS   Returns 0 on success or a negative value on failure.

Appendix B

1.0 NATIVE METHODS VS. JNI

Introduction

Since the Java Native Interface is greatly improved over JDK 1.0 `native` method support, is it worth discussing the two side-by-side in order to shed some light on possible migration paths from old to new.

From Chapter 2 you will recall a "Hello JNI World" method written to the JNI specification. Recall that all JNI functions are actually maintained in a function table pointed to by a `JNIEnv` pointer. This arrangement allows each JVM implementation to supply these functions in a way that makes possible native code binary compatibility across different JVMs on a given platform.

Although the JDK 1.0 approach is still supported in later versions of the JDK, there are plenty of reasons for making a ghost of the 1.0 implementation. The JDK 1.0 solution had a major shortcoming. It made assumptions about how the JVM laid out Java objects in memory. Since native code may directly reference fields in a Java object, any change to this layout on the part of the JVM would require that `native` method libraries be recompiled. Further, different implementations of the JVM for a single platform could arrange objects in memory differently. In this case, the user would need to support a different native library for each variant of the JVM.

Implementing native code using the JNI will allow you to write a single version of a native library that will support all implementations of the JVM for a given platform.

This appendix places examples of JNI side-by-side with the same functionality implemented using the 1.0-style `native` method techniques. Throughout this appendix the term "1.0-style" will be used to refer to the original `native` method implementation.

javah *Usage*

Both `native` method styles require the use of the `javah` tool. The `javah` tool is used for generating the support files necessary to provide linkage between Java classes and native functions. However, the use of `javah` differs slightly when used to support 1.0-style code vs. JNI code. Here is a quick look at the differences:

⟨ • **Difference Summary** ⟩

B.1 *Required* `javah` *Options*

Description	1.0-Style	JNI
Generate function prototypes	N/A	`-jni`
Generate stub files	`-stubs -o`	N/A

Two invocations of `javah` are required when writing 1.0-style `native` method code. First, the function prototypes need to be generated, and then, a *stubs* file created. JNI requires only the generation of the native function prototypes.

Consistent with continued support for 1.0-style native code, `javah` can generate both 1.0-style function prototypes and JNI function prototypes. If the `-jni` option is used, JNI prototypes are generated, otherwise 1.0-style prototypes are generated.

Using `javah` to Generate 1.0-Style Native Code

When writing 1.0-style native code two support files are needed to tie native code into Java. The first, called a stubs file, consists of wrappers around invocations of native functions. These stubs map the JVM stack elements to arguments of the native function. If you are really curious, take a look a `javah`-generated file and then the file $JDK_HOME/`include/interpreter.h`.

The command line to generate a single stubs file for classes `classX`, `classY` and `classZ` may look like this:

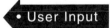
User Input   **Building a 1.0-Style Stub File**

```
% javah -stubs -o native_stubs.c classX classY
              classZ
```

In this example, the stubs are placed in the file native_stubs.c. When using the -stubs option, the -o option is required to name the stubs output file.

The second use of javah is to generate the include files that will contain native functions prototypes and the C struct definitions for Java classes.

To generate this include file for classes classX, classY and classZ, the javah command may look like this:

User Input   **Generating 1.0-Style Function Prototypes**

```
% javah classX classY classZ
```

The above use of javah will generate three header files: classX.h, classY.h and classZ.h.

Using javah to Generate JNI Function Prototypes

Only the include files which define the native function prototypes need to be generated for JNI native code. In this case, the -jni option is used with javah and relevant class file names are listed as command arguments. For each class file, classX, a file named classX.h is generated.

User Input   **Generating JNI Function Prototypes With** javah

```
% javah -jni classX classY classZ
```

Include File Requirements

javah takes care of generating the correct include directive for each file it creates. A different file is included depending on whether or not the -jni option is used with javah.

Both of these files can be found in $JDK_HOME/include. The JNI header, <jni.h>, also includes a file that defines some platform-dependent types. This file is jni_md.h. When building native code using JNI, your compilation line must know where find this file as well. It is in a directory named for the platform it supports (e.g. solaris or win32). For example, when building for Win32, you will want to point your C compiler to $JDK_HOME/include.

• Difference Summary

B.2 *Required* include *Directive*

Description	1.0 Style	JNI
Include file	`#include <native.h>`	`#include <jni.h>`

There are also other files in `$JDK_HOME/include` which are helpful for 1.0-style native coding. These file are:

- `oobj.h`
- `interpreter.h`
- `tree.h`
- `javaString.h`
- `typecodes.h`

and are included by `native.h`. For backward compatibility, these files are part of JDK 1.1 releases.

In any case, `javah` does the work of providing the right include file depending on whether the `-jni` option is used. This is significant because many a 1.0-style `native` method programmer has wandered around files like `interpreter.h`, `oobj.h` and `javaString.h` trying to figure out how to get done what needed to be done. If you are going to program to the JNI, such wandering must stop!

The Pieces, Side-by-Side

Before we look at the differences between building a 1.0-style native library and a JNI native library, let's look at the different building blocks. The table below summarizes the various files involved in building an application from `classX` which defines some `native` methods.

• Difference Summary

B.3 *The Pieces to a Java/Native Application*

Description	1.0-Style	JNI
Java Source	`classX.java`	`classX.java`
Function Prototypes	`classX.h`	`classX.h`
Function Definition	`classX.c`	`classX.c`
Stub Code	`classX_stubs.c`	`N/A`

The only difference is the need for the stubs file in the 1.0-style `native` method approach.

Building Native Libraries

The different set of files which make up the native code lead to slightly different requirements for building the native library. The difference, though, is only the omission of the stubs object from the link command.

For example, on Solaris, the commands to make the respective native libraries look like this:

> • **User Input**   **Building a Solaris 1.0-style Native Library**

```
% cc -I$JDK_HOME/include \
 -I$JDK_HOME/include/solaris \
 -G -o libNative.so classX.c classX_stubs.c
```

> • **User Input**   **Building a Solaris JNI Native Library**

```
% cc -I$JDK_HOME/include \
    -I$JDK_HOME/include/solaris \
    -G -o libNative.so classX.c
```

The idea is the same for other platforms: You don't need the stubs file when building a native library containing JNI code.

A `printString` Example

Let's look at a short example to expose some of the differences between 1.0-style native code and JNI code. We will then use this as a point of reference for further discussion.

Consider a Java class which declares a `native` method, `printString`.

Listing B.1 *Declaration of* `printString` *Method*

```
public class Native {
    public native void printString(String str);
}
```

`printString` simply accepts its `String` input argument and prints it.

Here is the printString implementation using 1.0-style native code.

Listing B.2 printString: *1.0-Style* native **Method Implementation**

```c
#include "Native.h" /* include native.h */
void Native_printString(struct HNative* thisObj,
        struct Hjava_lang_String * str)
{
   char* c_string = allocCString(str);
   /* makeCString() here would place
    * responsibility for collection of
    * allocated string on JVM runtime
    */
   printf("printString: %s\n", c_string);
   free(c_string);
}
```

The code for the equivalent functionality using JNI follows:

Listing B.3 printString: *JNI implementation*

```c
#include <jnih.h>
#include "Native.h"
JNIEXPORT void JNICALL Java_Native_printString(
        JNIEnv *env,
        jobject thisObj,
        jstring str) {
   char*       utf_str;
   jboolean    copy;
   utf_str - (char*)
      (*env)->GetStringUTFChars(env, str, &copy);

   printf("%s\n", utf_string)

   if (is_copy == JNI_TRUE)
     (*env)->ReleaseStringUTFChars(
                         env, str, utf_str);
}
```

In the following sections we will refer back to these two pieces of code.

The Execution Environment

Every `native` method called under JNI will receive a `JNIEnv` pointer as its first argument. This pointer is used to access JNI functions. If the `native` method is written in C, the `JNIEnv` pointer is treated as a pointer to a function table.

```
(*env)->jni_function(env,...);
```

If the `native` method is written in C++, the `JNIEnv` pointer acts like an object pointer and JNI functions are called as you would invoke a C++ method.

```
env->jni_function(...);
```

C++ avoids the redundant appearance of the `JNIEnv` pointer by providing in-line methods defined in `<jni.h>`.

The equivalent of the execution environment in JDK 1.0 is `EE()` macro. It is, however, always passed as `NULL` to the various functions made visible by the 1.0-style `native` method interface.

Function Specification and Naming

From the `printString` code above, you will note the difference in the function specification and naming. JNI declares `native` methods using a couple of `#define` macros as modifiers.

```
JNIEXPORT void JNICALL Java_Native_printString()
```

Whereas, in the 1.0-style the names did not contain any such fancy decoration.

```
void Native_printString()
```

The macros `JNIEXPORT` and `JNICALL` appear in the function specification of function prototypes generated for JNI native code. These macros have platform-dependent definitions and function, more or less as a concession to Microsoft Dynamic Link Library conventions. Chapter 2 gives more detail on these macros.

In both cases, the function name is created by prefixing it with the fully-qualified package name delimited by underscores. JNI function names are further prefixed by `Java`.

In both the interfaces, the `native` method name is prefixed by its fully-qualified class name with each path component separated by an underscore. Assume the `printString` `native` method above were defined in a class called `myPkg` as in the Java source below.

Listing B.4 *A* `native` *Method Declared Within a Package*

```
package myPkg;
public class Native {
    public native void printString(String str);
}
```

In this case, the function prototypes for the different native programming models would be generated as below.

Listing B.5 *JNI Function Prototype for* `myPkg.Native.printString`

```
JNIEXPORT void JNICALL
Java_myPkg_Native_printString();
```

Listing B.6 *1.0 Style Function Prototype* `myPkg.Native.printString`

```
void myPkg_Native_printString();
```

Data Types

JNI defines the Java Native Types which should be used by all native code. JNI defines types which map to Java primitive types and reference types. All of the JNI functions take these types as arguments and return these types as values. Similarly, when `javah` generates function prototypes, it maps the Java types in the method declaration to the corresponding native types in the prototype.

Note in the `printString` example above the appearance of `jobject`, `jint` and `jstring` as types of the function arguments. These are examples of JNI Native Types.

This, of course, differs drastically from 1.0-style where `javah` generates a different `struct typedef` for each Java class referenced by the native code. Under this scheme Java objects were treated as C structures, and Java primitive types mapped to C scalar types. The temptation in 1.0-style code is to treat a native `int` as the same size as a Java `int`. Depending on the platform, this is not always true. However, a native `jint` is guaranteed to be the same size as a Java `int`.

Details of the Java Native Types are presented in Chapter 4.

Argument Handling

Since JNI provides native data types for all arguments passed to native functions, the handing of these arguments is straightforward. What you see is what you get. A `jobject` represents a Java object, a `jstring` represents a Java string, etc.

In 1.0-style coding, the `unhand` macro is needed to change a C `struct` into something that looks and feels like an object. Referring back to `print-String`, for example, the `unhand` macro would have to be applied to the `thisObj` argument, of type `HNative`, before using it as an object.

Signatures

Amidst all this change, at least one thing has remained the same. A signature is a signature is a signature. The means by which a method is identified within native, namely its signature, does not change from the 1.0-style to the JNI. A method's signature was and is a function of the Java interpreter and not specific to native code.

Ah! The exception. As Listing B.17 and Listing B.18 below show, constructor signatures do differ across the two releases. `execute_java_constructor` identifies a constructor without a type for its return value. The JNI function `NewObject`, on the other hand, requires a `V` to denote a void return value.

Signatures are discussed in detail in Chapter 4.

Accessing Java Data Fields

The class `AppxEx` will be used to illustrate the difference between the ways in which 1.0-style code and JNI code access data fields in Java classes.

Listing B.7 *Class* `AppxEx`

```
public class AppxEx {
    private int anInt;
    private static int staticInt;
    private native void printInt();
}
```

Two examples are presented. The first shows native code accessing an instance variable. The second shows native code accessing a class variable.

A complete discussion of setting and getting Java data field values is in Chapter 3.

Accessing Instance Data

Accessing instance data using JNI requires three function calls. A 1.0-style access is simply a C struct field reference.

The following table compares both setting and getting instance data.

• Difference Summary

B.4 *Accessing a Java Instance Variable*

Operation	1.0-Style	JNI

set	C struct access	`GetObjectClass`
		`GetFieldID`
		`Get<type>Field`

get	C struct access	`GetObjectClass`
		`GetFieldID`
		`Set<type>Field`

The examples below only exhibit getting an instance variable.

The native code to print a field will first be implemented using the 1.0-style and then the JNI. Listing B.8 shows the C code implementing a 1.0-style access to Java instance data:

Listing B.8 *1.0-Style Access to Instance Data*

```
void AppxEx_printID(struct HAppxEx *thisObj) {
    ClassAppxEx* inst = unhand(thisObj);
    printf("id = %d\n", inst->anInt);
}
```

(1)
(2)

In [1], the `thisObj` "handle" is passed to the `unhand` macro to turn it into a class pointer. From there, as in [2], the instance variables are available as fields in a C structure.

Listing B.9 shows the `native` method implemented in C code using JNI functions.

Listing B.9 *JNI Access to Instance Data*

```
JNIEXPORT void JNICALL Java_AppxEx_printID(
JNIEnv *env, jobject thisObj) {
 jclass clazz;
 jfieldIDfid;
```
(3)
```
    clazz = (*env)->GetObjectClass(env, thisObj);
```
(4)
```
    fid = (*env)->GetFieldID(
                    env, clazz, "anInt", "I");
```
(5)
```
    jint x = (*env)->GetIntField(env, thisObj, fid);
    printf("anInt = %d\n", x);
}
```

The JNI approach requires calls to three JNI functions.

- `GetObjectClass` to return a `jclass` value in line [3]
- `GetFieldID` to return a `jfieldID` key to a Java data field in line [4]
- `GetIntField` to retrieve the value in line [5]

Accessing Class Data

The following C code implements a native function reference to a `static` variable. This code is written to the JNI API.

Listing B.10 *JNI Access to Class Data*

```
JNIEXPORT void JNICAL Java_AppxEx_printStaticID(
JNIEnv *env, jobject thisObj)
{
    jfieldID fid;
    jint    val;
    jclass clazz

    clazz = (*env)->GetObjectClass(env, thisObj);
    fid = (*env)->GetStaticFieldID(env, clazz,
                    "staticInt", "I");
    val = (*env)->GetStaticIntField(env, clazz, fid);
    printf("static ID = %d\n", val);
}
```

Invoking Methods

Let's add the following methods to the class AppxEx.

Listing B.11 *Java source for* AppxEx

```
public class AppxEx {
    private native void invoker();
    private native void staticInvoker();
    public void invokeMe() {
    System.out.println(getClass().getName()
        + " invokeMe called from native.");
}
public static void staticInvokeMe() {
    System.out.println(
        "staticInvokeMe called from native.");
}
```

The native methods, invoker and staticInvoker, will be used to call invokeMe and staticInvokeMe, respectively.

Invoking a Java Instance Method

Here is a quick comparison of the two means of invoking an instance method.

• Difference Summary

B.5 *Invoking a Non-Static Method*

1.0-Style	JNI
execute_java_dynamic_method	GetObjectClass
	GetMethodID
	Call<*type*>Method

A single call is all that is needed in the 1.0-style approach.

Listing B.12 *Using 1.0-Style Native Code to Invoke a Java Instance Method*

```
void AppxEx_invoker(struct HAppxEx * thisObj) {
    execute_java_dynamic_method(0,
            (HObject*) thisObj,
            "invokeMe", "()V");
}
```

Three calls are required when using the JNI. A class reference is obtained with a call to GetObjectClass [6]. A method ID is retrieved from Get-MethodID in [7]. Finally, in [8], the CallVoidMethod function is called.

Listing B.13 *Using JNI to Invoke a Java Instance Method*

```
JNIEXPORT void JNICALL Java_AppxEx_invoker(
JNIEnv * env, jobject thisObj)
{
    jmethodID mid;
    jclass clazz;

    clazz = (*env)->GetObjectClass(env, thisObj);
    mid = (*env)->GetMethodID(env, clazz,
                      "invokeMe", "()V");
    (*env)->CallVoidMethod(env, thisObj, mid);
}
```

(6)

(7)

(8)

CallVoidMethod is used to call Java methods that return a void value. The JNI supports a large number of method invocation functions that vary both by expected return type, argument passing mechanism and whether the method is a class method or instance method. A thorough discussion of JNI function naming conventions appears in Chapter 3.

Invoking a Java Class Method

Invoking a class (static) method is quite similar to invoking an instance method. The following table provides a quick comparison of the two coding approaches.

• Difference Summary

B.6 *Invoking a* static *Method*

Description	1.0-Style	JNI
Getting class	obj_classblock	GetObjectClass
Invoking a method	execute_java_static_method	GetStaticMethodID CallStatic<*type*>Method

Listing B.14illustrates calling a static Java method using the 1.0-style native programming model. The function execute_java_static_method at line [10] does the work.

Listing B.14 *Using 1.0-Style Native Code to Invoke a Java Class Method*

```
void AppxEx_staticInvoker(struct HAppxEx * thisObj,
        /*boolean*/ long invokeStatic)
{
    ClassClass* clazz = obj_classblock(thisObj);
    execute_java_static_method(0, clazz,
            "staticInvokeMe","()V");
}
```
(9)
(10)

Only when invoking a `static` method does the 1.0-style native function need to obtain class information. This is achieved with the macro `obj_classblock` [9]. The JNI analogue is `GetObjectClass` [11] below.

The C code for invoking Java class methods using JNI appears in Listing B.15.

Listing B.15 *Using JNI to Invoke a Java Class Method*

```
JNIEXPORT void JNICALL Java_AppxEx_staticInvoker(
            JNIEnv * env,
            jobject thisObj,
            jboolean invokeStatic)
{
    jmethodID mid;
    jclass clazz;
    clazz = (*env)->GetObjectClass(env, thisObj);
    mid = (*env)->GetStaticMethodID(env, clazz,
            "staticInvokeMe","()V");
    (*env)->CallStaticVoidMethod(env, clazz, mid);
}
```
(11)
(12)
(13)

Here, again, we see the common JNI idiom of getting a class reference [11], followed by getting a method ID [12] and, finally, invoking a method [13]. The JNI invocation function used to call a `static` method differs from the one used above [8] to call a non-static method, but a similar sequence of calls is needed to set up the method call. As with non-static methods, there are many flavors in JNI function for invoking `static` methods. They are discussed in Chapter 3.

Creating an Object

It may be necessary to create an object in native code for return to the Java side for further processing. Here is a quick look on how this is done using both 1.0-style native code and the JNI API.

• Difference Summary

B.7 *Object Creation*

Description	1.0-Style	JNI
Getting a class object	`FindClass`	`FindClass`
Get constructor	N/A	`GetStaticMethodID` `GetMethodID`
Create object	`execute_java_constructor`	`NewObject` `AllocObject`

In the example below we create an instance of the class `java.lang.Integer`. To do this we call the `native` method `new-Integer` from the class `AppxEx`.

Listing B.16 *Modified Class:* `AppxEx`

```
public class AppxEx {
    private native Integer newInteger(int val)
    // ...
}
```

Listing B.17 shows the 1.0-style coding steps to create an object. This is followed by the equivalent task using JNI code.

Listing B.17 *Using 1.0-Style Native Code to Create a Java Object*

```
struct Hjava_lang_Integer * AppxEx_newInteger(
        struct HAppxEx *thisObj, long val)
{
    ClassClass* c;
    struct Hjava_lang_Integer* obj;
    c = FindClass(0, "java/lang/Integer", 1);
    obj= (Hjava_lang_Integer*)
              execute_java_constructor(
                    0,"java/lang/Integer",
                    c, "(I)", val);
    return obj;
}
```

(14)
(15)

The creation of the Java object occurs in line [15] above and in line [18] in Listing B.18.

Listing B.18 *Using JNI to Create a Java Object*

```
JNIEXPORT jobject JNICALL Java_AppxEx_newInteger(
JNIEnv * env, jobject thisObj, jint val)
{
    jmethodID   mid;
    jobject     obj;
    jclass      clazz;
    clazz = (*env)->FindClass(env,
                        "java/lang/Integer");
    mid = (*cnv)->GetMethodID(env, clazz,
                        "<init>",
                        "(I)V");
    obj = (*env)->NewObject(env, clazz,
                        mid, val);
    return obj;
}
```

(16)
(17)
(18)

Findclass, although with slightly different arguments, appears in both examples ([14] and [16]).

In the JNI implementation, we see the need to obtain a method ID in [17] before calling the JNI invocation function. In this case, the method ID is returned for the specially named method <init> which designates an object constructor method. Note the difference in the method signatures for the constructor method in lines [15] and [17]. The JNI signature expects a V return value to signify that the constructor returns void.

Exceptions

Exception handling is much improved in the JNI API. Not only can you generate exceptions to pass on to Java code, but you can catch exceptions in the JNI functions. The following table compares the functionality of the two styles of `native` method programming.

• Difference Summary

B.8 *Exception Handling*

Functionality	1.0-Style	JNI
Generate an exception	`SignalError`	`Throw`
		`ThrowNew`
Catch an exception	`exceptionOccurred`[*]	`ExceptionOccurred`
Clear an exception	`exceptionClear`[*]	`ExceptionClear`
Exception message	`exceptionDescribe`	`ExceptionDescribe`

[*] Denotes C macro

The next two C code samples show how to throw an exception using each of the native programming styles.

Listing B.19 *Throwing a 1.0-Style Exception*

```
void AppxEx_thrower(struct HAppxEx *thisObj)
{
    SignalError(0,
            "java/lang/NullPointerException",
            "Bad Pointer Value");
(19)    /* code here gets executed
                        in spite of exception */
}
```

The exception generated by `SignalError` actually gets raised only upon return from the native code. Any code after `SignalError` and before return to Java code will get executed per comment [19] above.

The other three exception-related calls or macros are helpful for testing whether previous 1.0-style function calls into the JVM caused an exception. For example, after the call to `execute_java_constructor` at line [15] in Listing B.17 above, you could use `exceptionOccurred` to test for and handle exceptions at the native code level. In this case, `exceptionClear` is helpful to prevent the JVM from throwing an exception when control leaves native code.

Listing B.20 illustrates throwing an exception using the JNI functions.

Listing B.20 *Throwing a JNI exception*

```
JNIEXPORT void JNICALL Java_AppxEx_thrower(
        JNIEnv *env, jobject thisObj)
{
    jclass clazz = (*env)->FindClass(env,
            "java/lang/NullPointerException");
    (*env)->ThrowNew(env, clazz,
                        "Bad pointer value");
    /* code here gets executed in spite of exception */
}
```

(20)

As in the 1.0-style example, any code appearing after the ThrowNew at line [20] will be executed since the JVM does not actually detect the exception until its return to the Java code.

The JNI exception handling functions are given more detailed coverage in Chapter 7.

String Manipulation

String manipulation in the 1.0-style model is not a pretty sight. There are a slew of functions to manipulate strings, and their number complicates comprehension. Difference Summary B.9 lists the string handling functions for both styles of native function programming. The mapping from one to the other is rather imperfect since JNI makes explicit the distinction between UTF-8 strings and Unicode strings.

• Difference Summary

B.9 *String Manipulation*

Functionality	1.0-Style	JNI
Creating strings	makeJavaString	NewString
	MakeString	NewStringUTF
Converting	allocCString	GetStringChars
	makeCString	GetStringUTFChars
Freeing string memory		ReleaseStringChars
		ReleaseStringUTFChars
String length		GetStringLength
		GetStringUTFLength

Refer back to the `printString` examples in Listing B.2 and Listing B.3 that opened this chapter to view some simple string handling within native code.

Chapter 6 discusses JNI string manipulation functions in detail.

Arrays

A quick side-by-side comparison shows that the JNI provides a much richer set of functions for manipulating arrays than does the 1.0-style model. The following table lists the respective functions.

• Difference Summary

B.10 *Array Manipulation*

1.0-Style	JNI
AllocArray	NewObjectArray
	GetObjectArrayElement
	SetObjectArrayElement
	New<*type*>Array
	Get<*type*>ArrayElements
	Get<*type*>ArrayRegion
	Set<*type*>ArrayRegion
	Release<*pType*>ArrayElements
	GetArrayLength

1.0-style arrays are of type HArrayOf<*type*>. The following example shows an array of int values created using the 1.0-style programming model.

Listing B.21 *Creating an* int *Array Using 1.0-Style Native Code*

```
HArrayOfInt * AppxEx_buildArrayOfInt(
    struct HAppxEx * thisObj, long sz) {
    int i;
(21)    HArrayOfInt* ja =
            (HArrayOfInt*)ArrayAlloc(T_LONG, sz);
(22)    ClassArrayOfInt* clazz = unhand(ja);
    for (i = 0; i < sz; i++)
(23)        clazz->body[i] = i;
    return ja;
}
```

AllocArray returns a pointer to an HArrayOfInt struct [21]. This handle is used as an argument to the unhand macro to get a pointer to an array object [22].

Then, as with all 1.0-style objects, the data is accessed via normal C struct references [23]. In the case of arrays, body is the struct field which identifies the array data.

In the JNI example for array manipulation, an array object is allocated in [24]. Note that the allocation function is matched to the type of array it allocates. After the array object is allocated, native memory is allocated [25] and copied into the array object [26]. Of course, if a Java array object is passed as argument, as when Java code asks native code to populate an array, line [24] would be omitted.

Listing B.22 *Creating an* `int` *Array Using JNI*

```
JNIEXPORT jintArray JNICALL
Java_AppxEx_buildArrayOfInt(
        JNIEnv * env, jobject thisObj, jint sz)
{
(24)    jintArray ja = (*env)->NewIntArray(env, sz);
        jsize i;
(25)    jint * buf = (jint *)malloc(sizeof(jint) * sz);
        for (i = 0; i < sz; i++) {
            buf[i] = i;
        }
(26)    (*env)->SetIntArrayRegion(env, ja, 0, sz, buf);
        return ja;
}
```

In [26] the JNI function for setting array elements is also specific to a element type. Chapter 6 discusses array manipulation in detail.

Garbage Collection Issues

One of the nice features of JNI is its accommodation of the JVM garbage collection facilities without placing any burden on the native programmer. Unlike the 1.0-style implementation, the JNI does not expose JVM memory to the native code as anything other than object references. Since these references provide a level of indirection between the JVM and the native code, the native programmer is protected from garbage collection activity.

Even in the cases where native code places constraints on memory layout when it expects C/C++ strings and arrays to reside in contiguous memory, the JNI provides functions that are specially designed to meet these expectations. These functions are discussed in Chapter 6.

None of this can be said of the 1.0-style `native` method programming interface. The layout of Java objects is exposed to native code, and native pointers into Java objects have no special status. In other words, the garbage collection mechanism has no knowledge you may be using a pointer in native code to manipulate a Java object. Without this knowledge, it will have no qualms about moving that memory, invalidating your pointer.

Appendix C   *STRUCT*C*ONVERTER* R*EFERENCE*

> New things are made familiar,
> and familiar things are made new.
>
> Samuel Johnson
> *Lives of the Poets*

Command Syntax

```
java structConverter [-A] [-D] [-Csuffix|-c] [-E|-e]
      [-Iinclude_base] [-j]
      [-NoStrings] [-NocharArrayStrings]
      [-NocharStarStrings] [-NoFIDCache]
      [-f configfile] file
```

Synopsis: Generates Java source and JNI adapter code from C `struct`

file names a file generated by the C/C++ preprocessor using the `-E` flag (Solaris) or `/E` option (Microsoft C Compiler).

When compiling for Win32 platforms, use the `/W0` command line option with `cl` to suppress warnings caused by superfluous declarations.

463

Options

−f*configfile* Instructs `structConverter` which `struct typedefs` are of interest for conversion to Java. This file contains lines which look like:

> struct-name   package

where *struct-name* identifies a C struct name (e.g. `stat`), and *package* identifies the Java package in which the converted Java class will reside. By default all classes in the configuration file are `public`. The *package* value should use the dot notation for identifying a Java `package`.

The default configuration file name is `jclass.cfg`.

−A   Generates retrieve/commit `native` method declarations within the Java class. These are helpful for bulk read/write of C `struct` data to and from a Java object.

−C   Generate C++ code. All JNI calls are generated using the C++ calling syntax:

> env->GetFieldID(...);

This option also can take the form −C*xxx* where *xxx* is the suffix you want appended to the generated C++ files. The default is `cc`. This is handy on Win32 platforms when you are developing in Microsoft Development Studio which does not support the `cc` suffix.

−c   Generate C code. All JNI calls are generated using the C calling syntax:

> (*env)->GetFieldID(env,...);

−D   Prints lots of debug output.

−e   Generate exception checking code after every JNI call. The code

```
if (env->ExceptionOccurred()) {
      env->ExceptionDescribe();
      env->ExceptionClear();
      return;
}
```

is laid down after every JNI function call.

-E   Generate exception checking code as above but also generate an addi-
            tional `fprintf` reporting __LINE__ and __FILE__.

-I*include_base*

            Define the directory root for standard header file location.
            `structConverter` will look for this value as part of the include path
            name generated by the C/C++ preprocessor and convert the name to
            canonical form. E.g.

                    `"/usr/include/sys/types.h"`
                                `------> <sys/types.h>`

            In the above example, *include_base* would be `/usr/include`.

-j   Generate only a Java source file containing a class definition that include
            a setter/getter pair for each field in the input C structure. All the methods
            are declared `native`.

-NoStrings

            By default, each occurrence of `char*` and `char[]` is translated to a
            `java.lang.String`. If this flag is set, `char*` is treated as a Java
            `char` and `char[]` is treated as a Java `char` array.

-NocharArrayStrings

            `char[]` is not translated to `java.lang.String` and instead treated
            as a `char` array.

-NocharStarStrings

            `char*` is not translated to `java.lang.String` and instead treated as
            a `char` reference.

-NoFIDCache

            Normally all field IDs for a Java class are cached in `static` variables in
            the native code. This option prevents this. There is really no reason to ever
            use this flag. Performance is much better leaving things just the way they
            are.

Description

For each `struct` named in *configfile* the source for a Java class file is generated. The class consists of a member variable for each `struct` field and the corresponding setter and getter. For array variables, indexed setters/getters are generated.

For a C struct Person:

```
typedef struct {
    int             aa[10];
    unsigned int    x;
    long            z;
    char            *str;
    struct a_struct_in_foo {
        int         s_int;
        long        s_long;
    }               *a_struct_var;
    NoDeclare       ss;
} Foo;
```

Assuming `Foo` appears in the configuration file, the following Java class is generated:

```
public class Foo {
private int[]      aa;//  Converted from int[]
public void setAa(int[] _lcl_val_1) {
    aa = _lcl_val_1;
}
public void set_aa_Indexed(int ix, int _lcl_val_1){
    aa[ix] = _lcl_val_1;
}
public int[] getAa(){
    return aa;
}
public int get_aa_Indexed(int ix) {
    return aa[ix];
}
private long       x; // unsigned int

public void setX(long _lcl_val_1) {
    x = _lcl_val_1;
}
public long getX(){
    return x;
}
```

```
private long        z;

public void setZ(long _lcl_val_1){
   z = _lcl_val_1;
}
public long getZ() {
   return z;
}
private String     str;//  Converted from char*

public void setStr(String _lcl_val_1) {
      str = _lcl_val_1;
}
public String getStr() {
      return str;
}

// Converted from a_struct_in_foo*
private a_struct_in_foo    a_struct_var;
public void setA_struct_var(
   a_struct_in_foo _lcl_val_1) {
      a_struct_var = _lcl_val_1;
}
public a_struct_in_foo getA_struct_var(){
   return a_struct_var;
}
private NoDeclare    ss;
public void setSs(NoDeclare _lcl_val_1){
   ss = _lcl_val_1;
}
public NoDeclare getSs(){
   return ss;
}
private native static void initFIDs();
 static {
    initFIDs();
}
}
```

For a `struct` declared internally to a `struct` named in the configuration file, a Java class is generated regardless of whether the enclosed `struct` name appears in the configuration file. In the example above, Java source for the struct `a_struct_in_foo` is generated. Unlike `Foo`, this class is package `private`.

File Names

The name of the generated Java source file is *class*. java where *class* is the C struct name appearing in the configuration file. The JNI source file name is jni<*class*>.cc, and the corresponding include file is jni<*class*>.h. The suffix of the generated C/C++ file named may be changed using the -c option.

Type Modifications

- All unsigned types are promoted to the next larger Java type. For example, if an unsigned short appears as a C variable, it is converted to a int in Java.

- By default all char* and char[] variables are converted to java.lang.String object references.

- unsigned char variables are treated as the Java primitive type byte.

- All pointer variables are converted to Java references and the appropriate referencing is taken care of in the JNI code.

- Only one level of indirection is supported. If a C struct contains something like int**** foo, it is left as an exercise for the user to make sense of that in Java and JNI.

Java Native Interface Code

In addition to the Java class, C++ adapter functions are generated for moving data back and forth between the Java object and the C struct. For each variable a setter/getter is generated. Likewise, an aggregate setter/getter is generated.

Using the above example, the long variable x in Foo causes the generation of the JNI functions jniSetX_in_Foo and jniSetY_in_Foo:

```
void jni_SetX_in_Foo(
    Foo* __Foo_, JNIEnv *env, jobject thisFoo);
void jni_GetX_from_Foo(
    Foo* __Foo_, JNIEnv *env, jobject thisFoo);
```

The setter moves a value from the C struct pointed to by the first argument, __Foo_, to the Java object referred to in the third argument, thisFoo.

Conversely, the getter moves a value from the Java object pointed to by thisFoo into the C struct pointed to by __Foo_.

The naming convention for JNI adapter functions is:

```
jni_Setvar-name_in_class
jni_Getvar-name_in_class
```

where *var-name* is C variable name with the first character capitalized and *class* is the Java class (or C `struct`. They are the same.) name.

The aggregate setter/getters follow a similar naming convention:

```
jni_SetAll_in_class
jni_GetAll_in_class
```

Field ID Caching

For each Java class generated, a C/C++ routine

```
void init<class>FieldIDs(JNIEnv *, jclass)
```

is generated. This function initializes a `static jfieldID` variable for every data field defined in the Java class *class*. Also generated is the declaration for a `native` method, `initFIDs`,

```
private native static void initFIDs();
```

and its implementation which does nothing more than call

```
initclassFieldIDs();
```

The `native` method itself is called from a `static` block within the class for which the field IDs are initialized, *class*.`java`.

Global Variables

All global variables encountered will appear in the Java `public` class `AppGlobals`. No JNI code is generated for these variables.

Things Not Supported

- Currently only single dimension arrays of objects and pointers are supported.
- Function `typedefs`
- Anonymous `structs`
- `union` and `enum`

Appendix D   *JAVAH **REFERENCE***

> I have always wanted to do this. It's kind of a native thing.
>
> Dan Gardner
> *Three Ball Cascade*

Command Syntax

javah [**options**] *classname.* . .

javah_g [**options**] *classname.* . .

Synopsis: javah - C Header and Stub File Generator

javah produces C header files and C source files from a Java class. These files provide the connective glue that allows your Java and C/C++ code to interact.

Options

-o *outputfile* Concatenates the resulting header or source files for all the classes listed on the command line into *outputfile*.

-d *directory* Sets the directory where javah saves the header files or the stub files.

-td *directory*

Sets the directory where javah stores temporary files. By default, javah stores temporary files in the directory specified by the TEMP environment variable. If TEMP is unspecified, then javah checks for a TMP environment variable. And finally, if TMP is unspecified, javah creates the directory /tmp (Solaris) or C:\tmp (Win32) and stores the files there.

-stubs   Causes javah to generate C declarations from the Java object file. This is only relevant for 1.0 native methods.

-verbose   Causes javah to print a message to stdout concerning the status of the generated files.

-jni   Causes javah to create an output file containing JNI-style native method function prototypes.

-classpath *path*

Specifies the path javah uses to look up classes. Overrides the default or the CLASSPATH environment variable if it is set. Directories are separated by semi-colons. Thus the general format for *path* is:

```
.;<your_path>
```

For example:

```
.;C:\users\dac\classes;C:\tools\java\classes
```

Description

javah generates C header and source files that are needed to implement native methods. If 1.0-style code is generated the generated header and source files are used by C programs to reference an object's instance variables from native source code. The .h file contains a struct definition whose layout parallels the layout of the corresponding class. The fields in the struct correspond to instance variables in the class.

The name of the header file and the structure declared within it are derived from the name of the class. If the class passed to javah is inside a package, the package name is added to the front of both the header file name and the class name. Underscores (_) are used as name delimiters.

By default javah creates a header file for each class listed on the command line and puts the files in the current directory. Use the -stubs option to create source files. Use the -o option to concatenate the results for all listed classes into a single file.

The new native method interface, Java Native Interface (JNI), does not require header information or stub files. javah is used with the -jni option to generate native method function prototypes needed for JNI-style native methods. For a class named *class*, the result is placed in the file *class*.h. This file name can be over-ridden with the -o option. All the function prototypes for this book were generated using the -jni option.

javah_g is a non-optimized version of javah suitable for use with debuggers like jdb or dbx.

Environment Variables

CLASSPATH

Used to provide the system a path to user-defined classes. Directories are separated by semi-colons, for example:

```
.;C:\users\dac\classes;C:\tools\java\classes
```

TEMP

Determines directory in which javah creates temporary files. If it is not specified, the TMP environment variable is used.

TMP

Determines directory in which javah creates temporary file if TEMP environment variable is not specified. If TMP is not specified, javah creates the directory /tmp (Solaris) or C:\tmp (Win32) for locating of temporary files.

Appendix E *NATIVE METHODS, APPLETS, SECURITY*

> As long as this natural right of every man to every thing
> endureth, there can be no security to any man
> how strong or wise soever he be, of living out the time,
> which nature ordinarily alloweth men to live.
>
> Thomas Hobbes
> *Leviathan, Vol. III, Part I*

Introduction

No where in this book has there been a discussion of native methods and applets. Every example of loading a native library has been within the context of a Java application. This appendix is intended to serve as a jumping off point for the reader interested in using native code from within an applet.

The common understanding is that applets must play within the Java *sandbox*: they are limited in the operations they can perform so to not compromise the security of their host machine. For example, an applet restricted to the sandbox may not read a file on its host machine. The challenge facing an applet writer who wants to use `native` methods is how to get out of the sandbox. Specifically, an applet needs to be able to call `System.loadLibrary`.

This simple and very specific requirement is situated within a complex, general and evolving milieu of applet security that spans releases of the JDK and different browsers. That is why this appendix can serve only as a starting point. As such, a small example of calling `native` methods from within an applet will be accompanied by only a general discussion of security and lots of URLs that can serve as a self-directed tutorial on applet security and native code. Further, the discussion of browsers will be limited to Netscape's Communicator.

475

General JDK Security

The best place to start your learning about applets and security is the Security FAQ directly off of JavaSoft's home page or `http://java.sun.com/sfaq/index.html`.

The general point to learn from the series of questions constituting this FAQ is the difference between the Java *system class loader* and the *applet class loader*. The system or `NULL` class loader loads class files from directories, zip files or JAR files named in the `CLASSPATH` environment variable. The applet class loader is used to load applets specified by a URL, including those using the `file:` protocol.

In JDK 1.1 the differences in capabilities associated with a class loaded via the system class loader and an applet loaded via the applet class loader are summarized at `http://java.sun.com/sfaq/index.html#diff`. This table shows that an applet loaded by the class loader can not perform a `System.loadLibrary`. Simply put, the `SecurityManager` associated with the applet class loader *always* throws an exception when its `checkLink` method is invoked during an attempt to call either of the `System.load-Library` or `Runtime.loadLibrary` methods.

The JDK 1.2 security model complicates matters but, in doing so, provides more flexibility. Permission to access a named resource is determined by a *policy.* A policy is a runtime mechanism for determining which permissions are available to whom. The "who" is called a *principal.* A principal is typically a *signed object* (e.g. a class loaded from a digitally-signed JAR file) that requests access to some resource. A policy is determined by a *policy provider* which is named in a security configuration file. See the JDK 1.2 `javadoc` for the `java.security.Policy` class for details.

JDK 1.2 formalizes the notion of permission with the abstract class `java.security.BasicPermission`. For example, the class `RuntimePermission` extends `BasicPermission` and determines whether or not an applet can execute a `System.loadLibrary`.

With the new security APIs in JDK 1.2 the relevance of the sharp distinction between system and applet class loader gives way to the concepts of principal, policy and permission. This is how the advertised "fine-grain" security mechanism is implemented in 1.2: on a per policy basis a uniquely identified and trusted principal can be granted or denied specific permissions.

All the JDK 1.2 extensions are welcome since they represent the result of cooperation between Sun and Netscape to design a common security API. However, for today's writer of applets that want to play beyond the sandbox while running in Netscape's browser, they are irrelevant. Netscape has only recently incorporated JDK 1.1 into its browser product, so it may be a while before these extensions find their way into Communicator.

Current users of Netscape Communicator 4.03 and 4.04 products must rely on the Netscape security extensions to fine tune the capabilities of an applet. Recall that the basic JDK 1.1 security model prevents applets loaded by the applet class loader to play outside the sandbox. By extending the JDK security classes with the Netscape Capabilities API, Netscape allows applets to acquire permission to manipulate local resources, for example, reading and writing the local file system, as well as loading a native library.

Netscape Communicator Security

As provider of a JVM, a browser vendor is ultimately responsible for the implementation of any security mechanism. As long as the JVM meets the requirements for being called a Java Virtual Machine, a JVM implementor is free to extend its capabilities as desired. In the case of Netscape's Communicator, additional classes are provided as part of Netscape's Capabilities API. The Capabilities API supports Java developers who are writing applets or libraries that need access to local system resources, such as loading a native library. Microsoft provides similar functionality with its Internet Explorer but that is irrelevant to our discussion here since Microsoft does not support JNI.

Netscape Capabilities API and Object Signing

An introduction to the Netscape capabilities classes can be found at `http://developer.netscape.com/library/documentation/signedobj/capsapi.html`. From there you can also learn how Communicator verifies whether an applet is *trusted* and how it can then gain permission to play outside the sandbox. The following bullets minimally summarize the requirements for using the Netscape capabilities classes.

1. Obtain a code-signing certificate from one of the commercial distributors. For a list of certificate authorities see `https://certs.netscape.com/client.html`.

2. Write an applet using the Netscape capabilities classes, requesting the appropriate privileges. The capabilities classes are defined in the `netscape.security` package. A zip file containing these classes is available for download from `http://developer.netscape.com/library/documentation/signedobj/capsapi.html`.

3. Sign the applet class file using the Netscape Signing Tool, informally known as `zigbert`. (See `http://developer.netscape.com/library/documentation/signedobj/zigbert/index.htm`). This process requires the incorporation of your class file into a JAR archive file.

These steps result in a signed JAR file that Communicator clients can identify using a public key associated with the signing certificate. The distribution and managing of certificates and public keys is a study in itself. `http://developer.netscape.com/library/documentation/signedobj/trust/index.htm` is a good place to start on this topic.

The complete javadoc for the Capabilities API can be viewed at `http://developer.netscape.com/library/documentation/` `signedobj/javadoc/Package-netscape_security.html`.

Obtaining a certificate and doing the appropriate signing is a burden during your development and testing. Fortunately there is a better way, but before we learn how to avoid all the complexities of signing, certificates and public keys, a word about JNI is in order.

Discussion of Netscape security does not mention the JNI. The discussion applies just as well to 1.0-style native code. However, if you are using JNI, you will need either Communicator 4.03 or Communicator 4.04 and the JDK 1.1 patch. Evaluation copies of these products can be downloaded from the Netscape web site at `http://developer.netscape.com/software/` `index.html`.

Avoiding Signatures

For development and testing purposes, signing and certificates can be avoided by adding a single line to your Netscape preferences file, `prefs.js`. This file typically lives in `\Program Files\Netscape\Users\`*username* on Win32 systems and `~/.netscape` on UNIX systems.

The preference value you want to set enables codebase principals within Communicator. As mentioned above, in security vernacular, a *principal* is an object that needs access to system resources. A codebase is a URL. Enabling codebase principals, then, means that URLs can be considered as having or not having certain capabilities.

That said, to enable codebase principals, add the following line to your Netscape preferences files.

```
user_pref(
   "signed.applets.codebase_principal_support", true);
```

Communicator should not be running when this change is made, otherwise the setting will be over-written when you do exit. Also, be careful in your use of this setting. You should be sure to turn it off when you are finished your testing and return to using Communicator for general web browsing.

In the following example, the intricacies of signing and certificates will be ignored as the above shortcut is used to access native code from an applet.

Using Native Code With Applets

Two examples of calling native methods from an applet will now be discussed. The first illustrates how an applet itself can actually do a `System.load-Library`. The second example illustrates how a helper class loaded by an applet does a `System.loadLibrary`. Their appearance together is primarily a pedagogical device: the same security constraints must be met regardless of whether a native library is loaded by a remotely loaded applet or some other locally loaded class. The following assumes an applet is loaded from a remote machine. To view the applet and exercise the Capabilities API and Communicator's security support, the example applets could just as well reside on your local file system.

For either of the examples to work, the following three conditions must be met.

1. Codebase principals are enabled for Communicator.

2. The Netscape capabilities classes (`capsapi_classes.zip`) are installed and their location added to the `CLASSPATH` environment variable used by Communicator.

3. The native library to be loaded resides in the directory

`\Program Files\Netscape\Communicator\Program\Java\Bin.`

The first and second items revisit the immediately preceding discussion. The third item captures the Communicator requirement that all of its DLLs appear in a well-known location.

Let's turn our attention to the example source code.

Loading a Native Library From Applet Class

The first example will illustrate loading a native library directly from the applet class. This example applet displays a `java.awt.Label` in its `Panel`. The label contains a string generated by combining the name of the calling class, a string returned by a call to a native method, and the `getHost` and `getFile` components of the applet's codebase. The `native` method providing the second part of the string is declared in the Listing E.1.

Listing E.1 *Java Class With Native Method*

```
public class Native {
        public native static String getString();
}
```

This class lives on the local machine somewhere in the `CLASSPATH` environment of Communicator. The implementation of the `getString` method appears below.

Listing E.2 *Native Implementation of* getString

```
JNIEXPORT jstring JNICALL Java_Native_getString
(JNIEnv *env, jclass clazz) {
    return env->NewStringUTF("Applet Hello World");
}
```

This method is used simply to confirm a successful call into native code. The applet that calls this method, `RemoteLoad`, appears in Listing E.3. Its class file will live on a remote machine. As you can see, it loads a native library and calls `Native.getString`.

Listing E.3 *Applet Loading Library Using Netscape Capabilities API*

```
import java.applet.*;
import java.awt.*;
import java.io.*;
import java.net.URL;
import netscape.security.*;

public class RemoteLoad extends Applet {
  static {
    try {
      PrivilegeManager.enablePrivilege(
        "UniversalLinkAccess");
      System.loadLibrary("Chap15example1");
    } catch (ForbiddenTargetException e) {
      e.printStackTrace();
    } catch (Error err) {
      System.err.println(
        "Can't load native library");
    }
  }
  public void init() {
    String nmsg = Native.getString();
    URL cb = getCodeBase();
    String s = getClass().getName() + ":"
                 + nmsg + ":" + cb.getHost() + ":"
                 + cb.getFile();
    Label b = new Label(s, Label.CENTER);
    add("Center", b);
  }
}
```

(1) — `import netscape.security.*;`

(2) — `PrivilegeManager.enablePrivilege(...)`

(3) — `} catch (ForbiddenTargetException e) {`

(4) — `URL cb = getCodeBase();`

(5) — `String s = getClass().getName() + ":"`

What is relevant in this code really has nothing to do with JNI. Line [1] imports the required package from the Netscape Capabilities API. Line [2] enables a privilege associated with a specified *target*. A target is some thing for which some kind of access is requested. In this case, the target `UniversalLinkAccess` is requested. As its name implies, it is the target for loading and linking libraries from the host system. The lesson here is that certain activities require enabling the privilege for a specific target. There are lots of targets defined by Netscape. You can learn all about them by surfing to

http://developer.netscape.com/library/documentation/
signedobj/targets/index.htm.

Note that `enablePrivilege` is a method of the `PrivilegeManager` class. A `PrivilegeManager` tracks which principals may access which targets. Signed applets use an instance of class `PrivilegeManager` to request privileges for particular targets. Communicator associates each principal with a list of targets for which privileges may or may not be permitted. If the client's list of principals and their allowed targets include both the applet's principal and the requested target, the `PrivilegeManager` quietly grants the privilege. If the applet's principal has not previously been granted or denied a privilege for the requested target, Communicator displays a dialog box explicitly asking the user for permission to grant that privilege. When loading the example applets into Communicator, you will be asked to grant or deny the requested privilege for the `UniversalLinkAccess` target.

The `PrivilegeManager` makes a distinction between *granting* a privilege and *enabling* a privilege. To grant a privilege means a principal has been given the ability to perform a certain action. A privilege must be granted before it is enabled. Enabling a privilege is like turning it on. A granted privilege must be enabled before the privileged action may be performed.

Privileges can be granted in one of two ways. If the site at which the Netscape Communicator client runs is under the jurisdiction of Netscape's Mission Control suite of tools for configuring and managing Communicator clients, the system administrator may control the list of signers, the types of access each signer is allowed, and the list of certificates. Using Mission Control, the system administrator may also prevent individual users from changing signer privileges and certificate authorization for their client.

If the user is allowed individual control over signers and certificates, privileges may be granted using the Security button from Communicator's toolbar. From the initial Security page, follow the Java/JavaScript link to edit privileges assigned to different certificates. Additionally, there is the option of granting privileges in response to an explicit request in the form of a pop-up dialog when the signer is first encountered.

Returning to Listing E.3, since `enablePrivilege` may throw an exception, it is caught at [3]. Finally, as evidence that it is a remote applet that loads the native library, its codebase is retrieved at [4] and its components used in the `Label` string constructed in [5].

To run this example requires copying the `RemoteLoad.class` to a remote machine that serves HTTP, building an HTML file that loads the applet and pointing your Netscape Communicator 4.03/4.04 browser at the HTML file. The details of setting up the remote site are beyond the scope of this appendix.

As partial evidence that all this works as described, the `Label` string generated when the `RemoteLoad` applet is loaded from the author's unofficial and completely malnourished home page, appears below.

`RemoteLoad:Applet Hello World:members.iex/~rgordon`

This confirms that applet was loaded by the `RemoteLoad` class, the `getString` native method was successfully called and that the `Remote-Load` class file was loaded from my ISP's machine that hosts members' web sites, `members.iex`.

If you run the `RemoteLoad` applet, remotely or locally, while still viewing it, press the Security icon in the Communicator toolbar. When the Security dialog is presented, select the Java/JavaScript item on the left. You will be presented with a list of signed objects to which you have granted some privilege. Select one and press the Edit Privileges button. A description of the privileges granted to that signer will appear. You should not be surprised to see: Using native code stored in dynamically loaded libraries.

Loading a Native Library From a Helper Class

This discussion of loading a native library from a helper class will depend mostly on code listings. As mentioned above, the same security requirements must be met. In this example, the helper class `NativeWithLoad` resides on the client machine. When the applet, as before, calls the method `getString`, the `NativeWithLoad` class is initialized and the native library is loaded.

Listing E.4 *Helper Class* `NativeWithLoad` *Used to Load Native Library*

```
import netscape.security.*;
public class NativeWithLoad {
  static {
    try {
      PrivilegeManager.enablePrivilege(
             "UniversalLinkAccess");
      System.loadLibrary("Chap15example2");
    } catch (ForbiddenTargetException e) {
      e.printStackTrace();
    } catch (Error err) {
      System.err.println(
             "Can't load native library");
    }
  }
  public native static String getString();
}
```

The obvious thing to notice is that all of the Capabilities API code has been moved into `NativeWithLoad`. This is not an absolute requirement but it is an effective requirement. This is so for two reasons. First, privileges have lexical scope. Since they are recorded by annotating the stack frame, they exist for the duration of a method call. This argues for keeping the enabling of a privilege as lexically close as possible to the use of that privilege. This will ensure the desired operation is performed within the scope of the granted privilege. The second reason it is important to keep the enabling of a privilege as close as possible to its use is a general security issue. The shorter the period for which a privilege is enabled, the less susceptible the code is to security breaches. You should aim for "fine-grain" control over privileges. To refine privileges even further than the duration of a method, the Capabilities API provides `revertPrivilege` and `disablePrivilege`.

The Netscape page at

```
http://developer.netscape.com/library/documentation/
                   signedobj/capabilities/index.html
```

provides examples of various strategies for enabling and using privileges given different security and usability considerations.

Given that the privilege is enabled within the `NativeWithLoad` class, the new applet class that uses the native code, as defined by `LocalLoad`, appears as shown in Listing E.5.

Listing E.5 *Applet Using Helper Class to Load Native Library*

```
import java.applet.*;
import java.awt.*;
import java.io.*;
import java.net.URL;
public class LocalLoad extends Applet {
  public void init() {
    String nmsg = NativeWithLoad.getString();
    URL cb = getCodeBase();
    String s = getClass().getName() + ":"
          + nmsg + ":" + cb.getHost() + ":"
          + cb.getFile();
    Label b = new Label(s, Label.CENTER);
    add("Center", b);
  }
}
```

It should come as no surprise that all the Capabilities API code has been removed along with the `System.loadLibrary`. Otherwise, the code for `LocalLoad` is identical to `RemoteLoad`. Pointing to an HTML file that loads `LocalLoad`, you will see a message similar to the one printed by

RemoteLoad. The only difference is the class name part of the `Label` string.

`LocalLoad:Applet Hello World:members.iex/~rgordon`

How Did the Native Library Get There?

The foregoing discussion has entirely begged the question of how a native library loaded by an applet which itself was loaded from the network got there in the first place. The applet would have had to have some prior knowledge of the native library and would have to depend on the client machine to have the library installed in the proper location. This scenario violates the notion of "Write Once Run Anywhere" but it is not too far-fetched. One can imagine a web site vendor distributing software to clients in order to get the full functionality of its site. There is a precedent for this model with Netscape plug-ins. Perhaps to enhance my experience of a particular site, I may need to download Macromedia Shockwave.

Extending this model to native libraries, it is certainly possible, given the appropriate privileges, for an applet to first download a native library and then load it. To circumvent the Communicator requirement that dynamic libraries reside in a special directory, the applet could be written to do a `System.load` using an absolute path name after putting the native library in a well-known directory, say `/tmp`.

The details of this approach may make it cumbersome, but possible nonetheless. Additionally, its success depends on a great deal of trust between the client and the web server.

INDEX

> The people who stood at the forefront of the "communications age" had lost their ability to communicate with anyone but themselves. Their technical jargons were unintelligible to outsiders but immediately recognizable, as the badge of professional status, to fellow specialists all over the world.
>
> Christopher Lasch
> *The True and Only Heaven*

CREDITS

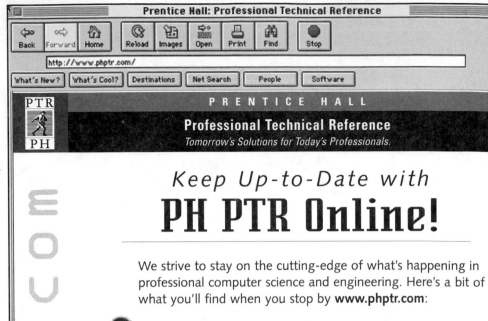